Encyclopedia of Haunted Places

Ghostly Locales From Around The World

Encyclopedia of Haunted Places

Haunted Places

GHOSTLY LOCALES
FROM AROUND
THE WORLD

COMPILED & EDITED BY
JEFF BELANGER

BY THE WORLD'S LEADING PARANORMAL INVESTIGATORS

CASTLE BOOKS

This edition published in 2008 by
CASTLE BOOKS ®
A division of Book Sales, Inc.
114 Northfield Avenue
Edison, NJ 08837

This edition published by arrangement with and permission of
The Career Press, Inc.
3 Tice Road, PO Box 687
Franklin Lakes, NJ 07417

Edited by Kate Henches
Typeset by Stacey A. Farkas
Cover design by Lu Rossman/Digi Dog Design

Library of Congress Cataloging-in-Publication Data:

Encyclopedia of haunted places: ghostly locales from around the world / compiled and Edited
by Jeff Belanger.
    p. cm.
    Includes index.
  1. Haunted places--Encyclopedias. I. Belanger, Jeff.

BF1444.E53 2005
133.1'09—dc22

                   2005048430

ISBN-13: 978-0-7858-2412-1
ISBN-10: 0-7858-2412-X

Printed in the United States of America

Acknowledgments

I'd like to thank the many people who contributed their writing and photography to this book. Though there are too many to list here, you'll see their bylines in each contribution. These paranormal investigators are always searching for answers to the unexplained, and I'm fortunate to have had the opportunity to work with so many of them to present some of their findings. This book simply would not exist without the hard work of all of the contributors from around the globe.

My wife, Megan, has my unending gratitude. She not only kept me sane through this project, she was always ready to lend her sharp editorial eye to help bring out the best in each submission.

A big thank you to Michael Pye at New Page Books, who played a significant role in making this book happen. I'd also like to thank Kate Henches and Stacey Farkas for their editing and design skills in bringing a ton of content together to form this book. All of the folks at New Page Books have really been behind those who work in this field of research. I'm grateful to everyone there for bringing this project to life.

Contents

Great Lakes, 111

Great Plains, 135

Rocky Mountains, 153

Southwest, 167

West Coast, 193

Alaska/Hawaii, 213

Western Canada, 219

Central Canada, 227

Eastern Canada, 243

Asia, 249

Jamaica, 259

South Africa, 263

Iran, 267

Oceania, 271

The United Kingdom, 287

Introduction

Ghosts are everywhere. Every town has its buildings, houses, and cemeteries about which locals whisper and which school children hurry past when walking by. Ghost legends are powerful—they're one of the few events today that still survive mainly by oral tradition. The tales of ghost encounters get retold, and soon certain locations get a "haunted" reputation. But those stories started somewhere. There is basis in fact behind every legend. And in many locations, people still experience the unexplained—they may tell one or two others about their experiences, and soon word of those encounters spreads and adds fuel to the supernatural fire that burns a haunted location into the collective memory of a region's folklore—almost as if the ghosts and spirits demand to be remembered and acknowledged.

Many people are afraid of ghosts, but fear comes from a simple lack of understanding something. Other people actually go looking for ghosts. These people have many labels: ghost hunter, paranormal investigator, ghost buster, or supernatural researcher. These are people who delve into the unexplained because they are seeking their own answers, and they're driven to help others who may be trying to cope with supernatural phenomena in their own homes.

Some paranormal investigators take a very technical approach—believing that if some form of spirit energy is manifesting itself to the point of moving a physical object, causing a cold spot, or even materializing in some way, then equipment should be able to measure and record the change in the environment. Digital thermometers, electromagnetic field (EMF) detectors, video and still cameras, and audio-recording equipment are all poised to capture a ghost in action. Other investigators take more of an esoteric approach, preferring channeling tools such as a talking board (better known by the brand name, *Ouija* board), a pendulum, dowsing rods, or a psychic person who can act as the go-between for the spirit world to establish contact and prove (or disprove) if a location is truly haunted.

All of these investigators, whether in an organized group or solo, are seeking answers, and it's a noble pursuit.

When studying the ghosts surrounding old buildings, battlefields, and other ancient locales, we're not only experiencing hands-on spirituality, but hands-on history as well. Even the legends themselves have something to teach us about our own past, and certainly about our future beyond the grave.

For people who are experiencing a haunting, it's difficult to know where to turn to for help. Those who are religiously affiliated may turn to their clergy who, hopefully, will take the situation seriously and get involved. But many others may feel embarrassed about openly discussing their unexplained phenomena for fear that they will be ridiculed. The concern is both understandable and valid. Even though every year millions of people have a brush with what they perceive to be the supernatural, open discussions still aren't happening in every office building and coffee shop.

This is where the paranormal investigators come in. They're ready to listen, and, in many cases, they have heard similar stories from others. Sharing the story itself can be part of the healing and understanding of the event. And the investigators can quite often offer validation of what you're experiencing.

The good news is that things are changing in our modern society. Though our technology and understanding of the universe around us increases every day, there is a growing trend in accepting at least the possibility of ghosts and hauntings. The evidence is all around us. When that evidence becomes proof is up to each individual to decide.

This book offers a peek into the case files of some of the world's most prominent paranormal investigators. The many contributors have written about some of their favorite haunts and the cases they know best. Additionally, there is a short glossary of terms in the back of this book to help you with some of the insider terms used in the entries. The book is a place to begin your own quest for haunted locations, ghostly lore, and a deeper understanding of both our past and our inevitable future.

New England

New England

Connecticut

THE WHITE LADY OF EASTON

UNION CEMETERY
INTERSECTION OF SPORT HILL ROAD AND
ROUTE 59
EASTON, CONNECTICUT 06612

The White Lady of Easton has been spotted walking along Route 59, Sport Hill Road, and within Union Cemetery. She's darted in front of passing cars, she's vanished when motorists pull over to offer help, and, according to one witness, she's been struck by a car—enough to cause damage to the vehicle. The driver, a local fireman, was stunned, believing he had just run over a person, but as he looked around he found no body—not of a person and not of an animal. But there was an unexplainable dent in the hood of his car.

Photo by Jeff Belanger

Union Cemetery is as scenic as it is historic. Headstones date back to the 1700s, some so weathered that they're no longer readable. Death's heads—cartoonish skulls with bat-like wings—adorn the tops of some of the old headstones. The small cemetery is still in use, but the living mourners aren't the only ones to walk the grounds.

Renowned ghost investigators and authors Ed and Lorraine Warren once showed me a video Ed had captured of the White Lady on September 1, 1990, at 2:40 a.m. He had his video camera set on a tripod at the gate of the cemetery that night.

"The only light was a streetlight that was 50 yards from where I was sitting," Ed recalled. "I heard a woman weeping, and I looked out and saw hundreds of ghost lights floating around and forming into a figure of a woman. I couldn't make out facial features, but I could see she had long, dark hair and she was dressed in white. I started to walk toward her and she disappeared. You never walk toward the ghost—you let the ghost come to you because you can change the molecular makeup and magnetic field when a ghost is materializing."

When watching the video, from the right-hand side of the picture, a misty white

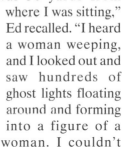

form takes shape into the outline of a human (presumably a woman), then weaves between several headstones and into the clearing just before the gate. As "she" gets closer to the camera, some dark blobs seem to jump at her from near her feet before she dissipates into the ground. The entire video lasts maybe five or six seconds but is among the most compelling footage ever shot.

The Warrens' book, *Graveyard* (St. Martin's Press, 1992), says the White Lady was a murder victim from the 1800s, and her body was dumped behind the Easton Baptist Church. The building is a picturesque white-steepled, old New England church that sits at the north end of the cemetery.

Today, the White Lady is a well-known piece of Fairfield County lore. As people drive by the cemetery (especially at night), many slow down and look around for the glowing white apparition.

—Jeff Belanger
Founder, Ghostvillage.com

DANIEL BENTON HOMESTEAD

160 METCALF ROAD
TOLLAND, CONNECTICUT 06084
TEL: 1 (860) 974-1875
WEBSITE: *http://pages.cthome.net/ tollandhistorical/ benton%20museum.htm*

Upon first glance at the Daniel Benton Homestead, it would appear a quaint, colonial home in a quiet setting. But there is a very tragic story held within its walls—a love affair involving two young people whose lives were cut short.

However, whether any living person is around or not, the house is alive with paranormal activity.

The Benton Homestead is a Colonial cape that was built in 1720. The original owner and builder of the house, Daniel Benton, had three grandsons who went off to fight in the Revolutionary War. Two died during the war while the third, Elisha Benton, contracted smallpox while being held as a prisoner of war. He was released and sent back home to Connecticut. Before he left for war, he had promised his heart to a young girl, Jemima Barrows. So, after waiting for her beloved to return, Jemima offered to care for him. Unfortunately, all of her love and nurturing could not cure him, and in 1777 Elisha died at the age of 29. As Jemima was the one to care for the ailing Elisha, she contracted the dreadful disease and subsequently died shortly before her 18th birthday, alone and with no one to care for her.

As the young lovers were never married, it would not have been proper to bury them side by side. Therefore, a carriage road divided their graves, which are located on the property. Some speculate that this separation caused their spirits to remain restless in the afterlife and that they continue to search the house for each other.

The house remained in the Benton family for six generations. In 1969, the Tolland Historical Society acquired it, and shortly thereafter it was opened as a museum. People who have toured the house have reported a gray shadow moving across the front bedroom (notably the room where Jemima and Elisha both died). Various guests staying in the house have reported seeing the apparition of a man—a soldier—and hearing rapping noises and unexplained weeping. Members of war encampments who have camped out on the property have seen lights flickering on and off in the house when no one was there.

Another interesting note is that the basement of the house served to hold Hessian soldiers during the war after they were surrendered to the United States during the victory at the Battle of Saratoga. It is said that the soldiers so enjoyed staying at the home that many did not leave the Tolland area as others moved on to Boston. Perhaps some enjoyed it so much that they have returned in spirit.

There is speculation as to whether Elisha or Jemima may be searching the house for each other in hopes of reuniting. Or, perhaps, a Hessian soldier has returned to the place where he found peace in life.

—Sarah Robinson

CAROUSEL GARDENS RESTAURANT

153 NORTH STREET
SEYMOUR, CONNECTICUT 06483
TEL: 1 (203) 888-2700
WEBSITE: *www.carouselgardens.com*

William H. Wooster came to Seymour in 1878, having been born in Waterbury, Connecticut. He was known as a captain of industry. He started a bank, the water company, a manufacturing company, and was involved with the schools and church in Seymour. He was often referred to as the founder of Seymour.

Mr. Wooster believed he should be living in the style to suit his stature in the community. In 1879, construction of the Wooster Estate began and continued until 1894. Wooster brought his wife, Anna, and their six children, Anna, Clara, Louise, Mabel, Helena Ruth, and one son Horace, into the estate with him. Ruth was the last surviving Wooster to live in the mansion. The estate was bought and sold several more times during its lifetime. The most recent owners, Paul and Debbie Schiarffa, bought the estate and have worked diligently to turn it into a very successful restaurant. Whenever Paul can tear away for a few minutes, he's got some great stories and pictures he loves to show people.

Various staff members and patrons have had experiences at Carousel—so much so that they have added a whole section of their Website devoted to the paranormal. On one occasion, several of the staff and clients heard a glass fall to the tile floor. When they went to pick it up, there was no glass to be found. People get tugged on and get the feeling of being watched, and a cat with glowing white eyes was seen, but no cat was found anywhere on the premises. Ghost investigators and Ed and Lorraine Warren investigated Carousel Gardens in 1990 and found it to be haunted by the spirit of Helena "Ruth" Wooster. But Ruth is not the only spirit still lingering; occasionally, William Wooster has been glimpsed out of the corner of the eye from the staircase, and Horace has made his presence known as well.

I actually communicated with Ruth on one of our visits. She is a very pleasant lady and loves that Paul and Debbie have turned the house into a restaurant. She gets to see many people enjoying themselves in her home once again (she loved to entertain). She doesn't mind the changes that have been made. We have found that if Ruth likes you, you are apt to find coins that appear from nowhere. Paul was being presented with dimes, another investigator kept finding dimes in her home, and I started seeing pennies everywhere I went. Coins are a common way for spirits to let us know of their presence. While investigating Carousel Gardens, we felt cold spots, saw curtains moving for no reason, felt our clothes being tugged on, and saw shadows. This is truly a delightful place to visit if you want to experience a haunting. Make your reservations, enjoy the food and the hosts, but don't forget to say hello to Ruth.

—Nancy Washell
Co-Director, Maine's
Paranormal Research Association

WINDHAM TEXTILE AND HISTORY MUSEUM

157 UNION STREET
WILLIMANTIC, CONNECTICUT 06226
TEL: 1 (860) 456-2178
WEBSITE: *www.millmuseum.org*

For almost 130 years, this building has stood on the corner of Union and Main Streets. Down the road are the rows of houses built to accommodate the workers. If you were a foreman, you could live further up in town away from the common workers. If you were an owner or manager, you lived in the "hill section" (still called that today).

The mills were worked by the immigrants who came to the area to try and make a better living for themselves and their families. Times were hard, and the work was even harder and more dangerous. The lighting was poor, the air choked with lint, it was cold in the winter and hot in the summer, and 12- to 14-hour days were the norm, even for the children. It was a hard way to make a living, but it was a job, and people flocked to Willimantic from all over to work at the mill.

The company was clever. By paying their workers with the company's own currency script, they were able to retain more profits because employees used the script to buy goods back from the company. Employees could buy everything they needed at the company store, from beef in the butcher section to bonnets and hats in the millinery section. A vault was installed to secure the script and other company money as a bank. The company also had its own warehouses, stables, a theater, and a fire department. The store was a place where the neighborhood came to shop, and there were thousands of people who went through its doors. Left behind were the energies of happiness for being able to provide for one's family with food and shelter, but also some disappointments of being unable to shop anywhere else in town, and the loss of individuality.

The museum still retains these energies through its wonderful exhibits and programs. There is a gift shop where friends come to share stories and history. There have been some strange occurrences in the building. When moving into the building to begin its use as a museum, the vault was discovered closed and locked and the combination could not be found anywhere. The next day, without human intervention, the vault was found open. There are cold spots when viewing some of the artifacts. There have been noises heard coming from the third floor, which used to house a library for the workers. No one has been up there in a very long time.

The second floor also has a strange feeling, almost as if you're being watched. If you visit the museum, be sure to bring your camera!

—Nancy Washell
Co-Director, Maine's
Paranormal Research Association

Boothe Homestead

134 Main Street
Stratford, Connecticut 06614
Tel: 1 (203) 381-2068

The town of Stratford, Connecticut, is home to a piece of property with a rich and mysterious history. The Boothe Homestead sits among 32 acres filled with a picturesque landscape, unique architecture, and an even more interesting history. Stratford was originally organized in 1639, and this property is perhaps the most remarkable in Fairfield County.

The original home dates back to 1663 and was built by Richard Boothe. Boothe was the first in his family to settle in the area, and local records suggest that Boothe was one of the first established families of the township. Today, the upstairs of the house is a museum that is open to the public during designated hours.

Many structures on the property were built and maintained by both David Boothe and his brother Steven, in the early 1900s. The siblings were often referred to as eccentrics, and the style of the property certainly reflects this notion.

Upon the grounds, a cathedral was assembled in 1933 and was dedicated to the Great Depression. It was entitled the "technocratic cathedral." The structure is made of solid redwood, its flat timbers representing a style very unusual in such a community as Stratford. A miniature lighthouse was also built on the property, although the ocean is not in sight. A rose garden and blacksmith shop add to the character of the premises as well.

Three large crosses stand on the grassy portion of land in between a rock garden and the rose garden. The Boothe brothers were said to be heavily involved with different types of spiritual practice and religious lore, and they embraced several of the religions of the world. The brothers often hosted Easter sunrise services. It is recorded that thousands of people from many different religious branches and societal classes attended the early morning event for the celebration of Jesus' resurrection. After criticism from many religious fanatics of the time, the Boothe brothers decided to end the unique event with its last gathering in 1938.

"Boothe [Homestead] is very unique to me," said paranormal investigator and Stratford resident John Zaffis. "My involvement stems from meeting with some of the psychic groups that met up in the main Boothe house on the property for a number of years. It seemed interesting to see what kinds of beliefs were out in society at this time, and I had been on several cases at this point in time and knew that there was more out there in the world than what the eye could see. I wanted to see if there were really those out there who were channeling, psychically reading, communicating with spirits in general, and experiencing things outside the five basic human senses. After attending the gatherings on the property, I realized that there was a possible reality to psychic experiences.

"There is so much in regards to psychic activity on that property. During many of my experiences up there I could definitely see as paranormal in nature. One nearby resident I was visiting the property with could actually see the silhouette of a woman looking down out of the window at everyone standing outside the home. She appeared to be keeping close watch on the happenings at Boothe, and she was as visible as you or I. There was also the appearance of an amber-colored light in the same window where the form had appeared.

"Another impression I can distinctly recall that was reported by a renowned psychic was the presence of what I believe to be Old Man [Richard] Boothe on the property. This man, witnessed by many, came out of the bathroom and walked by the doorway and up the stairs to the area that presently serves as a museum. Also, during the meetings, there would be frequent power surges, audible bangs, and cold spots.

"Another occurrence that puzzled me," John continues, "was the ringing of an antique phone that was not even in service at the time. Many antique items are located on the premises because there is a museum upstairs. During one of the discussion sessions, this phone started to ring uncontrollably. Also, the old grandfather clock would chime, although that was also not in use.

"This place is just so active and has been for years. Many reports come to me on a monthly basis from those who experienced something while visiting the site."

—*Brian McIntyre*
Researcher, The Paranormal
Research Society of New England

Maine

JOSHUA CHAMBERLAIN HOUSE MUSEUM
226 MAIN STREET
BRUNSWICK, MAINE 04011
TEL: 1 (207) 729-6606
WEBSITE:
WWW.CURTISLIBRARY.COM/pejepscot.htm

The house was built in the 1820s and was renovated by Joshua Chamberlain in 1871. It stayed in the family until 1939, when it was sold to a local landlord. The landlord turned the building into apartments and it remained that way until 1983, when the Pejepscot Historical Society bought the home and began renovations to restore it to resemble Chamberlain's time. The house is now almost completely restored, and it operates as a museum to help fund the ongoing renovations.

Walking into the house is like stepping back in time. You can feel Joshua Chamberlain all around. A sensitive in Maine's Paranormal Research Association saw him standing at the top of the stairs and watching us at one point. She also saw (and many of us less psychic could sense) Chamberlain's wife, Fanny. Pictures taken in the house revealed orbs and faces in the glass around the house. A pair of boots in a glass case appeared to have a face when the picture was viewed. In the parlor room, Chamberlain still enjoys entertaining. Our sensitive described a man standing near the fireplace to the tour guide, who said the description fit the profile of General Sherman, a friend of Chamberlain! As many know, Chamberlain had been shot in the hip, and two people in our group experienced severe hip pain inside the home. For one person, the pain was so bad that her leg became swollen and sore and she couldn't walk. This was the same place Chamberlain was shot.

The Chamberlains remain in their beautiful home, and their imprints as well as imprints of friends and family are also present here.

—Bill and Nancy Washell
Co-Directors, Maine's
Paranormal Research Association

THE DEVIL'S FOOTPRINT

NORTH MANCHESTER, MAINE

This cemetery in central Maine has been a hot spot of urban legend and the setting for strange happenings. As you go up the hill to the graveyard, woods line both sides of the road, and as you ascend, you can sense that something is not right.

Photo by Nancy Washell

The meeting house next to the cemetery was built in 1791 and was moved to its present location from the nearby town of Readfield. When the meeting house arrived at its new location, it was reassembled piece by piece. The cemetery is located right next to the building. This is the final resting place of the founding fathers of Manchester. One of these men built his home on top of a hill overlooking the cemetery and the lights of the capital city of Augusta.

The area is surrounded by a low rock wall with an iron gate that creaks almost as if on cue. A boulder in the wall near the entrance bears two footprints—a human and a hoofed print. There have been reports of strange lights and sounds coming from the woods around the cemetery. Ghostly figures have been seen walking through, including a lady in white. But it's not just inside the cemetery that strange things have occurred. Modern-day folklore tells of a brand-new van that pulled into the parking area next to the rock wall. It was late at night and all was quiet. While the occupants were sitting in the van, the windows started fogging up and a strange noise was heard by all. As they turned toward the window, they could see claw marks but no cause for them. Others have gone to the footprint to try and have their own brush with the supernatural only to get back in their vehicle and find that it will not start.

We have investigated this cemetery for more than seven years, and we always come away with some unique findings. We have seen cloaked figures walking the back corner and have heard strange voices. We were sitting in our car and saw a shadow dart behind the car and vanish. As we were wrapping up our investigation one night, everyone was outside the wall when we all heard and felt a thud hit the ground, as if a very large boulder or monument had been knocked over and had struck the ground nearby. We looked around but nothing was disturbed.

The ghost of a gatekeeper who stands guard near the gate wears dark clothing and a hat, and he can sometimes be seen holding a lantern. Wary of newcomers, he relaxes when he finds you are not there to cause harm. One woman from our group, who is quite empathic, started taking on labor pains near the back corner. We believe the spirit of a woman who is buried in an unmarked grave in the cemetery was trying to communicate through our sensitive that she died either during, or shortly after, giving birth. We have also sensed several portals where the air gets very cold and electrically charged. You can even see your breath in the middle of summer.

—Bill and Nancy Washell
Co-Directors, Maine's Paranormal
Research Association

CAPTAIN LINDSEY HOUSE

5 LINDSEY STREET
ROCKLAND, MAINE 04841
TEL: 1 (207) 596-7950
WEBSITE: *www.lindseyhouse.com*

Nestled among the historic seaport buildings of Rockland, Maine, the nine-room Captain Lindsey House, built in 1837, is one of Rockland's first inns. The house has served as the offices of the water company, a rooming house, and now an inn. At one time, traveling theaters were popular and actors went from town to town performing; many that came through Rockland stayed at the Captain Lindsey, and some of their gaiety can still be felt here.

The house is full of antiques, which tend to attract the spirit energy of the object's previous owners. The staff and owners will tell you right off the bat that the house has several unseen, permanent guests. Walking into the home, you can feel the energy all over and can be assured of having a hauntingly good time.

If you stay in one of the first-floor rooms, you can hear people walking around and furniture being moved when no one is upstairs at all. Each room seems to have its own story. In a few of the rooms, you'll first see the beds are made neatly, covers smooth, but if you go back into the room later, a handprint can be seen on one of the beds, or on other beds there are impressions as if someone had been sitting on it. A cabinet in the sitting room will show a woman's face. Faint voices have been heard, and pictures reveal many orbs in all parts of the house. You could say history is still alive at the Captain Lindsey House.

—Bill and Nancy Washell
Co-Directors, Maine's
Paranormal Research Association

Massachusetts

HOUGHTON MANSION

172 CHURCH STREET
NORTH ADAMS, MASSACHUSETTS 01247
TEL: 1 (413) 663-3486
WEBSITE: *http://houghton-mansion.tripod.com*

The Houghton Mansion is located deep in the Berkshires in North Adams, Massachusetts. It was the home of the former mayor of North Adams and wealthy patriarch Albert C. Houghton. On a warm summer's day in 1911, a family outing turned tragic. Chauffer John Widders was driving the Houghton family in a Pierce-Arrow when he was forced to drive around a work crew on a narrow mountain road. He hit the soft shoulder of the road, which gave way, sending the automobile rolling down the embankment.

Family friend Sybil Hutton was crushed and died at the scene. Mary Houghton, Albert's beloved daughter, was badly injured. The first doctor to arrive at the scene drove Mary to the nearest hospital, but she never made it. She succumbed to her injuries on the way. John Widders and Albert C. Houghton suffered only minor injuries and soon returned to the mansion.

John Widders could not forgive himself for what happened to Mary (after all, he was driving the automobile when the accident occurred). A short time later, his lifeless body was discovered in the barn behind the mansion. He was found with a bullet in his head, having committed suicide. Albert C. Houghton also never recovered emotionally from the accident and died soon after at the mansion.

The mansion soon passed to the Masons, who still own it today. Not only did they inherit the house, but reportedly a ghost or two. Members of the Masonic Lodge hear knocking on the walls and footsteps in the corridors, but when they investigate the sounds, there is no one there. Other members have even reported hearing a woman's or girl's voice echoing in some of the rooms of the mansion. There are also numerous cold spots and the lights seem to flicker at will. Orbs appear in photographs taken at the mansion,

and shadows are seen in the corner of your eye. Josh Mantello, one of the Masons, tells the story of a big, burly telemarketer who ran from the mansion late one night and refused to return. What did he see?

Are John Widders, Mary Houghton, and Albert C. Houghton still there? The evidence points to "something" there, but only the mansion holds the answers.

—Ron Kolek
Lead Investigator,
The New England Ghost Project

METROPOLITAN STATE HOSPITAL
475 TRAPELO ROAD
WALTHAM, MASSACHUSETTS 02154
WEBSITE:
www.metropolitanstatehospital.com

The Metropolitan State Hospital on the Waltham/Lexington line is one of several buildings designed and built by the late Dr. Thomas Kirkbride. Originally opened as a state-run mental asylum in 1930, the massive 490 acres of property has served many purposes since then: a haunted house for charity, a farm, and a school for juvenile offenders. Although the hospital is now closed and the land is being developed into a golf course, the torments that the residents endured have permanently left their mark on the area.

Like many asylums in Massachusetts, Met State has gained a steady reputation as a severely haunted location. In addition to the torments suffered inside the walls of the hospital, the spirits might be restless for other reasons. More than 350 former residents were placed in pauper's graves on the grounds of the hospital. Originally, none had proper headstones or even names attached to them. They were buried with only a stone to mark their number and their religion. In recent years, people have made an effort to give the souls a proper burial, but this does not seem to have slowed the hauntings.

Workers had reported hauntings in the buildings well before the hospital closed. Some dealt nightly with shadowy figures moving in and out of rooms and locked doors opening and slamming closed. For a while, electroshock treatment was used at the hospital. Years later, workers reported still hearing screams and seeing flashing lights from those areas. Activity was also reported in a series of tunnels underneath the grounds used by the workers to travel to different parts of the campus. Their passages were lit by single lightbulbs yards apart, and it was common for the workers to feel unseen hands grab at their feet or touch their faces or backs as they walked into the darkened areas.

Today the asylum is closed and is falling into disrepair. Its physical appearance and the legends surrounding the hauntings are enough to scare most people away, but the people who continue to walk the beautiful, scenic grounds say the emotions from the building are much more tangible. Most people feel like they are being watched and get uneasy, as if they are not wanted. Others feel physically sick and then return to normal as soon as they step off the grounds. A few local people have even had the overwhelming feeling of experiencing the actual emotions felt by the patients, and they could talk about procedures and practices of the hospital although they had never actually witnessed them.

—Christopher Balzano
Founder, Massachusetts
Paranormal Crossroads

THE REDHEADED HITCHHIKER OF ROUTE 44
ROUTE 44 NEAR THE
SEEKONK/REHOBOTH LINE
REHOBOTH, MASSACHUSETTS

One of the most popular and most notorious phantoms in Massachusetts walks along a dark stretch of road in the town of Rehoboth. For more than three decades, a redheaded man has been seen walking down Route 44, waiting to be picked up. At times he has been seen hitchhiking, and other times he has been seen walking into the woods or in the middle of the road, not moving as a car passes through him. At least once he was seen outside the window of a car that was moving at more than 40 miles per hour.

Who the man was is a mystery. Several people have died along that stretch of road, including a man matching the phantom's description, but no one can say for sure who the man is or when the haunting started. He is described as being more than 6 feet tall, well-built, and having red hair and a red beard. He is often seen wearing jeans or work pants, but he is always described as wearing a red flannel shirt, sometimes tucked in and sometimes left out. Some travelers see him as well-kempt, but he has also been seen with his characteristic red hair disheveled and dirty. People who come into contact with him can tell he is not human by his eyes, which are often described as lifeless.

Most of the encounters follow a similar pattern: Someone is driving along, usually alone, when they see a man in or alongside the road. They may either hit him or stop to pick him up. The hitchhiker will interact with the person and then eventually vanish before their eyes or will no longer be there when they turn to look. This is followed by some type of audio finale where he laughs, yells at them, or taunts them.

A woman once reported stopping to pick the man up. He disappeared as he went to grab the door handle. Her car battery then died, and then she heard a man laughing at her, although he could no longer be seen. Ten minutes later, the car started, but not before the woman broke down in fright. One man had been driving alone when he saw the redheaded man on the side of the road. He stopped and called out to the man, who started to walk toward him. As he got closer, the ghost slowly faded until he completely disappeared. Another witness had the hitchhiker appear in the backseat of his car through the rearview mirror. The radio started to scan the stations and then became so loud it shook the car. The phantom disappeared and began to laugh on the radio.

Local legend says that if three people are driving in the same car on Route 44, the redheaded hitchhiker will appear in the empty seat.

—Christopher Balzano
Founder, Massachusetts
Paranormal Crossroads

THE CHARLESGATE HOTEL

4 CHARLESGATE EAST
BOSTON, MASSACHUSETTS 02116

If only half of the stories about the old Charlesgate Hotel in Kenmore Square

were true, it would still be one of the most haunted locations in Boston. The building has seen the best and worst for the past hundred years, and its history represents the darker history of the city.

The building was originally opened in the late 19th century as a luxury hotel catering to only the most exclusive clientele. The original architect, J. Pickering Putnam, designed the six-floor building to be the centerpiece of Kenmore Square, but several of his designs for the building have never been explained. The top floor can-

Photo by Christopher Balzano

not be seen from the outside, and the east side of the building is shaped like a "C," allowing only the people across the way to see those apartments. One persistent rumor is that Putnam himself was a member of a cult, and the Charlesgate Hotel was designed and built with the right materials to act as a magnet for the paranormal.

From 1947 to 1972, the building acted as a dormitory for Boston University. The dorm quickly earned a reputation for being haunted, especially one room in which a student had killed himself. The building then became a tenement, servicing both upper-class college students and some of the more questionable residents of Boston. By the time Emerson College bought the building in 1981, it had seen its share of accidents, misfortune, and death. A small girl is said to have died in the elevator shaft. During a flood, several horses, and the young men who tried to save them, died in the basement. Cult activity, first hinted at when the building was a hotel, was now rumored to be full-on Satanic black masses with human sacrifices.

The arrival of the Emerson students did little to calm the evil spirits already attracted to the place. Charlesgate was now home to artistic residents who were known to practice alternative religions and engage in heavy drug use. The building seemed to feed off these students and become a full-fledged haunted building.

Students using *Ouija* boards have had direct questions answered in precise detail. On other occasions, the boards have flown across the room. Some students have seen dark figures in their rooms at night or have witnessed fogs moving in the halls. One student woke up to find a thick, black fog hovering above him. As he regained his ability to move, he watched it cross the room and disappear through the wall. After searching, the student found a secret room behind his wall. Other students have had their stereos and televisions turn on and off without explanation and have had things disappear and turn up at random. Over the years, the one constant has been the attraction of its residents to the black arts and Satanism.

In 1994, the dorm was sold and turned into condominiums.

—Christopher Balzano
Founder, Massachusetts
Paranormal Crossroads

SESSION HOUSE ON THE CAMPUS OF SMITH COLLEGE

109 ELM STREET
NORTHAMPTON, MASSACHUSETTS 01063
WEBSITE: *www.smith.edu/sao/reslife/houses/sessions.php*

The Session House dormitory is said to be haunted by two college students who died in a dark passage, two small children accidentally killed by their nervous mother, and two lovers whose doomed romance was never meant to be.

In 1700, John Hunt built a house for his family outside of the main military complex in Northampton. To protect against attack, he built a secret passage that went underground to the river nearby. During the Revolutionary War, British General "Gentleman Johnny" Burgoyne fought against the colonists and was eventually caught and held prisoner in the house. Burgoyne quickly fell in love with Hunt's daughter, Lucy, and although they were forbidden to see each other, the two would meet in the hidden passage. Eventually "Gentleman Johnny" was sent back to England, promising to return for young Lucy. He never returned and Lucy was heartbroken.

Ever since, the ghosts of the two lovers have been seen and heard from the passageway. There is not much detail about the nature of the hauntings, but what is also interesting is not just the ghosts that might exist in the hallway, but the ceremony that has evolved around them. Every Halloween, the young women at Session House are allowed to search for the hidden passageway and for the souls that are supposed to haunt there. For 20 minutes on that night only, they search the nooks and crannies of the house without any light, looking for the passage that contains the spirits. To find the passage is to be honored in the dorm and to be part of the larger tradition of the college.

The unlucky lovers are not the only ghosts said to live in the dorm. Another tale tells of a mother and her two children who were alone in the home one night telling ghost stories and scaring each other. The mother thought she heard a noise and grabbed an axe to protect her family. She began to search the house, eventually making it back to the room her children were in. Thinking they were intruders who had broken into the house, she killed them. When she saw her mistake, she killed herself in a room on the third floor of the house.

The other famous tale from Session House takes place after it had become a dorm and the passage hunt had already become part of its tradition. Two girls found the secret passage, but they fell into a hole in the staircase and either broke their necks or injured themselves and starved to death. Local lore says that the girls can be heard as you near the staircase.

Some say the ghosts might also try to push or drag you into the hole.

—*Christopher Balzano*
Founder, Massachusetts
Paranormal Crossroads

Photo by Jeff Belanger

STONE'S PUBLIC HOUSE
179 MAIN STREET
ASHLAND, MASSACHUSETTS 01721
TEL: 1 (508) 881-1778
WEBSITE: *www.stonespublichouse.com*

Built in 1832 by Captain John Stone, this public house has been an inn, a restaurant, a stop on the Underground Railroad, and a regular visiting place for the ghosts of John Stone, a traveling salesman who Stone accidentally killed, a little girl who died in the inn in the late 1800s, a former manager, and possibly some slaves who never made it to freedom.

Walking in to Stone's Public House today is like stepping back a century into the past. There's New England charm, creaking wood plank floors, and staff members who almost all have a ghost story to tell. I investigated the location in December of 2003 and toured the building from its low-ceilinged basement where a hole broken through the foundation reveals a hidden room used by the Underground Railroad; up to its charming main dining area; on to the second floor, which features smaller and more private function rooms; and a peek up the stairs to the third floor, which is no longer in use but at one time served as guest rooms when it was an inn.

Staff have reported smelling pipe smoke, even before the building opens for business for the day. Staff and patrons have both claimed to see apparitions and feel cold spots around the building, some have been tapped on the back, and some have even been pushed out of the way by an unseen force. Behind the bar is one very curious photograph taken from a night when a band was performing in the pub section. Within one of the vertical wooden beams, you can very clearly see the image of a man with a big, black mustache, dressed in old-fashioned clothes.

Jim Terlemezian has been working as a bartender at the restaurant since 2001. He said, "I definitely believe in ghosts, without a doubt. We came in on a Sunday to work a function, so I got in around 10 a.m. and worked until about 2 a.m., so I was exhausted. Everybody had cleared out, and it was just me and Marti [former owner, Marti Northover]. She was upstairs in her office, and I was on the first floor at the end of the bar. I went into the back to change my shirt and left the door open. As I take my shirt off, I hear a voice. I can't tell you what they said—I couldn't even tell you if it was a male or a female, but it was a young kid. I stopped what I was doing and came out [to the main bar] and said, 'Marti?' I thought maybe she said 'Jim' or something like that. But she wasn't even here; she was upstairs."

—Jeff Belanger
Founder, Ghostvillage.com

New Hampshire

WINDHAM RESTAURANT
59 RANGE ROAD
WINDHAM, NEW HAMPSHIRE 03087
TEL: 1 (603) 870-9270
WEBSITE: *www.windhamrestaurant.com*

The sign over the door of the Windham Restaurant says "Food & Spirits," and that may be truer than you think! The restaurant is located in an old house built around 1812 by the Dinsmore family. Issac and then Horace Dinsmore occupied the house for many years, but who "haunts" it now?

Three restaurants have occupied the house, and each has experienced some "unusual" events. First it was a Thai restaurant, then a French restaurant, and then finally the Windham Restaurant. While it was the French restaurant, the "spirits" singled out the blond waitresses. These women would have their hair played with by some unknown entity. It would also unclasp their jewelry—I was a witness to one such event.

While conducting an investigation there, one of the waitresses experienced a cold chill and then for no apparent reason, her necklace fell off her neck in front of me. She became hysterical and began to cry. This was not the first time it had happened, and she was getting tired of it; however, this was not the only game the unseen force liked to play.

Sometimes when the staff came in early in the morning, they would find the chairs moved and the knives and forks crossed on the tables. There were also a bunch of empty boxes wrapped like Christmas gifts on the third floor that were often moved. One time the boxes were stacked like towers and another time they were stacked wall-to-wall in mid-air across the stairs.

These unusual events continued when it became the Windham Restaurant. In addition to the chairs and place settings being moved, glasses would sometimes fly across the bar and dishes would shatter in the kitchen. Windows would open, lights would be turned on and off, and batteries in the deodorizers would drain at an unusual rate.

This is all interesting, but has anybody ever seen the "ghost"? The answer is an astounding yes! In addition to the staff, several customers have reported seeing the spirits—a little boy has been seen at the second floor wait station, a little girl has been seen wandering around the restaurant, and "Jacob," a man in a blue suit, has been seen several times. In fact, Lula, one of the current owners, saw a man in a blue suit fall down the stairs, but when she ran to help him, he had disappeared.

Is the Windham Restaurant haunted? Let's just say there is more truth in the "Food & Spirits" sign than meets the eye.

—Ron Kolek
Lead Investigator,
The New England Ghost Project

AMERICA'S STONEHENGE aka MYSTERY HILL

105 HAVERHILL ROAD
SALEM, NEW HAMPSHIRE, 03079
TEL: 1 (603) 893-8300
WEBSITE: *www.stonehengeusa.com*

America's Stonehenge has always been shrouded in mystery (hence the pseudonym Mystery Hill). Located deep in the woods of Salem, New Hampshire, this 4,000-year-old megalith site is a maze of stonewalls and trails punctuated with stone chambers. The main site contains a sacrificial altar, a working observatory, a burial chamber, and an oracle chamber, but little is known of who built the site or why it was abandoned.

The site is open to the public and self-guided tours are available. Although paranormal activity is not openly talked about, there are too many strange occurrences to ignore. People visiting the site have reported many unusual events (both physical and metaphysical). Some have felt as if they were being watched, while others have even seen what they describe as a pair of "red eyes" peering at them.

Neighbors have heard and seen strange sounds and lights in the woods surrounding the site. There is even a report that one of the employees there saw

Photo by Jeff Belanger

a stone turn into an old lady and walk across the parking lot. Stones taken from the site have been quickly returned by frightened visitors claiming that they have turned into 9-foot-tall Indians in their homes. These stories are reminiscent of the tales of ancient "shape shifters."

Blue energy fields have been witnessed and even photographed by many visitors to this ancient site. Batteries drain and even hot coffee goes cold quickly. Mediums and sensitives feel the presence of hundreds of spirits, but who are they? Phoenicians, Irish Monks, Native Americans, Vikings, or someone else? For now, at least, it looks as if the story of Mystery Hill will remain a mystery.

—Ron Kolek
Lead Investigator,
The New England Ghost Project

THE COUNTRY TAVERN

452 AMHERST STREET
NASHUA, NEW HAMPSHIRE 03063
TEL: 1 (603) 889-5871
WEBSITE: *www.countrytavern.org*

When you sit down to dinner at the Country Tavern, you can expect a wonderful entrée, a completely original soup, and a good ghost story. The owners are not afraid of their resident spirit; they advertise her on their menu.

Elizabeth Ford is said to haunt different rooms in the restaurant, most often the kitchen and ladies' washroom. Elizabeth's story begins with her marriage to an English sea captain who spent months at a time away from their New Hampshire residence. To ease his absence, he had a house built in 1741 on the land the Country Tavern now stands on. After one especially long trip, the captain came home to find his wife with a newborn baby that was not his. He killed them both and buried them on the property.

Photo by Christopher Balzano

Several buildings have been located on the property over the years, but the Country Tavern is the only one that has reported the mysterious activity of Elizabeth. She has been known to play with women's hair in the ladies' room and move plates and glasses. People have actually seen her in the upstairs dining room, and occasionally she has been seen from the outside windows. She has been described as having long, white hair and wearing a white dress.

One patron left the building to have a cigarette in the back parking lot. As he watched, the swinging door opened and closed a dozen times with no person coming through the door. When he went up to ask the staff about the strange occurrence, he was told the dining room was not in use that night.

—Christopher Balzano
Founder, Massachusetts
Paranormal Crossroads

Rhode Island

NINE MEN'S MISERY MEMORIAL

DIAMOND HILL ROAD
CUMBERLAND, RHODE ISLAND

The emotional and psychic impression left behind when opposite forces clash in mortal battle is one that usually well outlasts the memory of the actual event. The now-silent forests and meadows of Southern New England are no different. Cultural differences, personal tensions, and increasing violent incursions onto one another's lands ultimately climaxed into the two-year bloodbath historians would later name the King Phillip War. The ghosts of those bloody days often remind Southern New England residents and visitors alike of the carnage of those times.

Few public reminders exist that tell of this conflict. Perhaps this is one reason they annually report so many hauntings in the areas where these bloody battles between the Native American and his white adversary raged. Of the surviving reminders of this forgotten war, none has more paranormal activity associated with it than the wooded area surrounding the Nine Men's Misery memorial. The site's simple stone and mortar monument marks the area where Indian pursuers overran eight Rhode Island militiamen and their leader. Their flailed (skinned alive) bodies evidenced their slow, agonizing deaths, their only escape coming when their tormentors finally beheaded them and placed their heads on stakes.

For years, with reports reaching the Rhode Island Paranormal Research Group as recently as March 2004, paranormal activity has been verified in this area. Reported phenomena include sudden temperature drops and the audible, mournful sobbing of men. Visitors to the monument have submitted many photos containing questionable phenomena, including energy streaks in the immediate area.

However, of all the known ghosts of the war, these former monastery grounds still hold within their grasp one of the most disturbing. Sightings often confirm that one does not have to believe in ghosts to experience seeing one, including the ghost of a little girl dressed in mid-17th-century clothing whose presence we repeatedly see or feel on the grounds. The experience can leave one shaken, however, as witnesses always observe her desperately darting through the area's woods in a panic. Some have only heard her footsteps running toward them and heard her panicked panting. In either situation, the girl's ghost always and quite abruptly vanishes, perpetually fleeing her Indian pursuers.

—Andrew D. Laird
Founder and Director, The Rhode Island
Paranormal Research Group

THE GREAT SWAMP MASSACRE SITE

THE SITE IS ON ROUTE 2, JUST SOUTH OF THE ROUTE 138 AND ROUTE 2 ROTARY
SOUTH COUNTY, RHODE ISLAND

On a cold December morning in 1675, a large, heavily armed contingent of Colonial militia and regular British troops slipped silently through the morning mists toward a waking native encampment. It was their hope that they would catch what they regarded as renegade Indians off-guard and stop an impending Indian war before it could begin. This was the powerful Narragansett tribe's winter camp, and with the help of their Pequot and Mohegan scouts, the troops hoped that this secret sanctuary was to become the Narragansett's graveyard. The smoke from the inhabitants' cooking fires lingered like a specter above their wigwams and long houses. The occasional cry of an infant waking from his sleep betrayed the true nature of the "enemy" below. Suddenly, one of only a few younger braves left behind to guard the camp spotted the invaders and opened fire. The shot warned the camp of the impending danger, but it was too late. Volley after volley of "modern" musket fire sent waves of hot lead into the encampment, making quick work of running women trying to flee with children. Men bearing tomahawks and knives and using the butt of their rifles as clubs quickly dispatched the remaining old and sick. The target of their attack, Chief Metacom (King Phillip), was not at the encampment as their scouts had promised. Despite their losses at the hands of those few defenders, the war they had attempted to avoid had just begun by their own hand.

Today, an old and decaying memorial stands, where it was erected by colonists at the close of the war, shortly after 1675. Defiant of the facts, it tells of a great battle against the Narragansett, not of the massacre of unarmed innocents that really took place not far from that spot. More than a few visitors to the monument and to the surrounding hiking trails have told of an overwhelming sadness coming over them. More still have repeated how the area forests will suddenly fall silent for no apparent reason—often followed by the eerie sound of distant cries and even screams coming from the thick confines of a still almost impregnable swamp. Yet others have been driven back to their cars by the sudden chill coming over them and the endless and unnerving feeling that they were being observed.

Repeated investigations of the area by several serious groups have confirmed it as being a hotbed of paranormal activity.

—Andrew D. Laird
Founder and Director, The Rhode Island
Paranormal Research Group

Sprague Mansion
1351 Cranston Street
Cranston, Rhode Island 02920
Tel: 1 (401) 944-9226
Website:
www.cranstonhistoricalsociety.org

What, or who, is haunting Sprague Mansion? For many years, this large and stately mansion, now the home of the Cranston Historical Society, has had a reputation for being plagued by unexplained phenomena. Many visitors have reported hearing footsteps or seeing an astral presence. The apparition is often observed or heard descending the main staircase, or is felt as a passing breath of icy air. The wine cellar also has been a site of frightening occurrences, including the appearance of inexplicable orbs in photograph after photograph. Likely candidates for these hauntings are plentiful. Until several years ago, many believed that the ghost was that of John Gordon, convicted murderer of Amasa Sprague and the last person executed in the state of Rhode Island.

Amasa Sprague, a businessman and manufacturer from a politically powerful family, left his Cranston mansion one day in December 1843 to travel to Johnston. The following morning, his bludgeoned body (he had also been shot in the wrist and bitten by a dog) was found beside the road, almost within sight of his mansion. Gordon, an Irish immigrant and employee at the mansion, had been seen arguing with Sprague the day he was killed. Gordon was tried, found guilty of murder on the basis of circumstantial evidence, and hanged in 1845. Evidence later came to light that cast serious doubt on his guilt. Public indignation following John Gordon's execution led to legislation abolishing capital punishment in Rhode Island. Although the actual killer was never found, some scholars now believe that Amasa's brother, William, was behind the deed.

Besides Gordon and Amasa Sprague himself, other suggestions have included Amasa's father, William Sprague II, who died after a chicken bone lodged in his throat during a family breakfast; Kate Chase Sprague (daughter of Lincoln's Treasury Secretary and United States Supreme Court Chief Justice Salmon P. Chase, and wife of Amasa's son, Governor William Sprague IV), who lost her reputation and her beauty as she frittered away a fortune and died destitute and insane; and Kate's ne'er-do-well son, William Sprague V, who committed suicide while unemployed in Seattle in 1890.

Another addition to the possible uneasy souls connected to Sprague Mansion was revealed in 1968. A séance held by a Brown University student who lived in the mansion as a caretaker revealed the agitated spirit of Charles, the mansion's live-in butler during the 1880s. He had expected his daughter to marry one of the owner's sons (by then, the Sprague family's business had collapsed and they had moved out). Charlie's anticipated inheritance evaporated when the son married someone else. The séance climaxed when the *Ouija* began to move violently, spelling, "My land! My land! My land!" When the spirit was asked what it needed to be at peace, it responded, "Tell my story." Lydia Rapoza, the curator at Sprague Mansion, said that Charlie's ghost was trapped in the small "doll room" off the stair landing when a connector was erected between the original house (c. 1790) and the addition (1864), walling off what had been the servants' quarters.

The history of the mansion suggests that, throughout the 19th century, those associated with Sprague Mansion seemed to have more than their share of misfortunes and tortured personalities. Perhaps enough to create a host of restless souls.

—Michael Bell

RAMTAIL FACTORY
IN THE WOODS OFF OF ROUTE 6 AND RAMTAIL ROAD
FOSTER, RHODE ISLAND 02825

If there is one place in Rhode Island that deserves mention in the realm of ghosts, it is the Ramtail Factory. Not only do the locals have endless tales of the ghostly mill, the state even acknowledges the place as a haunted locale in the 1885 State Census, page 36. This makes it the only recognized haunted site in the whole state, if not all of New England, at that time.

In 1799, the Potter family ran a fulling mill. William Potter expanded the mill in

RAMTAIL FACTORY

1813 and took on his son-in-law, Peleg Walker, as a partner. The Potters ran the mill by day, and Peleg with lantern in hand would act as night watchman. At the break of dawn, he would ring the bell to summon the workers to their daily routines. All was well for several years until William and Peleg had some sort of disagreement. During this argument it was said that Mr. Walker stated that they would one day have to remove the keys to the mill from the pocket of a dead man.

This promise was fulfilled on the morning of May 19, 1822, when the bell failed to toll. They entered the mill and found Peleg Walker hanging from the bell rope, keys to the mill dangling from his pocket.

They buried him in the family plot, but he did not rest. That night the bell began ringing at the stroke of midnight. They checked out the mill but found no visible person who would have caused the sound. For a few more nights, the bell sounded at the witching hour, again, with no hand to pull the rope. This forced the Potters to remove the bell, but Peleg had more in store.

At midnight the next evening, the villagers were awoken by the clatter of the mill running full tilt. When they arrived on the scene, they stood agape as they watched the mill in full operation by itself with the great waterwheel used to run the mill moving in the opposite direction of the stream.

The villagers left the area for fear of their lives, and the mill soon closed for good. Witnesses reported seeing the specter of Peleg Walker meandering from building to building with a lantern in hand, creaking in the wind. In the 1880s, the factory burned to the ground, but the foundations still grace the forest to this day.

I did several investigations of the factory and proved it is still haunted. On one particular night, Rhode Island Paranormal saw a glowing apparition move about within the factory walls at the height the floor used to be. Another night we stood in the dark silence as the crunching of the leaves and the sounds of a swinging lantern moved by us into the foundation of the main building then move by us again to the smaller foundation just behind us. The sounds were recorded on tape and are distinct.

It seems that Peleg Walker still makes his eternal rounds in the dark of the Foster woods. This just proves that the Ramtail Factory is still alive and full of spirit.

The ruins of the Ramtail Factory are located in the woods of Foster, Rhode Island. Take Route 6 West. When you get to Hopkins Mill District in Foster, take a left onto Ramtail Road. The entrance to the trail leading to the factory runs along Dolly Cole Brook just before the little bridge on Ramtail Road.

—Thomas D'Agostino
Writer, Paranormal Researcher, and
Investigator, Rhode Island Paranormal

Vermont

THE ICE HOUSE RESTAURANT
171 BATTERY STREET
BURLINGTON, VERMONT 05401

Burlington, Vermont, is located in the northwestern tip of the state along the famed Lake Champlain—home of "Champy," the lake's infamous, and many say mythical, sea creature. It is also home to many land-bound oddities and eerie places. One such place is the Ice House Restaurant.

The history of the structure is born of tragedy. John Winan, a Burlington shipbuilder, erected his home on the site in 1808. That year he began construction of Lake Champlain's first steamboat. In 1868, fire claimed the home and was soon rebuilt from the foundation to serve as an icehouse.

The massive three-story building supplied ice year-round to the residents of Burlington for many generations with the chunks cut from Lake Champlain. It remained in operation well into the 20th century before being converted into retail property.

The massive square beams used to support the heavy ice still adorn the building as well as some entities from the past.

My wife's daughter and her fiancé had relocated to Burlington due to her job. Her fiancé, a chef, sought employment at restaurants in the area and was given a job at the Ice House. It wasn't very long before he had many a tale to relay to me.

One day as he was in the kitchen cleaning up, he spied someone out of the corner of his eye. To his amazement, he gazed upon a semitransparent apparition of an old lady swinging a bell. As he approached the figure, it vanished as silently as it had come. The wraith has been seen numerous times by other employees as well. A cook who has been there for many years is so accustomed to the haunted place that it seems lonely to him without something happening regularly.

The staff on duty has often heard the distinct sound of ice blocks being dragged across the floor. Objects that are put down in obvious places tend to disappear, only to be later discovered hidden in strange nooks of the kitchen and basement.

So, if you are in the area of Battery and King Streets in Burlington, Vermont, be sure to have a bite at the Ice House Restaurant. If you should feel a sudden cold chill while there, you'll know that it is not on account of any ice!

—Thomas D'Agostino
Writer, Paranormal Researcher, and
Investigator, Rhode Island Paranormal

LONG TRAIL

ROUTES 7 AND 9 BETWEEN GLASTONBURY MOUNTAIN AND POWNAL
BENNINGTON, VERMONT

It is apparent why Vermont is called the Green Mountain State as soon as one enters this New England parcel. Its rolling hills and draping fields have been the subject of many great photographs. Yet deep within lies a darker color that runs black with evil and mystery in many places. Restless spirits moan for justice in the howling mountain winds. One of those places is the Long Trail hiking path in Bennington, located in the southwest corner of the state.

Most recreational adventure seekers shudder at the very name, for they know that the path is cursed and the legend says that some who have chosen to ignore its evil have never returned. People seem to vanish into thin air on the trail without ever leaving the slightest trace of being there.

On November 12, 1945, Middle Rivers, a seasoned native to the area, disappeared without a trace while on the familiar trail. In December of 1946, Paula Weldon vanished from the trail while hiking it with some fellow college students when she wandered away from the group for a few moments. She, too, was never seen again.

James Telford fell victim to the trail in December of 1949 and Frances Christman in December of 1950. There are many other reports of disappearances on the trail dating back to the 1930s. Some are documented and some are not. There was one person who was found murdered on the trail—Frieda Langer was the only missing person to ever have been actually recovered from the bizarre path. Her untimely demise, however, remains a mystery.

A few locals swear that they have hiked the trail many times without incident. Most of them avoid the foreboding woods for fear of encountering the unknown that lurks within the deep thicket, awaiting the next unsuspecting hiker. Those who have hiked the woods and lived to tell about it are fortunate in that the woods were probably not hungry that day, or they had already had their fill.

—Thomas D'Agostino
Writer, Paranormal Researcher, and
Investigator, Rhode Island Paranormal

BOWMAN HOUSE AND LAUREL GLEN MAUSOLEUM
ROUTE 103
CUTTINGSVILLE, VERMONT 05738

As you drive on Route 103 in Cuttingsville, Vermont, an eerie sight may suddenly overtake you. It is the pale, white figure of a man crouching before the door of the Laurel Glen Mausoleum with a wreath and key in one hand

and a top hat in the other. The mournful figure is watching the door, as if waiting for its inhabitants to sally forth from the burial vault. No, the personage is not a ghost but the statue of John P. Bowman who, along with his family, is buried in the great vault.

The statue has graced the steps of the vault since 1881, when the wealthy farmer had the chamber built to house his wife and two daughters. Within the crypt that was erected with the help of 25 sculptors is the life-size statue of his oldest daughter, Addie, who died when she was an infant. Also within its walls are the busts of his other daughter, Ella, and his wife, Jenny, who tragically passed away within seven months of each other. The mausoleum would be the talk of Vermont. Ten years later, in 1891, Mr. Bowman himself passed on and was interred in the burial vault. The reason for the statue of his likeness at the steps of the chamber remains a mystery to this day.

Strange things have been reported around the mausoleum at night, but what is more horrifying is the Bowman House across the street from the cemetery, because it is extremely haunted. Many think it is the ghosts of Bowman and his family still dwelling within the mansion.

An unidentified woman has been seen on countless occasions in the house. A painting once flew off the wall at a little girl who stuck her tongue out at it. This phenomenon was witnessed by several people who were taking a tour of the great home. The mansion stood vacant for some years before it was recently purchased and renovated for its new owner. The woman now in possession of the home has reported seeing the spirits of the Bowman family everywhere in the house—so much so that she is afraid to venture forth from a special room after dark. She had to convert that area into a bedroom with a bathroom and even a little kitchenette, according to reports in the local Rutland papers. The spirits seem to have taken over the whole house, but they let her have her one little area after the sun's rays have fallen beneath the horizon.

The owners will no longer stay in the Bowman house after dark. It becomes vacant save for the ghosts who run its domain in the dark of the night.

—Thomas D'Agostino
Writer, Paranormal Researcher, and
Investigator, Rhode Island Paranormal

BOWMAN HOUSE/LAUREL GLEN

Paranormal Investigator Profile

Troy Taylor

TROY TAYLOR is the author of more than 30 books about ghosts and hauntings, including *The Ghost Hunter's Guidebook* (Whitechapel Productions, 1999), *Haunted Illinois* (1999), and *The Haunting of America* (2001). He's the president of the American Ghost Society and editor of *Ghost of the Prairie Magazine*.

Q: What is your favorite haunted place?

That's one of those questions I can't answer with one. There are a handful of places that I always go back to, that I never get tired of and not just because of the history and all of the years of ghost stories behind them.

One of them is the Lemp Mansion in St. Louis. It's one of those places where the tragedy of the place just lends itself to a haunting. Plus,

Photo courtesy of Troy Taylor

there have been really reliable stories over the years. It's a place that I'm fascinated with. And I know this sounds bizarre, but it's a place that I'm really comfortable with. I think my fascination with the history of the family and my respect for the family just makes me feel comfortable there. But I do honestly think it's a very haunted place.

Second would be a place in Illinois called the Old Slave House. I can't give you a town that it's near because it's just in the middle of nowhere. But it has a really horrendous history regarding a guy who leased slaves to work salt lands. He ended up kidnapping free African-Americans and pressing them into slavery. It's the only place in Illinois where slavery really existed. He kept the slaves chained up in the attic of the house. This sounds like an urban legend, but this is all really documented history and it's one of the only buildings—as far as I know, it's the only building in the state of Illinois—where official state records actually talk about the ghosts. That's how long the ghost stories have been around.

The Bell Witch cave in Tennessee is also very high on my list. I've been there probably a dozen times. I've spent the night in the cave, I've known the owners for years—it's just one of those places that has a great history behind it.

Finally, I'd have to say the first place where, I'm convinced, I actually saw a ghost. And that's the old Waverley Hills Sanitarium in Louisville, Kentucky. It's an old abandoned tuberculosis sanitarium with a dark history behind it, and there's just story after story there—more than just kids chasing down ghost stories. These are real people who've been there, who have had some really good documented encounters. One night, a friend and I were walking down the hallway there, and a guy walked across the hallway in front of us and disappeared into a room on the other side of the hall. I have no doubt that it was a ghost, considering the room was empty when we got there. I have to list that as one of my favorites.

Q: Why be a ghost investigator?

I'd love to say that I have some kind of really deep spiritual reasons for searching for life after death, but I don't. I've always just taken it as fact that there is life after death—that we're all going to end up somewhere. But preferably, I'm not going anywhere. I always tell people if it's possible, if you have a choice to be a ghost, I want to be one. So I'm not looking for proof, because I can't convince everybody. For me, it's just a lifelong fascination with the unusual and the unexplained. Yes, I'm convinced that there are ghosts and I'm convinced that there is life after death, but still, how does it work out? How does it happen? That's what intrigues me. If I had all of these answers, I probably wouldn't be interested.

Q: What are important items to bring with you on an investigation?

When I started out in this, I had a camera, I had a notebook, and I had a pen, and that's about it. That's why I think my belief system on the whole thing has never really changed. All of the gadgets and gear are great, but, for me, I find it hard to use electronic equipment and then offer that as any kind of proof. Only because there are so many things that can go wrong with electronics as far as trying to use them for evidence. Yes, it can be very compelling, but, for me, I'm always looking for the history behind the story. And by that I mean that if I can find a house, and that house turns out to have people who live in it now who claim that it's haunted, and I can go back through three previous owners and they all tell the exact same story, have the exact same things happening, without knowing that anyone else has ever reported it. For me, all I needed was a notebook and a pen to get what I consider to be "real proof" that the place is haunted. That's nothing that I [need to] use a magnetometer or a gauss meter or anything else to prove. I was able to do that with a pen and a piece of paper. People are the key behind the story—they are the essential element to all of this. People who get into this and don't have any kind of people skills are in big trouble. So that's really why I push with this kind of thing. If you have a video camera, bring it along, you want to remember what the place looks like. If you want to use electronic equipment, definitely use it if you know how to use it. But if you don't know how to use it, I tell people don't even bother.

Q: What's a funny thing that's happened to you during an investigation?

There've been so many things…. I always tell people, never go do this stuff by yourself. But, unfortunately, there have been a few times when I've gone and done it by myself. I had gotten a call from these people who were hearing foot-steps in their attic every night. They were sure that their home was haunted. And they had actually done some research into the history of the place. The real story behind it was that it had been owned by a farmer who had committed suicide when he lost his farm back during the Depression. He had gone up to the attic and hung himself. They were convinced that it was this guy's ghost and the foot-steps were happening every night—which obviously got my attention. Not only do they have a good story, but they have a good story that was happening every night. So I thought this was the perfect chance to get to really experience something.

So I went out to their house and it got late, and we were all sitting around in the bedroom being quiet and we started to hear footsteps walking around in the attic—I could hear them plain as day. I tried to get this woman's husband to go up there with me, but he was terrified—no way was he going to go up there. I climbed up into the attic with a flashlight (now a little nervous myself at this point), shined the light around, and I saw not one ghost, but two walking around. They were furry, they had tails—there were two great big raccoons in the attic. And every night, they would wake up when it got dark and go out to look for food. These things were so big that when they walked around up there, it sounded just like a person walking. You combine that with the story and suddenly you've got a ghost in the attic. I can laugh about it now. I always tell people you should never jump to conclusions.

Mid-Atlantic

Mid-Atlantic

Delaware

Fort Delaware

Delaware City, Delaware
Website: *www.del.net/org/fort*

Fort Delaware is located along the Delaware Bay, one mile east of Delaware City. It is also know by locals as Pea Patch Island because of a local legend about the origins of the island. The legend has it that a ship carrying peas ran aground on a river shoal and the peas sprouted, which started the formation of the island.

Construction on Fort Delaware was completed just two years before the Civil War and was to become a military POW camp. The pentagon-shaped building covers approximately six acres, the 32-foot-high walls vary from 7 feet to 30 feet in thickness, and the complex is surrounded by a moat 30 feet wide. The entrance is very imposing, with a drawbridge crossing the moat and torches on each side of the gate.

Photo by Joanne Davis

When you walk through the front gate of the fort, you get chills. If you listen closely, you may hear something from the past.

Living conditions were extremely harsh for the prisoners. An estimated 3,000 of them died here, so it is no wonder that it is considered one of the most haunted places in the Northeast.

In the dungeon, there have been reports of unexplained noises. People have heard moaning and chains banging. There have been reported sightings of Confederate soldiers running under the ramparts—it has been speculated that these may be images of prisoners trying to escape.

There have been many pictures taken at Fort Delaware that have unexplained features in them. Some have orbs, some have shadowy mists, and some have claimed to capture the ghost of a Confederate soldier standing in a doorway.

There is also a cemetery on the island where most of the soldiers who died there were buried, and it is also a noted haunted area.

Fort Delaware is now a state park. In September and October, they have candlelight ghost tours that have been quite eventful for the people brave enough to take them—some have had their own brush with the supernatural whether it be a strange photograph they took or spotting something ghostly. When talking to any of the employees or the people who do the reenactments at the fort, they all seem to have a few strange stories to tell. The spirits on the island are not harmful, but it is sad that, after all this time, they are still prisoners there. Apparently, for them, the war never ended.

—Joanne Davis

OLD NEW CASTLE
KENT COUNTY, DELAWARE

Old New Castle was founded in the 1600s by the Dutch who called it "New Amstel." It was later taken over by the Swedes and then the British in 1682 who renamed it "New Castle."

There are many homes that date back more than 200 years in age here. There are still cobblestone streets, old cemeteries, and churches around New Castle. When walking down the street, visitors get the feeling of being in a quaint, old colonial town.

There are also many ghost stories that come from this area. In some of the houses, footsteps are heard walking up and down the stairs with no living person to account for them. In Delaware, no smoking is allowed in public buildings, including restaurants and bars, yet some of the taverns in town report the smell of phantom pipe tobacco. Some people have even seen misty and shadowy figures by the old cemetery at night.

The most notable story in Old New Castle pertains to the Dutch soldiers. They are frequently seen walking up and down the old deserted remains of the docks at Battery Park, which is located on the Delaware River. The reported sightings are usually of full and occasionally of partial apparitions walking the old dock. Sightings of the Dutchmen have been reported throughout the year, but autumn is when the ghosts are most active. There are two soldiers who are often seen in the early evening, and there is one headless soldier who has been seen marching along the shoreline. There is not a lot known about these soldiers or why there are still here. Could they still be trying to protect their city from the Swedes? Could they still be waiting for a ship to dock? The only thing that is known for certain is that these spirits are persistent and very active.

—Joanne Davis

Maryland

LANDON HOUSE
3401 URBANA PIKE
URBANA, MARYLAND 21704
WEBSITE: *www.landonhouse.com*

In 1754 along the Rappahannock River in Virginia, the Landon House was built as a silk mill. In 1840, it was relocated to Urbana, Maryland, where it became the Shirley Female Academy and then the Landon Military Academy & Institute. At the time, slaves were commonplace, and the basement was used for their sleeping quarters. When the Confederates marched into Maryland, General J.E.B. Stuart took possession of the mansion. His calvary's encampment was located in the field adjacent to the mansion. On September 8, 1862, General Stuart initiated one of the most famous balls to ever take place during the Civil War: the "Sabers and Roses Ball." The next day, he and his calvary went off to fight in the Battle of Antietam, noted to be the bloodiest single day in American history. During the course of the Civil War,

Photo courtesy of WMGHS

the house served as a hospital for both Confederate and Union troops and still has original signed and dated Civil War sketches on the walls, drawn by Yankee and Rebel soldiers. Today, the Landon House is on the National Register of Historic Places.

Workers and visitors alike believe it to be haunted. One worker witnessed an apparition of a Civil War soldier in 2003. The entity walked in one of the front doors, paused in the foyer, continued up the staircase, and then dissipated into thin air. A direct quote (listed on the Sabers and Roses Website) from a worker in the mansion states: "People feel uneasy about being in the basement of the Landon House. This is where the worst spirits are. From

its days as a military hospital, the dead and the dying are felt in the depths of the basement. There is a feeling like the Amityville House. The dirt floors might still hold buried dead, and who knows what horror lurks from the days when the basement was used as the slave quarters for the mansion."

The West Michigan Ghost Hunters Society (WMGHS) performed a weekend-long investigation of the Landon House in April 2004. Paranormal activity was experienced in a majority of the rooms, along with the former calvary's encampment site. Intense temperature drops accompanied with feelings of being watched were both experienced in one of the archive rooms— a room that was documented as being used as the operating room when the mansion was used as a hospital. The basement, which housed the former slave quarters, held extreme feelings of negativity and anger. Unexplained footsteps were experienced in the hallways more than once during the weekend. WMGHS also photographed an abundance of orbs, mists, and vortices during the investigation.

—Nicole Bray
Founder, West Michigan
Ghost Hunters Society

BERTHA'S RESTAURANT AND BAR

734 S. BROADWAY
FELLS POINT
BALTIMORE, MARYLAND 21231
TEL: 1 (410) 327-5795
WEBSITE: *www.berthas.com*

Constructed around 1770, the restaurant known for its famous "EAT BERTHA'S MUSSELS" green bumper stickers has been through many incarnations since Colonial times. Built in Baltimore's

Historic Fells Point (Edgar Allan Poe's last stop before the afterlife), Bertha's has been a saloon, a boarding house, an eatery, and even a brothel at one time or another.

The atmosphere at Bertha's is a mixture of progressive art and attitude with a lot of old Baltimore nautical touches thrown in for good measure. Patrons are of all ages and backgrounds, and at any time a table can be hard to come by. Customers and employees have reported many strange occurrences over the years. One customer reported a man in 19th-century clothing near a downstairs window; another regular witnessed a woman in white descending the staircase from the restrooms upstairs. Employees have seen a woman with a wide-brimmed black hat in a studio upstairs and a child running along a hallway. Dark figures are seen quite often, and many have reported feeling uneasy, sensing they are being watched.

The Maryland Paranormal Investigators Coalition has done a few investigations and workshops there. On one investigation, a woman's voice can be heard laughing on a recorded EVP. During one of the workshops, a trunk on the second floor near the bathrooms shook and rattled while five people looked on.

—Vincent Wilson,
Founder and President, Maryland
Paranormal Investigators Coalition

New Jersey

HARRY'S ROAD HOUSE
662 COOKMAN AVENUE
ASBURY PARK, NEW JERSEY 07712
TEL: 1 (732) 897-1444
WEBSITE: *www.harrysroadhouse.com*

Made famous by Bruce Springsteen, the town of Asbury Park has a history beyond that of Palace Amusements and the Jersey shore.

November 15, 1910, marks the discovery of the mutilated body of 9-year-old Marie Smith. A student at Bradley School, she was on her way home that afternoon, but never made it. Eventually, 27-year-old Frank Heidemann, a German immigrant, confessed to her murder and was convicted and sentenced to death by electrocution. While this reads as a triumph for investigator Raymond C. Schindler, one finds many disconcerting discrepancies in the confession of Heidemann, leaving one to wonder if an innocent man was, in fact, put to death.

In July 2003, the New Jersey Ghost Hunters Society (NJGHS) was contacted by the public relations and event coordinator of Harry's Road House to investigate due to her own as well as the chef's experiences, and the manager's encounter, and patrons' reports.

She reported leaving her office in the basement one evening and while pushing the door closed, she felt it push back at her. She also experienced the feeling of dread overwhelming her one night with the thought repeating in her head of, "I shouldn't have been here."

One night in June 2003, the manager was closing up when he witnessed a white glow or aura coming up the stairs from the basement to the kitchen. On another occasion, he and two of the chefs went down to the basement to finish up and leave for the night. They witnessed an old woman at the end of the basement. The manager called out to her and advised her that the restaurant was closed and she needed to leave. She did not respond. He moved closer to her and said again, "We're closed, you cannot be down here." With that, she evaporated right in front of all of them.

A garbage collector had an encounter with the old woman ghost while making his pickup early one morning. The ghost even called him by name.

Several times, patrons have reported a female crying in one of the stalls of the ladies' room. Upon investigation, no one is ever found. A local police officer believes the ghost of the woman to be "Sara," the daughter of the shoe-store owner from when the building housed their store and a children's clothing store. Or could it be the ghost of Marie's distraught mother still searching for her little girl?

NJGHS historian, Stephen Goldner, researched tax records, sewer records, and interviewed a local historian. It's interesting to note that the maps of the area at that time indicate that Marie Smith should not have been in the Cookman Avenue area, as her walk home from school is on the other side of town. It's possible the public relations and event coordinator of Harry's Road House was actually picking up the ghost's thoughts and emotions.

—L'Aura Hladik
Co-Founder, New Jersey
Ghost Hunters Society

RIDGEDALE AVENUE AND SUMMERHILL PARK

RIDGEDALE AVENUE AND FAIRVIEW AVENUE
MADISON, NEW JERSEY 07940

Madison, New Jersey, was the town for millionaires such as the Vanderbilts to build their estates in and maintain commutable proximity to New York City. The town became known as "The Rose City" because the country's finest roses were grown here. Today, the serene park setting located on Ridgedale Avenue is the façade that masks the once-formidable Kluxen Winery.

On October 7, 1921, the suburban community was stunned by the brutal murder of 12-year-old Jeanette Lawrence. She was last seen alive that night waving good-bye to Mrs. Sandt, the woman whose 4-year old daughter she babysat. Her body was found at 7:30 p.m. in the woods by Chauncey Griswold and Walter Schultz, local Boy Scouts who were helping in the hunt to find the missing girl.

Although arrested and tried for the murder, Francis Peter Kluxen III was acquitted. The story of her murder, his trial,

Photo by L'Aura Hladik

and local politics reads like a made-for-television miniseries, and to this day, the case is "unsolved."

Over the years, reports of seeing Jeanette's ghost making her fateful trip home from her babysitting job on Ridgedale Avenue have been made by motorists who travel along Ridgedale and Fairview Avenues.

The New Jersey Ghost Hunters Society investigation included an interview with a family whose house is located across the street from the haunted Kluxen woods on Central Avenue. The family's son witnessed a little girl ghost who fits the description of Jeanette in their house. Their further investigation of the woods and surrounding streets did nothing more than to secure a few photos with orbs in them. Daytime photography of the woods shows the foundation remains of the Kluxen Winery.

—L'Aura Hladik
Co-Founder, New Jersey
Ghost Hunters Society

THE SPY HOUSE

119 PORT MONMOUTH ROAD
PORT MONMOUTH, NEW JERSEY 07758

Said to be one of the most haunted places in America, the Spy House in Port Monmouth, New Jersey, has quite a history behind it. Built around the year 1663 by a man named Thomas Whitlock, it has been a private home, a gathering place during the Revolutionary War, an inn, a pirates' hideout, a bordello, and a museum. Today, it unfortunately has been closed down, but visitors can still roam the outside area of the infamous house.

As legend has it, The Spy House was converted to an inn during the Revolutionary War in order to prevent it from being destroyed by British troops, who believed that the home was occupied by Colonial spies.

The building was first converted into a museum in the 1960s by Gertrude Neidlinger. In 1990, a woman named Jane Doherty started ghost tours at the infamous house. This was eventually stopped by the board of trustees, and the inside of the house is now closed to the public.

However, the house is still said to be inhabited by a number of spirits. Peter, a young and playful spirit, is known to cause disturbances with any electronic equipment used in the house. Abigail, probably the best known of the spirits, has been seen in the back upstairs window, staring out to sea—she has also been heard sobbing at times over her husband, a sea captain, who was lost at sea during the war. Other spirits that have been seen include that of a sea captain, the Reverend William Wilson (once an owner of the house), and the spirit of Thomas Whitlock himself.

During our investigations of The Spy House, many photographs of spirit orbs around the house were taken. Banging

Photo by Alison Lynch

noises were also heard coming from inside. The aura and feeling of the spirits of the house can definitely be felt. An EVP captured in the back of the house says, "I see you." Something or someone always seems to be around you there...watching.

—Alison Lynch
Lead Paranormal Investigator,
Real Hauntings

GRAVITY ROAD

EWING STREET EXIT OFF ROUTE 208 SOUTH
FRANKLIN LAKES, NEW JERSEY 07417

Franklin Lakes's "Gravity Road," as it has come to be called, is home to local lore that alleges a young woman was struck and killed by an unknown vehicle at the end of the exit ramp. According to legend, her spirit lingers at the intersection at the end of the ramp, hoping to prevent any future deaths. Visitors to the site claim that a force pushes your car back when you approach the stop sign, as if the young woman's spirit was trying to protect you from the bad intersection in which she was killed. Some also claim that, if you put your car in neutral, the car will roll backward up the hill. It is suggested by some that if a car's bumper is coated in talc or flour, a hand-print of the young woman can be seen, possibly from the force of the push. Skeptics claim the ramp and surrounding ground and hills create an illusion that looks as if it is sloping downward when, in fact, it is not. The police keep a close watch on the area, so attempts to visit are not recommended. Patrols have been known to ticket people whose vehicles linger at the spot and also fine those who try to walk to and explore the highly trafficked area. This could simply be a legend created to keep children away from a busy highway and intersection; however, a strange energy does seem to surround the site.

—Michael Pye and Adam Schwartz

BURLINGTON COUNTY PRISON MUSEUM

HIGH STREET
MT. HOLLY, NEW JERSEY 08060
TEL: 1 (609) 265-5858
WEBSITE: *www.burlco.lib.nj.us/county/ PrisonMuseum.html*

The Burlington County Prison Museum, located in Mt. Holly, New Jersey, was built in 1811 and was designed by the famous architect Robert Mills (the designer of the Washington Monument). It is a large, rectangular building made of stone and iron that looks more like a castle than a prison from the outside. It was used continuously as a jail until 1966. Since then, local legends have spoken of the ghosts that inhabited the building. One in particular was the ghost of Joel Clough, a convicted murderer who killed his mistress with a leg from a table. He was held in the death row cell, which consisted of an eyehook in the floor that he was always chained to and an extremely small window. He was eventually hanged in the 1850s and, since then, other guards and prisoners reported hearing his moans and chains rattling from that cell. The guards and inmates also reported seeing someone in the empty cell as well as objects levitating inside.

In 1999, the county began a restoration project, transforming the rundown building into a museum and returning it to its original condition. As the work progressed, the construction workers began reporting strange events such as loud noises, disembodied voices, and screams coming from various areas of the building. They also reported having their tools disappear when they'd turn their backs, only to find the missing items in another room or on another floor later on in the day. Eventually, some workers were leaving early so they would not be the last ones in the building. The county officials decided to contact our organization, South Jersey Ghost Research (SJGR), to see if we could verify the claims of the workers and put their minds at ease.

I was on each SJGR team that went out to the museum. I witnessed some of the supernatural events firsthand. On each investigation, I set up a motion detector in the death row cell. During each trip, the motion detector was set off by an unseen force. We were able to capture orbs on video and film simultaneously when the motion detector's alarm went off. On the second visit, I also obtained an EVP seconds after the motion detector went off. The recording was that of a man's voice saying, "Go out here." We did experience objects moving as well, as did three reporters from the *New York Times* who were there with us. A stretcher that was located in the cell next to the death row cell relocated itself and it was actually the reporters who noticed it first. Other members of the SJGR observed an apparition in one part of the building and found a single barefoot print on a dust-covered floor of

what was once the prison showers. The teams also obtained numerous photos, video clips, and EMF readings.

—Dave Juliano
Director, South Jersey Ghost Research

RINGWOOD MANOR
SLOATSBURG ROAD
RINGWOOD, NEW JERSEY 07456
TEL: 1 (973) 962-2240
WEBSITE: *www.ringwoodmanor.com*

Long before Europeans settled the United States, the land upon which Ringwood Manor now stands was considered sacred ground by New Jersey's native people. Oral traditions claim that tribes traveled from all over the East Coast to attend ceremonies here because of the many "unusual happenings."

A scientific explanation of these happenings may be the abundance of iron ore buried in the earth, which produces a powerful magnetic force. Certainly, the iron is what brought colonists such as Robert Erskine here. Erskine built the original manor in 1762 . By 1764, a town had been built to support the iron-making business at Ringwood. It was completely self-sufficient with stores, houses for the workers, a gristmill, a saw mill, farms...and a graveyard.

During the Revolutionary War, Ringwood Manor served as headquarters for General Washington, a supply center for troops, and a main transportation route. Many soldiers died here—and all do not rest in peace. When sick and wounded French soldiers died, they were buried in unmarked graves. Today there is still an indentation in the ground where they lie, and voices, speaking in French, are often heard at night. Horse hooves have also been heard crashing toward the bridge, and sometimes the scent of horse manure floats out of the adjoining field, though no horses have been there for a century.

One of the best-known spirits to haunt Ringwood Manor is Robert Erskine. In the early 1800s, people began to see Robert sitting on top of his tomb, holding a lantern. Sometimes he held a ball of blue light, which would follow people over the bridge leading out of the cemetery. A century later, the blue light stories persisted—now following cars. Bricks and mortar on Erskine's tomb appeared as though they have been chipped away—from the inside out. And don't go near Sallie's Pond... the spirit of the pond chases away visitors and has been known to steal fishing gear.

Think you'd rather go inside? Maybe not. Although the manor was completely rebuilt in 1807, ghosts from all times still congregate here. Psychics, paranormal investigators, and ghost hunters have all noted their presence. (Cameras are not allowed on the premises.) The second floor is especially active. Crying, objects falling and breaking, and thudding sounds have been frequently reported. They come from a small bedroom in which a maid was supposedly beaten to death. Footsteps, voices, and a clammy feeling all indicate spirits are present. In any part of the house, a frigid coldness, a light floral fragrance, or even a blue aura announces the presence of Miss Eleanor Hewitt, or Miss Nellie. Miss Nellie, the last private owner of the estate, often makes her presence, and her displeasure, known. When statues are moved, papers disappear, and books appear

opened to specific pages—Miss Nellie is trying to tell you something. Most people listen.

Indeed, the advice most heard from those who know Ringwood Manor is this: Leave before nightfall.

—Linda J. Rienecker

New York

THE COUNTRY WITCH
HIGH STREET AND BLANCHARD
FORT COVINGTON, NEW YORK

Shortly after moving to the quaint and historic village of Fort Covington, New York, my husband and I decided to open a small business there called The Country Witch (later renamed the Calico Cat Whatnot Shop). A wood-frame Victorian building that had once been used as a private residence seemed the perfect location for us. After converting the upstairs portion of this turn-of-the-century structure into a four-room shop, we were open for business, selling antiques, curios, and various occult supplies such as candles, oils, spell books, and tarot cards.

Not long after starting the business, strange and unexplained things began to happen—especially at night when I'd stay alone in the shop to do some work. Lights would sometimes turn themselves off and on, doors would open by themselves, and objects (including heavy ones) would mysteriously move from their shelves. One time, a radio that was playing in the room switched from one station to another all on its own.

THE COUNTRY WITCH

At the rear of the shop was a musty little room that was used for vintage clothing. No matter how high the thermostat would be set in the winter, that room would always remain chilly. And even on the warmest of summer days, a strange coldness would linger in the air.

On numerous occasions, I strongly sensed that something unseen was there in the shop with me, watching me. I admit that it gave me a very creepy feeling, but at no time did I ever feel really terrified or threatened by it. However, we did have a customer in the shop one afternoon who appeared to be extremely uneasy. She browsed around for a bit and then, with a terrified look on her face, ran out the front door and down the steps as fast as she could. It was quite a strange sight to see.

I've often wondered if anyone had died there in the past and remained as a ghost, or if maybe the occult items we were selling had attracted something supernatural. I've even pondered the notion that there might have been an earthbound spirit attached to some antique item that was brought into the shop. But one thing I do know for sure is that something, for some reason, haunted that building and wanted its presence to be known.

—Gerina Dunwich
Independent Paranormal Investigator

FORT ONTARIO STATE HISTORIC SITE

NEW YORK STATE OFFICE OF PARKS,
RECREATION AND HISTORIC PRESERVATION
1 EAST FOURTH STREET
OSWEGO, NEW YORK 13126
TEL: 1 (315) 343-4711
WEBSITE: *www.fortontario.com*

Fort Ontario, located in Oswego, New York, has a breathtaking view of some beautiful sunsets. As you enter the gates, you are taken back in time. The fort interprets life as it would have been in 1868. Many people immediately sense the supercharged atmosphere that has seen many conflicts.

Fort Ontario dates to the mid-1700s and has been held by the British, French, and United States at different times in its history. Fort Ontario has been held by the United States since 1796. The fort was also once a refuge to nearly 1,000 individuals who fled Germany during World War II.

Three ghosts that are prominent among the many that seem to remain here are Lt. Basil Dunbar, George Fikes, and a nameless ghost in a blue uniform. Lt. Dunbar was killed during a duel with Lt. Penier in 1759, and George Fikes died here in 1782.

Syracuse Ghost Hunters have reports of activity in all areas of the fort, but most predominantly in Officer Quarters #1. Many have reported doors slamming, footsteps, and the laughter of children. During an investigation, our team left a night-vision video camera on the third floor and left the building. When the team returned, they heard a banging that echoed throughout the building and seemed to be coming from all directions. They couldn't identify the origin and no explanation was found.

When the tape was played back, they heard the sound of footsteps during the time the building was empty. In October 2004, a local TV station did a report about the hauntings of Fort Ontario. An employee of the fort dressed in clothing from the late 1800s and was filmed walking down the stairs. During the filming, everyone could hear what sounded like a harpsichord.

Fort Commander Paul Lear reports that reenactors from both the Revolutionary and Civil Wars have had the same experience in Officer Quarters #2. Reenactors that spend the night here will awaken to the sound of voices. The men will yell, "Be quiet!" and attempt to go back to sleep. The voices will continue and get louder until they get up to investigate. The reenactors search for the culprit but never find anyone.

In the Enlisted Men's Barracks there is a story of murder. The barracks were the site of a conflict between Privates Marks and Clemmins. Apparently, Marks had turned in Clemmins for misuse of rations. Clemmins said, "Give me 50 cents for a funeral," and went to the second floor of the barracks where he shot and killed Marks. Clemmins was imprisoned in the guard house, where he drank poison and died shortly after.

A visit here will certainly pique your supernatural interest. Maybe you will see the phantom regiment on the parade grounds or the ball of light that is reported near the guard house.

—Laura Schmidtmann
Founder and Lead Investigator,
Syracuse Ghost Hunters

LAKE RONKONKOMA

ISLIP, NEW YORK
WEBSITE: *www.lakeronkonkoma.org/ tour_index.htm*

About 50 miles east of Manhattan, you can find the scenic residential village of Ronkonkoma. Located in the township of Islip, Ronkonkoma is home to the largest lake on Long Island, Lake Ronkonkoma. It is the lake and its shores that are said to be haunted by the spirit of an Indian princess.

In one version of the princess's story, usually referred to as "The Troubled Spirit of the Lake," the Indian maiden is sacrificed to appease a god, Manitou. In order to save her people from the rising waters, she ties herself down with stones, rows out to the middle of the lake, and slips over the edge into the water. Her lover dives in after her, unable to bear leaving her alone in the infinite waters (another legend connected with the lake is that it's bottomless—it's not).

Lake Ronkonkoma is what's known as a kettlehole lake. It was formed by an isolated piece of glacier about 20,000 years ago. When the ice melted, it left a depression behind, called a kettle. The depression filled with water to create a kettlehole lake. In December 1952, four members of a skin-diving team touched the bottom, disproving the old legend that the lake was bottomless.

Another version of this legend, often called "The Lady of the Lake," tells the tale of the princess and her love for an English settler. Their love was forbidden and she was set to marry another. One night, she attempted to swim across the lake to her waiting lover, but she drowned halfway across. The legend goes on to say

LAKE RONKONKOMA

that the princess returns to the lake once a year to look for a companion to join her in her watery tomb. Lonely and heartbroken, she has become like the Sirens of Greek myth, luring men to their deaths. Locals claim that there is at least one drowning per year at the lake, and most of the victims are male. Newspaper and police reports do seem to support the legend's claims in this area—the average, indeed, seems to be one a year and mostly male.

In addition to drownings, there are reports of odd moving lights and a misty fog that hangs over the lake. Cold fingers grab swimmers who venture out too far. The most common reported event is the sound of someone sobbing. Witnesses say that the weeping is heartbreaking and sounds as if it is everywhere. Is it the princess still mourning the loss of her life, or is she still looking for a beloved face among her victims?

—Nikki Turpin
Co-Founder, Long Island Ghost Hunters

THE HISTORIC OLD BERMUDA INN
2512 ARTHUR HILL ROAD
STATEN ISLAND, NEW YORK 10309
TEL: 1 (718) 948-7600
WEBSITE: *www.weddingcottage.com*

Owned by the Mesereau family, this enchanting mansion was built back in 1832. Rich in historic detail and charmingly enhanced with timeless antiques, the inn now serves as a restaurant, and wedding and party facility. Although the mansion has been extended to include new rooms, the original part of the mansion still remains intact.

In 1860, Mr. William Mesereau went off to war. Martha, his wife, stayed in the mansion, anxiously awaiting his return from the war. Looking out of her bedroom window (which overlooked the water) day after day, night after night, Martha kept vigil, waiting for her husband's ship to return. During the evenings, Martha kept a candle burning in the window so her husband could find his way home. One day, she received the terrible news that she had dreaded—Mr. Mesereau had been killed. Upon hearing this news, Martha retreated to her bedroom and, as the legend goes, died of a broken heart in that room.

Today, Martha's room is called "The Somerset Room." It is now a beautiful dining area, which, according to the lore, Martha still inhabits. Many people have claimed to see Martha's silhouette in the window as well as a figure walking about in the front part of the inn. Other reports from workers at the inn have included strange noises and locked doors opening by themselves. It is believed that Martha still waits patiently at the inn for her husband to return.

Photo by Alison Lynch

There is an oil painting of Martha Mesearu in the original part of the mansion. This portrait hangs in the first floor hallway and is quite an attraction to many visitors. Martha's beauty shines through in this portrait, which was painted at the inn those many years ago. However, the portrait also holds an experience of its own. When construction to expand the mansion was in progress, noises could be heard from the original part of the mansion. One evening, this portrait mysteriously caught fire! There was no one inside that part of the inn at the time. Luckily, a worker happened to walk through and saw the fire. Although the portrait was not destroyed, it still retains the burn marks on the bottom part. It is said that the reason for these unexplained noises and the fire was Martha, expressing her dislike to the changes which were being made to her home.

During Real Hauntings's investigation, we experienced many strange events. Cameras in Martha's room would often not work. Upon leaving Martha's room and entering the hallway, the cameras would work fine. Cold chills were felt in the room near one of the chairs where EMF meter readings were high. Many photographs taken throughout the inn showed only one spirit orb. That makes sense, because only Martha's spirit is said to haunt the inn. It was almost as if Martha was following us as we inspected her home. EVP captured in Martha's room included the opening and slamming shut of the closet door (no one was in the room at the time) and a woman's voice whispering, "Listen."

According to the inn's staff, another strange occurrence happens every night. In the hallway on the first floor of the original part of the mansion, one light on the chandelier hanging from the ceiling will not shut off. Even when the switch is flipped and the electricity is turned off, this one light stays on throughout the night. Many have inspected the chandelier and could find no cause for this to happen.

The Old Bermuda Inn's charm and elegance still shine through, as well as the spirit of Martha Mesereau.

—Alison Lynch
Lead Paranormal Investigator,
Real Hauntings

Roxy Studios
28-39 Review Avenue
Long Island City, New York 11101
Tel: 1 (781) 361-0965
Website: *http://roxystudios.8m.com*

For years, employees at Roxy Studios in Long Island City, New York, would tell stories about strange happenings in the studio. Apparitions would appear on video monitoring equipment, music would be heard after hours when no one was there. Footsteps would be heard above the studio (the only thing above the studio was a crawl space), and occasionally clocks would fly off walls. Employees told stories of books flying across rooms and strange cold spots. The studio cat would avoid certain areas—acting as if he were scared to death.

Roxy Studios became a music studio back in 1973 and has changed ownership four times since then. Two of the previous owners have died. The first died of a brain tumor and the second overdosed in the studio. It is believed that the spirits of both owners still linger in the building. Since 1973, these strange phenomena have occurred. Customers are not usually affected by the haunting and only a handful of them have actually witnessed anything unusual.

Recently, a longtime employee of Roxy was found dead in his home. The staff wonders if he'll be the next spirit to inhabit Roxy. Paranormal Investigation of NYC was asked to investigate these allegations and have found cold spots and have heard strange voices on the EVP recordings we captured there. One voice is of a child crying. The staff of Roxy Studios doesn't mind the haunting; they feel it adds personality to the studio. The spirits of Roxy have never caused any harm; people have always said that Roxy had a life of its own.

—Dominick Villella
Paranormal Investigator,
Paranormal Investigation of NYC

McCARREN PARK SWIMMING POOL

LORIMER STREET, GREENPOINT
BROOKLYN, NEW YORK 11222

The McCarren Park swimming pool opened in 1936 and was the brainchild of Robert Moses. In 1979, the city approved $100 million to restore all nine of New York City's pools so they would be ready for the 50th anniversary celebration in 1986.

The pool was closed in 1983 to begin the repairs, but then the community stepped in. A blockade of residents protested fixing

the pool, citing the petty crimes and undesirables it attracted.

The pool never reopened. It sits alone, a hulking, decaying mass, with razor wire fencing surrounding the entire pool and graffiti on every wall.

There are no public records of deaths at McCarren Park pool. But still, people have claimed to see the ghost of a little girl roaming the area at night and have heard her calling for help. Since the mid-1980s, numbers of homeless people have also died of various causes while taking refuge in the pool area.

Park permits do not allow entrance into the pool area. All investigations must be conducted on the outside perimeter.

Paranormal Investigation of NYC investigated the pool perimeter and picked up odd EMF readings and cold spots that would drop more than 50 degrees. Orbs were the only thing that showed up on film. EVP recordings were impossible due to heavy traffic noise.

—Dominick Villella
Paranormal Investigator,
Paranormal Investigation of NYC

WEST MIDDLEBURY CEMETERY

4949 WEST MIDDLEBURY ROAD
WEST MIDDLEBURY, NEW YORK

The West Middlebury Cemetery is one of Wyoming County's oldest and most spiritually active cemeteries. This cemetery, with just 100 plots and numerous unmarked graves, can be dated to the late 1700s—the very beginning of settlement in the area. The site has very little use now.

WNY Paranormal discovered during our investigations that there is a caretaker spirit in this cemetery known as Mary Chaddock. It was initially the team sensitive who discovered Mary by being drawn to a large pillar stone at the back of the cemetery. At this stone, we captured an incredible EVP, had a team member physically stopped in their tracks by an unseen force, and captured a moving partial apparition on video. The name on the stone was "Mary," and our sensitive confirmed that was the name of the spirit before reading the stone. Our research team then conducted some extensive research into Mary through local historical records and files from the gravesite. We initially had trouble finding a connection, but the information Mary imparted to our psychic did finally corroborate with the person named on the tombstone. It wasn't until we considered that maybe the name Mary was actually a nickname or short for another name that we made the breakthrough. Upon further research, we discovered that in that time period, it wasn't uncommon for a woman with the name Margaret to take the name Mary. Historical research uncovered that her name was actually Margaret Mary Chaddock—with that discovery, all the historical pieces fell into place. Our team sensitive then used dowsing rods beginning at the large stone pillar to have the spirit lead her to the gravesite. After a half hour of following the directions of the rods, we found Mary's site next to her husband. Mary continues to stay by the large pillar stone at the back of the cemetery. She likes to communicate through EVP, physical sensations, and can often be seen at night roaming among the trees and tombstones, watching both the living and dead. On many occasions, our sensitives have experienced the imprint of a murder that occurred, shadow figures walking the rows, and they have heard gunshots and screams while gathering some fantastic evidence including strong EVP, mist photographs, and a moving apparition on film.

WNY Paranormal believes the high paranormal activity at this site is due to the flow of an underground saltwater source and the kinetic energy generated by a nearby railway. The activity increases dramatically each time a train passes by the site, especially during the latter parts of the evening.

—Dwayne Claud
Investigator, WNY Paranormal

Pennsylvania

SACHS BRIDGE

OFF OF PUMPING STATION ROAD
GETTYSBURG, PENNSYLVANIA

Gettysburg, Pennsylvania, marks the site of the bloodiest battle of the American Civil War. More than 50,000 men lost their lives in the three-day battle, and thousands more were injured. There are many famous battlefields in Gettysburg, such as Little Round Top and Devil's Den; however, the entirety of Gettysburg was, in fact, a battlefield. To treat the wounded and dying, many makeshift hospitals were created. Barns, homes, and even a wooden covered bridge, Sachs Bridge, were used to treat the wounded.

The bridge was built in 1854 by David Stoner. It runs 100 feet long and was referred to as "Sauck's Bridge" during the time of the Civil War, and this pronunciation still continues, even with its current spelling of "Sachs." The bridge was used by troops during the war and provided an easy passage over the water below.

Many psychic photographs and electronic voice phenomena (EVP) have been captured at the bridge. There are even more accounts from believers and skeptics alike of strange occurrences happening all around the bridge. Many describe having uncomfortable feelings at the bridge, as if they are being watched. Others have described being touched by unseen entities. Some people have even reported witnessing apparitions and unexplained sounds and smells at the bridge.

On an investigation at Sachs Bridge in Gettysburg in May 2004, members of the Paranormal Research Society of New England and Central New York Ghost Hunters experienced a ghostly reenactment of a battle in the middle of the night. John Zaffis, founder of the Paranormal Research Society of New England, said about the event:

"It was a perfectly clear night, and a fog rolled in very quickly and the temperature also dropped quickly. A few minutes later, we could all hear loud booms coming from the field adjacent to the bridge. There were 10 of us there that night, and everyone was hearing the booms. They were so powerful that you could feel it hit your chest. We could see orange bursts of light coming from the field that occurred with the booms. Others could hear gunfire and the sound of running horses. Even though Brendan Keenan had a video camera running throughout the phenomena, none of the sounds or orange lights showed up on film. About 15 minutes after it began,

the fog lifted and the booms, orange lights, and all the other phenomena stopped. The temperature also increased significantly. I turned and looked at everyone and said, 'This is just like it's out of a movie.' Some of the researchers there that night have been back to the bridge since, but they have not experienced anything to the magnitude that we experienced that night."

—Brendan Keenan
Investigator, The Paranormal
Research Society of New England

THE LEGENDARY TANNERSVILLE INN

ROUTE 611
TANNERSVILLE, PENNSYLVANIA 18372
TEL: 1 (570) 629-3131
WEBSITE: *www.tannersvilleinn.com*

The Legendary Tannersville Inn is located in the beautiful Pocono Mountains of Pennsylvania. Built in 1825, the inn put the town of Tannersville on the map, as the town was actually built around the inn and its original 98 acres. This historic inn has welcomed generations of locals and travelers who have passed through its doors for the past 200 years.

The inn has been owned by the Jakubowitz family for the past 34 years. Besides the wonderful atmosphere, great entertainment, and fine food, the inn is also host to the Pocono Mountain Film Festival—but that isn't all. The inn is also said to be inhabited by a number of spirits, most likely of former owners and guests who find the inn too enchanting to ever leave.

The Legendary Tannersville also has its dark side. This was the site of what is known as "The Learne Massacre." The

Learne family, who had owned the building, were all killed by the Indians who inhabited the area. Mrs. Learne was hung from a tree and her children were murdered.

On a Real Hauntings investigation, we did find much evidence of spirits following us throughout the evening. My hair was pulled, and cold chills and cold spots were felt in certain areas. EMF readings were high in certain spots. Also, as we were filming an interview with a worker at the inn, we got a shot of an orb in motion on video camera while the worker and interviewer were sitting in a carriage said to be haunted. Right above the worker's head, the spirit orb appeared, moved around a bit, then disappeared. Another employee at the inn also reported strange happenings, such as objects being thrown off shelves and unexplainable noises in the night.

From this investigation, we concluded that many spirits do still haunt The Legendary Tannersville Inn. We believe that, besides the massacre that took place there, many travelers and locals still find this an attraction and tend to "visit" the inn often in spirit form.

—Alison Lynch
Lead Paranormal Investigator,
Real Hauntings

BARCLAY CEMETERY

APPROXIMATELY 3 TO 5 MILES UP BARCLAY MOUNTAIN OFF ROUTE 514
BRADFORD COUNTY
LEROY, PENNSYLVANIA

Hiding in the hills of the abandoned mining town of Barclay sits a cemetery and the foundation of a long-fallen church. Amongst these falling-down graves walk the former residents of this forgotten town. Wiped out by the Black Plague and the Industrial Revolution, the once-bustling town is now appropriately named a ghost town.

The first time Ghost Hunters Incorporated ventured into this cemetery was back in 1999, and it would be the stepping stone from which all of our other investigations would grow.

Greg Newkirk, one of our team members, had discovered the cemetery while researching a location to conduct our first real investigation. He led us on a late-night excursion there. The cemetery has a history of strange occurrences unrelated to the paranormal, including grave robbing and, disturbingly, a murder.

Standing at the very front of the cemetery is a large gate with the name of the graveyard you are about to enter. As you cross this gate, you begin to notice how vastly large and spread out this resting place really is. Now mostly overgrown and barely remembered, it is here that many hear the sounds of human footsteps when no one is there. It is also where people have claimed to hear the sounds of tunes being whistled in the night when no one is around to do so. Some have reported seeing phantom women dressed in long, white gowns walking amongst the trees there. Others have claimed to have heard the sounds of children laughing.

One particularly odd event that has taken place many times during our numerous investigations there is the sounds of pickaxes hitting the ground in a town that has not had miners in it for more than 100 years. The unmistakable clang of the metal hitting the ground resonates through the air, leaving the hair on the back of your neck standing on end.

BARCLAY CEMETERY

Nick Foust of Ghost Hunters Incorporated recounts the first night he experienced something in the cemetery:

"Barclay Cemetery is located basically out in the middle of nowhere. As we entered, I was really uneasy about everything. It seemed like this place was forgotten about a long time ago, and when you can't really see that well—yeah, you can say that I was scared. As the night went by, all of sudden you could hear a noise out in the woods, and everyone just stopped dead in their tracks and listened. As we listened, Greg said, 'You know this town was full of miners!' or something like that. Not two seconds after he said that— PING!—it sounded exactly like someone hitting a rock with a pickaxe."

Barclay is a definite hot spot of haunted activity with a dark past full of plague, death, and obvious heartbreak. The spirits who walk the grounds have made their presence felt and continue to carry on in the afterlife. Will they ever find peace and be able to cross over, or is this their eternal fate to walk the abandoned hills of their once-busy town?

—Jason Gowin
Ghost Hunter,
Ghost Hunters Incorporated

BURLINGTON METHODIST CHURCH
U.S. ROUTE 6
BRADFORD COUNTY
WEST BURLINGTON TOWNSHIP,
PENNSYLVANIA

The Burlington Methodist Church was built in 1822 on the grounds where two former churches and a school once stood. Today, the building no longer holds regular services, but it does serve as the home for several entities. Set back along the rural U.S. Route 6, you may miss it if you blink as you pass by. The church sits majestically, almost terrifyingly, on the hillside. A small graveyard surrounds the path as you walk up its lawn and reach its doors—and you realize you may be in for more than you bargained for.

Reports of ghostly figures walking through the cemetery at night have always been plentiful. But the most bizarre supernatural account involves a former clergyman who, while preparing for the day's services, went to his car to retrieve supplies. He was gone only a matter of a minute, he returned to find every Bible in the building had been turned to the same page—a creepy passage in Revelations. In the time that he was gone, no man would have had the time to complete such an act. And no one had entered or left the building while he was at his car.

In April of 2003, Ghost Hunters Incorporated ventured to the church for the first time. From the minute we set foot in the place, things seemed eerie. From the balcony, stomping could be heard. But upon inspection there was nothing that could have caused such a noise. A short while later, a green mist began to form on

Photo by Jason Gowin

the stairway of the pulpit. It was clearly visible by all who were in the room. Things then turned for the worse—the cameraman who had been filming this entire event suddenly began to choke for what seemed to be no reason. The group rushed him outside, and we immediately left.

Another incident that happened to our group involved a book being hurled across the room after we provoked the inhabitants. Nick Foust, one of our team members, had this to say about the church:

"When the book was thrown, it made such a loud noise that I didn't know what the hell was going on. Fear just took over me, and I didn't know what I was doing. The next minute, I'm just out the door—screaming like a little girl and running for my life."

A few months later, Bill Angove of Ghost Hunters Incorporated and I found that upon our arrival, the entities immediately began to make themselves known by stomping violently in the upstairs of the church. When I stepped through the door, I was violently thrown into a wall by an unseen force. We scrambled to get ourselves to safety and away from there.

The church has been haven to a host of unusual EVP, some of which can be heard to say: "Just the ghosts are looking," "You're going to get it," and "You are being too loud."

—Jason Gowin
Ghost hunter,
Ghost Hunters Incorporated

ANDREW BAYNE MEMORIAL LIBRARY
34 NORTH BALPH AVENUE
PITTSBURGH, PENNSYLVANIA 15202
TEL: 1 (412) 766-7447
WEBSITE: *www.einpgh.org/ein/andbayne/*

" Amanda's ghost has been around as long as this place has been a library," said Sharon Helfrich, director of the Bayne Library. "It's just a case of different sightings here and there. And she seemed to be very active right around the time that our Lone Sentinel was dying. I think it's probably because part of the trust is that no tree in the park is allowed to be touched. Trees and nature and things like that were very important to her."

The Lone Sentinel was a 300-year-old giant elm that graced the library's property right up until tree surgeons had to remove it in 1998 due to excessive decay.

Amanda Bayne was born in 1846 to Andrew and Mary Anne Bayne. Andrew Bayne owned several acres of land north of Pittsburgh—land that became a precious commodity as the city of Pittsburgh rapidly expanded. Bayne gave his two daughters some land upon which to build their own homes.

In 1870, Amanda married a prominent local architect named James Madison Balph. Balph set to work designing and building his dream house, and, in 1875, the building that would go on to become the library was completed. The home is a stately three-story brick Victorian mansion that sits on a hill overlooking what is now a two-acre park.

Amanda was widowed in 1899 and lived out her remaining 13 years in the mansion. She had a vast collection of books and adored looking out her bedroom window at the majestic elms on her property. When she died in 1912, her will stipulated that her home and property would be donated to the town so long as they promised to use the building as a library and to never harm the elm trees.

Ghost sightings and strange sounds have been reported for decades at the library—the sounds of footsteps walking across the second floor when there was no one in the library above the first floor, strange numbers being typed on the computers by unseen forces, and lights being turned on and off, especially in the attic.

A portrait of Amanda Bayne Balph hangs over the fireplace near the library's charge desk, so the staff and patrons there know what she looks like. One staff member actually saw Amanda behind her one day in the late 1990s. "I've only seen her once," said Linda Momper, assistant director of the Bayne Library, who has worked there since 1993. "I was in the library by myself and was turning on the computers, and I looked up at the window and saw a reflection in there of a woman. I looked behind me and I thought, 'Who's in here?' but nobody was there, and I looked again and I saw the reflection again. It looked just like her picture."

—Jeff Belanger
Founder, Ghostvillage.com

SLEEPY HOLLOW
PA 2034
KULPMONT, PENNSYLVANIA 17834

If you live in, or around, the Northumberland County area of Pennsylvania, you may have heard of the legend of Sleepy Hollow. There is no headless horseman in this legend, however. The place known as Sleepy Hollow rests in a wooded area behind the Kulpmont Cemetery located just outside of Kulpmont, Pennsylvania, near a town called Den Mar Gardens. The area is eerie, silent, and still considered to be part of the Kulpmont Cemetery. Numerous decapitated tombstones lie in a thick overgrown area of broken-down trees and weeds. When entering Sleepy Hollow, you find yourself walking under what seems to be a tunnel of trees.

The story of Sleepy Hollow sounds like that of a local legend, but curiosity has taken over many individuals who have decided to venture to this location. The legend says that many years ago, three young men ventured into the cemetery, that at the time was not overgrown. The three young men, for reasons unknown, decided to tear down a large, cement cross, which stood in the center of the cemetery on a cement platform. They destroyed the

Photo by Jess Kroh

monument. After wrecking the cross, it is said that they got into a deadly car accident, and all three died. There is another local legend stating that in the 1980s and the early 90s, this location was used to perform Satanic rituals. It is believed that numerous Satanic symbols can be found carved on trees here—though we did encounter carvings on the trees, we couldn't be certain of their meaning.

There are numerous unexplained accounts that come from this location. One popular legend states that at exactly midnight, you can hear an old organ playing. There have been other reports of hearing strange noises here as well.

My group, the Eastern Pennsylvania Ghost Researchers, ventured into this location on two different nights. When entering Sleepy Hollow, an eerie feeling had taken over. We felt as though we were being watched as we walked along the long, tunnel-like path. Various tombstones were barely visible in the thick brush along the path. Some of the tombstones were destroyed and looked very aged, while others looked as if they had been recently placed there. We then entered the center of the Hollow, which is where the large cross once stood. The cement platform is still there. We proceeded to walk along the path. While doing this, we received a few electromagnetic field spikes, and we were startled after hearing a few awkward noises after passing a fallen tree that had blocked off the path. An uneasiness followed us throughout our investigation until we left Sleepy Hollow.

—Jess Kroh
Co-Founder,
Eastern Pennsylvania Ghost Researchers

THE ANGEL ROSE BED & BREAKFAST

616 WEST MARKET STREET
POTTSVILLE, PENNSYLVANIA 17901
TEL: 1 (570) 628-4850
WEBSITE: *www.geocities.com/ angelrose_17901/*

Owned and operated by Diane and Bob Karpulk, the Angel Rose Bed & Breakfast is located in downtown Pottsville near Garfield Square. The inn's name stems from the owner's interest in angels. The bed and breakfast offers its guests a sense of being transported back to the Victorian era.

"The house feels like it's 100 years back in time. Guests are reluctant to leave for that reason," Diane Karpulk said.

The home is beautifully decorated—decorative curtains and rugs adorn the building, and each bedroom where guests stay is also beautifully appointed, including the room called Victorian Orchard, which contains antiques from the late 1800s.

But the Angel Rose B & B also has another history, a ghostly one.

The first signs that showed the Karpulks that they might not be alone in their spectacular retreat began shortly after they had moved in. They said the presence wasn't a worthy cause for concern. They describe it as an energy that seems to inhabit the home.

The first supernatural incident happened when Bob was in the basement and he smelled a perfume aroma. He described it as a Victorian lady's perfume—something unlike any that his wife, Diane, wears. Bob also stated that it was a very heavy aroma. During another incident in the basement, he picked up the pungent aroma of body odor.

ANGEL ROSE BED & BREAKFAST

Bob and Diane are two sensible adults and were not swayed by just two inexplicable instances, but other unexplained things kept on happening as they began to settle in.

Major appliances would suddenly turn on without any reason, even after electricians were called and could find nothing wrong with any of them. Other electrical occurrences continued to manifest.

Diane said, "We felt we were being checked out. It was as if someone is here and continues to test us."

As all of the electrical appliances seemed to have a mind of their own, Bob and Diane pulled the plug—literally—on the appliances they rarely used to ensure they would not switch on unexpectedly.

Bob does not rule out the possibility of previous owners' restless spirits still watching over their home.

Once, Bob found a cassette tape in the downstairs area, so he put it in the tape player and he began to hear church music playing. He flipped the cassette over and the "Notre Dame Fight Song" started to play. Bob stated that the previous owners were Italian-Americans, and they didn't like hearing the "Notre Dame Fight Song" and probably acted up when the song played.

Family members of Bob and Diane and even guests still sense signals that the Angel Rose is indeed occupied by something that none of them can explain.

—Tom Brobst
Co-Founder,
Eastern Pennsylvania Ghost Researchers

EASTERN STATE PENITENTIARY

HISTORIC SITE OFFICES
2124 FAIRMOUNT AVENUE
PHILADELPHIA, PENNSYLVANIA 19130
TEL: 1 (215) 236-5111
WEBSITE: *www.easternstate.org*

Eastern State Penitentiary is one of the largest and most famous prisons in the world. Opened in 1829, it quickly became the model for prisons of its time. Eastern State was built on more than steel and stone. It was built on principle. The prison conducted itself on the principle that given the right "motivation," a criminal would see the errors of his ways and repent. The criminal would be penitent. This brought on the birth of the word "penitentiary."

Although based in righteous methods and good intentions, ill will found its way into Eastern State Penitentiary. A commonly used device in containment, the strait jacket, was used quite frequently, although not always with its intended purpose.

Inmates would be bound tighter than was needed, and soon their body would become numb. Inmates were kept in this state until they passed out. Another feared method was known as the "iron gag." This device was attached to the inmate's tongue while his hands were folded behind his head. The restraint was then tied behind the man's neck. Any movement of the arms would strain on the tongue, causing severe agony.

Though Eastern State housed thousand of prisoners over the years, none is more famous than Al Capone. Capone served eight months in Eastern State for a concealed weapons charge with his bodyguard, Frankie Rio. Capone, responsible for the famous Saint Valentine's Day massacre, reportedly began being harassed by a supernatural being named "Jimmy." Capone later revealed that "Jimmy" was James Clark, one of the victims of the infamous massacre. Prisoners reported hearing Capone's screams, apparently begging to be left alone. This activity allegedly continued even after Capone was released and followed him until his death.

Photo by Tom Iacuzio

But Capone is not the only one to report ghostly activity behind Eastern State Penitentiary's walls. Although it is no longer an active prison, Eastern State is still used as a tourist attraction, and the experiences continue to this day. Cell Block 12 is reported to be one of the most haunted sections of the prison. Some visitors have reported the sound of laughter as well as the appearance of a shadowy figure roaming the upstairs hallways. On a recent investigation, I myself encountered a strange mist coming from Cell Block 12. Even an experienced investigator such as myself was prone to goosebumps in the dark, murky corridors of Eastern State Penitentiary.

—Tom Iacuzio
Founder, Central Florida
Ghost Research

Washington, D.C.

FORD'S THEATRE
511 10TH STREET NORTHWEST
WASHINGTON, D.C. 20006
TEL: 1 (202) 347-4833
WEBSITE: *www.fordstheatre.org*

A shot rang out through this crowded theater on April 14, 1865. The shrill screams that followed, bouncing off the walls and piercing the very soul of a nation, can still be heard to this day. The lives of individuals in attendance at this rendition of *Our American Cousin* were forever stained with the blood of the United States's 16th president.

Ford's Theatre is the historic location of one of the most tragic assassinations in American history. It's no wonder, then, that this old theatre in downtown Washington, D.C., is known to house a vast array of ghosts.

The spectral appearances of Abraham Lincoln, among others, spark interest in history buffs and ghost hunters alike. The final moments of President Lincoln's life will forevermore be played out on the ghostly stage of this diminutive theater in the heart of the nation's capital.

John Wilkes Booth, a well-known actor at the theater, approached President Lincoln from behind and proceeded to shoot him in the back of the head near point-blank range. The bullet entered the President about 3 inches behind the left ear and traveled about 7 1/2 inches into his brain. Lincoln's muffled cry was cut off at the moment his head declined toward his chest. Mrs. Lincoln screamed.

Ten days before his assassination, Lincoln had a prophetic dream of his own

FORD'S THEATRE

demise. He wrote about this dream in detail in his journal.

Since the assassination, it is believed that Ford's Theatre has become very haunted. There have been reports of voices and laughter on numerous occasions. John Wilkes Booth's footsteps have been heard running up the back staircase toward the presidential box, and the sound of a gunshot followed by someone screaming, "Murder!" has also been reported.

The ghost of Mrs. Lincoln is said to lean out of the box with ashy cheeks and lips, and with a hysterical cry, she points to the retreating figure of Booth, shouting "He has killed the president!" Lights have been reported to turn off and on, icy sensations have been felt in certain spots, and apparitions appear at center stage.

The fatal shot heard that fateful night in 1865 silenced the nation. Lincoln's blood will forever stain this historical landmark.

—Jason McCurry
Founder, Haunted Lives
Paranormal Society

DECATUR HOUSE
1610 H STREET, NW
WASHINGTON, D.C. 20006
TEL: 1 (202) 842-0920
WEBSITE: *www.decaturhouse.org*

The United States capital has its own blend of haunted history and ghostly manifestations. Many of the apparitions documented here were prominent citizens of the area. Such is the case at the Decatur House, where dark clouds of conflict still hover over this distinguished neoclassical structure.

The Decatur House is located on Lafayette Square just one block north of the White House. The grand mansion was designed by Benjamin Henry Latrobe, often referred to as the father of American architecture. In the 1800s, this area was the heart of the social scene in Washington, D.C. Stephen Decatur and his wife, Susan, enjoyed celebrity status during their lives here—that is, until a violent confrontation ended Decatur's life abruptly.

The duel between Stephen Decatur and Commodore James Barron is a historical fact. Barron was the commander of the ship the *Chesapeake*, and had been the subject of a scandal in 1807. According to history, Commodore Barron failed to prepare his ship for battle, and it was easily defeated by a British warship. This incident led to Barron's court marshal in 1808. Decatur's naval duty at the time was to attend this court marshal.

Decatur agreed to a verdict that discharged Barron from the Navy for a period of five years. This action led to a 13-year dispute between the two that eventually ended in death.

A letter written by Barron to Decatur stated: "You have hunted me out, have persecuted me with all the power and influence of your office; and for what purpose or from what other motive than to obtain my rank." He then requested that their dispute be settled by a duel.

"If we fight, it must be of your seeking," replied Decatur, in a letter addressed to Barron.

Barron responded with this statement: "Whenever you will consent to meet me on fair and equal grounds, that is, such as two honorable men may consider just and proper, you are to view this as that call."

On March 22, 1820, Stephen Decatur and James Barron met on the dueling ground in Bladensburg, Maryland. The duel that followed mortally wounded the Naval hero, Decatur. The nation mourned.

The night before the duel, Stephen Decatur stood at his window silently peering out. After his death, he was spotted so many times by onlookers at this window that it was eventually walled up.

Decatur's wife, Susan, also haunts the residence. So upset was she when her husband died that, to this day, you can still feel a sense of sadness in the air when you enter the house, and you can hear the sound of her desperate cries.

—Jason McCurry
Founder, Haunted Lives
Paranormal Society

THE WHITE HOUSE

1600 PENNSYLVANIA AVENUE NW
WASHINGTON, D.C. 20500
TEL: 1 (202) 456-2121
WEBSITE: *www.whitehouse.gov*

The President of the United States lives in a very historic and very haunted home. Construction on the "President's palace" began in 1792 and was overseen by George Washington—though Washington never lived long enough to spend a single night in the home. On November 1, 1800, President John Adams and his wife, Abigail, would be the first to get the honor of sleeping there.

The history of the White House is a direct reflection of life in the United States. The mansion has always been center stage for celebrations, mourning, controversy, and perseverance. It was completely gutted by fire set by the British during the War of 1812, and some have reported seeing a ghostly Redcoat still wandering the grounds.

Some presidents bore the weight of the nation on their shoulders during times of crisis. But no president has had to deal with the pressures that Abraham Lincoln endured—trying to hold a country together that was at war with itself. Not surprisingly, Lincoln is the most prominent spirit encountered in the White House today.

What is now the Lincoln Bedroom was actually the executive office when Lincoln served as president. The room is a hot spot for paranormal activity—staff have reported the lights turning themselves on and off, and doors opening and closing. But Lincoln is seen in other parts of the building as well.

Tony Savoy, White House operations foreman, discussed his encounter with the ghost of President Lincoln in an interview on the official White House Website:

"It was early one morning, and I was taking care of the plants up on the second floor. I used to come in early in the morning and turn the lights on and walk down the hall in the dark. When I turned the light on one morning, he was sitting there outside his office with his hands over top of each other, legs crossed, and was looking straight ahead. He had a gray, charcoal [colored] pin-striped suit on, and he had a pair of three-button spats turned over on the side with black shoes on. He was sitting there, and he startled me and I stopped. And when I blinked, he was gone. And I left there and went down the stairs and told assistant usher Nelson Pierce what I had seen. And he said I'm just one of the other ones that had seen him throughout the house over the past years."

Other notable specters reported at the White House include Dolley Madison's

THE WHITE HOUSE

angry ghost standing by her beloved rose garden when some groundskeepers were coming to remove it, and the ghost of Lincoln's son, William Wallace, who died in 1862. The young boy was one of the earliest ghost reports at the White House—even making it into Mary Todd Lincoln's personal correspondence.

—Jeff Belanger
Founder, Ghostvillage.com

South

South

Florida

PILGRIMS REST CEMETERY

CORNER OF NOVA ROAD AND GRANADA
BOULEVARD
ORMOND BEACH, FLORIDA

This image was taken at Pilgrims Rest Cemetery in Ormond Beach, Florida. After doing background research, the Daytona Beach Paranormal Research Group, Inc. (DBPRG) came to find out that an African-American man was hanged in the tree in the back corner of the cemetery for "crimes" he allegedly committed. He was hanged by the neck in this spot before the land was opened as an actual cemetery. After his death, it was discovered that he was not the man that committed the crime of which he was accused.

It is believed, by some, that one of the most elusive phenomena to photograph in the spirit realm is the spirit of an African-American.

Photo by Doris "Dusty" Smith

This photo was taken with a Pentax IQ Zoom 35mm camera, using Kodak 800-speed film. The original photo was scanned into the computer, resized, and the final photo was cropped out and enlarged. No other enhancements were made to this photo.

The spot at which this photo was taken is also notorious for having frequent "hot spots." DBPRG members have recorded temperature fluctuations that increase by 20 to 40 degrees on numerous occasions. Several small animals, such as birds and squirrels, have been found dead in this exact location, and strange mists have been photographed in this area as well.

—Doris "Dusty" Smith
Founder & Chief Researcher, Daytona Beach Paranormal Research Group, Inc.

APPROACH OF THE ORANGE AVENUE BRIDGE

DAYTONA BEACH, FLORIDA

On the northeast side of the Orange Avenue Bridge, just at the bridge approach, there have been many reports of a cloaked young woman with long, dark hair over the past few decades. No one is quite sure who this young woman was, but her spirit is very active, and sometimes violent.

Three theories as to her identity include a young maid who worked on the peninsula at an affluent home and was killed on the ferry coming home from work one night. She fell off the edge of the ferry and was crushed to death between the dock pilings and the end of the ferry.

Another theory includes a young runaway who made her temporary home under the Orange Avenue Bridge while working and panhandling in the business district. Apparently, in the early 1980s, she figured out that her home life may not have been as bad as she thought. She bedded down under the bridge one night and was joined by an uninvited stranger who sexually abused her and took her life.

The third and most likely candidate for the identity of this entity is a young girl who was raised by her grandmother. Her name was Rose and she adored a long cloak that her grandmother had given her as a gift. She wore this cloak one night as she walked across the bridge to attend her high school's homecoming dance. At the top of the bridge approach, she was struck by a car and killed instantly. Her shoes wound up under the bridge and her cloak looked as if she had laid it lovingly across the bridge's handrail.

The sighting of this entity seems to increase during homecoming season. She is always seen wearing a long cloak and has been picked up by many drivers going across the Orange Avenue Bridge. When the vehicle reaches the peninsula side of the bridge, she is no longer in the vehicle. She has also been known to throw soda bottles and cans, shoes, and even lawn furniture at passing cars.

At the Daytona Beach Paranormal Research Group's investigation during homecoming week of 2000, we quickly discovered that this particular entity is indeed quite active. We set equipment up at the base of the bridge where the majority of sightings have been reported. We recorded temperature drops of 25 to 30 degrees, EMF fluctuations from 0.2 to 7.6 miligauss, an overhead streetlight that flickered on and off with no set pattern, and one of our male researchers was hit in the back of the head with an empty soda can as he got in his vehicle to leave.

—Doris "Dusty" Smith
Founder & Chief Researcher, Daytona
Beach Paranormal Research Group, Inc.

MARRERO'S GUEST MANSION

410 FLEMING STREET
KEY WEST, FLORIDA 33040
TEL: 1 (305) 294-6977
WEBSITE: *wwww.marreros.com*

The magic of Marrero's Guest Mansion can be felt the minute you pass through its double front doors. This is a house that was truly built for love. In 1889, Francisco Marrero hoped to entice his young love, Enriquetta, to settle in Key West to continue their life together. Apparently, his strategy worked, as they were said to be happy and their union produced eight children. At that time, Key West was a center for the cigar industry, and Francisco was a very successful cigar producer. Originally from Cuba, he often made trips there on business. On one ill-fated trip, he died under what some felt were suspicious circumstances. Soon after receiving this tragic news, Enriquetta was dealt another blow. It seemed that Francisco had a wife, Maria, in Cuba that he never divorced. She arrived in Key West and laid claim to his estate in court where she won that claim. Enriquetta and her eight children suddenly found themselves homeless and penniless. As she left her home for the last time, Enriquetta was said to have made the promise that she would always remain in spirit in the home she loved.

Photo by Kathy Conder

To many of us who have been guests in this charming house, now Marrero's Guest Mansion on Fleming Street, Enriquetta appears to have kept the pledge she made that day more than a hundred years ago. Her presence is pervasive yet benevolent, and numerous guests have experienced it over the years. Owner and innkeeper John Diebold said that guests staying in rooms 17 and 23 have reported

hearing the sound of babies crying at night. Marrero's is an adults-only establishment, so there are no children on the premises. Neighbors have no children either. Interestingly, the rooms in which the sounds occurred were once the Marrero children's nursery. John added that, "My experiences involve doors and locks. Doors get locked from the inside with the secondary lock, which can only be locked from the inside... but nobody is in the room. This usually happens when people have been talking about Enriquetta in a skeptical way." Guests have also reported seeing the spirit of Enriquetta in what was once her bedroom—room 18. She has been seen passing through the door that connected her room to the nursery.

Today, Marrero's is a welcoming getaway that gives its guests a true taste of Key West. The ample front porch welcomes you to sit back and enjoy the warm, tropical air as you sip a cocktail each evening. Several of the graciously appointed rooms open to verandas while some open to a secluded pool area. Care is taken to make each guest feel welcome with attention to detail and an emphasis on hospitality. As Enriquetta continues her vigil over the house she loved in life, she must be pleased that it continues to be a place of which she can be proud.

—Kathy Conder
Lead Investigator, Encounters
Paranormal Research and Investigation

MARRERO'S GUEST MANSION

CAPTAIN TONY'S SALOON
428 GREENE STREET
KEY WEST, FLORIDA 33040
TEL: 1 (305) 294-1838

Built in 1933, Captain Tony's was the original "Sloppy Joe's" in Key West and is said to have been frequented by the great author Ernest Hemingway. It once served as the town morgue and ice house. It is also home to the hanging tree that was used to bring pirates and criminals to justice. Seventeen people are said to have been executed there. The tree continues to claim its prominent spot in the center of the building next to the bar, as the building was constructed around the tree.

Photo by Kathy Conder

It is one of these unfortunate people hanged from this tree who is said to linger there today. A woman who murdered her husband and son was dragged from her bed and lynched at this spot. Today, she is known as the "Lady in Gray" and has been seen wearing the nightdress she had on at the time of her hanging. While excavating, Tony uncovered the remains of 16 bodies, and it is said that when the bar served as a morgue, the coroner buried his daughter there. Encased in the walls of what is now

the pool room are bottles of holy water. Customers frequently report sensing a spirit presence in the women's restroom. Given its gruesome history, it's no wonder that this bar is one of the most haunted in Key West.

—Kathy Conder
Lead Investigator, Encounters
Paranormal Research and Investigation

RIDDLE HOUSE
YESTERYEAR VILLAGE, PALM BEACH COUNTY FAIRGROUNDS
9067 SOUTHERN BOULEVARD
WEST PALM BEACH, FLORIDA 33411

Something or someone in the Riddle House, a historic Victorian painted lady built in 1905, doesn't like men. Dangerous ghostly phenomena, directed toward males visiting the house, often turn physical.

Today the house sits in Yesteryear Village—a living museum of a late-1900s-era Florida town nestled on five acres and containing 30 buildings either moved intact from their original, historic sites or reconstructed from original blueprints upon the fairgrounds property.

"I'll never go into the Riddle House again," stated carpenter Steve Carr during a phone interview. He was doing restoration work in a first-floor room when the lid from an iron pot lifted three feet off its base, flew across the room, and struck him in the head. He never saw the lid, but a second man did and dragged the unconscious Carr outside the house.

Since then, male security staff and visitors are not allowed to go into the attic, a particularly active hotspot for paranormal activity believed to be the work of a man who hung himself and whose image often appears in the north or west attic windows to people below. In January 2003, one of our team members, Jack Rodriguez, saw the solid head and torso of a black-suited man against the north window with a noose around his neck and the end attached to an attic beam as he peered down at him.

Photo by Christine Rodriguez

A few days later, interviews with Yesteryear volunteers first verified that the ghost of a man wearing a black frock coat is believed to be a former boarder who hung himself in the single-room attic of the three-story house. His apparition is also seen on the lower floors and walking the Village grounds.

Riddle House, so-called since 1920, was originally named the Gate Keeper's Cottage because it functioned as a place for parlor funerals and the management of the Woodlawn Cemetery across the street from 327 Acacia (its original location) in downtown West Palm Beach. It was built on land owned by Joseph Jefferson, the most famous actor of his day. The house itself was erected by Henry Flagler's construction workers with some materials left over from Flagler's Palm Beach motels.

When Karl Riddle became the first city manager and superintendent of Public Works, the house served as his home. In the 1980s, Riddle House was a girl's dormitory for the Palm Beach Atlantic College until it was abandoned, fell into disrepair, and faced demolition by the city. Finally, the city donated the building to John Riddle, nephew to Karl, and it was divided into three sections and moved to Yesteryear Village. Karl Riddle's diary actually tells of the death of an itinerant man on the property but gives no details.

Witnesses say that only days after its arrival, unexplained incidents began inside the house. Psychics, parapsychologists, and paranormal investigators have been brought into the attic, and orbs, unexplained temperature increases near the west window, anomalous streaks of spirit energy, and even spirit communication with a man who hung himself in the attic because he "took the fall" for a crime he didn't commit and which involved financial wrongdoings with Flagler funds have been experienced by our team or reported to us.

—Christine Rodriguez
Parapsychologist, East Coast
Hauntings Organization (E.C.H.O.)

RIDDLE HOUSE

NICHOLS CREEK ROAD

MILTON, FLORIDA 32583
TEL: 1 (850) 623-4460
EMAIL: RAIMIKE@BELLSOUTH.NET

On a piece of property in the Nichols Lake area of East Milton lie some very haunted grounds. Since Michael Wright and his family moved to the property more than a decade ago, they have experienced apparitions, cold spots, and poltergeist activities. By digging through historical records and speaking with previous owners as well as other locals, Wright believes their property was once home to a graveyard for slaves called "Holley Cemetery," from the days when a large plantation stood nearby many years ago. The location of his property is close to where historical documents have speculated this cemetery would have been. Wright believes that one of the previous owners removed any headstones or markers that might signify that a cemetery once stood there so they could sell the land without relocating the graves. Wright has taken to snapping photographs around the property when the paranormal activity stirs up.

Photo by Michael Wright

He has hundreds of anomalous photos taken from on the property. In the image above, he believes he has caught an apparition that seems to be hanging from the tree in his backyard. He has speculated that this could have been the victim of a lynching. Wright is open to allowing others to come on his property to investigate by appointment only.

—Jeff Belanger
Founder, Ghostvillage.com

Georgia

BONAVENTURE CEMETERY

330 BONAVENTURE ROAD
SAVANNAH, GEORGIA 31404
WEBSITE:
www.bonaventurehistorical.org

Photo by Jason McCurry

"America's Most Haunted City," Savannah, Georgia, is home to more than its share of ghostly inhabitants. Among the noted hotspots is Bonaventure Cemetery, home of Gracie, the weeping monument, and the "Bird Girl" from *Midnight in the Garden of Good and Evil*. The "Bird Girl" statue was recently moved to the museum downtown, because curiosity seekers and vandals would not leave it alone.

This cemetery, with its moss-covered trees and serene atmosphere, is as frightening as it is beautiful. According to a well-known authority on paranormal phenomena, this site was once a lavish plantation, beautifully landscaped. During a dinner party held at the estate, a fire broke out and the immense mansion burned to the ground. Visitors have since told tales of spirit laughter and the clatter of dinnerware, when no one was actually present to account for the phenomena.

The creepy statue of a small girl named Gracie Watkins allegedly cries during the night within the cemetery. People who visit the grounds often place presents in Gracie's hands, such as money and trinkets. When one of these items is taken out of her hands, it is said that she weeps tears of blood.

Several other ghosts are also believed to haunt this old cemetery, including a pack of ghost dogs. These spectral hounds have been known to run after visitors, snarling and barking.

Savannah's history shines at this historic landmark, listed on the National Register of Historic Places. Many noted and locally influential people such as former mayors, clergy, writers, and military officers share this burial ground. In addition, millions visit Bonaventure Cemetery each year just for the sheer beauty of the location.

—Jason McCurry
Founder, HauntedLives
Paranormal Society

The Old Tallapoosa Jail

Tallapoosa Police Department
32 Alabama Street
Tallapoosa, Georgia 30176

The Old Tallapoosa jail is located underneath the chief of police's office today. The area that is the old jail is no more than a storage room, since the current department was constructed. We are unclear on an exact construction date for the original jail cell, but it's possible it was as early as 1880. Since its construction, three inmates have died inside the jail, and two police officers have been shot at its gate. This area is thought to be haunted

Photo by Scott McClure

by as many as four ghosts, two are possibly the slain officers, and the other two were killed by an officer before he died from a fatal gunshot wound.

The first officer who was slain at the jail was Mr. William H. Maeger. Officer Maeger never carried a gun; he always trusted his skills as a conversationalist to solve his issues. The murderer thought otherwise. He was killed by a man they called "Boss" Cason. Mr. Cason shot him in the chest near his heart. Maeger died on Sunday, February 13, 1910. Before his death, Maeger said to fellow officers, "Boss Cason shot me, I'm done for."

THE OLD TALLAPOOSA JAIL

The second officer who was killed at this location was Officer Henry C. Pope. According to information gathered, it seems that Officer Pope had arrested the nephew of Mr. and Mrs. C. W. Ledlow.

Mr. and Mrs. Ledlow requested that Officer Pope allow them to post bond for their nephew. He agreed to do so. While filling out the bond papers, apparently a verbal argument took place between the officer and the relatives of the prisoner. The story then says that Mrs. Ledlow pulled a gun and shot Officer Pope from point-blank range. Fatally wounded, the officer was able to draw his weapon and he shot Mrs. Ledlow in the mouth, killing her instantly. When Mr. Ledlow then attempted to pry the gun from his wife's dead fingers, the officer shot him between the eyes. Officer Pope died shortly afterward.

Witnesses have reported hearing strange noises from the jail cell, and unexplained things occur in the Chief's office. It seems that the officers are still taking care of unfinished duties, and the others are condemned to jail for eternity.

—Scott McClure
Lead Investigator, West Central Georgia
Investigators of Paranormal Activity

DEVIL'S KITCHEN

OLD RIDGEWAY ROAD
1 MILE OFF OF U.S. HIGHWAY 78
TALLAPOOSA, GEORGIA

The area known as Devil's Kitchen in Tallapoosa, Georgia, was thought to be named for "The Devil's Water," or moonshine that was made in the creek valley. There are alleged stories of Satanic worship and witchcraft that have taken place in this area that also add to the legend be-

hind the name, though nothing of that nature has ever been proven. The area is about one mile off of U.S. Highway 78 on Old Ridgeway Road. The actual "kitchen" is a beautiful, secluded area. There is a winding creek that falls away into the deep canopy of oak trees, and as you follow it down, the creek then runs into a small canyon of sorts. This is where the moonshine was made. Many bootleggers tried their luck in this area, and the revenuers caught every one of them.

Key's Castle, as it is known, was a grape vineyard in the late 1800s. It has always been an area of spooks and ghosts, according to legend. This home is a large mansion off to the left side of the road before you make it to Walker Creek—the source that feeds the Devil's Kitchen.

Many hayrides and ghost stories have been given and told about this area, and many articles have been posted on paranormal Websites that know nothing of the area and its real history. The other stories tell a tale of a woman who was killed because she was a crime witness—this is untrue. The real story of Devil's Kitchen is more of a tragedy.

The legend of the ghosts at Devil's Kitchen started in 1962. A woman named Mary Moore Newman was taken to an area just behind Key's Castle and was strangled because of an affair that wasn't going as

Photo by Scott McClure

planned. Two men watched Mary as she left to go to the store for groceries, and they entered her home to await her return. Upon her return, the men forced her into their car and drove her to the Kitchen where they strangled her to death. They then took her body to a well, near Friendship Church, in Muscadine, Alabama, where she was later found by the game warden in 1963. He had been stalking poachers who were in the area and smelled the decay as he walked by the well. Around her body were deer heads that had been placed there by the poachers.

The legend says that you can hear her screams for help in the woods around the area of the Kitchen.

A few years after the Mary Newman murder, teenagers were playing a prank on a buddy. They left him at Walker Creek Bridge, where he later stumbled into the creek and drowned—or did he? It is said that you can see his figure awaiting the return of his friends who abandoned him that night.

Then, in the mid-1980s, there was a large flood in the area. A mother and her two children rounded the curve, not knowing that the water was raging over the bridge. Her car was swept downstream. The mother managed to get the children out of the car and placed them atop the roof. She went for help. When she returned, her two children had been swept away, far down to the depths of the Kitchen.

The Kitchen has been filled with death and mystery for years—enough to make you wonder if there is more to it than just a name. Sinister as it sounds, the Devil's Kitchen has been a den for death and mystery, tales and legend, and still is today.

—*Scott McClure*
Lead Investigator, West Central Georgia
Investigators of Paranormal Activity

Kentucky

THE BELLE OF LOUISVILLE

LOUISVILLE, KENTUCKY
WEBSITE: *www.belleoflouisville.com*

Docked along the Ohio River near downtown Louisville, Kentucky, this paddlewheel steamboat dates to 1914 when it was originally named the *Idlewild*. The boat was renamed the *Avalon* in 1948, and in 1962 it was purchased by the city and renamed once again, this time to *The Belle of Louisville*.

Through the years, the boat has developed a reputation of being haunted, especially by those who have worked on the boat for any amount of time. *The Belle of Louisville* has been the site of several deaths, including that of the captain. In 1948, Captain Ben Winters suffered a fatal heart attack in the wheel house and died shortly thereafter in the captain's quarters. According to a former employee of the boat, on at least two separate occasions, workers have died in both the engine room and near the paddlewheel. One was crushed to death when machinery was turned on accidentally, and another died when the paddlewheel was inadvertently placed into motion while he was performing routine maintenance in the area. Paranormal activity has been reported in these areas by long-time workers, and many of these events are said to take place in the early morning hours when the boat is nearly deserted.

According to former employees of *The Belle of Louisville*, newly hired workers are advised of potential paranormal occurrences aboard the boat. They are told they can talk about what they see or hear among themselves, but that no "official record"

BELLE OF LOUISVILLE

of such an event will be recorded in the log for fear of driving away the public or having government funding revoked. Therefore, any official statement regarding a haunting or paranormal activity aboard the boat has never been released to the general public.

One former employee of the *Belle* reported that he was alone in an office late one evening completing some paperwork when he had the sense that he was being watched. He had looked down to file some papers into a nearby drawer and when he look up again, he claimed he was looking directly at the late Captain Ben Winters. The encounter lasted several seconds before the apparition faded away. During that time, the former employee said he was paralyzed with fear and could not take his eyes off of the ghost. The same employee stated that the late captain has also been seen in the wheel house where he suffered his fatal heart attack back in 1948.

The Louisville Ghost Hunters Society has investigated *The Belle of Louisville* a number of times, the last being on July 20, 2004. We have recorded cold spots on the upper deck of the boat and numerous unexplained EMF readings throughout the entire structure. Although no apparitions were recorded during these visits, the history of the boat and the credible sightings from former employees make the *Belle* a top prospect for further study.

—Louisville Ghost Hunters Society

Louisiana

Magnolia Mansion
2127 Prytania Street
New Orleans, Louisiana 70130
Tel: 1 (504) 412-9500
Website: *www.magnoliamansion.com*

Entering Magnolia Mansion in the Garden District is like a step back in time. Decorated in beautiful antiques of impeccable style, it is reminiscent of the pre–Civil War grandeur that the richest town in the country, New Orleans, could afford. But not just the sheer grandiosity captures you—it feels like a time portal.

As I wandered room after room, I could tell that the spirits of yesteryear still cling onto the home where they, too, had once held many a lavish affair. The parlors were thick with guests, both seen and unseen, and a definite welcome was heard and felt. Upon wandering the guest rooms on the second floor, the boudoirs were calling to me, and some rooms felt more active than others.

Because my first entering of the 1857 Magnolia Mansion was during a party to boast about in this day and age, it was of course something the spirits would want to attend—and did! From floor to floor and even out on the grounds, the crème-de-la-crème were there following me, both in flesh and not. Upon returning home that evening, my astral travel lured me back upstairs and to the last bedroom on the right at the end of the hall (I believe that was my room long ago in a past life). I found this especially interesting because of all the rooms I explored at the party, that was the room that felt the most clear.

Hollie Diann Vest, the mansion's current owner, was gracious enough to invite me back and let me stay in that room where I encountered the sleep of the dead—my best sleep ever. I truly believe I had stayed there before. In the morning, when the house was quiet, I could talk to Hollie about the unusual encounters at Magnolia.

Built by Alexander Harris in 1857, the mansion was meant to be a home for his young bride, Elizabeth Johnson Thompson. The home stayed in the Harris family until 1879. Yellow fever took its toll on the Harris clan. In 1869, Alexander died in the mansion within 24 hours of his brother who also lived in New Orleans. After 10 years of fighting and lawsuits among the widows, the estate broke up. Throughout the coming years, the home saw more good times than bad, but the mansion did have its share of death and funerals. The building served an altruistic calling between 1939 and 1954 when Red Cross volunteers spent their time preparing bandages, schooling nurses, and helping the World War II and Korean War recovery effort.

Hollie and her mother bought this mansion in October of 2001 and worked seven 12-hour days a week with a crew of hard-boiled construction men to complete their renovations. This hard work continued until February of 2002, when the mansion opened her doors to guests. The result was fabulous, and you would think the house spirits would have approved—after all, Hollie verbalizes her thoughts out loud letting everyone in on her plans. But at least one spirit was unsure of intent, or perhaps did not take to the burly crew helping Hollie renovate. The renovations were halted one day in early November 2001 when the crew encountered an unexplained oily substance all over the walls and floors. Hollie announced to the house that she was there to make the mansion better and that the entity can't scare or harm any of her guests or friends. This seemed to settle things down for a while. But more spirit encounters continued even after all of the work was completed.

In the kitchen, which adjoins the active dining room area, there was a large Cajun man on the phone. A very large 300-pound door, hard to maneuver on its own, slammed with such veracity to the level that the housekeeper thought a gun had shot off, and the Cajun man promptly left the premises. He had been talking to his girlfriend quietly on the phone and with no source of wind, this violent slam made him check out right away.

The dining area and the downstairs parlors where so many parties were held seem to still hold the spirits dear, but the upper floors are not without their spirits, too. Some say a spirit or two may slip into bed with you in some of the guest rooms. Icy chills down the spine and occasional forms of pressure upon the chest have also been reported.

As time goes on, many supernatural visitors show themselves now and then to the guests. A spectral housekeeper has been known to tuck some of the guests in bed at night, and a little girl has also been seen wandering the halls. But if a party is in the house, all of the spirits come out and the place slips into another dimension. The Magnolia Mansion's spirits are clearly fond of a soiree, fine dining, and all the splendor of 19th-century New Orleans.

—Bloody Mary
Mystic, Medium, Paranormal
Investigator, Bloody Mary's Tours

MAGNOLIA MANSION

BLOODY MARY'S HOUSE

(PRIVATE RESIDENCE)

NEW ORLEANS, LOUISIANA

In a rather quiet mid-city area of New Orleans, you may be surprised to find a haunted house, but not I. New Orleans is haunted beyond the French Quarter and Garden District—the ghosts are spread all over town. Why not? In a city with the highest mortality rate in North America for two centuries, where a cemetery—a city of the dead—guards nearly every neighborhood, in a town that was a giant swamp and an early Native American trade route, there should be no surprise at what lingers behind.

Most of us have spirits that travel with us whether we know it or not—mainly guardian angels, spirit guides, ancestors, and occasionally something not so beneficial. I know that the house I live in is haunted with those I carried with me, some of the spirits who lived and visited this house in the past, as well as a few hitchhikers I may bring home with me after introducing tourists to graveyards and haunted sites. I am a medium, paranormal investigator, psychic, and tour guide, so there are many hitchhikers who latch onto my light. Houses I live in can become crowded, especially if the previous tenants were waiting to greet me or perhaps even lured me there to begin with. The dead can be lonely and need to have someone to help and listen to their needs, too.

The little old lady who lived here for years walks and watches the house and causes no trouble at all; in fact, she protects it. I see her as a very short woman mainly in the hallways; my husband and child see her, too. Also seen now and then is Thomas, a rather thin 35-year-old man who may have a bit of protective/jealous

streak. He did not like my ex-boyfriend, and whenever he came over, the electricity would always go out in the bedroom/parlor section of the house. The second the ex would leave, everything was fine again. I have had many fights with the electrician who could never fix the issue because by the time he got here, everything worked fine.

The ghosts in the attic are now sealed in with holy oil; though we have heard them on many occasions. We recently moved my child's bedroom to the rear of the house—to the room with the attic entrance. In this room, my son had his first encounter as the attic door creaked open on its own. In five years, the incredibly stubborn attic door, which has always taken a lot of strength to open, never ever opened on its own. After the incident, I sealed the door with holy oil and forbade anything but protective spirits to enter through there again. I have to go up there to store stuff soon and will have a further talk with the spirits.

In my home, I constantly see orbs at night—they are green balls 7 to 12 inches in diameter floating around the bedroom and living room. There are a few spirits who hide things and an occasional one that fixes things. An occasional negative spirit may slip through, but, because I sense them, I can battle them away.

Early on, there were many more spirits than there are now. There were so many filling the hall that I had to clean house. It was like a spirit party—they were dressed as clowns or costumed (after all, it is New Orleans) and were dancing about—they were happy and loved my child who was six at the time. My son was expressing a bit of fear on the overload of the spirit activity, so I had to settle them all down. I still occasionally invite outside and inside spirits to parties, but you just can't have everyone over all the time—that goes for the living and the dead.

—*Bloody Mary*
Mystic, Medium, Paranormal
Investigator, Bloody Mary's Tours

JEAN LAFITTE'S BLACKSMITH SHOP BAR

941 BOURBON STREET
NEW ORLEANS, LOUISIANA 70116
TEL: 1 (504) 523-0066

Jean Lafitte's Blacksmith Shop Bar is the last bar to discover at the end of Bourbon Street and is actually the oldest pub in the country. A New Orleans brick en poste building dating from around 1722, the pub is one of the three oldest buildings in New Orleans and houses many lingering spirits from that early period to modern day. Spirits love spirits, and I refer to this establishment as the "ghost watering hole." Some still arrive on horseback, others just pop in and out, and a few seem to reside permanently.

Master Jean Lafitte, buccaneer of high seas and low bayous, appears with pirate hat and is seen side by side with some of his cohorts from days of ole. But those aren't the only ghosts here—generations of happy customers who have passed on in flesh still frequent his pub.

Once a place to move contraband for the Lafittes, the building was a real blacksmith shop and also served as a front for the Gentleman Pirate. Much booty has made its way through here, and some say treasure is still hidden within. The first time in this lifetime that I entered Lafitte's, I was compelled to stare into the dual smithy (now turned fireplace). Staring back at me from the center was a pair of eyes—free floating, with no face to be seen. My eyes and his were locked in a trance for some time until the eyes simply *poofed* into two bursts of flame and disappeared. That, of course, broke my trance, and when I bent down again to recheck the scene, nothing was to be seen. I checked for mirrors, candles, and such mundane things that might explain what I saw, but I found none. Shrugging my shoulders, I simply decided it was a sign of welcome. I was indeed welcomed by those who run the bar and those who may sometimes remain unseen.

After this encounter, I began to feverishly research pirates, treasure, Jean Lafitte, and such to find the meaning of my visitation. The common consensus was that when a pirate buries a treasure, he kills someone on the spot, and thus turns that person's spirit into a ghost slave to guard the treasure so no one can tamper with it besides the one who placed it there to begin with. The trouble is that Jean Lafitte is dead, but his spirit was not released from his guard duty. The only way that Jean Lafitte can be released from the curse is when someone of noble heart finds the treasure that was bought with blood and puts it to good use. The way that Jean tries to help those few he finds with a heart of gold is by pointing his long and bony finger and having eyes that burst into flame and drip with blood. I researched this information for years after I saw those eyes. Some research indicates that whatever treasure was left behind is indeed within the fireplace.

There is one account of fear related by one of the bartenders who was working in the building late one rainy night. The bartender was alone and a short, stout man walked out of the fireplace, walked to the end of the bar, and simply disappeared. Most of the ghosts here are less of an ominous fare and are just there like the rest of the patrons. Here they wander in and out, enjoy a brew, and mingle with the humans like they used to do.

—Bloody Mary
Mystic, Medium, Paranormal
Investigator, Bloody Mary's Tours

THE MYRTLES PLANTATION

P.O. BOX 1100
7747 U.S. HIGHWAY 61
ST. FRANCISVILLE, LOUISIANA 70775
TEL: 1 (256) 635-6277
WEBSITE: *www.myrtlesplantation.com*

The Myrtles Plantation has been called "One of America's Most Haunted Homes." It was built in 1796 by General David "Whiskey Dave" Bradford, who was driven to the Louisiana Territory from his home in Washington County, Pennsylvania for his role in the Whiskey Rebellion. Bradford originally purchased 600 acres from Spain and built a modest, eight-room home there that he called "Laurel Grove." Bradford died in 1817, but the plantation stayed in his family. Eventually his daughter, Sarah Mathilda, and her husband, Clark Woodruff, took over the land and planted indigo and cotton. Many slaves were brought in to work the land, and though the exact history is fuzzy, depending on who you ask, most agree the many ghostly legends trace their beginnings from when this was an active plantation.

The most predominant legend at the Myrtles is that of a slave girl named Chloe, who was a house servant. The legend says that Clark Woodruff was a bit of a philanderer, and he began having a sexual relationship with Chloe. Chloe didn't protest the affair because her alternative was to live a much harder life working in the field. Eventually Woodruff grew tired of Chloe and started to take up with another slave woman. Chloe was then caught eavesdropping in the home while trying to find out if Woodruff was indeed going to send her to the fields. As punishment, one of her ears was cut off. She would forever wear a green turban to cover the disfigurement.

The local lore says that Chloe then poisoned a birthday cake for the children with the hope of making them ill so she could be useful and help nurse them back to health. But she used too much poison and wound up killing all three children. The other slaves, fearing reprisal from the family, dragged Chloe out and hanged her from a nearby tree. After she was dead, her body was weighted down with rocks and thrown into the river.

Visitors and staff have reported seeing the ghost of a turban-wearing woman all over the grounds of the plantation. Additionally, there is a mirror by the staircase in the mansion where the spirits of those who were murdered at the plantation are said to manifest themselves. Phantom handprints on the mirror and unexplained smells and noises are also part of the Myrtles Plantation's ghostly experience.

—Jeff Belanger
Founder, Ghostvillage.com

North Carolina

FORT FISHER CIVIL WAR BATTLEFIELD
HIGHWAY 421
KURE BEACH, NORTH CAROLINA 28449
TEL: 1 (910) 458-5538

Fort Fisher is widely known for its role as the protector of last trade stronghold of the South during the Civil War. Wilmington was the last of the Confederate South's trade ports to remain open during the end days of the Civil War, and Fort Fisher allowed it to stay open to blockade runners and to Robert E. Lee's army.

Two major battles were fought there. On Christmas Eve 1864, the first attack came in the Union's effort to close down the South and win the war. In the next assault, January 12, 1865, a massive bombardment began as the fort was assaulted from sea and land. General William Whiting was injured on January 15th. To literally add insult to injury, General Whiting was forced to officially surrender. Fort Fisher had been defeated and, with it, the Confederate South.

Only a few months later, the South would also surrender. In all, during the second attack, the Fort Fisher garrison lost almost 2,000 men, 500 of which were killed in battle. The Confederate army as a whole lost more than 2,200 men during these attacks, and the Federal forces lost more than 1,500. General Whiting was taken to a Union prison and left there to die.

With so many violent and emotional deaths, it is no wonder the locations of battles seem to have ghosts everywhere you turn. Fort Fisher's best-known ghost is General Whiting himself. Seen on the parapet and walking the ground, his ghost still commands the fort. Does he blame himself for the fall?

The staff at the fort tells of another sighting of a Confederate soldier standing watch in the pine grove north of the fort. Other reports sent to us include the sounds of footsteps on the wooden walkways, the appearance of an apparition going from the ocean toward the fort, and the sounds of battle over the ocean at night.

In October 2004, Cape Fear Paranormal Investigation went to investigate the legend of General Whiting. We had a rather high electromagnetic field reading on top of one of the dirt mounds as well as in the pine grove just outside the fort. This area is said to be an old road that led from the fort to Wilmington. A photo taken from this spot showed a human-shaped mist, while other photos taken showed orbs. Could this be General Whiting still watching over his fort, or one of the many soldiers who died defending the South?

—Stanley Wardrip
Cape Fear Paranormal Investigation

SPENCER MOUNTAIN HAUNTED HOUSE
SPENCER MOUNTAIN, NORTH CAROLINA
WEBSITE: *www.spencermountain.com/hh*

How ironic! Used as a haunted fun house around Halloween to raise funds for the Spencer Mountain Volunteer Fire Department, this house, situated on a hillside overlooking the South Fork of the Catawba River, really *is* haunted. Tales of ghostly activities in this house have been well-documented. Significantly, many of the reported paranormal encounters occurred during the hours in which the haunted house was not open to

SPENCER MOUNTAIN HAUNTED HOUSE

admission-paying thrill seekers, eliminating the possibility that these paranormal encounters could be merely encounters with costumed actors.

Photo by Scott Schneider

The most dramatic report of a ghost sighting happened on October 11, 2002, as a fireman dressed as Freddy Krueger positioned himself in an upstairs corner shortly before the public was allowed inside that evening. The fireman states that he came face to face with a woman wearing a white lace garment, the type, said the fireman, that would have been fashionable in a bygone day. In addition to seeing the apparition, the fireman also noticed during the encounter that the strobe lights and fog machine had stopped working (*Gaston Gazette*, October 20, 2002, 1B). Too terrified even to scream, he bounded down the stairs and breathlessly told his colleagues on the front lawn what he had witnessed. That firefighter refused to re-enter the house. The volunteers preparing the house for the 2004 Halloween season claim that there has never been an actress attired to look like that apparition in the old, white lace dress.

A team from the North Carolina Piedmont Paranormal Research Society investigated the house on September 25, 2004. The firefighters graciously disconnected the electronic devices, such as strobe lights

and simulated train whistle, which would have interfered with the equipment used in the investigation. Although no apparitions appeared that night, the team did photograph a white, string-like image in three pictures taken in an interior room. This string-like image cannot be dismissed as merely a decoration for the fundraiser, because in two pictures the string appears in front of an investigator standing in the middle of the room. The investigator who took these pictures did so because a pair of dowsing rods, previously calm, had begun to swing.

Writing in *The Architectural History of Gaston County*, Kim Withers Brengle states that the house was built in the late 19th century, although some of the volunteers assisting with the fundraiser believe that the part of the house referred to by Brengle as "a multi-sided bay" dates to the mid to late 1700s. The house has been vacant, except for the Halloween fundraiser, for more than 25 years. As for the woman in the white lace gown, although a few people have seen her and one man even spoke with her, no one knows who she is or why she has chosen to remain in the house.

—Scott Schneider
Investigator, North Carolina
Piedmont Paranormal Research Society

PRICE-GAUSE HOUSE
514 MARKET STREET
WILMINGTON, NORTH CAROLINA 28401

This location is one of the most active in all of Wilmington. Prior to a house being built on the site in 1843, the property was the site to Wilmington's Gallows Hill. Many men were hanged at this location. It was customary for the bodies to be buried right on this site if no one was there to take them after the hangings.

Photo by Josh Braathen

When Dr. William Price decided to build his home on this property, he planned enough room for both his office and living space. Immediately after the Price family moved into the house, they experienced strange and unusual occurrences. To this day, sounds of footsteps have been heard walking up the stairs along with the smell of pipe tobacco. Doors have also been seen opening and closing with no rational explanation.

One of the most active rooms is the upstairs office, which, for many years, was used as a bedroom. It is almost usual for the windows to frost up on hot summer nights. They can be seen from the outside, and on a clear night you can see the world "HELP" written in the frost in the upper-left window. There is no explanation for the phenomenon.

Activity has also been seen outside next to the house. J & J Ghost Seekers have taken some strong EMF readings in this area during our investigation. We have also captured photographs of colored orbs and what looks like a shadow of a person peeking through a window and pulling a curtain open. Visitors have reported feeling a pressure build over them while spending time in the side yard. This is no surprise

because there are a number of unmarked graves in the area.

The house is now an office for an architectural firm. The paranormal activity continues just as it has for the past 150 years. The employees of the architectural firm have taken to calling their resident ghost "George." This site is also a stop on one of Wilmington's local ghost walks.

—Josh Braathen
Co-Founder,
J & J Ghost Seekers and Associates

South Carolina

BLACKSTOCK BATTLEFIELD
BLACKSTOCK ROAD
UNION, SOUTH CAROLINA

On November 20, 1780, a major skirmish broke out between 270 British troops and 1,000 American troops at Blackstock Plantation in Union, South Carolina. The battle was short but fierce, and in a matter of hours, Colonel Banastre Tarleton, commander of the 63rd British regiment, retreated, leaving 50 of his British troops wounded or dead and at the mercy of Thomas Sumter and the American troops. Only three American soldiers were killed. The British soldiers killed in the battle were buried where they fell on the battlefield, where their bodies remain to this day.

Today, Blackstock Battlefield is part of a national park and still looks very much as it did that November day in 1780. The site is extremely isolated and remote, located far from the beaten path. Driving down the 1 1/2-mile gravel road to the battlefield, it is easy to grasp a sense of the history and timelessness of the place. Not much has changed in the last 225 years. Blackstock Plantation house is long gone, but the battlefield remains virtually intact. Standing atop the hill overlooking the site of the battle, it is a simple matter to imagine the battle raging below—to imagine the smell of gunpowder, the shouts of troops, the screams of wounded men and horses. Some people have claimed to have heard that very thing. Visitors to the battlefield have reported hearing phantom troops marching and some have had sightings of shadowy apparitions. Unfortunately, visitors to the site are fairly rare, and reports of ghostly sightings are few and far between.

However, one often-reported encounter that stands out as particularly odd is the sighting of a mysterious large, black dog that appears out of nowhere and follows visitors' cars as they leave the battlefield site. One such report indicated that a black dog appeared alongside a moving car in one spot on the gravel road, disappeared back into the woods, and reappeared a couple of minutes later when the car stopped at the stop sign at the end of the road. Not very odd until you realize that the dog would have had to have traveled at a rate of more than 30 mph for a distance of more than a mile to reappear that quickly.

According to folklore, phantom black dogs are sometimes guardians of the dead. Do the restless dead of Blackstock have their own guard dog keeping watch over their final resting place? No one knows for sure, but a visit to the Blackstock Battlefield just might bring you face to face with a mysterious black dog if you are lucky (or unlucky) enough.

—*Melanie Billings*
Independent Paranormal Investigator

ST. PHILIP'S CEMETERY
146 CHURCH STREET
CHARLESTON, SOUTH CAROLINA 29401
WEBSITE: *www.stphilipschurchsc.org*

Photo by Joanne Davis

The city of Charleston, South Carolina, is rich in history, culture, and hauntings. St. Philip's Church is located in the French Quarter, the oldest part of the city. The current church was built in 1823, replacing the previous church that was destroyed by fire. Even though this is a working city, it is very quiet at night in the French Quarter.

There are many reminders of the past as you walk through the French Quarter. As you walk, you will see very decorative posts where horses were once tied up and boot scrapers by the front doors of some of the homes. Some of the brick sidewalks and cobblestone streets still remain. It is almost as if time has forgotten this area.

St. Philip's Cemetery is along the side of the church, and there is also a section that is across the street. This is the section where I took several paranormal photos. It was approximately 10 p.m. when I took them. I took the above picture not expecting anything to show up because it was so dark out, and there was nothing out of the ordinary in the cemetery. After I snapped the picture, I saw the vortexes on the camera screen and immediately took another picture. The second picture also showed similar light streaks, though they appeared to have moved from the first position.

Many people have reported capturing strange phenomena in the pictures they have taken here.

Charleston is a great place to visit for anyone who has an interest in ghosts. There are several different books about the Charleston ghosts, and there are still many more stories left to be told.

—Joanne Davis

CIRCULAR CHURCH CEMETERY

150 MEETING STREET
CHARLESTON, SOUTH CAROLINA 29401
WEBSITE: *www.circularchurch.org*

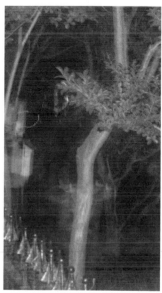

Photo by Joanne Davis

The city of Charleston played a major role in both the Revolutionary War and the Civil War, so it is no surprise that it is one of the most haunted cities in the country.

When walking down the city streets, you can feel the history surround you. Many of the buildings have historical markers on them that also include information about the resident ghost of that building. The people of Charleston are very proud of their heritage and of their ghosts. The citizens there are very friendly people who, when asked, are happy to talk about the hauntings.

The Circular Church cemetery is the oldest burial ground in Charleston. There are graves dating back to 1695. This picture was taken around 10:30 p.m. with my digital camera. I first noticed the three shiny metal buttons on the upper-left portion of my camera's screen and quickly took another picture of the same area. I was surprised to find what looked to me like a Revolutionary coat and shirt. In the second picture I took of the same area, the figure is higher up in the air and seems to be fading.

There have been more reports than can be counted of activity in this area. Orbs are frequently seen dashing through the cemetery and beyond. There have been reports of apparitions, voices, vortexes, and misty forms throughout the grounds.

Even knowing the history of the area and how haunted it is, you never feel afraid when walking the streets. The people of Charleston always show their Southern hospitality and apparently their ghosts do too!

—Joanne Davis

Tennessee

Tootsie's Orchid Lounge
422 Broadway
Nashville, Tennessee 37203
Tel: 1 (615) 726-0463
Website: *www.tootsies.net*

Because of its proximity to the Ryman Auditorium, just across an alley, Tootsie's became the "green room" to many Grand Ole Opry performers, and it's possible that some of them are still hanging around waiting for their next performance.

Purchased by Tootsie Bess in 1960, the bar originally opened as Mom's, but Tootsie was soon inspired by a local painter to change the name. After hiring the gentleman to paint her establishment quickly but cheaply, Tootsie came to work one morning to find her place painted orchid—thus the name, Tootsie's Orchid Lounge.

Famous early customers included Kris Kristofferson, Willie Nelson (who received his first songwriting job after singing his original songs at Tootsie's), Faron Young, Tom T. Hall, Waylon Jennings, Patsy Cline, and many more. Charlie Pride, another Tootsie's regular, was said to have given Tootsie the jeweled hatpin that she used to stick unruly patrons with, and it's rumored that Roger Miller wrote "Dang Me" about his exploits at Tootsie's.

An early customer of Tootsie's was Hank Williams Sr., and many believe his spirit still visits the honky-tonk on a regular basis. Shortly after Tootsie's opened, numerous customers began reporting seeing the lanky country singer sitting at the bar ordering a drink. Some years ago, a patron took a photo, later published in a national magazine, of the front stage that included a plasmic mist said to resemble Williams. The figure appears to be playing a guitar and singing.

But the bar isn't the only thing haunted at Tootsie's. Kristofferson and Nelson both lived in the upstairs rooms at an early point in their respective careers, and both reported more than one instance of unexplained noises and figures.

The alley between Tootsie's and the Ryman is also the scene of an occasional encounter, with a patron seeing the ghost of Williams there in September 2002. Hank Sr. was said to be wearing slacks, a long-sleeved white shirt, and cowboy boots. The polite ghost vanished before the startled man's eyes.

Tootsie Bess was well-known and well-loved in the country music business. She would hire down-on-their-luck writers and pickers so they could support their families, feeding them while they worked, and often slipping $5 and $10 bills in their pockets as they left for the night. She kept a cigar box full of IOUs from those very same artists under the counter, and it's said that, at the end of every year, grateful Opry performers would band together to pay off those IOUs so that Tootsie could afford to stay in business.

Though she passed away in 1978, employees say Tootsie is still at her beloved honky-tonk, watching over the hopeful artists and wannabe songwriters, appearing when a new singer takes her fancy.

—Donna L. Marsh
Founder,
Adsagsona Paranormal Society

THE HERMITAGE

4580 RACHEL'S LANE
HERMITAGE, TENNESSEE 37076
TEL: 1 (615) 889-2941
WEBSITE: *www.thehermitage.com*

Once known as the Southern White House, the Hermitage was home to Andrew Jackson and his wife, Rachel. When she passed away on December 22, 1828, Rachel left a much-saddened man to become the seventh president of the United States on March 4, 1829. While in Washington, Jackson, also known as "Old Hickory," hired Nashville architect David Morrison to dramatically enlarge the mansion and to construct a Grecian "temple and monument" for his beloved Rachel. The domed limestone tomb with a copper roof was constructed in the garden from 1831 to 1832.

Jackson retired from the U.S. presidency in 1837 and returned to the Hermitage, where he resided until his death on June 8, 1845. He was laid to rest two days later next to his adored wife. At that time, the plantation passed to Jackson's adopted son Andrew Jackson, Jr.

While he did make some improvements to the property, the younger Jackson was not an effective manager, and debts soon forced him to begin selling off parcels of land and mortgaging the remainder. In 1856, Andrew Jackson, Jr., sold what remained of the Hermitage to the state of Tennessee for $48,000. The state first proposed using the property as a school, but lack of funds allowed the Jacksons to remain there as tenants until both Andrew Jackson, Jr., and his wife, Sarah, passed away.

Lack of money also meant that the property was allowed to slowly fall into disrepair, although occasional funds could be found for small repairs, such as to the Jackson tomb. In attempt to utilize the property, Tennessee politicians proposed converting it into a hospital for invalid Confederate soldiers in 1888, but a public outcry ensued, and the response was to create an organization of Tennessee women who would fight to save the Hermitage.

In April 1889, the Ladies' Hermitage Association (LHA) was charted by the state of Tennessee, and they took immediate possession of the house by sending two ladies to spend the night. The ladies, however, did not spend a peaceful night, reporting to their fellow LHA members that they were kept awake for most of it by Old Hickory riding his horse up and down the stairs.

Other haunting activities have been reported since, although Old Hickory quieted down once restoration was complete, and a photo of a full-bodied apparition captured in one of the bedrooms was once featured on a Nashville news broadcast.

The Hermitage has operated continuously as a museum since 1889. It continues to offer daily tours, closing only on Thanksgiving and Christmas as well as during the third week of January.

—*Donna L. Marsh*
Founder,
Adsagsona Paranormal Society

STONES RIVER NATIONAL BATTLEFIELD

3501 OLD NASHVILLE HIGHWAY
MURFREESBORO, TENNESSEE 37129
TEL: 1 (615) 893-9501
WEBSITE: *www.nps.gov/stri/*

The site of a bloody Civil War battle from December 31, 1862, to January

2, 1863, the 350-acre Stones River National Battlefield was established as a national park in 1927, and it contains the Stones River National Cemetery, established in 1865. With more than 23,000 estimated casualties during this four-day battle, it's no wonder that many sites along the six-stop driving tour have been reported as haunted.

Tourist stop number two is known as the "Slaughter Pen." This rocky, wooded area full of sinkholes was the site of a horrific loss of life. Many of the wounded and dead were not found after the battle was over, and they lay in the open air for days. Quite a few wounded here died for lack of prompt medical attention. It is at this stop that many visitors report hearing footsteps behind them as they walk the paths. Some visitors have also reported seeing men in Civil War–era uniforms when no scheduled reenactments were taking place.

Farther along the trail at stop number six is the site of a park ranger's run-in with a ghostly soldier. The ranger was camping near here with friends when he noticed his canteen was empty. Heading to the administration building to refill it, he came around a bend in the path only to see a man standing behind some bushes. Thinking his friends were playing a joke, the ranger called out for the man to come out in the open. As the man approached him, he raised first one hand and then the other, as if to surrender. Fearing for his safety at this point, the ranger called out to the man that he had a gun and would shoot. Just as he uttered the last word, the man fell to ground, disappearing into the darkness. Upon investigation of the site, no evidence of the man could be found—no footprints, not even a single broken twig.

—Donna L. Marsh
Founder, Adsagsona Paranormal Society

THE THOMAS HOUSE HOTEL
530 EAST MAIN STREET
RED BOILING SPRINGS, TENNESSEE 37150
TEL: 1 (615) 699-3006
WEBSITE: *www.thethomashouse.com*

In the mid-1800s, people came to believe the mineral waters in a sleepy little hamlet in northern Tennessee had medicinal qualities, and it wasn't long before word spread around the nation and a thriving industry began to build. By the beginning of the 20th century, Red Boiling Springs had gone from a hole in the road to a thriving town boasting a lake, dance hall, bowling alley, shooting gallery, skating rink, and swimming pool. It was best known, however, for its gracious hotels and bathhouses, where people, including such notables as President Woodrow Wilson, would spend the summer months relaxing and partaking of the healing waters. In the midst of it all stood the Cloyd Hotel, built around 1890 by Henry Cloyd.

The era of summer-long retreats and mineral baths ended after World War II, however, and it wasn't long before Red Boiling Springs soon settled into a quieter state. As time passed, so did most of the hotels, with only three of the originals remaining. Now owned and operated by the Thomas family, who also live on the premises, the Cloyd has been renamed the Thomas House Hotel. This pleasant establishment has seen its share of emotion and tragedy, including two fires, and this may explain why some of the former employees and guests have remained.

The spirits of the Thomas House include a former cook who lived over the kitchen and who still calls that room home, and a whistling gentleman who is frequently heard in the hallways during the day, as well as a gentleman who has been seen leaning against the front desk by some of the guests.

But the ghost who seems to touch the most hearts is that of a little girl. Thought to be a child brought to the hotel to partake of Red Boiling Springs' healing waters, she passed away within its walls, and, while many sensitives feel sadness associated with her spirit, others believe she is rather mischievous, choosing to spend her time knocking on doors and running down the hallways of this historic landmark.

—Donna L. Marsh
Founder,
Adsagsona Paranormal Society

running along the bridge in her white wedding dress or hanging from the bridge from her hanging rope.

This is an extremely active site for the supernatural. Please note, however, that in an effort to keep ghost hunters and thrill seekers (many of whom have painted racial slurs on the bridge) away from the site, the road sign on one side of the road has been changed from Crawford Road to Crafford Road. The road goes straight through to the highway and on the other side of the road, the sign reads "Crawford Road."

—Valkerie Carver
Tidewater Paranormal Investigators

Virginia

CRAWFORD ROAD
OFF OF HIGHWAY 238
YORKTOWN, VIRGINIA

Crawford Road, located in Yorktown Virginia, has a colorful and jaded past and is an active hotspot for those in the spirit world. The land was part of a battleground during the Revolutionary and Civil Wars. Many people have reported hearing the ghostly sounds of a battle as well as sighting spectral soldiers in the area. Today, this road is a favorite for young dragracers, occasionally leading to a deadly car crash. It is also reported to be a favorite dumping ground for those wishing to dispose of murder victims.

However, the most famous ghostly resident is that of a young black woman who was left standing at the altar on her wedding day. She hung herself from the bridge in a fit of sorrow, shame, and desperation. Her restless spirit can be seen

WESTWOOD HILLS BAPTIST CHURCH
865 WOODSTOCK ROAD
VIRGINIA BEACH, VIRGINIA 23464
TEL: 1 (757) 420-2186

Mr. Arthur S. Ward was a religious man who was devoted to his family and to his lifelong church, Westwood Hills Baptist Church. When Mr. Ward died, the people of his church erected a beautiful memorial garden in his honor. The garden had a stone cross surrounded by roses and

27 1:03PM

Photo by Valkerie Carver

other beautiful flowers. For many years, this garden grew and flourished. It was a beautiful place to go to for reflection and to remember the man who the garden was made for.

As time went by, a new preacher took over at the church. He began to claim that he was having dreams about the garden and the evil that it brought to the church. He told his congregation that because the roses had grown up and around the cross that this was a sign of the occult and that God wanted him to tear down this garden of evil. He said that dark forces were at work here and must be destroyed! Others in his congregation said that they too were having dreams of the dark place.

So early one day, the preacher and some of his followers went to the garden with pickaxes, shovels, sledgehammers, and other tools and tore the monument down to the ground, then dug everything up. What once had been a beautiful and peaceful garden now laid in ruins. There is still a large moon-shaped hole and a wooden cross stands in the place where the garden once stood. But what will strike you most about the spot is the overwhelming feeling of sadness that fills the area. During an investigation at the site, I captured a photograph of an entity (page 101). Perhaps it is that of Mr. Ward who undoubtedly is saddened that something that was so lovingly created in his memory could be labeled a place of evil.

—Valkerie Carver
Tidewater Paranormal Investigators

OLD HOUSE WOODS

DIGGS, VIRGINIA 23045
(TAKE HAVEN BEACH ROAD TO THE STOP SIGN AND MAKE A LEFT AT THE PUBLIC BEACH SIGN. THE ROAD WILL CHANGE TO A DIRT ROAD AND OLD HOUSE WOODS IS ON THE LEFT.)

Diggs is a picturesque little coastal town that at first glance looks like any other rural Virginia town. However, there is more here than meets the eye. Located deep in the woods on an unpaved back road is one of Virginia's most haunted hotspots, which is known as Old House Woods.

For more than 200 years, people have been reporting sightings of green ghost lights; skeletal sword-wielding pirates; spectral British soldiers; headless dogs that will attack your car; a ghost ship that appears before a coming storm, sailing from the bay up and over the tree tops; as well as a woman in white who wails from the trees during a storm. There are also reports of a mysterious fog that appears and just as quickly disappears, as well as headless pirates that come out of the bay searching for their buried treasure. It is also said that there is a time vortex in the woods that has taken people away, never to return.

—Valkerie Carver
Tidewater Paranormal Investigators

YORKTOWN

COLONIAL PARKWAY
YORKTOWN, VIRGINIA 23690

Yorktown, Virginia, is most famously known as the site where Lord Cornwallis surrendered to General George

Washington on October 19, 1781, bringing about the end of the Revolutionary War and the birth of a new nation.

Nearly 81 years later, the town would once again be at the center of military conflict during the Civil War. Though there was not an actual battle in Yorktown, many soldiers met their end there from disease and exposure to the elements.

These events have not only secured Yorktown a place in the history books, they have left the tiny colonial village haunted by its past. Today, the village, with its population just over 200, is a living postcard to a sometimes ghostly past.

CORNWALLIS'S CAVE

On the shore of the York River, there is a small manmade cavern. During the Revolutionary War battle, many of the townspeople sought shelter inside this cave. It is rumored, however unlikely, that Cornwallis himself was huddling in a corner. The cave became known as Cornwallis's Cave. Since that time, residents and visitors to Yorktown have claimed to hear sounds of panicked voices and screams coming from inside. Upon investigation, the cave is found to be empty.

NELSON HOUSE

Without a doubt, the grandest home in Yorktown is the Nelson House on Main Street. Built in the early 18th century, it was once home to Thomas Nelson Jr., a signer of the Declaration of Independence. During the Revolutionary War, the house served as Cornwallis's headquarters. In the Civil War it was used as a hospital. Crude medical procedures were conducted there, including amputations. Many men lost their lives in the house, but it seems not all of them left. Inexplicable gusts of wind

and the smell of rotting flesh are not uncommon occurrences. People have experienced hearing voices and seeing men of the Civil War era when they are alone in the house. There is also an occasional sighting of a British soldier on the first floor of the home.

GRACE CHURCH

Grace Church dates back to 1697. It was destroyed and rebuilt twice and still serves the people of Yorktown today. There has been a phantom Colonial-era funeral seen in the cemetery surrounding the church. The first recorded sighting of this was in 1791. There is also an apparitional woman holding a dead infant seen inside the church.

OTHER HAUNTED SITES

Other haunted sites in Yorktown include a field across from the Nelson House. Men dressed in red coats have been spotted running around the property and ducking behind trees. On the battlefields, Civil War soldiers have been seen marching around and still on guard. At the Moore house, there is a woman in white who wanders the grounds and a man seen inside the house.

But perhaps the most paranormally active spot in Yorktown today is a narrow trail that leads through the woods from the waterfront to Main Street. It is called Great Valley Road. It is not uncommon to experience cold spots and unexplainable mists on the trail. There have also been several instances of voices being recorded on tape that were not heard until the recording was played back.

—Belinda Swindell
Lead Investigator, Hampton Roads
Paranormal Research Group

YORKTOWN

FORT MONROE
CM 20 BERNARD ROAD
FORT MONROE, VIRGINIA 23651
TEL: 1 (757) 727-3391
WEBSITE: *http://fort.monroe.army.mil/ monroe/*

Fort Monroe, an irregular hexagon-shaped stone fortress that is completely surrounded by a moat, is located in Hampton, Virginia, on a spit of land called Old Point Comfort. It is the largest fort in the United States and has been continuously occupied since 1823. It is one of only four Southern forts never captured during the Civil War.

While they may have been successful at keeping the Confederate army out, they have not been able to stop the ghosts from making the fort their home.

The ghost sightings at the fort read like a who's who in American history. In a plantation-style house called Old Quarter's Number One, the spirit of Abraham Lincoln was said to have been seen standing by a fireplace appearing deep in thought. Lincoln visited the fort in May of 1862 to help plan the attack of Norfolk. The ghost of General Ulysses S. Grant has also been spotted in the house.

Confederate President Jefferson Davis was imprisoned at the fort from May 25, 1865, until May 13, 1867. Davis's first year of captivity was spent in a cell in Casemate Number 2. A vision of a woman is commonly seen staring out of a second-story window in a quarters across from the casemate. It is thought to be the spirit of the Confederate president's wife, Varina, who fought for better treatment of her husband during his imprisonment. Davis has also made spectral returns to the fort, though not in his cell or at Carroll Hall where he was eventually moved. He is seen walking near the flagpole.

But the most well-known hauntings at Fort Monroe don't involve famous people. One of these specters is known as the Luminous Lady. According to the legend surrounding this spirit, she was the wife of a much older officer who was insanely jealous and often threw fits of rage. She eventually found comfort in the arms of another man until one night when her husband returned early and found them together. The husband drew his pistol and shot his wife dead. She now walks the alley behind the quarters they once shared.

The former Chamberlain Hotel on the base has its own legends of the spirit of a woman who roamed the eighth floor. Her appearances were so common and so disturbing to guests that the floor was eventually closed. The Chamberlain is currently being renovated into housing for retired military. I have no doubt that we will soon know if this lady still wanders the once-grand hotel.

Numerous other buildings at Fort Monroe also house unexplained phenomena. In the Old Slave Quarters, residents tell of finding furniture moved around and objects mysteriously flying through the air. Residents of the home where General Robert E. Lee lived during his time at the fort in the 1830s acknowledged that they have experienced hearing mysterious footsteps and voices during their time in the house. I recently spoke to a family who said their young child's battery-operated toys often turn themselves on and off, even after they remove the batteries.

—Belinda Swindell
Lead Investigator, Hampton Roads
Paranormal Research Group

West Virginia

MOUNDSVILLE PRISON

878 JEFFERSON AVENUE
MOUNDSVILLE, WEST VIRGINIA 26041
TEL: 1 (304) 845-6200
WEBSITE: *www.wvpentours.com*

Moundsville, West Virginia, resembles so many other small towns along the Ohio River. There is, however, something that makes this place unique; it contains one of the largest burial mounds in the United States.

Between 250 to 150 C.E., the Adena mound builders constructed the largest conical burial mound known. Typically, the people of that time were cremated after death and placed into small logs that were then covered with dirt and rocks. Inside the log, the Indians would place their native jewelry, pipes, and other various ornaments. This was their death ceremony. In the 1800s, this particular mound was measured at 69 feet in height and 295 feet at the base.

Directly across the street from this structure sits the now-abandoned West Virginia Penitentiary, also called Moundsville Prison. Built to resemble the Gothic architecture of Europe, this prison was completed in 1876. By the 1990s, overcrowding in the nation's prisons led to an all-time high in prison violence. More than 400 inmates died during Moundsville's tenure—and only 98 of those were state-sanctioned deaths.

Considering the amazing history of the area, Deadframe Paranormal Research was anxious to see what, if any, traces of the past might still be lingering in this aging building. The infirmary, located upstairs, seemed fairly inactive during the first investigation, but while walking through the second time, I immediately felt as though she was being "piggybacked," a term used by paranormal researchers to indicate the presence of a spirit making physical contact. I became nauseous and dizzy, and immediately went back downstairs to the main entrance and sat on one of the provided benches. The feeling, whatever it may have been, passed within 30 minutes.

Most remarkably, during the first visit to the penitentiary, Deadframe made our way out to the prison yard, which was once the site of the "Death House." When West Virginia abolished the death penalty in 1959, many of the inmates voiced their concerns over the electric chair and the building which housed it—perhaps they considered it a grim reminder of their once-possible future. The state agreed and removed the building, replacing it with a basketball court for recreation. The court is surrounded by razor wire, and upon finding the surrounding fence unlocked, Deadframe entered the area to look around. Suddenly the wind, which had been calm, picked up to an alarming speed. Debris began flying, forcing our researchers to shield their eyes. It almost seemed as though the sky was growling. The moment our team left the yard, the wind halted. It didn't just slow down gradually, it literally stopped as though it had never started. Upon inspection, there was not a cloud in the sky that night, not a storm in the area. Who or what caused this phenomenon? One of the many prisoners who drew their last breath in this location, or perhaps the millennia-old spirits of the Adena people, reminding all who enter that this was—and maybe is still—their land?

—Jennifer S. Smith
Lead Investigator, Deadframe
Paranormal Research Group

MOUNDSVILLE PRISON

HILLTOP HOUSE HOTEL
400 EAST RIDGE STREET
HARPERS FERRY, WEST VIRGINIA 25425
TEL: 1 (304) 535-2132
WEBSITE: *www.hilltophousehotel.net*

The town of Harpers Ferry is settled in the junction of the Shenandoah and Potomac rivers. First established in 1734 by Robert Harper, who ran a very successful ferry for a number of years, the town is as picturesque as it is historically significant. The area has been called the birthplace of the Civil War because of a skirmish that took place in town on October 16, 1859 between abolitionist John Brown, his army of 18 men, and Lt. Col. Robert E. Lee's cavalry of 90 men. Brown was attempting to arm the slaves in town to lead a revolt, though he didn't get the flood of people he thought he would when he came into town with a wagon full of weapons. Not surprisingly, Lee's men made quick work of the revolt. But the seeds of revolution were already planted.

The Hilltop House Hotel was built on a bluff in this historic town in 1888. The building has 65 guest rooms and offers views of three states, two rivers, and some majestic mountains. The Hilltop has played host to such notable guests as Alexander Graham Bell, Mark Twain, and President Woodrow Wilson. Today, the building plays host to guests of the ghostly kind who have been known to pass by the grounds, through the halls, and in some of the corners of the hotel today.

One of the more vivid encounters occurred near the front desk when a woman in period dress walked through and into the dining room. When the staff went into the dining room to ask this woman if they could help her, she was gone.

Carroll Easton has worked at the Hilltop Hotel since the early 1980s. She didn't know of the building's haunted reputation until she started working the front desk there. She said some guests who stayed in the room above the kitchen would say they heard laughter, pots banging, and voices between 2 and 3 a.m.—even though the kitchen was completely empty and silent. Today, Easton is the sales manager for the hotel and has heard many of the first- and secondhand accounts of ghostly activity. "Civil War soldiers have been sighted walking along the property," Easton said. "It's also been reported several times that there's a phantom regiment that marches up and down our street periodically."

Easton herself has joined a local paranormal group and has had some unexplained experiences during her own investigations. "We have one room up on the top floor, and three of the other employees and I were doing our own investigation," she said. "The ghosts were actually beginning to materialize in this one room for us. There was one man who was over in the corner with white hair and a white beard—a really kind-looking man. We called him John. And in the same room, there was a lady who started to materialize in the corner."

—Jeff Belanger
Founder, Ghostvillage.com

Paranormal Investigator Profile

Ed and Lorraine Warren

FOR MORE than 50 years, Ed and Lorraine Warren have been investigating the paranormal. In 1952, they founded the New England Society for Psychic Research, and they have investigated more than 4,000 hauntings around the world. They're the authors of nine books including: *The Haunted* (St. Martins Press, 1989), *The Ghosthunters* (1990), and *Graveyard* (1993). The following interview was conducted with Lorraine Warren.

Q: How can people know if their homes are haunted?

They should look for any type of abnormal infestation, which can include scratching sounds, it can be movement of objects or things dematerializing and reappearing—making you think you've really lost it. It can also include seeing ghostly forms. Cabinet doors or other doors within the home may be opening and closing on

Photo by Shannon Hicks

their own. People might notice changes in temperatures. Change in temperature is something that happens quite readily in these homes—in certain areas they describe it as "cold spots." It's not that they are really cold spots, what's happening is the energy is being drawn from you or from the heat in that room in order to allow something to manifest because it needs energy. If it doesn't have energy, it can't do anything. These types of things can especially happen during the psychic hours of the night, which are from 9 p.m. to 6 a.m.

Q: What should people experiencing a haunting look for in investigators?

They should look for the credibility of the investigators. We are listed in the governor's library in Connecticut. I don't know how many paranormal investigators are listed in the governor's library, but we are listed based on our credibility. There are people now referring to themselves as demonologists—they're not demonologists. My God, do you know the amount of knowledge you have to have in the area of religious demonology? They just like the idea of calling themselves that.

You can also call the universities in your area. That is usually a good place to start. And then there is clergy. Clergy are very important because they are the ones who can help clean the house of what is going on, be they Catholics, be they Christians, Jewish faith, or whatever. It is so important to reach out to the right people when trying to find your help.

Q: What was your most compelling case?

There have been so many, but Amityville is a case that affected our personal lives more than any case we've ever worked on. Because it followed us. It followed us right here to our home, it followed us on the road. We had very dangerous things happening to us as a result of the Amityville case.

That was a very outstanding case—it's probably the most haunted house in the world. It got the most publicity, and there's not one part of the world where Ed and I have ever traveled, no matter what their language, that they don't know about Amityville. The infamous Amityville horror.

Why should that home have been any different than any other home we ever investigated? It shouldn't have. It was just another case. But when that call came in, there was a very threatening, ominous feeling that came over me. I didn't know what it meant.

When Ronald DeFeo, on November 13, 1974, murdered every member of his family in that home, we were lecturing at a school in West Virginia. When we got there, the dean of students came to our hotel room and told us that Ed's mother had passed away. It was at the exact time that Ronald DeFeo had murdered every member of his family. Don't ask the meaning of it, because we don't know the meaning of it.

Before we left the house, I had called some clergymen and asked them if they would go into that home with us in spirit. Why did I do it? I don't have the answer myself. We went into the Amityville home and spent a couple of days there. We were trying to figure out why a family was murdered there 13 months before and then another family moved in and fled after 28 days. On the way home, Ed hardly talked to me, which is unlike Ed. He didn't stop for coffee, which is unlike Ed. He was out of character where I was concerned.

When we got back, he went down to his office off of our museum and I got in bed. And I had both my dogs with me. I start reading but I couldn't concentrate on the first paragraph, and I knew that was bad, I knew that was a sign that there was a real problem—that something was reaching me, affecting me. So all of a sudden there was this incredibly loud noise; it sounded like somebody shaking sheet metal, it was a deafening sound throughout the house. And out of the corner of my eye, I could see the two dogs and they were acting like they were drugged, just like two statues. They weren't moving. All of a sudden, there was a cyclone of wind or energy and it seemed to come from the lowest level of the house, and it came up into the bedroom area. I looked and, in the doorway, there's this huge black mass. I made a big sign of the cross in the air and I said, "In the name of Jesus Christ I command you to leave and go back to where you came from." And it recoiled like a snake. It went right up through the wall and out of the top of the house.

Within seconds, Ed came in and said it sounded like wild animals fighting—big animals—but there was nothing there. He walked into the bedroom, laid down on top of the blanket next to me, and put his hand on my hand and he said, "You have no idea what just happened to me." I said, "You have no idea what just happened to *me*."

What happened to me in that room was the same thing that happened to him. That huge black thing also appeared to him. Both of us came under attack in our home that night. We got to a point where we realized that it plagued us. It would take away our peace.

Q: What have you seen change in this field?

The public is far more aware than they were 35 years ago. People were very closed-minded then. There is more information out there, and people are reading more, becoming more aware. But then you worry, too, about the foolishness that's being done by people who are going into these houses. They are calling themselves "ghost hunters." They're going in for the thrill. They can't document a case, they can't bring closure to a case, they don't know what they're doing. And that's the sad thing.

Q: What role does your faith play in your investigations?

Our faith is our guidance and protection in our work. But every family whose home we enter is not necessarily a Catholic or even a Christian family. So we became very ecumenical where our work was concerned. But we remain steadfast to our Catholic faith. Our faith plays a very big role.

Great
Lakes

Great Lakes

Illinois

ASHBARY COFFEE HOUSE

8695 SOUTH ARCHER AVENUE
WILLOW SPRINGS, ILLINOIS 60480

The Ashbary Coffee House is in the legendary haunted area of Archer Avenue in Willow Springs, Illinois. I came upon this location when I was looking for a meeting place for my organization's members.

It seems I was drawn to the location. I didn't know it was haunted, but that soon changed. The manager, Deanna, informed me that many strange things go on that the employees have witnessed. One employee says she will never use a *Ouija* board inside there again because the planchette, untouched, was spinning in circles. Another employee

Photo by Edward Shanahan

took the talk of spirits as being a product of others' imaginations and would joke about it. He changed his mind when a cup flew by him from off of a table.

When I asked about running a séance there, Deanna said our psychic fairs are fine, but no séances.

I brought our psychic feeler there—her name is Amy Cooper, and she is an American Indian and very spiritual. She and I team up together when we venture out to locations with paranormal activities that we document.

Also joining us was LuAnne Patno, a solitary Witch, who I felt was an asset to have along for providing a circle of protection. Amy picked up on the spirits as soon as she entered the location. She said they are a family of four spirits: a father, mother, a son about 10 years old, and a daughter about 5 years old. The son is afraid of the father, and the daughter is very sad. The mother also fears her husband.

The father seems to be the dominant one. As we video-recorded this day, every time Amy would describe the father, the microphone would shut down. Amy and I even changed seats, and when we did, we could hear the wooden floor creak as the father's spirit would also change and move to the side of Amy. She was able to describe all other spirits and the camera recorded.

Amy and LuAnne wandered the second floor together, and they discovered that cold spots showed up in areas they moved to.

The spirits are friendly, however, and no harm has ever come to any person there. The spirits are older than the building the coffee house is located in. Amy feels the family is from a building that was on the land earlier, around the late 1800s, as that is the time Amy picked up that the spirits were from.

During one of our psychic fairs at the coffee house, our Tarot reader, Annette, had a very peculiar experience. She held a Tarot card in her hand during a reading for an individual, and they both stared in amazement as the card bent back on its own until the top of the Tarot card touched the table.

—Edward L. Shanahan
Spiritual Psychic Investigator,
The Unexplained World
and Amy Cooper,
Spiritual Paranormal Investigator

RICO D'S PIZZA RISTORANTE

8933 SOUTH ARCHER AVENUE
WILLOW SPRINGS, ILLINOIS 60480

In the Willow Springs section on the south side of Chicago, along a stretch of infamous Archer Avenue, is a haunted building that stands alone, considering the legendary reputation of the mobster who once owned it. That mobster was Al Capone.

The basement of the building held the illegal alcohol, the first floor is where the bar was (and still is) located and was also the area for illegal gambling, and the second floor was also used for profit, as it housed a brothel.

I first came upon the location back in 2003, when it was a local pizza place called Cavellone's West. I was shown only the restaurant eating area and the basement. I took a photo of a picture of Al Capone and now, when viewed, there is a pitchfork running across the image.

In the basement one can feel the impressions of emotions left due to fear or acts done upon others. There are bricked-up areas sealing off passageways to tunnels that ran to the woods, allowing those inside an escape route when the law came knocking.

It is said that in those woods is an area where Capone's gang did some of their dirty deeds to others. Individuals have captured on film the many orbs that show in the woods just beyond the location.

The new owners call the place Rico D's Pizza Ristorante. They reopened the location with a 1920s feel—and the legend of the spirits that call the location home resurfaced. For the first time, in January 2005, I was shown the second floor by General Manager Don Kress. I saw what were bedrooms, a kitchen, a bathroom,

Photo by Edward Shanahan

and what seemed to be sitting rooms for the gentlemen, and it was like stepping back in time.

I was feeling the spirit side of what was once there. In a closet in one of the bedrooms, I picked up the feeling of one being strangled there. In the bathroom, I picked up the feeling that something happened to a female employee of the brothel by a not-so-friendly client. In one area of the room's floor, I psychically picked up the outline of a body.

On the main floor in the restaurant area, the body of a woman dressed as if she were in the 1920s has been seen by employees. She appeared out of the section of the room where a painting once hung of who some people claim to be Capone's aunt, and who others claim to be the madam of the brothel.

This female specter spoke to the employees, saying that "they" are happy with the new owners, as "they" feel the owners will bring class back to the place that was there when "The Boss" owned it. Upon saying those words, she walked toward the stairway leading up to the brothel, and as she stepped upon the stairs, she vanished.

—Edward L. Shanahan
Spiritual Paranormal Investigator,
Creator, The Unexplained World

Indiana

Seven Pillars

On the old Frances Sloccum Trail
3 miles east of Peru, Indiana

For the tribe of Miami Indians that inhabited the Mississinewa River valley, "Seven Pillars" was more than a landmark of natural beauty. It was a "gateway to the other world." Here the Tribal Council would meet within the grotto-like alcoves, feeling that their ancestors would be present to help guide them with their wisdom. It was also where criminal proceedings were held, and where those found guilty of the most grievous of crimes against the tribe would be beheaded.

Seven Pillars also served as a type of trading post, due to its excellent position on the river and its easy access for French traders. The site made an impression upon the French who, according to local legend, bore with them religious icons to ward off the spirits of the dead that lingered around the rounded buttresses carved by nature into the jointing and bedding of the limestone cliffs.

Until recently, Seven Pillars was a popular camping and fishing site for the inhabitants of Miami County, and many an adventurous camper has braved the night to sleep within the limestone chambers of the pillars—and just as many have left with tales of fright.

Bruce S. was one of the more adventurous. "There's ghosts in them there woods," he said with a grin. "There I was, sleeping under the main pillar, when I was snapped awake by a sense of, I don't

Photo by Nicholas Moore, Junior Investigator,
Nightstalkers of Indiana

know…it was something that wasn't right. I saw it hovering over the water. It was a ghost…it was like what I always thought a ghost would look like, I guess. It drifted along the bank. It was beautiful, but scary…know what I mean?"

Shannon D. saw something similar. "It was a mist, roughly in the form of a man, swirling among the pillars. We were camped on the south bank when we were awakened by the sound of someone running through the water. We went to look and saw the apparition moving in and out of the limestone pylons on the north side of the river. I'll never forget that as long as I live."

The area has recently been repurchased by the ancestors of the Miami as part of their bid toward having their tribal status reinstated by the United States Government.

—Bob Freeman
Senior Investigator,
Nightstalkers of Indiana

THE GRAVESITE OF JAMES DEAN
PARK CEMETERY, 1/2 MILE NORTH OF SR 26 ON CR 150
EAST FAIRMOUNT, INDIANA

In the 1950s, James Dean was the living embodiment of teen angst and swaggering cool. In death, he became a larger-than-life legend, forever young and rebellious. And some would say that Dean's restlessness in life carried over to his afterlife as well.

James Dean was born in Marion, Indiana, on February 8, 1931, though by the time James turned 5 years old, the Dean family had moved to Los Angeles. He returned to

Indiana following the death of his mother and was raised on a farm in Fairmount by his paternal uncle and aunt. After graduating high school, Dean pursued his dream of acting, first by attending UCLA and James Whitmore's acting workshop, then by joining Marlon Brando and Juliet Harris in the prestigious Actors Studio in New York.

Following rave reviews on Broadway, James Dean got his big Hollywood break and filmed *East of Eden* and *Rebel Without a Cause* in quick succession. He used his new-found fame to finance the one thing he was more passionate about than acting: fast cars. He bought his first Porsche and began entering road races across Southern California.

Dean was killed on September 30, 1955, in a freak highway accident. He was driving a rare, silver Porsche Spyder that he had nicknamed "the Little Bastard." The car has become almost as legendary as its owner and is said to be "cursed."

Despite having only filmed three movies in his short career, James Dean was catapulted into legendary status, due in part to his untimely death at the tender age of 24. Dean was a maverick, with a reputation of being a hellion off-screen.

Photo by Nicholas Moore, Junior Investigator,
Nightstalkers of Indiana

He became in death an immortal icon symbolizing American youth and the rebel mystique. Some would say James Dean's spirit refused to die, and one need only visit his grave in Fairmount for the proof.

Long-time fan Marc F. stated: "James Dean's tombstone is a mecca for people that want to keep that fire alive, you know. We come there to feed off of that 'something' that he had…that perpetual cool. People leave their little mementos. Lipstick kisses on the headstone, flowers, photographs, beer, and cigarettes. It's a ritual. And you can feel him there. His presence is strong. One night, as we started to leave, I thought I smelled a cigarette burning… just a whiff. I turned around, and the smoke I had left for Jimmy was gone and I could see a pinpoint of fire just off by the old Sycamore tree. I called out and it disappeared."

James Dean's gravesite is open to the public year-round, and a festival is held in his honor annually.

—*Bob Freeman*
Senior Investigator,
Nightstalkers of Indiana

MISSISSINEWA BATTLEFIELD

STATE ROAD 15

SEVEN MILES NORTH OF MARION, INDIANA

In the early morning hours of December 18, 1812, the cacophony of combat echoed across the Mississinewa River. Lt. Colonel J.B. Campbell and his beleaguered Dragoons found themselves assaulted by an outnumbered but desperate band of Miami Indian warriors. There would be no winners on this bloody day.

After an intense battle that lasted for one hour, the Dragoons were left with a dozen men dead, 75 men wounded, and more than 100 horses slain. The Indians fared no better, though their numbers could not be accurately calculated. Lt. Colonel Campbell estimated their casualties to be between 30 and 50, though historians consider this to be boastful on his part.

The battle would be remembered as one of the most significant chapters in the War of 1812, and certainly one of the most remarkable and dramatic events in the history of Grant County. It was a day of bloody deeds that forever left its mark on the field of battle, tainting the landscape for all time. After nearly 200 years, the banks of the Mississinewa are still marked by the spirits of the fallen warriors of both sides of the conflict.

The battle site is now home to an annual battle reenactment and a popular camping site for those who make Miami and Grant County their home. It has been reported by those brave enough to camp through the night that the sounds of battle still reverberate through the woods. As one camper stated: "One night back in 1992, I was camping back by the battle site when I got woken up by what I thought were firecrackers. Hell, I could smell the sulfur. Then I saw the smoky fog along the river and

Photo by Nicholas Moore, Junior Investigator,
Nightstalkers of Indiana

MISSISSINEWA BATTLEFIELD

heard the sound of running feet in the water. I swear, it was like the smoke from a muzzleloader, man. I packed up and got the heck out of there." Other campers have reported similar sounds, as well as the additional cacophony of war cries, presumably from the Native Americans who lost their lives in the battle.

Cassie M. added: "You can hear their voices. You can't make out what they're saying, but it's there, whispering through the trees. You never feel alone. It's like there is always something there beside you. Every time I'm out there, it raises the hair on my arms."

—Bob Freeman
Senior Investigator,
Nightstalkers of Indiana

REEDER ROAD
GRIFFITH, INDIANA

Reeder Road, also known as Redar Road, is a well-known haunted location in Northwest Indiana. This five-mile road meanders between Griffith and Merrillville, though it isn't listed on every area map anymore. It is located south of Oak Ridge Park off of Colfax Street in Griffith and is nestled within the confines of mysterious-looking woods.

According to accounts of teenagers in the vicinity, the main story of this "haunted" stretch of road concerns a teenage youth in the 1970s who encountered a specter as he drove home from a date. As he was racing down the road, a beautiful young woman with long, blonde hair traversed his path. He was forced to stop his vehicle as she instantaneously entered his car. She proceeded to tell him that her car had veered off the road and that she needed a ride home. While she was giving him directions to her home, the young man drove by Ross Cemetery. To his horror, he discovered that his mysterious guest had vanished. Local lore states that this young woman was buried in this cemetery in 1955 after a car accident had sent her hurtling to her death face-down into a nearby swamp.

Another local legend claims that if you walk down Reeder Road for about an hour and a half from the direction of Griffith, as you look to the right, you may spot a white church dating back to the early 1900s. Some say that a passerby can hear the screams of the congregation that an insane pastor had killed many years ago.

Other local accounts have stated that at night, if you pass the railroad tracks that run parallel to Reeder Road, you can see a man in black clothing slowly walking toward you from the direction of the center track.

Photo by Sharon Blumberg

Many people say Reeder Road used to be a heavily traveled road that teenagers would frequent, because it was so dark and desolate. There were no streetlights on the road. They say that the mob used to throw dead bodies along that area. One account tells of a body that actually fell on the car of a teenage couple who were "necking" in a lonely spot.

One local teen stated that she had visited the road with some friends. They had driven down the road until they encountered a chained-off section blocking the road. She said that the road appeared to look forgotten and was covered with wild grassland. She said that they had felt a distinct "presence" while they were there. Consequently, they left the area quickly.

Whatever you may find while visiting Reeder Road, you must come with an open mind. According to my own observations of this location, this unkempt stretch of road is indeed from another era. Since the late 1980s, the road has been closed. It is chained together by yellow barricades that imply: "Please stay away." Whatever remains of this legendary, ghostly road is now swallowed up by the surrounding woods that embrace it.

—Sharon Blumberg

STEPP CEMETERY

MORGAN MONROE STATE FOREST
SOUTH OF MARTINSVILLE, INDIANA

Stepp Cemetery has a long reputation for being haunted. Today, the grounds are tucked away five miles inside the dark Morgan-Monroe State Forest. The cemetery was originally a pioneer cemetery started in the early 1800s.

Locals tell the sad story of a woman who tragically lost her baby son during the mid-1930s and had the baby buried in the nearby Stepp Cemetery. She then became a recluse, spending most of her time at the cemetery watching over her baby's grave and singing to it. She, too, eventually passed on, and that is when the accounts of ghosts began to roll in. Around the mid-1950s, visitors to the cemetery began to report seeing a woman in black sitting on a tree stump in the cemetery near a baby's grave. People would witness her sitting there one second and being gone the next. Rangers have said they've heard the cry of a woman in the woods, but upon inspection, they found nothing. Also, there have been reports of a black ghost dog, watching over the baby's grave and protecting it.

Being five miles back into a huge, dense forest doesn't always make for the easiest investigation of a two-century-old cemetery. PROOF Paranormal had seen photos of a gate in front of the path to the cemetery and we were thrown off a bit because there are actually two almost identical gates that are about a quarter mile from each other. At the second/correct gate that marks the path to Stepp Cemetery, we proceeded down the path for about 200 yards or so before we started seeing the first of the headstones. History and possible hauntings aside, this place is very impressive. A feeling of walking back into the past is in the air as you stroll into the clearing deep within the woods.

During a second investigation of Stepp Cemetery, we captured a strange, red glow in one of our numerous photos. Strange noises were heard throughout the investigation, as well as several footsteps passing by at least one member. This was, interestingly enough, in the same area of the cemetery as we had previously experienced

STEPP CEMETERY

a cold spot. Maybe we were hearing the infamous Black Lady on her nightly walk to her favorite spot by the child's grave?

—Justin Hammans and
John-Michael Talboo
Co-Founders, PROOF Paranormal

Michigan

GRAND RAPIDS HOME FOR VETERANS
3000 MONROE AVENUE NW
GRAND RAPIDS, MICHIGAN 49505
TEL: 1 (616) 364-5300

The Grand Rapids Home for Veterans (a.k.a. Michigan Soldiers' Home) was built soon after the Civil War. While no battles were fought in Michigan during this war, an estimated 90,000 men from the Great Lakes State enlisted to fight for the Union. More than 15,000 of them never came home. The Michigan Soldier's Home was created for the wounded and sick soldiers that could no longer take care of themselves. Adjacent to the home, the state of Michigan set aside five acres of land to be used as a cemetery/memorial to the soldiers who passed on. Today, 4,000 soldiers from other wars lay buried beside the 214 Civil War soldiers who went before them.

As soon as the home opened, reports of paranormal phenomena began, and they continue to this very day. The West Michigan Ghost Hunters Society (WMGHS) continually receives e-mail from people visiting or working in the home. They include accounts of unexplained cold spots, strange electrical disturbances, footsteps and other unexplained noises, and the intense feeling of being watched. In the cem-

etery, ghostly apparitions in full uniform have been seen around the Civil War gravesites. Common occurrences that cannot be explained include moaning noises, sudden chills, and flashlights that suddenly quit working.

In November 2004, WMGHS investigated the Soldierss Home Cemetery. We experienced intense feelings of being followed and had constant unexplained equipment malfunctions. The home itself has never been investigated for paranormal activity because it remains in full use today, home to almost 300 veterans.

—Nicole Bray
Founder, West Michigan
Ghost Hunters Society

LAKE FOREST CEMETERY
FERRY HILL, LAKE AVENUE

Photo courtesy of WMGHS

GRAND HAVEN, MICHIGAN

On the top of Ferry Hill in Lake Forest Cemetery rests one of the founding fathers of Grand Haven. Rev. William M. Ferry was born in 1796 and was the first Protestant missionary to work with the

American Indians. Together, he and his wife founded an Indian Mission on Mackinac Island in 1822. In 1834, their "calling" took them further south in Michigan where they cofounded the city of Grand Haven with Rix Robinson. This was followed by the neighboring city of Ferrysburg.

Lake Forest Cemetery has a high hill with wooden stairs leading up to a fenced-off area named Ferry Hill. The hill contains the remnants of the founding fathers of the Grand Haven community and their families. In the late 1940s, Ferry Hill was horribly vandalized, especially Rev. William Ferry's flat slab gravestone. It is believed this may be the reason why Rev. Ferry may not be able to rest and why he haunts his gravesite to this day. Sightings of a pale, bluish male apparition has dated back to the 1950s. This apparition is always spotted hovering over the flat slab grave stone. Many teenagers, armed with *Ouija* boards, have run away from Ferry Hill swearing never to return. When visiting the cemetery at night, others have had their cars stall out and die, as if the battery had been drained, at the bottom of Ferry Hill.

The West Michigan Ghost Hunters Society (WMGHS) has periodically visited Rev. Ferry's gravesite on Ferry Hill from 2000 to 2004. Investigations have led WMGHS to believe that Ferry Hill, in itself, holds much paranormal activity. This includes orbs, mists, black shadows, voices, and extreme temperature and geomagnetic variances. WMGHS will continue to investigate this site many times in the future, in hopes of capturing the apparition on film or video.

—Nicole Bray
Founder, West Michigan
Ghost Hunters Society

DORR E. FELT MANSION

SHORE ACRES TOWNSHIP PARK
STATE PARK DRIVE
SAUGATUCK, MICHIGAN
TEL: 1 (616) 896-7860
WEBSITE: *www.ebold.com/~mansion/
FeltMansion.html*

Inventor and millionaire Dorr E. Felt built the Felt Mansion in 1928. This "summer home" was to be a gift for his wife, Agnes, and was affectionately dubbed "Agnes's House." Sadly, she passed away in her new bedroom only three weeks after the mansion was completed. Dorr remarried, but his new wife refused to spend any time in the home. Upon Dorr's death in August 1930, the estate was turned over to his daughters. The family retained ownership until 1948, when it was sold to St. Augustine Seminary. The seminary, also a boys' school, added several buildings to the property in the 1960s. Due to the declining enrollment in the 1970s, the seminary was forced to sell the land and buildings to the state of Michigan. The state turned the main dormitory into the Dunes Correctional Medium Security Prison. The mansion was used for offices and the state police post. Due to budget cuts, the prison was closed down in the late 1980s. The land was sold to Laketown Township on the stipulation that the old prison would be torn down due to asbestos contamination. Left standing today is the 80-man trustee building and mansion.

Official investigations for paranormal activity started in November 2001 when the West Michigan Ghost Hunters Society (WMGHS) had full access to the grounds of the mansion while giving "ghost tours" to help raise funds for the restoration.

DORR E. FELT MANSION

During this time, WMGHS was able to pool a large amount of data to prove the mansion is haunted. These investigations continued until October 2002. A wide variety of paranormal activity was witnessed, including positive photos, physical touching, and the moving of objects.

Apparitions were witnessed in the library, ballroom, and Agnes Felt's bedroom. WMGHS determined that the most active room in the mansion is Agnes's bedroom.

Activity included mists, extreme temperature variances (documented 15- to 52-degree Fahrenheit temperature drops), lights turning on and off, and windows opening on their own. WMGHS also caught on video Agnes's French doors flying open on their own. Many volunteers who were working to restore the mansion have reported hearing footsteps, seeing doors opening by unseen forces, and witnessing apparitions. Some restorers refuse to work in the ballroom for this very reason.

WMGHS has deemed this location the most paranormally active building we have found to date. We believe the Felt Mansion holds both residual and intelligent hauntings. WMGHS also considers the last remaining building of Dunes Correctional Prison to be paranormally active. Footsteps in the hallways, doors slamming, and unexplained voices are continuous occurrences in this building. WMGHS believes, however, that this building is mostly classified as a residual haunting.

—Nicole Bray
Founder, West Michigan
Ghost Hunters Society

Minnesota

RILEY'S FINE FOOD & DRINK
46551 STATE HIGHWAY 6
DEER RIVER, MINNESOTA 56636
TEL: 1 (218) 832-3656

About 16 miles north of Deer River in northern Minnesota sits a small, unassuming bar and grill that possesses a spirit other than the alcoholic kind. It is the spirit of a woman that has become affectionately known as "The Blue Lady." This property's past is very obscure, and the investigations into the bar and the history of the land are ongoing.

Photo by Brian Leffler

The Blue Lady seems to like crowds, as it is during times when many people are around that most of her sightings seem to happen. When the kitchen is really hopping, the Blue Lady loves to play with the staff and push things onto the floor. The staff picks up whatever fell, makes sure that it won't fall again, and a few minutes later they find that it's right back on the floor. The restaurant's "to go" boxes seem to be the favorite items for this spirit to play with.

There have also been staff reports of hearing a woman's voice. They weren't able to make out exactly what was said, but upon investigating, they found no one there—no one who could be seen anyway. There have also been many reports of the staff being touched, and this has actually provoked some yelling at the Blue Lady by some of the restaurant's staff members.

The investigations of our own group, Northern Minnesota Paranormal Investigators (N.M.P.I.), as well as investigations by the owners, have provided some nice pictures of orbs flying around the bar. Most of these pictures with orbs were taken when there were customers in the bar, supporting the theory that the Blue Lady likes to show up when Riley's is busiest.

—Brian Leffler
Founder, Northern Minnesota
Paranormal Investigators

LAKEVIEW CEMETERY

MORSE ROAD
BUHL, MINNESOTA 55713

Lakeview Cemetery in Buhl is one haunted location that is not for the faint of heart. The Northern Minnesota Paranormal Investigators have been there many times and have experienced several different supernatural events. We have encountered full-bodied apparitions, heard

Photo by Brian Leffler

voices, smelled strange, unidentifiable odors, and always have had a feeling of unwelcome and dread.

The burials began in Lakeview Cemetery in 1913—about the time the Shaw Hospital was built. Shaw housed people who were sick with tuberculosis and mental illnesses—the dregs of society. When these people died, there was no money for a "proper" burial, so they received a simple plot in what is known as Potter's Field. These men and women weren't even buried with a name, simply a number on a cast-iron cross. Potter's Field is adjacent to the main cemetery.

An investigation in June of 2003 resulted in a very strange video. I was filming in infrared and asking questions. I said, "If there are any spirits here, show me a sign." I started filming, and a single flag began to wave, though there was no wind. I panned the camera around and found many other flags sitting perfectly still, including the large flags on their poles sitting 25 feet in the air. This anomaly was confirmed when I listened to the audio from my micro cassette tape and found I had captured some EVP. I discovered that immediately after I had asked for a sign, two different ghosts had a conversation. The first ghost said, "There's no harm in that," followed by the second ghost replying, "Yeah, show 'em the flags, Roy."

Another trip to Lakeview in June of 2003 handed me my first full-bodied apparition experience. I was sitting in my vehicle loading my camera when a man walked out of the main gate. I was mildly upset, thinking that someone had come to lock up the cemetery. He walked right across the small dirt road that my car was sitting on and vanished. He was a younger man wearing a touring cap, a light-colored shirt, and dark pants—he looked to be from about the 1920s.

Our entire group feels that the "sanctuary" is the strangest place of all within this location. It is actually known as the "Veteran's Memorial." We feel that this area was blessed and the spirits don't tread there. This is a simple area containing a crucifixion statue, about 50 white wooden crosses, and a concrete, box-like memorial with a veteran's medallion on it. It is closed in on all sides with a white picket fence. In front of the area is a dirt roadway, and a row of pine trees run along the back. Immediately upon stepping into this area, the feelings of dread leave you. We took temperature readings inside the sanctuary and then again when we stepped out. We found a 10-degree difference.

Why is Lakeview Cemetery so active and spooky? I can't answer that question, but I can tell you that there is something there. Everyone who has passed through its simple gates have taken something away from there, good or bad.

—Brian Leffler
Founder, Northern Minnesota
Paranormal Investigators

Emmitt House. James was a banker, and in the midst of the Civil War, he built his hotel in 1861. Now, almost a century and a half later, it seems as though the ghost of James Emmitt himself still walks the halls of his hotel.

When you first walk into the restaurant, you get the feeling that you just stepped off a horse and buggy and into late 1800s. The main room is almost as it was back then and retains many of the era-style fixtures, wallpaper, and woodwork. It is hard not to imagine that it is haunted. There seems to be an aura of the people who stopped by there in the early days, where traders, the wealthy, and war soldiers came to eat and sleep.

As you walk from room to room, you get the feeling that someone is behind you, and you catch yourself looking back to see if someone is there. To the employees of the Emmitt House, it is more than just tall tales of footsteps and creaking doors. "I was in the kitchen working," says an employee, "when an old woman walked by the hall. I told her we were not open yet, and asked if I could help her, and she said, 'no.' She walked by a second time, and I knew her clothes were out of place for this time, and when I immediately looked down the hall, she was gone." This is only one of

Ohio

THE EMMITT HOUSE
123 MARKET STREET
WAVERLY, OHIO 45690
TEL: 1 (740) 947-2181
WEBSITE: *www.emmitthouse.com*

With the completion of the Erie Canal in 1832, Waverly was the perfect place for the honorable James Emmitt to build a hotel that is now known as the

Photo by Rob Husak

many sightings and experiences that people have witnessed, which include the smoky smell of the cigars that James enjoyed and the aroma of floral perfume in areas that are off-limits to anyone except staff.

Our team went in to do an overnight investigation, and while there, we witnessed a doorknob turn on its own in the attic. We captured many EVP there, including that of a growling voice upstairs in one of the many guest rooms. The sounds of children's voices laughing and playing were also recorded. Among the many photographs that were taken by our team, we captured blue mists and red glows, and right above Mr. Emmitt's portrait, a photo reveals an ectoplasmic mist. Our team psychic reported the presence of a young girl and the smell of bubble gum in the main hallway.

There are many who claim to have seen the ghost of James Emmitt and other visitors from the past, but all agree that whoever or whatever is in the Emmitt House is there to stay. If you happen to drive by and look up in the windows, you may just get a glance of Mr. James Emmitt himself!

—Rob Husak
Founder, Lead Investigator,
TRP Paranormal Investigations

farm. The road was never built because in 1832, the Ohio and Erie Canal was completed. But the canal had not brought sufficient agricultural and economic activity to the area to warrant an effort for building the road.

In 1840, Ira Hawkins requested for the road again. Conditions had changed significantly and the road was built—the Everett Pike cut through the Cuyahoga Valley and connected the towns of Boston and Peninsula. What is today a quiet valley byway was then a main road, but there was no bridge. Tragedy would eventually change this condition.

On February 1, 1877, John Gilson and his wife were returning home from visiting friends down south. A winter storm had caused the waters of Furnace Run to churn furiously. As they approached, they found a large piece of ice that blocked their way on the road and they had to edge around it through the water. When they were passing, Mrs. Gilson was thrown into the rapidly rising stream. John lost his footing and was dragged by his horse into the deeper water, which was cold and swirling with ice. Mrs. Gilson was rescued by a local resident, but John's body wasn't recovered until four days later. The death of this citizen was believed to be the reason for the construction of the Everett Road covered

EVERETT ROAD COVERED BRIDGE
CUYAHOGA VALLEY NATIONAL PARK, OHIO

In 1810, Jonathan Hale, one of the earliest settlers of the Cuyahoga Valley, had requested for a road to pass through his

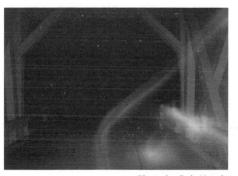

Photo by Rob Husak

bridge. The bridge has been a part of the Cuyahoga Valley for more than 100 years.

Today, some witnesses report seeing a faceless man in gray coveralls with an old straw hat standing by the bridge. The sound of hooves has been heard, though no animals were anywhere near the bridge, and others have spotted lanterns by the bridge at night, only to find the lights gone when they approached. When our team went up there, we were able to catch a few photos that showed some paranormal activity. There are also reports of a cemetery being on the right-hand side of the bridge that has a dozen or so graves without headstones.

—Bea Brugge
Co-Founder,
World Paranormal Investigations

OHIO STATE REFORMATORY A.K.A. MANSFIELD REFORMATORY

100 REFORMATORY ROAD
MANSFIELD, OHIO 44905
TEL: 1 (419) 522-2644
WEBSITE: *www.mrps.org*

Built in 1886, the Ohio State Reformatory was designed to humanely rehabilitate first-time offenders and was initially applauded as a positive step toward prison reform. However, conditions rapidly deteriorated. After 94 years of operation, the prison's legacy became one of abuse, torture, and murder. Now, within the decaying walls of this abandoned prison, the restless spirits of its prisoners and workers are said to still remain confined.

The imposing architecture, modeled to resemble old-world German castles and Victorian Gothic churches, succinctly conveys the atmosphere of the prison. Inmates recall deplorable conditions, including rats, inedible food, and disease. Violence among prisoners was an everyday way of life. Tales are told of inmates being sliced by shanks, beaten by soap bars, or thrown from six-story walkways, all over petty grievances. One African-American inmate reported being disciplined by being placed in a "sweatbox," a special type of torture that white prisoners escaped.

But perhaps the most terrifying prospect for prisoners was "The Hole": an area of solitary confinement cells equipped with nothing but a toilet and where prisoners sometimes had to sleep on the bare concrete floors. On one occasion, following a riot, approximately 120 prisoners were confined to "The Hole" for 30 days, with only 20 rooms to hold them. During this time, at least one inmate was alleged to have been murdered, his body hidden by other inmates under some bedding for several days.

Prisoners were not the only victims. In 1948, escapees brutally murdered a farm warden's family. In 1950, the warden's wife died under "mysterious circumstances." She had allegedly died after a gun accidentally fired while she was searching for items in her closet. The warden later suffered a heart attack at the prison and died soon thereafter.

Denounced by civil rights activists for its "brutalizing and inhumane conditions," the prison eventually shut down in 1990. After taking over ownership of the prison in 1995, the Mansfield Reformatory Preservation Society (MRPS) unsealed the prison for ghost tours.

Since the prison opened its gates to the public, it has been considered among ghost hunters as one of the most active haunted places in the United States. Paranormal investigators have captured numerous orb photographs and haunting EVP. Many report unexplained cold spots and equipment malfunctions.

One of the most active areas of the prison is the warden's administration section. Here, visitors report hearing the voices of the warden and his wife. The faint smell of perfume can be sensed in the "Pink Room," the warden's private bathroom. Others report activity in the prison's Chapel and, of course, sense an ominous presence in "The Hole."

Currently, the MRPS holds regularly scheduled overnight ghost tours for those brave enough to explore the remains of this dark, foreboding prison. A schedule of the tours can be found by accessing the MRPS Website.

—Stephanie Lane
Webmistress, DeadOhio.com

PROSPECT PLACE

MAIN STREET
DRESDEN, OHIO
TEL: 1 (740) 754-4314
WEBSITE: *www.prospectplace-dresden.com*

In 1856, Abolitionist George Willison Adams built a mansion in Dresden, Ohio, that would ultimately serve as a safe haven for slaves traveling north along the Underground Railroad. This house, known as Prospect Place, would become one of the largest stations for liberating slaves in the entire state of Ohio.

The mansion features intricate framework, ceilings, and towering windows reminiscent of days long since past. A large staircase leads up to the second floor, where the atmosphere changes from warm and inviting to cold, dark, and unfamiliar. The building is being renovated, and the difference between the phases is very noticeable. Aging wooden floors echo every step taken into the dark recesses of the house. Some rooms are barely lit, others infinitely dark, and all uncomfortably quiet.

Deadframe Paranormal Research Group was given a tour of the house and grounds prior to an investigation. According to Randy Mullinnex, one of the co-owners of the mansion, the building allegedly houses many different ghosts; as many as eight spirits are said to haunt the third-floor ballroom. Another legend says that a bounty hunter, looking for slaves in the area, was captured and later hanged from the rafters of the neighboring barn. "Some people won't even go inside the barn," he explained. "The energy is that heavy."

—Jennifer S. Smith
Founder, Deadframe
Paranormal Research Group

REPUBLIC GHOST TRAIN

BALTIMORE AND OHIO RAILROAD
REPUBLIC, OHIO

Along the old Baltimore and Ohio Railroad, in and around the small town of Republic, is the site of one of Ohio's first documented hauntings. A ghost train repeatedly travels its ill-fated route, and the guardian spirit warns too late of a fatal disaster that occurred more than a century ago.

REPUBLIC GHOST TRAIN

On the cold evening of January 10, 1887, a passenger express train was traveling west at 60 miles an hour. It was due to arrive at the Republic train station at 2 a.m. On the same tracks, and from the opposite direction, a slower-moving freight train was heading east. The freight train was supposed to arrive and pull off at the Republic station well ahead of the passenger train.

Workers on the freight train grossly miscalculated the time and distance between them and the speeding passenger train.

At just past 2 o'clock that morning, one-half mile west of Republic, the passenger train rounded a bend and violently collided with the freight train. It is said that the force of the head-on collision was so great that both engines rose in the air and crumpled into one another. An engineer was impaled by steel beams that lifted him more than 10 feet. He died a slow, painful death three hours later.

The crash site was overcome by a massive fire, which quickly consumed the sleeper cars containing 15 people. Most did not survive and were burned beyond recognition. Among the dead were two young boys and their father, who had just sold the family farm and was carrying the proceeds with him. His wife and daughters, who were in a different sleeper car, survived the accident but were left penniless. It is unknown exactly how many persons died that night. Many human remains that were recovered consisted of nothing more than burnt fragments.

Since the disaster, a "ghost train" has been witnessed in and near Republic. Its lights glow in the night as it races along the tracks and over the trestle, reenacting the events leading up to the accident.

Reports of another haunting came just weeks after the accident. As reported in a Tiffin newspaper article on March 4, 1887, submitted to me by railroad engineer Fritz Keunzel, train workers repeatedly witnessed a ghost at the scene of the disaster: "[T]he engineer saw a red light, the danger signal ahead, and applying the brakes and reversing the engine, the train came to a stand still on almost the exact spot of the great wreck. Strange to say, when the train came to a stop, the light had disappeared, and could nowhere be seen. Before stopping, both the engineer and fireman noticed that the light appeared to be carried by a woman wearing white. Puzzled by the disappearance of the signal, the conductor walked over the track for some distance ahead, but could discover nothing." Workers witnessed the same ghost on three separate occasions.

—Stephanie Lane
Webmistress, DeadOhio.com

FRANKLIN CASTLE

4308 FRANKLIN BOULEVARD
CLEVELAND, OHIO 44113
TEL: 1 (216) 631-2582
WEBSITE: *www.franklincastleclub.com*

Built in 1865, this Gothic mansion was home to German businessman Hannes Tiedemann and his family. The mysterious deaths of the Tiedemann family mark the beginning of the castle's ghastly reputation. Strange voices coming from empty rooms and behind the walls, sounds of children crying, faces suddenly materializing in the woodwork, spinning chandeliers, cold spots, and ghostly ectoplasm—these are but a few of the bizarre occurrences at Franklin Castle, one of Ohio's most notorious haunted places.

Photo by Stephanie Lanie

Although unverified, many believed that Tiedemann was abusive toward his family. These rumors intensified following the deaths of his four children, wife, and mother. While their causes of death were officially natural, many quietly suspected that Tiedemann was responsible.

After Tiedemann died, the castle was sold to the German Socialist Party. During this time, not much is known about their activities, although many speculate that the party held secret meetings, built hidden tunnels, and even conducted a mass political assassination.

The party later rented out the castle to boarders, one of whom was believed to be a doctor who performed "strange" experiments using human specimens. Oddly, in the 1970s, one owner found skeletons of a dozen babies inside a sealed room. The coroner examined the remains, but could make no conclusive determination. Another owner, Sam Muscatello, reported discovering a skeleton inside a hidden panel. He later became physically ill and invited a local news crew to investigate. They reported strange events, including spinning chandeliers and equipment that moved on their own accord.

A young girl haunts the fourth floor ballroom. She may be the ghost of a servant who was allegedly murdered, or Tiedemann's niece. A large blood stain still appears on the marble floor.

The Romano family, who owned the home from 1968 to 1976, claimed they were visited by the ghost of a young girl who interacted with the children. The family later moved out of the house after receiving warnings of a future death by the ghost.

One former neighbor reported to me that when he was a child, he and his sisters played with three children in a room at the castle. "The next day, our parents took us to the Castle. We met the owner. He allowed us in and we walked through the door we had entered before. However, this time, there was a closed, locked door at the bottom of the staircase. He unlocked it and opened it to show us. The steps looked very old, as if they were not used in many years. The owner informed us that no one uses or even goes up there much any more."

Following the fire that nearly destroyed Franklin castle in 1999, it has been closed and undergoing extensive renovations. The new owner, Charles Milsaps, hopes to reopen the castle as a private club. It remains to be seen if the ghosts of Franklin Castle have other intentions.

—Stephanie Lane
Webmistress, DeadOhio.com

FRANKLIN CASTLE

Lock 4 Canal Park

Ohio and Erie Canal, Lock 4 Canal Park
Erie Avenue
Lawrence Township, Ohio
Tel: 1 (330) 477-3552
Website: *www.starkparks.com*

Photo by Stephanie Lane

Upon its completion in 1832, the Ohio and Erie Canal established a major transportation route that promised great social and economic growth for cities situated along its 300-plus mile route. For many years, it did just that. Yet, the success of the canal system was built upon the sweat and blood of hundreds of Irish immigrant workers, some of whom are said to have never left the now-decaying waterway.

"For every mile of the Canal, an Irishman is buried."

This is a popular expression associated with the Ohio and Erie Canal, and for good reason. The canal workers were mostly Irish immigrants. Their job was grueling and dangerous. For over a 12-hour day of strenuous labor, the canal worker received a pittance in pay, slept in a tent or shanty, and ate meager meals that consisted mostly of coffee, bacon, beans, potatoes, and, on every other day, maggot-ridden meat.

Not surprisingly, there were several labor uprisings as a result. In addition, many internal conflicts brewed among the workers that often turned violent, even deadly. This may have been due to the "daily jigger of whiskey" allotted to the men as part of their compensation. Some local law enforcement officials attributed as much as 90 percent of homicides to drunken canal workers.

Hundreds of young men died from various microbes festering in the mud and stagnant water, such as malaria (or "Canal Fever") and acute diarrhea. Some local towns refused to accept their bodies for burial. When they were accepted, the bodies were often buried in mass paupers' graves. Other times, the men were simply buried in shallow, unmarked graves along the canal.

Many tales are told of the restless spirits of canal workers haunting the many locks along the canal from Cleveland to Columbus. But Lock 4, located just south of Canal Fulton, has an especially grisly haunted reputation. In 1857, it is said that the canal manager of Lock 4 learned that the lock was about to be shut down permanently. Enraged at the prospect of losing his job, the operator brutally killed some of his workers and then took his own life by pouring acid on himself. Even in death, he still refuses to leave the lock and nearby lock tender's cabin.

The mass murder and suicide could not be verified, and we have investigated Lock 4 on two separate occasions, but we did not encounter the spirit of the canal manager. Yet, the lock tender's cabin—which is still standing today—seemed to carry an ominous, almost malicious presence.

Lock 4 is now part of a park that is free and open to the public. Contact the Stark County Park District for hours and more information.

—Stephanie Lane
Webmistress, DeadOhio.com

CONFEDERATE STOCKADE CEMETERY

JOHNSON'S ISLAND
SANDUSKY BAY, LAKE ERIE, OHIO
WEBSITE: *www.johnsonsisland.org*

How long, O fate, shall I remain
In this dark place, my lot to mourn?
How long shall I endure this pain
Which I already long have borne?

—Levi Branson Williams,
2nd Lieutenant, Company E,
Fourth North Carolina Calvary
Died September 26, 1863,
Johnson's Island

Photo by Stephanie Lane

Johnson's Island served as a Civil War prison camp from 1862 to 1865. During its relatively short existence, the stockade held thousands of Confederate POWs. Sadly, Levi Williams, like hundreds of other Confederate prisoners, never left the island alive. In death, some say, they still march the grounds of the former prison.

The stockade was comprised of about one dozen barracks, hastily built to contain the Union's growing Confederate POW population. While the prison was designed to hold approximately 2,500 Confederate prisoners, it quickly became overcrowded. During the 40 months of operation, more than 10,000 prisoners passed through its gates.

The Union's version of the prison's history tends to downplay the living conditions and treatment of its prisoners. To be sure, the Confederate prisoners did create their own community of sorts. They developed their own trade system, and even established a theatre.

However, life was particularly harsh for the soldiers. Credible stories were found of prisoner abuse during the latter years of the stockade's operation. Food and other resources grew increasingly scarce as the prison population increased. Furthermore, the barracks were not designed to withstand Lake Erie's extreme climate changes—prisoners suffocated in the summer and froze in the winter. Many died from disease and illness.

Today, the barracks and other prison structures no longer exist. In their place stand private homes. The only evidence of the prison is the Confederate Stockade Cemetery. The marble gravestones are not original but were carved in the early 1900s to replace the old wooden grave markers that had rotted away. Many graves within the cemetery remain unmarked.

Officially, 209 soldiers are said to be buried in the cemetery. However, it is widely believed that the remains of other soldiers are buried throughout the island. Recent archaeological research (including infrared scans of the island) strongly suggest that more than 100 additional, unmarked graves exist.

Not surprisingly, the cemetery has a reputation for being haunted. The spirits of uniformed Confederate soldiers are seen marching around the island. One well-known legend states that the ghostly soldiers can be heard singing Dixie.

A memorial statue of a Confederate soldier is also said to be haunted. Named "The Lookout," he stands watch over the remains of the soldiers and inexplicably changes position at midnight.

The Confederate Stockade Cemetery is open to the public. Access to the cemetery itself is free, although there is a $1 toll fare to access the island. Donations are encouraged to assist in ongoing preservation efforts.

—Stephanie Lane
Webmistress, DeadOhio.com

Wisconsin

THE FORMER ROGERS THEATRE
310 NORTH FOURTH STREET
WAUSAU, WISCONSIN 54403

Like many old theatres, the Rogers Theatre is no exception when it comes to claims of it being haunted. The theatre has been the site of various unexplainable phenomena. Apparitions, electrical disturbances, and the feel of veiled forces are all but commonplace here. Located in the historic downtown Wausau area, the theatre has played host to a variety of tenants over the years.

Built in the early to mid-1920s, records show that the building was first utilized as Ammenthorp Tire Shop and Helke's Funeral Home, which was later changed to Helke's Furniture. These businesses operated there until approximately 1940. The building then lay vacant for a number of years; however, it was reportedly used as a brothel during that time. In 1945, it opened as the Hollywood Theatre and then in 1960 it became the New Wausau Theatre. In 1979, it opened as the Rogers Theatre and has been known by that name since.

Even though the theatre officially closed its doors in 2002, many feel that the building is still a flurry of activity. The Wausau Paranormal Research Society conducted an official investigation in October of 2003. Our findings were minimal; however, what drew our interest was the fact that many witnesses had reported similar incidents in the past.

Most of the reports seem to emanate from the basement auditorium. Former employees commonly referred to the spirit as "Bob." One former employee reported that while working alone in the basement projector room, he saw a man dressed in a black suit cross the stage area. The employee checked the theatre, but no one could be found. He continued his work in the projection room only to be frightened nearly to death. When he looked through the projection window, the same man in the black suit was staring back at him.

Another account tells of two employees who were working in the basement auditorium removing rows of seating from

Photo by Shawn P. Blaschka

the floor. Both men heard a thumping sound from the stage area, and when they looked up, they noticed that the first few rows of seats were bouncing. At once the men threw their tools to the floor and hurried out of the theatre only to be frightened by the seats rocking violently behind them as they ran.

On another occasion, a night manager was locking the front door for the evening when he was "pushed" from behind by imperceptible forces. Other unexplainable activities include: projectors shutting off simultaneously, lights being turned on and off by unseen visitors, and rapping noises that radiate from seemingly nowhere. Currently the theatre is for sale and remains vacant.

—Shawn P. Blaschka
Lead Investigator,
Wausau Paranormal Research Society

UNIVERSITY OF WISCONSIN MARATHON CAMPUS

518 SOUTH SEVENTH AVENUE
WAUSAU, WISCONSIN 54401
TEL: 1 (715) 261-6100
WEBSITE: *www.uwmc.uwc.edu*

During the 1970s, a female custodian by the name of Annie worked for the university. She was best-known for her habit of starting out her workday with a trip to the cafeteria for a morning cup of coffee and some friendly conversation— she was frequently joined in her quest for coffee by other members of the custodial staff. While chatting before work, Annie would occasionally slip into a distinctive laugh. Her colleagues described her laugh as sounding like a chicken cackling. Sadly, Annie died of cancer of the throat; however, according to some, she never left campus.

Soon after her death, several people reported hearing Annie's distinctive laugh in the building. The library director at the time said she "distinctly heard a woman's laugh" while in the cafeteria. When she turned to the custodian with her and asked if he had heard the laugh as well, he answered that he had.

Annie's presence isn't confined only to ghostly laughter. Custodians working on

Photo by Shawn P. Blaschka

the late shift reported hearing footsteps in the hallway above the maintenance office and break room. When they left to investigate, no one could be found. A custodian at the time related the following: "We would hear footsteps coming from the hallway above the break room, and a couple of us would run up different staircases to try and trap whoever it was between us. But when we reached the top of the stairs, there would be no one there. This happened quite a lot."

Another custodian described the following: "Sometimes when I am in the break room at night, I hear what sounds like a wooden chair being dragged across the tile floor above, but when I go up to check it out, there is nobody there." As in the previous case, more than one person has heard this phantom chair-dragger.

—Todd Roll
Investigator,
Wausau Paranormal Research Society

Great Plains

Great Plains

NEWTON COMMUNITY THEATRE

1701 SOUTH 8TH AVENUE EAST
NEWTON, IOWA 50208
WEBSITE:
www.newtoncommunitytheatre.org

" Theater people" are a very special breed. While some people only devote themselves to an occasional production, others make it their life. And in some cases, their *afterlife* too!

The Newton Community Theatre got its start in October of 1963, with productions held in the old Maytag Ballroom. In late 1965, the theater group purchased the former Four Square Church building. This served as its home until a power failure and fire occurred during a production in 1971. The community of Newton raised funds for a new auditorium, and, in 1976, a theater was built on to the west side of the town's new YMCA building.

The theater now consists of a 250-seat auditorium, with sound and lights controlled from an upper balcony. The basement houses dressing rooms, a makeup area, storage, a small kitchen, and a workshop.

In the tradition of all good theaters, they also have a long-time resident ghost. No one seems to know the ghost's identity, or when he was first reported. He is usually just referred to as T.G. (Theater Ghost). Rather than being an actor, this spirit seems to prefer the technical aspect of the theater. There have been sightings of a shadowy male figure, both backstage and in the light booth. But T.G.s most common prank is to play havoc with stage and auditorium lights.

For years, the lights near the sound and light balcony have behaved strangely. Many people have witnessed these lights flickering. The lights have also often refused to turn off during performances, despite being on the same switch as properly functioning lights. Electricians had been called to inspect the wiring, but no defect was ever found to explain this behavior. Recently, a new lighting system was installed, but even this didn't stop the pranks. Now besides causing an occasional flicker in the house lighting, T.G. has computer-controlled stage lights to play with.

One night after a rehearsal, the directors and some cast members stayed late talking. Suddenly, a stage light moved loudly along its track. This was not a technical possibility, as the computer that controls those lights had been shut down an hour prior.

T.G. was particularly active during the 2001 investigation that the Central Iowa Ghost Hunting Team conducted. The light in the men's dressing room turned on by itself, a wire stretched above the auditorium began to vibrate violently, and an apparition was sighted backstage. The house lights also started to flicker for us before we left.

Other reports from actors and stagehands include unexplained smells, the sensation of being touched by an unseen hand, set pieces moving by themselves, and unusual sounds. A children's group that was staying overnight in the theater's basement reported hearing a few notes from a piano and muted voices coming from the stage above. A search showed the auditorium to be empty—of any earthly presences, that is.

—Lynette Baker
Leader, Central Iowa
Ghost Hunting Team

FORMER JASPER COUNTY CARE FACILITY
5245 LIBERTY AVENUE
NEWTON, IOWA 50208

The site, often referred to as the County Home, was originally built as a county "poor farm" back in 1867. The original building was replaced in 1896 and has been built on to many times since. It became "home" to the unfortunate people who had nowhere else to go, to those who were mentally or physically handicapped, to the orphaned, and to the elderly. In the 1800s and early

1900s, inmates who could do so helped raise crops and stock to help pay for their keep. When residents died with no families to provide for them, they were buried in unmarked graves as late as 1962.

Thankfully, situations had been much improved and modernized in the last 40 years, but this was still not a place most people wanted to end up in.

The home closed a few years ago and has sat vacant since. Well, not completely vacant...some troubled former residents seem to have remained—some merely as place memories absorbed by the building, some as restless spirits.

A few previous workers at the facility told us that they had seen people they thought were residents vanish while walking down a hallway, or they saw them turn and go through a closed door. More than one unsettled employee quit.

After obtaining police approval, the Central Iowa Ghost Hunting Team did some preliminary investigations on the outside grounds. We obtained one photo showing the apparition of a young boy in a

Photo courtesy of Central Iowa Ghost Hunting Team

white T-shirt looking out of a window. He was not visible to the investigators when the photo was taken.

In the spring of 2004, we obtained permission for a second visit to investigate inside. It was a very unsettling experience for the psychically sensitive people in the group.

In an area in the former Alzheimer's ward, I suddenly smelled the very strong metallic scent of blood. Another member of our group came into the room and commented on the same smell before I had said anything. A picture taken in the room at the time showed some unusual anomalies. The scent of blood then vanished, and subsequent pictures showed nothing unusual.

We recorded many places where the temperature would drop by as much as 20 degrees, and abnormal readings were obtained on the EMF meters. Other members captured photos of strange mists and light energy. Two members of our group even experienced unusual spirit activity in their own homes shortly after the investigation.

The former care facility is now in the process of being redone to serve as a center and storage area for various public works. Hopefully, it will soon be filled with a new lifeforce.

During our visits, we were lucky enough to capture some very intriguing photos, giving some proof of those former residents who would not be forgotten and still remain (page 138).

—Lynette Baker
Leader, Central Iowa
Ghost Hunting Team

THE HIGHWAYMAN
INTERSTATE 80
MITCHELLVILLE, IOWA

The history of the Des Moines, Iowa, area can be traced back to 1600s, when Trappist Monks (Moines de la Trappe) who lived in huts at the mouth of the Des Moines River lived and died there over the course of many years while trying to convert the Iowa Natives to Christianity and the European way of life.

Later, French Colonial voyagers went up and down the many rivers around what would later become the city of Des Moines. These Colonial French trappers worked the Des Moines area for many years, fueling the lucrative fur industry that focused on buying and selling pelts to Natives for the European fur trades. Iowa has a colonial past that stretches as far back as some of the earlier original colonies.

There is a ghostly legend that has its roots in Iowa's Colonial past. This story has been going around for many years and tells of a walking spirit out looking for something on a lonely stretch of Interstate 80 in Mitchellville—a few miles northeast of Des Moines.

Who knows if the Colonial apparition is just trying to get home or is searching for someone. Maybe he's looking for his lost horse that left him stranded in Iowa's open plains?

Sightings of this ghost have been reported by dozens of people over many years in the section of highway between Mitchellville and Des Moines. A man dressed in colonial attire has been seen walking across the interstate and along the side of the road searching for something.

THE HIGHWAYMAN

Many people who have seen him initially believe he is a Colonial reenactor or someone dressed for a costume party. However, this entity is seen for only a few brief moments before he vanishes into thin air as onlookers watch in horror and disbelief.

The Des Moines Iowa Extreme Paranormal Advanced Research Team interviewed a couple we personally know and work with who verified that this story isn't just a local legend, but is actually still happening today.

The woman told us that one cold night back in 1998, on the way home from a basketball game in Des Moines, she and her husband were driving home and both saw the image of a man dressed in full Colonial garb walking east on I-80 just west of Mitchellville. It was late at night between 10:30 and 11 p.m.

She went on to say they couldn't see the man's face, but they did notice how he had a kind of faint glow when she first saw him.

As they got closer, almost a hundred feet or less, she flicked her lights on bright to get a better look at the man, and that's when he suddenly disappeared right before their eyes. She turned to her husband who was sitting beside her, and his mouth was wide open. They both talked to other people including friends, family, and co-workers about this incident that left them both in shock and awe. They soon learned that they were some of the many who have seen this phantom.

—Joe Leto
Founder, Des Moines Iowa Extreme
Paranormal Advanced Research Team
(DIEPART)

THE VILLISCA AXE MURDER HOUSE
508 EAST 2ND STREET
VILLISCA, IOWA 50864

On June 10, 1912, sometime between the hours of midnight and 5 a.m., a string of gruesome murders took place at the two-story, humble white house of J.B. Moore in the small town of Villisca, Iowa. This would soon come to be known as the worst mass homicide in Iowa history. The eight victims, all bludgeoned to death, were Josiah B. Moore (age 43), his wife, Sara Moore (age 39), their children Herman (age 11), Katherine (age 10), Boyd (age 7), and Paul (age 5), and two guests in the home, Lena Stillinger (age 11) and Ina Stillinger (age 8). The murder weapon was located by police; it was a large axe owned by Josiah Moore. The axe was found in a small bedroom downstairs, propped up against a wall, next to the dead bodies of Lena and Ina Stillinger. There were many suspects in this gruesome murder, but no one was ever charged, and the case remains unsolved to this very day.

The J.B. Moore residence, currently uninhabited, is known as a hotbed of paranormal activity. The current owner has restored the home to the way it looked in 1912 and, for a small fee, rents the house out to anyone who dares to spend the night.

The Villisca Axe Murder House has been investigated by many ghost hunters and paranormal investigative teams from all around the Midwest. Many have spent the night in this house and reported similar experiences. Some of these experiences include the feeling of a heaviness reported around the main stairwell of the house and a strange change in appearance of the upstairs bedrooms at night. Various video and still shots have been taken with orbs and light trails appearing in them, and numerous EVP have also been captured in the house.

The real thrill ride of a night spent at the house begins around 2 a.m. It is at this time of the night when a train passes through the town of Villisca, and the whistle of the train is thought to trigger the residual events of the murder that took place back in 1912. It is widely believed that the killer(s) used the masking sound of the locomotive to sneak throughout the house and murder all its inhabitants, one by one. Many investigators have noticed a light fog filling up the master bedroom at the point when the train whistle is first heard. This fog moves from room to room, just as the killer(s) might have. Once the fog dissipates, it is followed by the sound of dripping—the sound those eerily inclined have assumed to be blood.

—David P. Rodriguez
Founder and Lead Investigator,
Paranormal Research & Investigative
Studies Midwest

Kansas

CAFE ON THE ROUTE & THE LITTLE BRICK INN BED AND BREAKFAST
1101 MILITARY AVENUE (ROUTE 66)
BAXTER SPRINGS, KANSAS 66713
TEL: 1 (620) 856-5646
WEBSITE: *www.cafeontheroute.com*

My wife Debra and I were out driving and exploring and found our way to Baxter Springs, Kansas. Hungry, we found a remarkable restaurant downtown called Cafe on the Route & The Little Brick Inn Bed and Breakfast of Baxter Springs. We had a wonderful meal. The music playing out of the wall speaker was right out of the 1920s era, and the clarinet was a jumping joy to listen to.

The building was once the Crowell Bank, built in 1870. It is said that Jesse James and Cole Younger robbed the bank in 1876. The old building was restored with the lower floor for dining and the upper floor for bed and breakfast guests. My wife and I savored the quietness of the old structure and our lunch. As a sensitive, I could feel other presences in the area, but I saw nothing.

We walked up the wooden staircase to see what the bed and breakfast rooms looked like. I sensed a presence in the first room off to the right of the stairs, but when I pursued it, it evaporated like a soft breeze. Again, I could sense several presences in the upstairs area, but I could not see them.

There was a friendliness about these ghostly presences, a sweetness and kindness that was genuine. I mentally wished them peace, and my wife and I went through each open room and viewed its contents.

It was a nice visit with ghosts. I wonder if those Missouri outlaws, Jesse James and Cole Younger, were among them? It was a memorable meal and a memorable encounter.

—Lee Prosser

CAFE ON THE ROUTE

Old Highway 40
5 miles Southeast of Hays, Kansas

It was late afternoon when I pulled off onto the shoulder of Highway 40, not far from Hays, Kansas. I had passed the area of Victoria and what is called the Cathedral of the Plains. Tired, I drifted off into a mild sleep. The day was clear. There was no traffic.

I awoke to the sound of voices. To the left, outside my car window on the open road, was a couple in what could best be described as a surrey with a fringe on top. It was a genuine four-wheeled, two-seated carriage with a brown top. Two brown horses pulled it.

The couple was studying me, and I was studying them. The man reminded me of the late actor William Holden, and the woman beside him was dark-haired and pretty. I would say they were in their mid-30s. Their clothes were of the fashion found in the 1890s. I waved and they waved back. But when I rolled the car window down to speak, they slowly faded into the flat nothingness that surrounded me and then vanished within a few seconds.

The fact that I had been acknowledged by the couple in the surrey in such a manner led me to reflect on ideas concerning a time vortex. Is it not possible that a sensitive to such encounters, under the right conditions, could also be sensitive to a time vortex? Is it not possible that as I was seeing the couple in the surrey, the couple in the surrey was seeing me at the same time? In this instance, was I their ghostly encounter and they were my ghostly encounter?

I drove on into Hays, Kansas, and had a nice meal at an old restaurant. I never forgot the incident of this contact, and the reality of the situation was that I almost stepped into a different time stream and a different era.

I have had other such encounters, and I know the difference between a ghostly encounter and an encounter with a time vortex. Someday, I might come across a time vortex that appeals to me and step into it, and thus become another unexplained disappearance.

—Lee Prosser

Missouri

The Armor Home for the Aged
Kansas City Home for Orphans
(Western Baptist Bible College)
2116 Tracy Avenue
Kansas City, Missouri 64108

On a hill just off the Paseo Boulevard stands two 100-year-old buildings. Though the sign on the driveway proclaims it as the Western Baptist Bible College, the buildings have seen much better times and once served a much different purpose.

Photo by Tim Pool

What is called the residence hall is simply falling apart. Columns have been replaced by two-by-fours, there is little glass left in the windows, bricks are falling by the handful, and the roof has only a few of its shingles left.

Originally built by a prominent Kansas City family, the Armors, its purpose was to provide an eternal home for retirement. Shortly afterwards, it was sold to a charity, which in turn sold it to the college. The education building was built as Kansas City's orphanage, and its walls show the scars of the terrible fire in which many children were lost during the blaze that tore through the building in 1903.

Though the college served its purpose well, today it seems that no one cares for its buildings as they fall into ruin and decay. Oddly, the grass is mowed with regularity but little is done for either building. As dusk comes, the windows seem to have shapes and shadows peering out at those below.

In the education building at night, screams are heard, allegedly from the children who were caught in the fire. Strange lights and orbs are seen and photographed around its walls where the marks of fire are still seen.

The residence hall once had marble fireplaces, chandeliers, ornamental iron, crown molding, along with a small kitchen and many other amenities. Now the basement has nothing on its wall but black mold. Any marble or other fixtures were ripped out for replacements in rehabbed homes.

Through the building's skeletal windows, the shadows seem to be full of anger. When the home was sold to the charity, nothing was ever heard about what happened to the elderly inhabitants. Rumors of the time tell of someone dragging all of them down to the basement and locking doors until nothing lived. Many orbs can be easily captured at dusk and nighttime. Those that live a short distance away tell of the apparitions of old people that wander around the house and are seen late at night. Just coming close to the building fills one with dread.

New projects, housing, and roads creep closer to the two buildings, and what their ultimate fate will be will only be known with the passing of time. Until then, one can still drive up to the old buildings at dusk and see what comes out to greet them.

—Tim and Sueanne Pool
Kansas City Ghost Hunters

CHRISTIAN CHURCH HOSPITAL

2697 WEST PASEO BOULEVARD
WEST PASEO AND 27TH STREET
KANSAS CITY, MISSOURI 64108

Anyone who comes close to the hospital immediately feels the sorrow, the loss, and the sense of death from the many

Photo by Tim Pool

spirits who still inhabit its crumbling façade. Any digital camera that takes a picture at any time can catch hundreds or even thousands of orbs that swirl around the exterior. Pictures taken at dusk reveal even more strange and sinister shapes and shadows in its windows.

The ghost of Dr. Patterson can sometimes be seen in the windows of the staff offices.

Some said it was a bad choice to open the hospital on October 31, 1914, but to the serving veterans and poor alike, it became well-known for its exceptional healthcare. It was so well-known that hundreds of citizens flocked to its corridors seeking cures during the 1919 flu pandemic. Unwilling to turn any away, the hospital took them all in. With little understanding of the flu virus, more died than survived.

Then, in the years that followed, the hospital was sold to the federal government, then abandoned, and finally bought in 1927 by Dr. Robert Patterson, a European-trained and locally well-known psychiatrist.

Though trained in the most advanced theories of the day, methods of cures still included using chains, cages, wet sheets, beatings, and some say the worst of all, the ice pick method of frontal lobotomies for unruly and unresponsive patients.

For 30 years, Patterson continued using these methods. In 1957, even though he was in fine health, Patterson suddenly went insane and after all attempts at trying to cure him failed, his own staff made him victim of his own method, the ice pick lobotomy. Patterson didn't live long afterward, and shortly after his death, the build-

ing was again abandoned. The city stepped in, bought the hospital, and converted it to hold the criminally insane.

For 20 more years, the city used the same methods that Patterson had used. Even though cruelly efficient at "cures," the city decided it didn't need the costly upkeep of the building and moved out of it in 1975.

Thus it now stands crumbling and empty of the living. The marble exterior is slowly yielding to the elements, and its windows are empty of glass. But it hasn't succumbed yet. The city finally sold the buildings to a private concern, and it is now surrounded by a fence, as steps are being taken to turn the main hospital into retirement apartments. Progress seems to be very slow, because no one wants to keep working in its haunted corridors.

With doors opening and closing, unknown sounds, and tools being moved and thrown at workers, it may be quite a while before the hospital is redone.

—Tim and Sueanne Pool
Kansas City Ghost Hunters

Nebraska

BALL CEMETERY
20999 SOUTH 176TH STREET
SPRINGFIELD, NEBRASKA 68059

The Ball Cemetery began as a family cemetery—its oldest grave marker is dated 1869. Over the years, the cemetery grew to include individuals such as William "Rattlesnake Pete" Liddiard, a United

States Marshal and implement dealer who left his home of Springfield, Nebraska, to join up with William "Buffalo Bill" Cody. He had a large handlebar mustache and became known as one of the fastest on the draw of all the U.S. Marshals. When he later died on the West Coast, his body was brought back to Ball Cemetery for burial.

Various apparitions have been seen at the cemetery. The ghost of a tall male figure has been seen walking around the cemetery after dark. This ghostly apparition is known to have a rather bad temper, and there have even been reports of phantom, physical attacks dealt to some of the people who dare to visit this cemetery late at night. Other visitors have found unexplainable bruises on their arms and legs after entering the cemetery. Could this be the work of Rattlesnake Pete?

Another spirit roaming this cemetery by night is thought to be Mary Mumford, one of Ball Cemetery's interred residents. Visitors have reported hearing the faint voice of a woman emanating from somewhere in the cemetery, and some have even felt their clothing being tugged, followed by a woman's laughter.

More strange reports from Ball Cemetery include those who say they have witnessed headstones tipping over and then rising back up on their own and strange ectoplasm mists appearing in photographs taken among the gravesites.

Visitors beware! Ball Cemetery is guarded by its next-door neighbors, who won't think twice about brandishing a shotgun if they catch you hanging out in this cemetery in the middle of the night.

—David P. Rodriguez
Founder and Lead Investigator,
Paranormal Research & Investigative
Studies Midwest

HUMMEL PARK
11808 JOHN J. PERSHING DRIVE
OMAHA, NEBRASKA 68112

Hummel Park, which is said to be one of the most haunted places in Omaha and is rumored to be an ancient Native American burial ground, was once the site of a fur trading post run by Jean Pierre Cabanne in 1823. It was later named in tribute to J.B. Hummel, a longtime superintendent of the Omaha Parks and Recreation Department.

The park has a very eerie feel to it. Spread over 200 acres, it is filled with steep hills and winding dirt roads. An area at the eastern edge of the park is known as "Devil's Slide" because of the many suicides that have taken place there. Erosion

Photo by David P. Rodriguez

HUMMEL PARK

has washed the area free from trees and resulted in steep cliffs and sharp drop-offs.

One of Hummel Park's most mysterious characteristics is the trees that bow over the road entering the park. It is believed that many black men and women were hanged from these trees in the early 1900s by local racist lynch mobs—and their ghosts still dangle from the trees. Park visitors claim to hear screams and cries coming from this park late at night.

Another of Hummel Park's well-known mysteries is the "Morphing Stairs," a long, stone staircase located at the top of the park. These stairs are said to "morph" because nobody knows the exact number of stairs in the staircase. Each time a person counts the number going up or down, a different number is counted on the return trip.

The "Morphing Stairs" lead down a large hill into a valley containing a decrepit pit area with a deteriorating shelter house. Spray-painted markings in this area, such as inverted pentagrams and swastikas, along with the presence of dead animal carcasses, indicate that Hummel Park is a place where occult rituals and devil worship have taken place.

In addition to these satanic rituals, numerous murders have been committed in the park. One of these murders involved an Omaha prostitute named Laura LaPointe who, in 1983, was sexually assaulted and then robbed of $25 by four other prostitutes. She was beaten to death with a 6-foot tree limb and a softball bat and was later discovered in a roadside ditch located in a heavily wooded area of the park.

The screams and cries heard by park visitors, coupled with local ghost hunters' claims of unexplained electromagnetic readings and sightings of various ghostly apparitions, indicate a high level of paranormal activity at Hummel Park.

—David P. Rodriguez
Founder and Lead Investigator,
Paranormal Research & Investigative
Studies Midwest

Oklahoma

VINA RAE'S GRILL 'N GRAZE
AVARD, OKLAHOMA 73717
TEL: 1 (580) 435-2382

Vina Rae's Grill 'N Graze is home to several past residents of the tiny town of Avard, Oklahoma (population: 34), as Tulsa Ghost Investigators (TGI) discovered during an investigation on Halloween, 2003. Avard is a rural town located between Alva and Waynoka in northwestern Oklahoma. The café is located in the old high school gymnasium.

The property was donated to the town in the late 1940s to build a gymnasium. With such a small population, the gym eventually closed down. Nan Wheatley set up her café in the west end of the building in 1995. Since then, she and her patrons have experienced voices, footsteps, objects moving, and mists. Many photos taken inside reveal orbs and plasmoids. In 1995, shortly after the café opened, a ghostly woman in a green dress was seen sitting in one of the booths. Also a headless woman was reported floating through a wall.

Our group arrived at Vina Rae's at approximately 3:30 p.m. and began a preliminary walk-through of the building after a light supper of Witch's Brew Stew.

The ELF and Profi meters were very quiet—surprising because I was expecting them to behave radically due to the recent solar flares hitting the earth during the previous week. After the seemingly quiet walk-through, we slowly headed up the staircase leading to the attic area. Much energy was captured on camera in the form of orbs and plasmoids. However, the meters remained quiet. Temperature was maintained at 55 to 65 degrees.

That evening, our schedule included a set of three 30- to 45-minute presentations by TGI and subsequent tours of the main hallways.

During the first walk-through, the area designated "vortex" was active. The air, upon approach of the vortex, was clear, but upon entering the vortex, our eyes fogged over. Members of the tour group also experienced the "fog." Thinking this optical event may have been caused by a single black light set up at the end of the hall, we turned away, but the fog was still enveloping. There was no fog, smoke machine, or foggy weather reports. This fog was very dense in spots, but not visible unless you stood directly in it. I sensed it was indeed the "vortex."

During the second expedition, the fog appeared at the same location. On this tour, researcher Amy Plank walked through one of the side rooms with a small group of folks from the tour. Her ELF meter spiked to five and a feeling of oppression overcame the group, Amy's chest tightened, and boxes fell on the floor, blocking the path into the room. The group quickly ran out and a few screams were heard.

During the third group tour, the fog came and went again. The tour group was advised not to enter the rooms along the main hallway, as the managers were concerned somebody might get hurt.

There are many supernatural phenomena still waiting to be discovered at this very haunted café in the small town of Avard.

—Vicky Glidewell
Psychic/Medium and Founder, Tulsa
Ghost Investigators

The Mancill House

(Private Residence)
909 S.E. Cherokee Avenue
Bartlesville, Oklahoma 74003
E-mail: jana.majors@sbcglobal.net

Mancill House was erected in 1918 by Howard E. Mancill and has served 14 families, two of which were headed by Episcopal priests. The house is of Middle European design, made of brick and wood, with the distinction of two front doors.

Previous owners have made changes to the original construction—the screened-in back porch was converted into a breakfast nook in the 1970s, the original kitchen layout was disturbed, and a small room upstairs was opened into the master bedroom.

The current owners since 2003 are Keith and Jana Majors, who have twin 12-year-old children and a Shih-Tzu dog. The children's mother (from a previous marriage), Lindsey Majors, frequently visits from out of town. The Majors family is undertaking a restoration project on Mancill House.

THE MANCILL HOUSE

Tulsa Ghost Investigators were contacted after the family continued to experience many unexplained events, including "heat shimmers," loud knocking on bedroom doors, music that continues to play after the stereo is turned off, strange dreams, being tripped on the staircase, and the sighting of a tall man with a beard. The family also reported a sense of being watched. Mists have been seen in the upper hallway, and the chandelier in the master bedroom moves by itself.

One of the most profound events occurred at 3 a.m. in early fall of 2003. The current Mrs. Majors and the dog were alone in the house. Both heard a "man" entering the home using a key. The man came up the staircase and then quietly knocked on a door down the hallway. Later it was revealed that two blocks down the street at the same time as the encounter, a drunken man used a key to let himself into the home he once owned and was shot dead on the staircase by the new homeowner, who mistook him for a burglar.

The incident coincided exactly with the event Mrs. Majors experienced.

Tulsa Ghost Investigators investigated Mancill House on Friday, August 13, 2004. The initial sweep produced normal readings—there were no unusual spikes from the ELF or geomagnetic meters. However, there was a definite feel of energy on the staircase and in the upstairs hallway, as felt during the preliminary investigation.

That evening, we conducted three one-hour sit-down sessions where we turn off all power in the building, set up our equipment in pertinent locations, then sit quietly and record what happens. We received several knocks and pops. Visible points of light were witnessed on the staircase as was a mild mist and some dark shadows.

During the investigation, TGI researcher Becky noted her setup time as 9:03 p.m. At 10:56 p.m., she noticed her watch had stopped at precisely 9:03 p.m. Her watch began working normally after the investigation was finished.

Becky's psychic impression was that of a small child on the staircase. The spirit was too shy to visit with Tulsa Ghost Investigators.

Eight EVP have been recorded to date at the Mancill House. Seven are male voices, which is important considering that all present for the investigation were female. The name Ally was spoken in the first hallway EVP. Approximately three minutes later, a second "Ally" was recorded but this time a spike of the ELF meter was also recorded. EVP were recorded on Olympus and RCA digital recorders.

Several photos of orbs were taken by both the Mavica Digital and the 35mm 800 speed cameras. One taken by the 35mm shows a potential vortex in the daughter's bedroom. The orbs range from clusters to faces with beards and lips protruding to large, milky orbs with apparent movement.

—Vicky Glidewell
Psychic/Medium and Founder,
Tulsa Ghost Investigators

OVERHOLSER MANSION

405 NW 15TH STREET
OKLAHOMA CITY, OKLAHOMA 73103
TEL: 1 (405) 528-8485

Overholser Mansion was built in 1903—four years before Oklahoma received its statehood—by a very prominent Oklahoman named Henry Overholser. He was a wealthy businessman and the first president of the chamber of commerce. As the epitome of high society, this Victorian beauty is a site to behold. Many of the family's original antique furnishings still reside in the home, which is now under Oklahoma Historical Society care.

Photo by Laura Smith

When Henry passed, the front parlor was where his wake took place. His casket lay amongst sprawling masses of flowers as many famous and important individuals paid their respects.

Volunteers, tourists, as well as our own paranormal research team, have all reported various types of supernatural phenomena over the years. While working in the house, volunteers have reported body-shaped impressions on freshly made beds, brooms being found mysteriously laying in the middle of the hall, and unusual sounds from unoccupied areas.

Overholser Mansion's parlor also happens to be the site of the Oklahoma City Ghost Club's highest electromagnetic field variance ever recorded. At 150 mg, it was well above baseline and was obtained while the building was locked down and empty. On another occasion, while we were touring the ballroom floor, a closet door opened right in front of me. Every attempt at recreating this was unable to make the phenomenon reoccur.

—Erik Smith
Director, Oklahoma City Ghost Club

FORT WASHITA

3348 STATE ROAD 199
DURANT, OKLAHOMA 74701
TEL: 1 (580) 924-6502

Established in 1842, Fort Washita was once the western-most front on the American frontier. The fort was initially used to keep peace between the resident Plains Indians and the Native Americans who were coming into the area via the Trail of Tears. It served as a Union fort at the beginning of the Civil War, but the order was given to quickly abandon the site in order to defend other more prominent forts. The Confederate Army moved in, and it became a major base of operations almost overnight. For this reason, the fort has both a Union and a Confederate cemetery on opposite ends of the site.

Beyond the many accounts of hauntings by the fallen soldiers, the fort also holds the legend of "Aunt Jane," the headless woman who has been seen wandering about. Some say she was beheaded and robbed for the gold she was known to carry. Others say that she was beheaded one night after she was discovered having an affair at a nearby encampment. Still others believe the story was only a ghost story concocted by the soldiers during campfire ghost stories.

Photo by Andy Selfridge

The Oklahoma City Ghost Club had the privilege of an overnight investigation at this site. The first phenomenon that was noted was the lower torso of what appeared to be a woman in a white gown floating across the road within the fort. Witnessed by four investigators, the image disappeared as one investigator ran toward the anomaly to get a closer look. Throughout the night, other phenomena were also experienced, such as vibrating stairs at the barracks, as if people were walking down. Drums were heard in the distance, a bugle was heard at exactly 10 p.m., and unusual electrosensor and trifield meter activations and readings were noted in and near the front of the south barracks.

—Erik Smith
Director, Oklahoma City Ghost Club

South Dakota

THE BULLOCK HOTEL
633 MAIN STREET
DEADWOOD, SOUTH DAKOTA 57732
TEL: 1 (605) 578-1745
WEBSITE: *www.heartofdeadwood.com/ bh.htm*

Wyatt Earp, Doc Holliday, Wild Bill Hickok, Calamity Jane—these old West names may be more familiar than Seth Bullock's, but the first sheriff of Deadwood, South Dakota, had just as strong a presence as these luminaries... and perhaps an even stronger one in death.

Seth Bullock, former sheriff of the Montana territory, followed the Gold Rush to Deadwood intent on becoming a businessman. With partner Sol Star, he opened a hardware store on the corner of Wall and Main Streets in 1876 and did well in the mining camp.

But the burgeoning town was wild, rough, and lawless, and when Wild Bill Hickok was shot in the back of the head during a poker game in August 1876, Bullock agreed to become Deadwood's first sheriff. Renowned for his ability to stare down lawbreakers, Bullock backed his natural law enforcement talents by hiring skilled deputies. Deadwood settled down under his firm gaze. In fact, he never killed anyone while serving as Deadwood's head lawman.

In 1894, after the hardware store fell to fire, he decided to build a luxury hotel. Completed in 1896, the three-story Bullock Hotel was—and is—famous for its amenities. Bullock died in room 211 in September 1919, at the age of 70. But he apparently didn't leave.

Hotel workers and guests have reported a strong presence in many rooms as well as the hotel restaurant. Photos taken in room 211 occasionally include misty anomalies. In 305, the Bullock Suite, an antique clock that doesn't work sometimes chimes of its own accord. There are frequent reports of Bullock sightings as well, and the staff feels that he's watching to make sure they're working. Laziness increases paranormal activity, including lights and appliances turning off and on, crockery flying in the restaurant, and items being moved by unseen hands. Sometimes showers turn on by themselves.

You can pay Sheriff Bullock's grave a visit in nearby Mt. Moriah Cemetery, where he lies in the company of people such as Wild Bill and Calamity Jane. But if you stay at the Bullock Hotel, the sheriff is more likely to pay *you* a visit.

—Tamara Thorne
Author,
Independent Paranormal Investigator

THE BULLOCK HOTEL

Rocky Mountains

Rocky Mountains

Colorado

The Hearthstone Inn

506 North Cascade Avenue
Colorado Springs, Colorado 80903
Tel: 1 (719) 473-4413
Website: *www.hearthstoneinn.com*

The stately Hearthstone Inn is comprised of two Victorian mansions. The first was built in 1885 and was home to the Judson Moss Bemis family. The second was constructed in 1900 and became a tuberculosis boarding house—serving as the final refuge for many patients who sought the cool, dry Colorado air to help relieve the symptoms of the often-fatal disease. Since 1978, the mansions have been home to the Hearthstone Inn—a bed and breakfast that offers many relics of the past—old, cast-iron radiators, hardwood floors, antiques, and even some ghosts.

David Oxenhandler and his wife bought the inn in 1999, but they weren't aware of its haunted nature until they started working there. "When somebody tells you an experience in the inn—whether it's an employee or a guest—your first reaction is, is there a problem with my inn or a problem with the person telling me this?" Oxenhandler said. But over time, he noticed people began to relay very similar experiences. Considering they didn't publicly talk about their ghosts, there had to be something more to the story.

The encounters picked up after lightning struck a tree outside of the building in the summer of 1999. The bolt knocked large sections of the tree into the street and was close enough to damage computer and phone equipment inside the Hearthstone. The following day, someone checked into the inn and was given a room on the third floor. Within minutes, the guest came down and asked if they could change rooms. "We put them in a new room," Oxenhandler said, "and the front desk person went back to the first room and saw that there was a mahogany mirror face-down on the floor. She just assumed it was smashed. She picked it up and it wasn't broken. So she hung it back on the wall. The next night, somebody else checked in to the same room. They again asked to be moved. This time they said the mirror floated off the wall and down to the floor."

After the lightning strike, Oxenhandler phoned his insurance company to report a claim for some of the electrical equipment that had been damaged by the lightning.

But he also asked his insurance company about another problem. He said, "I said to them, 'If we had a problem with one of our rooms since the lightning strike and can't use it, would that qualify?' And they said, 'Sure. What, does it have a leak in the roof or something?' And I said, 'No, it's haunted.' Needless to say, faxes went all over the world from the insurance company laughing about this thing. They sent down an electrical engineer to examine everything and absolutely nothing happened."

The Hearthstone Inn has been investigated by paranormal investigators and psychics who feel the haunting stems from several former tuberculosis patients, the spirit of Alice Bemis Taylor, daughter of Judson Moss Bemis, and a man who may have hung himself on the third floor landing. During her life, Alice Bemis Taylor donated two other buildings in the Colorado Springs area: Colorado College's Bemis Hall, and the Fine Arts Center in Colorado Springs. Both buildings also have reports of Alice Bemis Taylor's ghost still wandering through—on some occasions, she's been reported in both buildings and the Hearthstone Inn on the same night.

—Jeff Belanger
Founder, Ghostvillage.com

St. Elmo

Colorado

(To get to St. Elmo, take US 285 South from Buena Vista and then Country Road 162 West for 16 miles.)

Founded in 1878 during the height of the Gold Rush, the town of St. Elmo, Colorado, is rumored not only to be one of the most well-preserved ghost towns in the United States, but also one that truly lives up to its title of "ghost" town. The lively ghost of one-time resident, Annabelle Stark, roams the deserted streets and buildings of St. Elmo, still carrying out her job as self-appointed caretaker of the town.

Annabelle grew up as the town was suffering through the downfall of the short-lived Gold Rush during the early 20th century. As the prospect of gold dried up, residents quickly vacated the town in search of work. Annabelle and her family were some of the few people stubbornly clinging to their old way of life in the dying town. Annabelle left the town once for a period of two years to work in a nearby town where she became engaged. The engagement was short-lived, however, and Annabelle soon returned to St. Elmo without a husband or explanation, seemingly resigned to the fact that she would never leave the town again.

By the mid-1930s, the population of St. Elmo had dwindled down from 2,000 to fewer than 10. After Annabelle's parents died, only Annabelle and her brother Tony were left in St. Elmo, and their mental state slowly deteriorated along with the town. They isolated themselves in the town's hotel without running water or electricity and allowed the building to fill with trash and debris. Annabelle, with her unkempt appearance and straggly hair, became known as "Dirty Annie" and was sometimes sighted patrolling St. Elmo with rifle in hand. Despite her appearance and mental state, Annabelle was regarded as a kind and vigilant soul.

Annabelle Stark never left St. Elmo until her death in 1960, and it seems that even that does not deter her from her self-appointed caretaking duties. Soon after Annabelle's death, the new owners of the hotel began the difficult task of cleaning decades' worth of dirt and grime from the building. It wasn't long before Annabelle made her presence known by rearranging cleaning supplies, including moving them out of a padlocked closet several times. The apparition of a ghostly woman has been spotted in the hotel on occasion, one of the most notable being in the late 1970s, when someone caught sight of her peering out of an upstairs window. Following her intent gaze, the person found a group of snowmobilers down the street. After the person confronted the snowmobilers and informed them that snowmobiles were not allowed in the town, the apparition disappeared. A subsequent search of the upstairs room in which she had been spotted revealed that no one had been in that room at the time.

Annabelle "Dirty Annie" Stark seems determined to continue on indefinitely guarding her beloved town.

—Melanie Billings
Writer/Paranormal Investigator

STEVE LEE HOUSE

(PRIVATE RESIDENCE)
BLACK FOREST, COLORADO
WEBSITE: *www.haunted-places.com/ black_forest_haunting.htm*

The home of Steve and Beth Lee in Black Forest, Colorado, is possibly one of the most haunted locations in the world. The two-story log house and the five acres it is situated on is the site of some of the most incredible paranormal activity ever witnessed. Balls and streaks of light flit through the trees in the yard, the sounds of unexplained footsteps echo through the house, ghostly mist and apparitions show up in photographs, and a 100 year-old mirror seems to reflect otherworldly faces and figures. Even more intriguing is the fact that a lot of the paranormal activity has been witnessed by more than one person and also caught on film and videotape, including by the crew of the TV show *Sightings*.

Soon after moving into their new home in 1991, Steve and Beth Lee at first assumed someone was trying to scare them away when odd occurrences began to take place. The El Paso County police department investigated 64 unexplained reports of "break-ins" but failed to find any evidence of criminal activity. Frustrated, Lee hired private investigators who set up cameras and motion detectors on the property. The videotape and photos did not show any suspicious activity of human origin but instead showed unexplained streaks of light and even phantom transparent faces. After conducting his own experiments to determine where the strange images originated, Lee finally came to the conclusion that paranormal forces might be responsible. Over the years, Steve Lee has amassed more than 3,000 photographs and dozens of hours of videotape showing evidence of paranormal goings-on.

The paranormal activity has been documented and experienced by several individuals outside of the Lee family, lending even more credibility to their story. The Lees contacted *Sightings* in 1995 and over the next two years, *Sightings* conducted several investigations of the Lees' home with the help of paranormal investigators Echo Bodine and Peter James. Echo

STEVE LEE HOUSE

Bodine called the haunting "monumental" in scope and detected more than 20 different spirits. *Sightings* also consulted a Hopi Shaman who was familiar with the area who told them that the Lee home was located on the site of a "rainbow vortex"— a sort of doorway between this world and the next.

To further validate their experiences, the Lees even contacted a state senator, Charles Duke, and invited him to come and take photographs. He did so and captured several anomalous images with his own camera, including a very clear image of an apparition of a dog. Intrigued by his own findings, Senator Duke contacted the FBI, who declined to investigate but told the Lees that "poltergeists" might be the cause.

It is still not clear what is responsible for the paranormal activity in the Lees' home, but judging from the sheer volume of evidence and first-person experiences, it is obvious that something unexplainable is going on. Perhaps the home is indeed the site of a "rainbow bridge," a gateway to the afterlife, a sort of ghostly train station for traveling spirits just passing through.

—Melanie Billings
Writer/Paranormal Investigator

sets in right away, and maybe you should listen when every fiber of your being tells you to leave. Who is the elderly woman that sits on a bench in the cemetery late at night when all others have been in bed for hours? And where does she go when you look away and then turn back to find that she has just vanished? How about the midnight female jogger who vanishes from the road behind the cemetery after your car has passed her, and how is that she is able to jog...without any legs? Is she also responsible for the reports of automatic car windows going up and down on their own?

The cemetery dates back to the 1800s, and there are some very sad stories behind some of the people who are buried there. There are suicide victims, murder victims, and even a woman who was killed along with her five children when their car went off the road and plunged into the water.

Stephen Cuff, a lifelong resident of Caldwell, has heard these tales from the time that he was a little boy growing up in the area. His friends would take trips to the cemetery just to see if they could catch a glimpse of the jogger or the elderly woman.

On December 11, 2004, members of the Idaho Spirit Seekers team went to the cemetery around 8 p.m., hoping, once again, to find more evidence that there is paranormal activity taking place in this

Idaho

CANYON HILL CEMETERY
2024 NORTH ILLINOIS AVENUE
CALDWELL, IDAHO 83606
TEL: 1 (208) 455-3055

Walking this cemetery at night is eerie enough to give even the most experienced ghost hunter the chills. The fear

Photo courtesy of Idaho Spirit Seekers

spot. When members of the team walked into the cemetery, there was a noticeable drop in temperature. One of the members had a strong sense of someone or something watching them in the shadows and suggested they walk in that direction. When one of our members experienced a strong feeling that someone was in the area, a second member began taking pictures. Immediately after taking the pictures, she reviewed them and noticed that she had captured what appeared to be an eerie, white mist wrapped around the trees and a green mist surrounding the headstones. In one of the pictures, there appears to be the face of an angry man. In further review of the pictures, there were numerous orbs captured, and four others contained an eerie, white mist as well.

Investigators from Idaho Spirit Seekers have been to this site numerous times on investigations and will continue to go back until they are able to get some idea of who these haunted spirits are.

—*Marie Cuff and Kelly Winn*
Idaho Spirit Seekers

of 88. Or could this be George Hamilton, who designed the dining hall and was so distraught over having been ordered to leave Idaho after his release that he committed suicide the same day that he was released from the prison? Did he come back to the prison, calling it home in life and in death? Maybe it's the inmate who hung himself in 1971 with a rope made from his pants while on death row in maximum security.

The penitentiary was built in 1870 when the Idaho Territory was only about 10 years old. It began as a single cell-block and grew into the several buildings that are now on the property. Sandstone was used to construct the walls, and many of the building materials were mined from the local area by inmates sentenced to hard labor here. Throughout the years, it held approximately 13,000 prisoners, 215 of which were women. The prison closed on December 3, 1973, because of riots resulting from the conditions of the prison. It is one of only four territorial prisons still standing in the United States. In the main courtyard, you can see where buildings were burned in the riots, yet the first and oldest cell blocks still stand. The prison has

OLD IDAHO PENITENTIARY

2445 OLD PENITENTIARY ROAD
BOISE, IDAHO 83712
TEL: 1 (208) 334-2844

There are spirits who walk the cell blocks and entertain those lucky enough to sense them with glimpses of their shadows. Is this the spirit of Harry Orchard, convicted of murder? He served 46 years at the prison, trying for parole numerous times but being turned down. Then, when he was finally offered parole, he refused, only to die in prison at the age

Photo by Kelly Winn

OLD IDAHO PENITENTIARY

been investigated by Idaho Spirit Seekers on multiple occasions.

Driving up Old Penitentiary Road gives you the feeling of having stepped into the past. The road is graveled and narrow. Still standing are the warden's house (1902), the bishop's house (moved to the site in 1975), the guard house (1912), and oddly enough, the cell block that held the women's ward (1906) sits outside of the main walls. The rose gardens inside the complex were tended to by inmates, and there have been reports of ghostly prisoners still tending to the roses they loved so much.

The women's ward is the first building you see when you approach the complex. It is also open to the public. The ward was built in 1920 after a female inmate, who was housed in the main section of the prison, became pregnant. The ward is surrounded by a sandstone wall and has an open walkway into the yard of the cell block. The cell block itself is very small. It does not take long before you feel some of the loneliness that these women must have felt being imprisoned there. I have sensed this on my many visits to the prison. The cells are cramped and cold. Just inside the courtyard there have been reports of cold spots, the feeling of being watched, and an apparition was seen standing by the door going into the front of the building.

The prison was a lonely place for a prisoner, and conditions were harsh back when it was built. There have been 10 executions at the prison—all were by hanging, and all were punishment for the inmate having committed murder.

Past and present staff have reported smells, voices, shadows passing by, cold spots, alarms that have been deactivated and dismantled going off, and the sound of footsteps in the cell blocks.

The most recent investigation of the Old Pen conducted by Idaho Spirit Seekers took place on November 27, 2004. Two team members were touring the maximum security part of the prison when one member took a picture with her digital camera and saw that she had an orb. Her batteries for the camera had been fully charged before they entered the building, and when she snapped this picture, her battery drained to zero. The other member was doing EVP work at the same time and when he got home that night to review his tape, he discovered that he had captured what appears to be someone saying "I'm here," when asked if there are any spirits present.

We look forward to returning to this location in the future with the hopes of obtaining more evidence of paranormal activity.

—Marie Cuff and Kelly Winn
Idaho Spirit Seekers

ENDERS HOTEL & MUSEUM
76 SOUTH MAIN STREET
SODA SPRINGS, IDAHO 83276
TEL: 1 (208) 547-4980

The spirit who haunts Enders Hotel is someone who was shot at "The Office." "The Office" was a bar that existed in the building in the past.

The Enders Hotel, built in 1917, is a three-story building with the second floor serving as a museum and the third floor containing hotel rooms. The Ghosts of Idaho staff investigated the building because there have been many claims of phantom footsteps, objects being moved by invisible forces, and an image was captured in the basement showing a hazy male face in it with no logical explanation as to why the face would be there. Though that picture was taken in the basement, we decided to investigate the rest of the building first.

One of our sensitives had the feeling that someone had fallen down the staircase from the first floor leading to the second floor, and their spirit was lingering because of the accident. We investigated the second and third floors but didn't pick up any supernatural phenomena, though we did encounter a dead-end hallway where the air was very thick and hot. We also noticed that the hallway was very calm and quiet. We called our sensitive over to check it out, and when he walked down the hallway, he saw a blue flash in the mirror, which he described as the same color of electricity arcing. We left the hallway, and another of our psychics had an intuition that the ghost in the hotel was a clean-shaven, middle-aged man dressed in a black suit. One of our members pointed to an old picture that had a family in it in which one of the men was wearing a black vest and was clean-shaven. Our psychic stated that the man he envisioned was missing the jacket but was wearing the same style clothes. After investigating the second and third floors, we went downstairs to the lobby and spoke with an employee. She stated that there was a hotel employee named Penny who would see someone come into her room and feel them sit on her bed. Many of the Enders Hotel staff have had unexplained experiences while working here.

—Ghosts of Idaho Staff
Ghostsofidaho.org

AMMON PARK

AMMON STREET
POCATELLO, IDAHO 83202

Ammon Park is a small park that is a stone's throw from Interstate 15. The park is home to the ghost of a girl in a blue dress. The Ghosts of Idaho staff have collected several accounts regarding her sightings.

A typical encounter with this young girl's specter involves being in the park and hearing a girl playing on the swings. The witness may turn to look, see the girl in a blue dress swinging, and then watch her disappear. Another encounter reported to us involved a utility shed in the park that was left open by the caretakers. Two kids were playing inside when the door closed and locked without explanation. The kids, who were not easily frightened, suddenly became very afraid. Later on, other local kids arrived to let them out and explained that the latch had been flipped firmly over the catch that holds the door shut.

After multiple of investigations conducted in the park, our group has had a few experiences. Two of our sensitives both had the feeling that the little girl in the blue dress was present. They described her as having brown hair just below the shoulders, and they said her dress was like an Easter Sunday dress—baby blue in color, with white lace.

We feel that she was killed there either in the little tool shed or in the vicinity of the park. Toward the end of the investigation, we felt that she was hiding by a tree. Upon examination of the tree, one of our sensitives had the strong feeling that he was intruding, and she wanted him to leave the area surrounding the tree. While returning to the car, we felt that she was following us and she wanted us to stay in the park, though away from her tree. We did not want her to follow us back to our homes, so we kindly asked her to stay there and then left.

—*Ghosts of Idaho Staff*
Ghostsofidaho.org

Montana

HOTEL MEADE

BANNACK STATE PARK
4200 BANNACK ROAD
DILLON, MONTANA 59725
TEL: 1 (406) 834-3413

As you walk the creaking boardwalk through the ghost town of Bannack, you can almost imagine a time when its buildings and streets were bustling with gold miners looking to strike it rich on the gold-laden banks of Grasshopper Creek. You can also understand why this town is still "occupied" by ghostly residents from a time long gone by, when so many died as a result of lawlessness, rampant illness, and harsh climate.

Photo by Greg Burchfield

One such occupant can be found in the once-stately Hotel Meade, which operated on and off until the 1940s. On the afternoon of August 4, 1915, Dorothy Dunn, Fern Dunn, and Cousin Ruth Wornick were bathing in an abandoned dredge pond along nearby Grasshopper Creek when the girls stepped off a ledge into deep water. A young boy courageously dove in and was able to pull the three girls out of the water. However, 16-year-old Dorothy had already succumbed by the time she was pulled onto shore.

Possibly due to the dreadful nature of her death, Dorothy has since been haunting the second floor of the Hotel Meade where she spent much of her time while her mother worked in the hotel. There have been numerous accounts of visitors seeing a young girl sitting at the top of the grand staircase and of children visiting with parents who seem to be chatting with no one but insist they are talking to a young girl.

Although state-of-mind plays a large role in our perceptions, I have been in other purportedly haunted places where I didn't feel the same palpable presence that I felt as I crested the spiral staircase to the second floor. The feeling was quite overwhelming, and I actually needed some coaxing to continue down the hallway, as there were no other visitors in the park and no personnel in the hotel, yet I knew I was not alone. Armed with my digital voice recorder and what little nerve I had left, I proceeded to record silently for a few minutes as I slowly walked the hallway. I encountered an area roughly the size of a person that was markedly colder than the rest of the building, and as a wave of chills washed over me, every hair on my body stood on end. Returning to the end of the hallway where I started, I playfully asked if she was a "little chicken" with a purposeful pause, giving her a chance to reply, then prodding a bit more by saying, "I think she's a little chicken." With dozens of photographs in addition to 30 minutes of recordings in the hotel and other buildings in town, I called it a day and headed home. As I played back the recordings, I was literally in tears as I heard a young girl giggle and respond to my taunts by saying, "Little chicken from the farm," in a playful voice.

—Greg Burchfield

LITTLE BIGHORN BATTLEFIELD NATIONAL MONUMENT

EXIT 510 OFF I-90 ON HIGHWAY 212
CROW AGENCY, MONTANA 59022
TEL: 1 (406) 638-3204

On June 25, 1876, General Custer led 647 soldiers of the 7th Calvary in an attack against a village of more than 8,000 Sioux, Arapaho, and Cheyenne Indians. After the smoke cleared, General Custer lay dead on the battlefield along with 263 of his men. Situated near the Little Bighorn River 15 miles outside the town of Hardin, Montana, Little Bighorn Battlefield is now a national monument that attracts nearly 400,000 visitors each year.

Paranormal activity has been reported by both employees and visitors to the park. Perhaps the most well-known of these reports is that of Christine Hope, an employee who lived in an apartment near the battlefields in the mid-1980s. She awoke one night to see the ghostly figure of a man sitting at her kitchen table. The man wore a military uniform and had a long handlebar mustache. The apparition did not speak to her but looked directly at her for several moments before he faded away. Later, while visiting the marker of Lt. Benjamin H. Hodgson who died in the battle, Hope became intrigued by his story and looked up further information on him. Her search yielded a photograph of the Lieutenant, who seemed to be the same man who had appeared in her apartment.

A former park ranger had a startlingly vivid encounter late one night with two Indian warriors on horseback, seemingly dressed for battle in feathers and shields, sitting atop a bluff overlooking the battlefield. The apparitions clearly saw her, as one of them raised up in his saddle ostensibly to get a better look at her. The next day, the ranger climbed the bluff to check for hoofprints or some sign that someone had been there but found nothing.

Visitors to the park have reported seeing ghostly soldiers marching across the battlefield and Indian warriors galloping on the backs of their war ponies, in some instances being so vivid and solid-looking that they were mistaken for reenactors. Some have even reported hearing the sounds of battle and men screaming. The Stone House, built in 1894 for the cemetery's caretaker, is the site of various types of paranormal happenings, including phantom footsteps, apparition sightings, strange knocking on the walls, and even disembodied voices. A shadowy figure dressed in a brown shirt and cartridge belt has been reported in the visitors center and another apparition, rumored to be that of General Custer himself, has been seen making inspection rounds of the center late at night. The cemetery has its own share of paranormal activity, including cold spots and apparitions of Indians on horseback charging through the cemetery grounds.

Is the Little Bighorn Battlefield truly haunted? The various personal accounts and the bloody history of the location combined certainly make for a very convincing case. At the site of what has been called the "worst military disaster in U.S. history," it is not hard to imagine that restless spirits still roam the battlegrounds.

—Melanie Billings
Writer/Paranormal Investigator

BUTTE-SILVER BOW ARCHIVES

17 WEST QUARTZ STREET
BUTTE, MONTANA 59701
TEL: 1 (406) 782-3280
WEBSITE: *www.co.silverbow.mt.us/
archives.htm*

The Butte-Silver Bow Archives is a treasure trove of artifacts from these famous mining towns. Even the building itself is a relic—originally the Quartz Street Fire Station built in 1900, it was the fire chief's headquarters until the 1970s. The two-story brick building with its four garage bays housed 22 men and the fire chief. Since 1981, the building has been home to the Archives—a living testament to the region's history. There are many documents; personal artifacts including jewelry, mining tools, and clothing; family heirlooms donated to the Archives; and many old photographs, newspapers, and other documents. But according to many local legends and even some of the staff who work at the Archives, this building holds many relics of the ghostly kind as well.

Shain Wolstein has worked at the Archives since 2001, but didn't know anything about the ghosts there until his second day of work. "I was down in our basement," Wolstein said, "and we've got these old fire bells that are physically disconnected, but they tend to just go off at random times. Finally, I came upstairs and asked about them and my boss just said, 'Don't worry about it—it's fine.' Sure enough, she finally told me that they go off all of the time and it's our cue to get out of the basement, that they [the ghosts] just don't want us there at that particular time."

Wolstein may have started the job a bit of skeptic, but he's a believer now. He says he experiences something unexplained almost every day. Some supernatural events were as simple as seeing a darting shadow out of the corner of his eye, but others were a bit more significant, such as doors opening and closing on their own, hearing disconnected telephones ringing, phantom footsteps, and murmuring voices. But one strange event repeated itself every single day. Wolstein said, "Every morning I'd come in, and on my desk I'd have this picture of one of our ex-mayors. It was hanging on the wall, and my desk was probably about four or five feet away from it. Well, this picture would be on my desk every morning for about a year. Finally, one time I was here late at night because we were doing a film project, and I actually saw the picture fly off the wall about five feet away, and land on my desk."

Up to this point, Wolstein had experienced a lot of strange phenomena, but he had never seen any of the spirits present in the old fire house. That changed on Halloween of 2002. He said, "I decided to come in the building late—it was probably 11:30 p.m.—and right away I could hear what sounded like people running up our stairs. I was with one other person and I had a digital camera, so I was taking a lot of pictures and I didn't turn the light on. So that kind of freaked me out. I went back outside for a second, and as I came back in, there was the fire chief who had died here in 1915 after falling from the back of the truck and suffering a brain hemorrhage that killed him."

The chief isn't the only ghost spotted inside. People have also seen old miners who may still be drawn to their old tools or heirlooms, a woman in period dress, and a man in the reading room who vanishes when you take a second look. Certainly all of the items in the Archives hold a lot of memories for the region and for the people who owned them long ago.

—Jeff Belanger
Founder, Ghostvillage.com

Wyoming

IVY HOUSE INN BED AND BREAKFAST
815 SOUTH ASH
CASPER, WYOMING 82601
TEL: 1 (307) 265-0974
WEBSITE: *www.ivyhouseinn.com*

66 We didn't believe in ghosts or hauntings until we moved into this place," says Tom Johnson, owner of the Ivy House Inn.

Tom and his wife, Kathy, soon changed their minds when they began renovating the turn-of-the century Cape Cod bed and breakfast inn in Casper, Wyoming. The paranormal activity started up soon after the renovations began.

Strange odors began to turn up in odd places. The scents of burning rubber,

mentholatum, talcum powder, and even the smell of dead fish came and went with no rational explanation. "Things disappeared. Electrical plugs pulled out of the walls. Doors opened and closed. Footsteps could be heard walking on floors where nobody was," Tom explained.

Still not completely convinced they were sharing their home with ghosts, the Johnsons began taking photos of the renovations. They were shocked at what turned up on film. The Johnsons have numerous photos that show ectoplasm, orbs, faces, and even full apparitions. The investigative team from Denver Haunted History has captured several anomalies in photographs and a TV crew once caught orbs on tape.

The Johnsons firmly believe that Mrs. White, the former owner of the house, is one of their ghosts-in-residence. "I think that Mrs. White doesn't believe that she is dead," Tom said. "This house was her life. She cared for it, and even the year before she died at age 92, she got on ladders and climbed 18 feet to clean out gutters."

Mrs. White also had a reputation for being a bit nosy, which might explain the nature of some of the paranormal activity. According to Tom, "She walked in on her tenants at any time of the day or night to make sure that they were not abusing her house, and she is still nosy enough to check up on who is in her home. Especially in the Blue Rose Room, where there are knockings on the door."

The apparition of an old lady has been witnessed in the inn by several different people, including family members, friends, and guests. A dinner party guest saw a short old lady with red hair staring at her in the bathroom. Another guest at the inn witnessed an old lady walking down the hallway.

After researching the history of the Ivy House Inn, the Johnsons have a theory as to why there might be more than one spirit occupying the inn. Between the years of 1902 and 1940, there were no less than 26 different owners, and the town of Casper itself also has an interesting history, as Tom explained: "Casper sits on several trails. The Mormon Trail, California Trail, Oregon Trail, Pony Express, and cattle trails all come through here and probably through this property." Perhaps some of the spirits present are there because they once traveled along these trails and thought Casper was a good spot for a rest.

The ghosts do not frighten Tom and Kathy. In fact, they have made the haunting part of their lives at the inn, even hosting a "Haunted Slumber Party" each Halloween.

—Melanie Billings
Writer/Paranormal Investigator

Southwest

Southwest

Arizona

THE JEROME GRAND HOTEL

200 HILL STREET
JEROME, ARIZONA 86331
TEL: 1 (928) 634-8200
WEBSITE: *www.jeromegrandhotel.net*

In 1927, the United Verde Hospital was opened by the Phelps Dodge Mining Corporation in Jerome, Arizona. The 30,000-square-foot Mission-style building, made of poured concrete thick enough to withstand mining blasts felt 20 miles away, is located atop mile-high Cleopatra Hill.

By 1930, the hospital was considered to be the most state-of-the-art in Arizona. But times change. Mining dwindled and the hospital closed in 1950, though it was kept ready for use, stocked with beds, equipments, and linens. The 1926 self-service Otis Elevator was parked at the top of the fifth level, and for 44 years, everything remained as it was, ravaged only by time.

The building had been considered haunted even when it was a hospital, and during the years of desolation, the reputation grew—no surprise, as people frequently heard the groan of the elevator going up and down by itself, though it never actually moved.

In 1994, the Altherr family bought the building and began a loving, precise restoration. Today, the Jerome Grand Hotel crowns the little town, dominating it with grandeur and ghosts. This is no small feat, because the entire town of Jerome is infested with ghosts.

Standing on the third-floor balcony and gazing at the red rock peaks of Sedona 40 miles north, it's difficult to believe this building contains so

Photo by Tamara Thorne

many secrets, so many deaths. It doesn't seem like you're leaning against the same wrought iron railing where at least one victim met a violent death. When you ride the original elevator, it's an adventure in time, but by day, you don't think about its haunt, the ghost of Claude Harvey, a handyman murdered in 1935. His head was positioned beneath the elevator to simulate a suicide, and most believe he hangs around to clear his name. Mr. Harvey is an active ghost, sometimes bedeviling the lobby staff with all manner of noisy phenomena and poltergeist activity.

There are many other ghosts within the Jerome Grand. Over the years, screams of the injured from hospital days, whispers, and squeaking gurney wheels have been heard. Apparitions have been noted in many places, particularly on the third and fourth levels. The most-seen phantom is thought to be a nurse. One room on an upper floor contains the spirit of a suicide who hanged himself from a heating pipe near the ceiling.

The Jerome Grand is a lovely, peaceful place by day, but once you're in bed, you may find yourself thinking about using a nightlight. My own experiences include multiple minor cold spots and insistent phantom footsteps moving up and down the empty corridor outside my room. I have yet to experience major phenomena, but one night a guest down the hall awoke when he heard a voice loudly whispering his name in his ear. He sat up and turned on the light—and it happened again. He spent the rest of the night on the sofa in the lobby. If only I'd known, I would have offered to trade!

—*Tamara Thorne*
Author, Paranormal Investigator

BIRDCAGE THEATER
SIXTH & ALLEN STREET
TOMBSTONE, ARIZONA 85638
TEL: 1 (520) 457-3421

The adobe building on the southeast end of Tombstone's Allen Street that would eventually become the Birdcage Theater opened on December 23, 1881. It served as a burlesque hall with a stage, bar, casino, and dance hall. Cage-like cribs hung from the ceiling where the "soiled doves" entertained the miners, cowboys, drifters, and home boys as long as they had money in their pockets to spend.

Photo by Janice Cottrill

It was a place that was only in business for nine years, but the building knew what violence was all about. The Birdcage has 140 bullet holes in the walls and the ceilings, evidence from the many shootings that happened there. It was also a witness to the murder of Margurita, who was mortally stabbed by Gold Dollar for sitting on the lap of Billy Milgreen, whom Gold Dollar considered to be her man.

Hundreds of tourists visit the Birdcage, and many tell the same stories and see the same things: they speak of the "cold spots" and invisible people who sing and talk in rooms that are empty. Some have seen a woman singing and then the sudden appearance of a crowded room, complete with cigar smoke, liquor, and loud voices in a room that a moment earlier was completely empty.

A man with a celluloid visor who carries a clipboard walks across the stage and is seen by many, along with ghosts who like to wear old-fashioned clothing and who appear so real, tourists think they are part of the Birdcage staff until they walk right through the walls.

Not all of the ghosts are on the inside, as is evidenced by this picture I took outside the Birdcage on my last visit to what I feel is the most haunted town in the West—Tombstone, the town known as "too tough to die." Be sure to notice the pair of boots in the middle of the doorway. It must be someone who died with their boots on.

—Janice Cottrill
Investigator, Researcher,
and Writer, Cottrill Investigations

Nevada

CARLUCCIO'S TIVOLI GARDENS

1775 E. TROPICANA
LAS VEGAS, NEVADA 89119
TEL: 1 (702) 795-3236
WEBSITE: *www.lvrg.com/carluccios*

Carluccio's is a local Las Vegas favorite that serves up superb Italian food. Located across the shopping center from the world-famous Liberace Museum, the restaurant was part of Liberace's dream for an entire center dedicated to his genius. His untimely death left the dream unfulfilled. He purchased the restaurant in 1982 and renamed it Liberace's Tivoli Gardens. The flamboyant entertainer wanted his restaurant to resemble those fine establishments he had eaten in while abroad. In an attempt to capture that elegant European ambiance, he did much of the interior decorating himself. Some of his lavish touches remain today. The sparkling overhead lighting and the mirrored walls in the piano room are two examples of Mr. Showmanship's decorating flair.

Liberace was a hands-on owner who left nothing to chance. He proudly oversaw menu planning and liked to entertain showbiz pals such as Dolly Parton and Debbie Reynolds at the restaurant whenever they were in town. It was not uncommon for him to drop in at the Tivoli Gardens after a performance in one of the large showrooms on the strip. To the delight of his patrons, Liberace occasionally entertained them with an impromptu piano selection. After his death in 1987, Carluccio's purchased the restaurant. Some believe the ghostly Liberace is overseeing his beloved restaurant still.

Several patrons have reported seeing Liberace's apparition in the piano lounge or standing near the window. A waiter who has worked at Carluccio's for 14 years told of seeing glasses clinking together and hearing noises such as silverware moving around. One night while cleaning mirrors in the piano lounge, he saw the reflection of a rhinestone-covered cape. No one was wearing the cape. He turned around to see what it was, but nothing was there. A few weeks later, he was asked to lead a Spanish language tour of the Liberace Museum. While leading the tour, he saw the cape he'd seen in the mirror.

A patron even asked a pianist to play a certain selection, only to have him vanish before her startled eyes. Kelly, a bartender who has worked at the restaurant for more than 16 years, believes the entertainer is still in residence. One evening several years after his death, bottles toppled at the bar and the power went out. Someone casually remarked that it was Liberace's birthday and he might want that fact remembered. Everyone at the bar wished him happy birthday. Suddenly the power came back on and no more bottles fell. Members of the American Ghost Society and Las Vegas Paranormal Investigators conducted two separate ghost investigations at the restaurant. Electro Magnetic Field detector readings were especially high in the back hallway and the women's bathroom area. Dowsers were also on hand and their findings closely matched those of the EMF meters. These findings bear out the bartender's experience with toilets flushing of their own accord and water faucets turning on and off by themselves. Several photos were taken during the investigations. Orbs showed up in some of them. During one session, world-famous magician Dixie Dooley conducted a séance in the mirrored piano lounge. No significant findings were reported.

—Janice Oberding
Author, Las Vegas Haunted

GOLDFIELD COURTHOUSE

GOLDFIELD, NEVADA

It's hard to imagine that the near-ghost town of Goldfield, Nevada, was once the largest city in the whole state. Now, only a few old-timers hang on in what was once a promising community. Many ghost hunters who visit focus on the four-story Goldfield Hotel, long rumored to have several persistent phantoms, including that of a prostitute murdered in one of the rooms. The old hotel has changed hands several times over the decades but so far it is still boarded up. Far more haunted, and still open to the public, is the old courthouse. This two-story stone building has the look of a castle and if the evidence is true, it's a haunted castle as well. It was built in 1907 when the mines were going strong. Sadly, by 1913 the bloom was off the rose and Goldfield went into steady decline.

Goldfield is the county seat for Esmeralda County (the smallest population of all the counties of Nevada). The old courthouse is a living relic of another day. The lamps are original, as are many of the furnishings. The courtroom on the second floor is rumored to be haunted by a phantom trial with voices heard from time to time. Shadows walk the hardwood floors, and there is even a tale of a ghostly hangman's noose seen on one of the chambers. The ghostly chair is perhaps the most interesting of all the supernatural events linked to the courthouse. When the staff come in each morning, they find it has moved. Once they even locked it in the vault on the first floor. The door was closed and locked but the next morning the chair was back by its desk—somehow it had moved through the steel door of the fireproof vault.

The whole town of Goldfield is a ghost hunter's delight, with a rich history and haunted buildings. Be sure to visit the courthouse and ask about the haunted chair. If the clerks are not too busy, they will tell you the tale of the chair with a mind of its own.

—Richard Senate
Psychic Investigator/Author
Carson Valley Ghost Stalkers

THE DAKE HOUSE
2242 MAIN STREET
GENOA, NEVADA 89411

This Victorian home stands in the small town of Genoa, Nevada, and was the first established community in the Silver State. The Dake House now serves as an antique store and may be one of the most haunted places in northern Nevada. The house was once the home of the local undertaker, which might account for some of the odd goings-on that take place at the site. The first reported supernatural event reported happened when a large painting, a still life of roses in a vase, flew from the wall. The owner later learned the painting was a "spirit painting" done at a séance by a well-known San Francisco medium at the turn of the 19th century.

Footsteps echo in the antique store, and phantom shadows are reported by the staff. There are also ghostly smells in the place. The strangest story was that of a visitor who was walking on the second floor. In the master bedroom, now filled with antiques, he paused to look out the window. Just as he did, the man was slapped. He turned and discovered he was quite alone in the room. He ran from the house vowing never to return. Many ghost hunters and local TV crews have visited the place over the last two years, and each one has come away convinced that the place is haunted by several ghosts. The most prominent spirit is that of an older woman.

—Richard Senate
Psychic Investigator/Author
Carson Valley Ghost Stalkers

GOLD HILL HOTEL
1540 MAIN STREET
VIRGINIA CITY, NEVADA 89440

This site has long been rumored to be haunted. The old two story hotel was in business when Mark Twain was a reporter in Virginia City, and it is possible he visited the place in years gone by.

Today, the hotel features a fine dining room and lobby right out of the glory days of the Comstock Lode. The building also houses two well-known ghosts: a man and a woman. Some say the male spirit is that of a con-man who was killed when he was caught cheating at cards. Others say that the ghost is the unhappy shade of William, the original owner of the hotel. Whoever it is, he has manifested as footsteps and the pungent smell of a cigar. The other ghost is the better known of the two. She is called Rosie and is said to have been a lady of the night who plied her trade at the hotel long ago. She was murdered here or took her own life (you take your pick) and now haunts room number 2. She might also be the spirit of a red-haired Irish cleaning woman who once worked here. Whoever she was, she has mostly manifested as the smell of cheap rose perfume. I spent a long night here, investigating the psychic smell. While bathing in the large claw-footed tub, I smelled the strong rose smell. It wasn't like a real smell—it was overpowering. I checked the soaps, the windows, everything, and then the aroma vanished instantly in an unnatural way. I believe I was visited by Rosie. This took place about 2 a.m. I made sure no one was about the hall or balcony trying to hoax me with a spray bottle of perfume. I believe the hotel is haunted, but more work will be needed to find out the identity of the ghost.

—Richard Senate
Psychic Investigator/Author
Carson Valley Ghost Stalkers

New Mexico

THE ST. JAMES HOTEL

ROUTE 1 (HIGHWAY 21)
CIMARRON, NEW MEXICO 87714
TEL: 1 (505) 376-2664
WEBSITE: *www.stjamescimarron.com*

The St. James Hotel opened first as a saloon in 1872 and then expanded into a hotel in 1880. Built by Frenchman Henry Lambert, the elegant St. James was a popular stop between Denver, Colorado, and Albuquerque, New Mexico, attracting the likes of Buffalo Bill Cody, Annie Oakley, Black Jack Ketchum, Jesse James, and Wyatt Earp. At least 26 people died violently, most of them in the gambling hall and saloon. During a 1901 reroofing, more than 400 bullet holes were discovered in the ceiling, and some of the scars remain today as silent evidence in the original pressed tin ceiling of what is now the Lambert Dining Room.

Several well-known ghosts call the hotel home. The first floor is home to the mischievous "Little Imp," a glass-breaking, object-moving trickster often described as a small wizened man. Upstairs, room 18 holds a notoriously rough ghost said to be fond of throwing people across the room. The hotel keeps the room locked and never rents it. I even offered to sign a waiver in order to see into the room, but was refused. The employees appeared to genuinely fear the room.

Instead, I spent the night in room 17, home of the benign ghost of Mary, Henry Lambert's young wife. The room is often reported to be filled with her perfume. I didn't experience that, but as the evening wore on, the number of small cold spots manifesting throughout the room became so annoying I went downstairs and played pool for a couple hours, hoping to deprive the phenomena of energy. However, when I returned they were still extant. The "heart" of the haunt seemed to be the bathroom, where a very large cold area formed. I took a photo of the area and saw, through the lens, a bright white area surrounded with red. Though striking, I would have assumed it was the glare of the flash, but my roommate, standing behind me, screamed. She described the same phenomenon.

I took the film to a photo shop for hand development. There was absolutely nothing there but a blank wall and towels, not even a reflection from the flash on the pane. I'm impressed, but I still want a chance to be tossed across room 18.

—Tamara Thorne
Author Independent
Paranormal Investigator

THE WEEPING WOMAN
PUBLIC EMPLOYEES RETIREMENT ASSOCIATION BUILDING

1120 PASEO DE PERALTA
SANTA FE, NEW MEXICO 87501

New Mexico is a favorite haunt of La Llorona, and she is often sighted along the Rio Grand. In Santa Fe, the skeletally thin wailing woman has been repeatedly sighted in and around the Public Employees Retirement Association (PERA) building. The five-story structure, near a tributary of the Rio Grande, is built over an old Spanish graveyard. The two bottom floors are underground, deep in the graveyard. Employees report hearing sobbing echoes through the corridors and sometimes feel unseen hands push them on the stairs. Many locals refuse to go anywhere near the building.

The timeless legend of the Weeping Woman, La Llorona, originated in South America and traveled to the American southwest via Mexico. La Llorona is always said to be tall and thin, with long dark hair and a flowing white gown. She is the ghost of a mother who drowned her own children in a creek and now eternally sobs as she searches for them along creeks and rivers.

The finer details vary, but while the Weeping Woman is most often thought of as a tragic figure, she is also portrayed by parents of disobedient children as a banshee who will come for them if they don't behave. In fact, the California Milk Advisory Board sometimes runs a "got milk?" ad that features La Llorona.

La Llorona is also a prominent figure in Taos and Taos Pueblo, Guadalupta, and Colfax, a ghost town near Cimarron, New Mexico.

—Tamara Thorne
Author Independent
Paranormal Investigator

LINCOLN, NEW MEXICO

THE TOWN OF LINCOLN IS LOCATED ON ROUTE 380 IN THE CENTRAL PART OF THE STATE, ABOUT 180 MILES SOUTHWEST OF ALBUQUERQUE.

During 1995, while living in Roswell, New Mexico, my wife, Debra, and I spent much time at Lincoln, New Mexico, which was best known for its bloody gunfights and conflicts involving Billy the Kid.

Lincoln was the site of one of the bloodiest gunfights in American West history, taking place during July 1878, although the area had been troubled by killings and shootouts prior to this. After a five-day battle that killed the major participants, Billy the Kid was among the few to escape, only to be killed later by his friend, Sheriff Pat Garrett.

With the passage of time, ghosts still prowl that area. Today, Lincoln is a small village setting with an excellent museum, a store, restaurants; with many of the buildings still intact; and a small population. For my wife and I, it became a nice getaway spot and a place to walk in peace and quiet, simply enjoying the setting.

Since childhood, I have had the ability to see ghosts, although it is not a perfect sense of paranormal sight. My Uncle Willard explained to me that it was all right to see such things and urged me to enjoy such encounters and learn from them. Lincoln is a place where this extra sense has been well-utilized.

I recall several ghost encounters during the times visiting Lincoln. An elderly Mexican man with a beige cowboy hat and Western clothes walked by me on the sidewalk but never looked directly at me, and curious, I turned to look back at him, but he had vanished. Near the museum, I encountered a young woman in a Western gingham dress who vanished upon my approach. In several instances, I saw cowboys riding on horses down the main street only to have them fade and vanish into thin air without a trace as well. A small boy, probably 10 years old, was playing by himself in a yard by the old church. I approached, he looked up into my face, smiled, and disappeared. A group of three women in Western dress crossed the street in front of me only to disappear as they reached the other side of the street—I still recall the vivid black hair of one woman who was smiling and looked my way. In one part of town, I was given directions by a young man with a broken sort of smile to the gunfight scene where Billy the Kid escaped. Thinking he was part of the personnel or staff for the museum, I thanked a museum staff member for this person's courtesy, but the woman said there was nobody there who fit my description. Maybe it was Billy the Kid? I do not know. I only know what I encountered.

Lincoln, New Mexico, remains one of the most haunted historical sites of the American West. I have seen ghosts in many places and at different times, but Lincoln was one place that I will always recall with fondness.

Despite its violent past, today Lincoln is a serene, peaceful place to visit. It's also a place where the ghosts still walk the streets.

—Lee Prosser

Texas

CARTER GHOST TOWN
CARTER ROAD
SPRINGTOWN, TEXAS

The only proof that Carter, Texas, once a town of 80 residents, still exists is the old church building and the historical marker. Rumors of a little girl killed in an Indian raid and an old minister who still paces the church draw ghost enthusiasts from all over North Texas.

Carter was established in 1866 and once had a flour mill, cotton gin, blacksmith shop, school, and a church. It sits in a rural area off Highway 51 in Parker County. The old church still stands and, next to it, a covered meeting area perhaps used for picnics. A dirt road runs in front of the church, sectioning it from a grouping of trees that forms a canopied walkway. Where the walkway led is now anyone's guess.

Dotting the grounds are granite markers, not unlike gravestones, that describe historic events that happened here. One boasts the site of gun battle between two cattlemen in 1878, leaving one man dead. Another lists the names of "Seven Rugged Riders." Some of the last skirmishes between white men and the Comanche nation occurred here. Perhaps these seven lost their lives fighting for the land where Carter sits or maybe trying to recapture the little girl said to have been captured by the Comanche.

The voice of a little girl has been captured on tape as EVP. Michelle DePaul of Mystic Ghost took a photograph at Carter that contains three female faces close to the ground. Is this little girl still trying to show herself to us?

Inside the church, if you sit quietly, you will start to hear footsteps evenly pacing

Photo by Kira Connally

the floor from the front to the back of the building. Once, a man wearing a low-rimmed felt hat—Quaker style—was seen in the shadows of the church. Is he the ghost of a minister that refuses to go on, choosing to watch over his house of worship?

We may never know the answers to these questions, but certainly there is ghostly activity to be experienced at Carter. Photographs taken here have revealed bright orbs and unexplainable streaks of light. Video taken at Carter also reveals these streaks of light, darting hither and to, across the field. Investigators with Mystic Ghost have witnessed blue lights appearing in the brush, shadow figures moving amongst the trees, and even felt the heat rising over a spot that might have been an old fire pit directly across from the church. Psychic and Mystic Ghost investigator Wendy Gunderson felt she had contact with a stern man named Lily inside the church itself. Could Lily be the aforementioned dead cattleman?

Carter's decline as a town began in 1907, though no history research reveals why. Many questions about the town remain unanswered, though maybe the ghosts will one day be able to tell us their story.

—Kira Connally
Paranormal Investigator, Mystic Ghost

THE VON MINDEN HOTEL

607 LYONS AVENUE
SCHULENBURG, TEXAS 78956
TEL: 1 (979) 743-3714

Four stories high and 77 years old, the Von Minden Hotel towers over the other buildings in downtown Schulenburg.

It's the last standing combination hotel/theater of its kind. Like most hotels that have been around for a while, this one has seen its share of death.

One room, dubbed the "Jumper's Room," belonged to a paratrooper from World War II who lost his leg and was badly disfigured when his plane was shot down during military service. On his way back home, he stopped for a night at the hotel. Upon his arrival, he was given a batch of letters written by his girlfriend, now known as "Miss Polka Dot," so named because of the polka-dotted dress she was last seen wearing. One of the letters was a "Dear John" letter. Although she had changed her mind, the veteran read that particular letter out of sequence. Dismayed, he jumped to his death from his fourth-floor window. Miss Dot showed up the following afternoon hoping to reunite with her lover. Since that time, there have been reports of the Polka Dot lady wandering the hallways looking for her man.

In another room, a railroad worker died suddenly while standing behind his door, effectively blocking it so no one could get in when they discovered what happened. A skinny hotel worker climbed over the transom above the door so he

Photo by Ginger Pennell

THE VON MINDEN HOTEL

could get inside, move the body, and unlock the door.

One of the current owners, Garret Pettit, tells the story of his mother's ghostly experience one night. "This particular night," Pettit said, "Mom finished cleaning up the theater and turned off the lights. She was making her way up the dark aisle by trailing her hand across the seat backs when her fingers brushed against the hand of someone else. She knew without a doubt she was the only one left in the building. She also knew without a doubt she'd just brushed the hand of a ghost."

My husband, Chris, and I have investigated the hotel several times with excellent results. One night we were in the lobby talking about the former deceased owners, and as soon as their name left our lips, Chris's EMF meter began chirping loudly. A photo later revealed a good-sized orb above his left shoulder while the light on his meter flashed.

One morning, after a long night of strange noises and occurrences, Chris and I gave up on sleep and wandered down to the hotel lobby. I relaxed in a comfortable chair hoping for a catnap while Chris snapped random pictures. The atmosphere suddenly seemed to feel "heavier." A photo taken at the time showed a very faint round orb next to my foot. In the middle of the orb is a tiny, brilliant spark of bright blue light.

Subsequent visits generated more paranormal photos and video. We've even orchestrated a very successful ghost conference there. Many guests had their own ghost stories to tell after that hauntingly fun weekend!

—Ginger Pennell
Co-Founder, Spirit Quest Paranormal

THE FORT WORTH STOCKYARDS
121 EAST EXCHANGE AVENUE
FORT WORTH, TEXAS 76106
TEL: 1 (817) 626-7921
WEBSITE: *www.fortworthstockyards.org*

Any native of Fort Worth will tell you that the city is where the West begins. Strolling through the Stockyards section of town offers a ride back to memories of cowhands and cattle drives up the Chisholm Trail. It's where a small fort was built to fend off Indians, where fortunes were made and lost, and where many riders left on their last trip heading to Kansas with the cattle herds. It's Hell's Half Acre, and it contained as many bordellos, gambling halls, and saloons that could fit on that patch of land.

Photo by Henry Bailey

Today, the Fort Worth Stockyards look almost identical to the way they did during the heyday of the cattle drives. Hotels, restaurants, and shops still share the same streets, the same old wood frames, and possibly some of those same old trail hands and outlaws that once walked down Exchange Avenue.

When the old steam locomotive, the Tarantula Train, pulls into town on its run, not everyone who steps off has paid for a current ticket—some are phantoms from a bygone era.

Ghost stories are plentiful in the Stockyards. It was regularly home to outlaws and gunfights. From the General Store to Miss Molly's Hotel, one walk down Exchange Avenue might have you wondering if the cowboy next to you is an actor or an actual ghost from the past.

Miss Molly's Hotel, a former bordello, is still maintained the way it was when it was first visited by cowhands making a last visit to see the ladies before they hit the trail. At least two rooms and the kitchen are reputedly haunted, with a visiting reporter once waking up in the middle of the night to find a former blond employee from the hotel's glory days sitting on his bed.

The Stockyard's hotel has recorded at least two ghosts sighted by the staff. It had been the hotel of choice for Bonnie and Clyde, who spent a night in room 305 Butch Cassidy and the Sundance Kid also favored the Stockyards for a resting place, along with other members of the Hole in the Wall Gang.

Walk into any store or restaurant and one of the old-timers will have a ghost story to tell. After all, with Billy Bob's—the world's largest Honky Tonk—in town, maybe some of the old cowpokes couldn't bear to head out before one more round.

—Henry Bailey
Independent Investigator,
Conjecture.com

MISS MOLLY'S BED AND BREAKFAST

109 W. EXCHANGE AVENUE
FORT WORTH, TEXAS 76106
TEL: 1 (817) 626-1522
WEBSITE: *www.missmollyshotel.com*

Located in the middle of the Fort Worth Stockyards, Miss Molly's is the oldest bed and breakfast in Fort Worth. Established as a boarding house in 1910 and originally called the Palace Rooms, it went through the Prohibition period being called the Oasis and later it served as a bordello in the 1940s when it was called the Gayatte Hotel. Miss Molly's is just old enough to have caught a glimpse of the Wild West as well as all of America's speak-easy and bordello days. Because of the building's long history as a boarding house, it has been home to a vast number of residents. Apparently, some have decided to extend their stay. Perhaps the large amount of antiques and period pieces in the hotel remind them of the bawdy times that they shared there.

Photo by Henry Bailey

The seven themed rooms in the hotel all share stories of paranormal activity, with the Cattlemen's and Cowboy rooms having some of the more famous sightings of apparitions. Visitations have also occurred in the current owner's private rooms: numbers eight and nine. The ghost is that of a young girl, who many believe was a former tenant of the hotel—though most of the sightings have involved the former working girls from the hotel's days as a bordello.

The phenomena at Miss Molly's includes full-bodied apparitions, unexplained scents, items disappearing and reappearing, toilets flushing on their own, lights turning on and off, cold spots, unlocked doors refusing to open, and a variety of unidentified but entertaining sounds. According to the current owner, Dawn Street-Boyd, one housekeeper quit because she kept finding coins in rooms even though there had been no guests in that room. She would finish cleaning only to return and find the coins where she had just cleaned.

Miss Molly's has been visited by a number of paranormal investigation groups and is listed with Texas Christian University's paranormal activity class, which makes regular visits to record the phenomena. Copies of unusual photos and tape recordings, as well as statements of the investigators and results, are kept prominently in the common living area.

The hotel situated above Fort Worth's Star Café takes visitors up a staircase to another era. Period furnishings, furniture, and a number of stories about unexplained happenings are provided with firsthand accounts by the owner. Miss Molly's is considered one of the most haunted properties in Fort Worth and one of the most active paranormal sites in Texas.

—Henry Bailey
Independent Investigator
Conjecture.com

La Carafe

813 Congress Street
Houston, Texas 77002
Tel: 1 (713) 229-9399

La Carafe sits in the oldest commercial building in Houston, still resting on its original foundation. The building was built for Irishman John Kennedy about the year 1860 and may have been erected by developer Nathaniel Kellum. Kennedy, a baker, came to Houston in 1842, and after operating several businesses in the area, he erected the building housing La Carafe to function as a steam bakery. Known originally as the Kennedy Bakery, it served that function for a number of years. The structure remained in the Kennedy family until 1987, when the present owners purchased it. It became La Carafe in the 1950s and has served the bakery, bar, and restaurant function since its original construction.

The hauntings of La Carafe include encounters with a well-liked former bar manager named Carl, whom many have either seen looking out of the window on the second floor or they have felt his presence. Other reports include the sound of a ball being rolled on the second floor, a bar glass being thrown that was captured on the audio piece of a video shot by a Canadian TV crew, and many other encounters.

When interviewing Gavin, the bar manager at La Carafe, he told me of a story regarding Carl. Gavin said that a La Carafe bartender was closing up one evening and was walking to his car. He felt as if someone was staring at him, so he looked over his shoulder back at the bar and saw a man in the window. Thinking he locked someone in, he went back. Upon entry, he asked the person to come downstairs.

When no one responded, he went upstairs, but found no one there. "That bartender didn't work nights again," Gavin said. Patrons have reported cold spots in the restrooms, glasses breaking, and footsteps either upstairs or on the stairs. If you like your spirits with spirits, this is a great haunt.

—Peter James Haviland, Adv.C.H.
President, Lead Investigator,
Lone Star Spirits

JEFFERSON HOTEL

124 W. AUSTIN STREET
JEFFERSON, TEXAS 75657
TEL: 1 (903) 665-2631

The Jefferson Hotel—sometimes referred to as the New Jefferson Hotel or Historic Jefferson Hotel—was originally built in 1851 as a cotton warehouse. At the turn of the 20th century, it assumed its current function and became a hotel. During the roaring 20s, according to locals, it was known as the Crystal Palace.

Many ghostly sightings have been reported throughout the years here at the hotel, and each room has its own personality. When investigating the hotel for a TV shoot, Lone Star Spirits found cold spots where there were no drafts, and while a medium was communicating with a spirit of a prior bordello employee in room 14, EMF fluctuations were recorded on key words. As the communications continued, the EMF readings continued their fluctuations—all of this was caught on film. Among the other experiences that are reported there include the sounds of chil-

dren playing when no children are staying there, a floating apparition of a female, slamming of doors by unseen forces, and the sounds of a scuffle in a room that is above the restaurants. This same medium picked up on residual haunting phenomena from when the place burned when it was a cotton warehouse. This is energy that does not have intelligence but is rather a kind of tape loop that plays itself over and over again. Some of the phenomena sensed were the sounds of cracking timber, screams, a feeling of anxiety, and other effects relating to the fire.

One of the encounters told to our team during the filming involved a former desk clerk named Michael, who was ending his shift. It was the middle of a slow week, and there were no "living" guests staying at the hotel overnight. Michael made his rounds upstairs, turning off lights and locking rooms before leaving for the night. He was closing the last door in the long, dark hallway when the doors opened and then slammed shut all at once.

Lights turned on and off as Michael dashed downstairs and phoned his friend Phyllis, a desk clerk at the Excelsior Hotel across the street. Phyllis reports that Michael was in a complete panic when he called, screaming that he was alone in the hotel but that "all heck" was breaking loose upstairs! He said he could hear doors slamming and the sound of footsteps and someone dragging furniture. Ongoing weekly investigations are currently being performed.

—Peter James Haviland, Adv.C.H.
President, Lead Investigator,
Lone Star Spirits

JEFFERSON HOTEL

THE UNIVERSITY OF TEXAS MEDICAL BRANCH (UTMB) FACE

EWING HALL
301 UNIVERSITY BOULEVARD
GALVESTON, TEXAS 77555
WEBSITE: *www.utmb.edu/rumor/ ewing.htm*

For years, people spoke of an old sea captain—some say maybe even gentleman pirate Jean Lafitte himself—who willed his land to his children and asked them to keep it in the family. But eventually one of his heirs sold the land, against the captain's wishes, making his spirit angry. This was the land Ewing Hall was built on.

The urban legends surrounding the identity of the original landowner range from a pirate to historical figures from Galveston's history. But the presence of the face on the building is difficult to deny. This is an awesome picture on a building with some questionable facts surrounding it.

Ewing Hall was built upon an accretion into the bay. The state essentially piled up silt and used it for construction, so the story of a prior landowner is urban legend.

According to fellow researcher, Jerry Drake: "I was working on a file regarding land about three miles or so east along the bay from UTMB. It struck me as odd that this survey was in the name of William A. A. Wallace—the famous 'Bigfoot' Wallace from Texas history. He's not typically associated with Galveston Island. And that's when it hit me...the face looks like Bigfoot Wallace. According to research, he, his attorney, and an adjoining canal company had a hell of a time getting their land out of the state of Texas. Perhaps this is Bigfoot's way of taking revenge."

When granted access to Ewing Hall for a television shoot, shots were taken of the exterior, and Channel 2 Houston broadcasted the photo you see below, only enhanced slightly to bring out "the face." Nothing was added or subtracted to create the image. Upon further investigation, a medium pointed out that they felt that the death of a child happened on the spot, and that the face was the last thing that the child saw. Upon looking into crime records in that area during the time period given by the psychic, the search came up as inconclusive, although there were missing children reports from the area at the time. In December of 1992, while trying to look at the face, a nurse lost her life in a strange automobile accident caused by her own hand, only adding to the legend. This property is posted "No Trespassing," so if you want to see it for yourself, you will have to gain permission from the University.

—*Peter James Haviland, Adv.C.H.*
President, Lead Investigator,
Lone Star Spirits

Photo by Brendan Keefe

THE BAKER HOTEL
201 EAST HUBBARD STREET
MINERAL WELLS, TEXAS 76067

The Baker Hotel is a 14-story brick giant looming over the town of Mineral Wells. Built in 1929 and opening its doors just two weeks after Black Monday, the hotel boasted 280,000 square feet, 450 guest rooms, and a whole floor dedicated to spa treatments. It was billed as a resort hotel, offering mineral water treatments touted to cure ailments from rheumatism to insanity. The hotel now stands in near ruin, inhabited only by a few spirits.

The Baker Hotel register book was graced by such famous names as Bonnie and Clyde, Judy Garland, and Clark Gable, yet it seems to be the local ghosts who have stayed on. Hotel magnate T.B. Baker, who built the hotel, haunts the Baker Suite, a lavish apartment on the 11th floor. Tour guides knock on the carved oak door before entering, and often his cigar smoke lingers in the air. Small items go missing from purses while ghost tour groups visit this room; occasionally, a tour guide will find the missing item at the threshold to the suite when closing the building up hours later.

Probably the most famous ghost in local lore is Virginia Brown, mistress to T.B. Baker. She kept a corner suite on the seventh floor, and while in these rooms, people have reported the smell of lavender perfume, soft touches on the shoulder, and even seeing the old windows rise and fall of their own accord. Virginia is rumored to have committed suicide from the bell tower of the hotel in despair over her illicit love affair. On moonlit nights, locals say that you can see the form of a woman in white leaning over the edge of the bell tower, and they have reported seeing a soft glow in her window, as if she were holding vigil there.

In the basement of the hotel, a young bellhop met an unfortunate death. His name was Douglas, and he was trapped in the elevator cage as it was rising. He was severely crushed at the midsection and died several hours later. There is a rumor that his death was no accident, but rather a way to hide illicit knowledge about gambling and prostitution. Whatever the intent behind Douglas's death, the air is colder at the base of this elevator shaft, and on occasion the lucky observer can witness the cage doors sliding open with no physical aid.

Maybe the saddest and strangest ghost of the Baker Hotel is that of the Unnamed Prostitute. She was suffocated to death with her own pantyhose, and when found, no one was willing to volunteer her name. Hotel management had her body embalmed and displayed her in the lobby under glass, hoping someone could identify her. A week went by, and no one claimed her. She was buried in a local cemetery, but her spirit can be heard crying in the hotel lobby on quiet nights.

—Kira Connally
Paranormal Investigator, Mystic Ghost

Utah

THE GRIST MILL INN
300 EAST 100 SOUTH
MONTICELLO, UTAH 84535
TEL: 1 (435) 587-2597
Website: *www.thegristmillinn.com*

The Grist Mill Inn is located about 280 miles south of Salt Lake City in Monticello, Utah, just off Utah's legendary highway 666. The inn is owned by Glen and Phyllis Swank.

Photo by Kelly Flynn

The original building was built in 1933 and was a working mill called the Monticello Flour Mill. In its time, the mill produced nearly all of the flour that was sold by the U.S. government to the Navajo nation. The mill was closed down after an unfortunate accident cost a young Boy Scout his life while he was touring the mill with his Scout pack. The 1963 accident polarized the town of Monticello, pitted neighbor against neighbor, and eventually led to the closure of the mill.

In 1985, the mill was turned into a bed and breakfast with a beautiful old-fashioned country appeal.

Its seven bedrooms are each designed to make you feel like you have taken a trip back in time. The mill has retained the look of a working flour mill, and guests wake in the morning to a gourmet breakfast. While staying at the inn, a guest might encounter one of the many ghosts who still call the Grist Mill Inn home.

In the mill's breakfast room, guests will often see the specter of an old man in coveralls walking between the bagging machine and back door.

In the inn's lobby, people have reported seeing the ghost of a young boy (thought to be the ghost of the Scout) playing ball near the elevator where he was killed. The small ghost likes peeking around corners at visitors and hiding in the stairways. He also appears in the kitchen area whenever chocolate chip cookies are being baked.

In the Corbin Room, there is a dark, even frightening, presence. Guests report a "dark" man wearing work clothes and boots who looms over the bed of guests, walks in and out of the room, and occasionally slams the bedroom door.

In the Nielson Room, people often find an old man sitting on the bed, staring out the window. The bedspread is often messed up as though someone had been sitting on the bed. The inn's co-owner, Phyllis, said that she frequently had to go up to the Nielson Room several times a day and straighten the bedspread. Phyllis says that she's learned to just leave it be. She said, "There's no sense smoothing it out just to walk past the room 10 minutes later and it's messed up again!"

On October 25, 2003, the Utah Ghost Hunters' Society (UGHS) investigated the Grist Mill Inn and during the investigation, we recorded an astonishing amount of electronic voice phenomena (EVP). But the most remarkable evidence collected during the investigation was this photograph taken by UGHS researcher Kelly Flynn of an upstairs bedroom window. The photograph shows what appears to be a ghost starring back at her through the window.

—Chris Peterson
President, Utah Ghost Hunters' Society

UNION STATION

2501 WALL AVENUE
OGDEN, UTAH 84401
TEL: 1 (801) 269-8444
WEBSITE: *www.theunionstation.org*

The old Union Pacific Station in Ogden, Utah, was the hub of transcontinental railroad traffic for a little more than 50 years. The current structure was erected in 1924 after the original building was destroyed by fire. The grand lobby of the station is typical of train stations that were built in the early 1900s. The structure is a Mediterranean-style building with large murals at each end of the main hallway, which depict the completion of the transcontinental railroad in Utah.

Once an active railroad station, Union Station is now home to several museums: the Utah State Railroad Museum, the Browning Arms Museum, the Browning Kimball Car Museum, the Natural History Museum, and the Gallery at Union Station.

There are many ghost stories that surround Ogden's Union Station. The one most often told is the story of the lady in blue. The particulars of the legend depend upon who tells you the story; however, no matter what version you hear, there are many aspects all of the stories have in common: A beautiful woman wearing a radiant blue dress is jilted by her lover. Blinded by tears of sorrow, she runs, wailing, across the yard. In her grief, she doesn't watch where she is going. She steps in front of an oncoming train and is killed.

Another version of the story claims the woman in the blue dress and her lover are arguing in the station yard, and he takes back her engagement ring and throws it away. The woman, in tears, runs to recover the ring and (again, not watching where she is going) steps in front of an oncoming train and is killed.

Regardless of how the story is told, visitors to Union Station are frequently terrorized by the sound of a wailing female voice and by the sight of a woman in a blue dress dashing through the rail yard.

"The woman in blue" is not the only specter at the Union Pacific Station. During several investigations of the old building, the Utah Ghost Hunters' Society (UGHS) have recorded many instances of EVP and have even seen strange mists floating down the stairs and across the great hall on the ground floor. During one investigation, Chris and Nancy Peterson (of the UGHS) actually heard a woman's voice speaking in the ground floor hallway by the restrooms.

The station has a rather grisly past that may account for some of the activity that haunts the old building. In the 1960s, during the Vietnam War, the station received the bodies of many American soldiers who were killed in the conflict. At times, the loading docks were piled high with coffins. Each coffin had a routing tag on it, routing the coffin through the Utah hub to its final destination.

Another section of the building of supernatural note is the Browning Arms

Museum inside Union Station. The museum is a comprehensive collection of the firearms produced by Browning Arms. It is thought that some of the firearms in the collection have ghosts of their own. Visitors and security guards tell of seeing a few men dressed in old military uniforms, including one gentleman with a long handlebar mustache dressed in a Civil War uniform.

—Chris Peterson
President, Utah Ghost Hunters' Society

THE CAPITOL THEATER
50 WEST 200 SOUTH
SALT LAKE CITY, UTAH 84101
TEL: 1 (801) 355-2787

The Capitol Theater is an operational theater that plays host to the arts. From Shakespearean theater to the ballet, to the opera, a modern dance company, the Capitol Theater has it all, including several rather famous (or infamous) ghosts.

The Capitol Theater began as the 2,000-seat Orpheum Theater in 1913. In its early days, the theater featured some of the "highest standard acts and greatest stars of the stage."

Capitalization of the project came from the Walker Estate in Salt Lake City. G. Albert Lansburgh, a San Francisco architect, designed the building with its tapestry brick, polychrome terra cotta, and steel reinforcement. The theater was one of only two buildings in the city using the new terra cotta material on its exterior. The Orpheum Theater was significant for introducing innovative architectural features in theater construction and the most

modern mechanical contrivances of its time to the Intermountain West.

In the early days, the theater hosted Vaudevillians who entertained crowds of theatergoers who paid 10 cents, 25 cents, 50 cents, and 75 cents (depending on the performance and the type of seat) for tickets.

In 1923, the Ackerman Harris Vaudeville chain purchased the theater, and Vaudeville continued to reign as king-of-the-house until 1927 when the theater was again sold. In 1927, the theater sold to Louis Marcus, who was mayor of Salt Lake City. Marcus, who was a movie pioneer in Utah, enlarged the seating capacity to 2,260 and installed the "Wurlitzer" with Alexander Schreiner as its spotlighted musician.

When the theater finally raised its curtain on September 29, 1927, the Orpheum Theater had become the Capitol Theater. The Capitol Theater introduced "talking pictures" to Salt Lake City in 1929.

Capitol Theater got a facelift in 1947, and talking pictures continued to be the main attraction at the theater, with the occasional live performance staged as they became available. The theater hosted such names as Stanley Holloway, who played in *My Fair Lady*, Judith Evellyn in *A Streetcar Named Desire*, and Frank Fay in *Harvey*.

In December of 1975 when Salt Lake County residents passed an 8.6-million-dollar bond to renovate the old theater, it became, and is now, the center for the performing arts.

The most interesting thing about the theater, however, is its haunted history. In 1947, fire broke out in the theater and claimed the life of a young usher. Nighttime patrons of the theater, theater staff, and theater security all claim to have had various run-ins with a playful ghost they all call George.

George enjoys a good joke, such as unplugging extension cords and reaiming lights and spotlights moments before a performance. George seems to enjoy the panic-stricken rush to put things right before the curtain goes up. He has also been known to lock and unlock doors. Many people have found themselves helplessly trapped between two locked doors beneath the stage when the doors seem to magically lock themselves.

George is just one of many spooks who inhabit the halls of the old Orpheum Theater. For years now, the Utah Ghost Hunters' Society has conducted an ongoing investigation into the strange events inside the building. We have conducted many eyewitness interviews and have recorded hours' worth of Electronic Voice Phenomena there, especially on the stage and in the catacomb-like hallways, passages, and dressing rooms beneath the theater. "Theaters just seem to attract ghosts," the UGHS's Nancy Peterson said. "Maybe it's an attraction to the limelight. When actors and actresses leave this world, maybe the lights, the stage, and the energy of the audience draws them back to the theater."

—Chris Peterson
President, Utah Ghost Hunters' Society

THE CAPITOL THEATER

Paranormal Investigator Profile

Loyd Auerbach

LOYD AUERBACH is the director of the Office of Paranormal Investigations and the author of *Ghost Hunting: How to Investigate the Paranormal* (Ronin Publishing, 2003) and *Hauntings & Poltergeists: A Ghost Hunter's Guide* (2004). His first book, *ESP, Hauntings and Poltergeists* (Warner Books, 1986), deals with the ways parapsychologists investigate psychic phenomena outside the laboratory and the misconceptions of the phenomena held by the public. It was named the "sacred text" on ghosts by *Newsweek*.

Q: What drew you into parapsychology?

What drew me into the field was really an interest that came out of science fiction. I used to watch the old *Topper* TV show in the 60s, and *Star Trek* certainly got me there too. Comic books, science-fiction literature, really all of that kind of put me into the interest. And then *Dark Shadows* and a show in the early 70s called *The Sixth Sense* all kind of really formalized my interest into parapsychology.

Photo courtesy of Loyd Auerbach

Other than knowing who was on the phone occasionally [before picking up] or things like that, I really didn't have any sort of psychic experience until I got into graduate school.

Q: Did you actually see something?

I actually saw folks move some objects in college. This was a series of seminars run by a couple of folks at Mundelein College in Chicago. They brought in some parapsychologists and did some work on PK (psychokinesis). So I did see some movement of objects that way.

Q: What kind of evidence do you consider credible in determining if an area is haunted?

Evidence is the right word. We're really talking about peoples' experiences here, so when you're talking about a ghost experience or a ghost sighting, it's a person who has that experience. There's no technology involved. For a place to be haunted, you're typically talking about a history of peoples' experiences, but most important are current experiences. There are many places that are no longer haunted— they were, at one point, according to the local histories, but it doesn't do any good for anybody who's doing an investigation, or who is even interested, unless the folks who witnessed the phenomena are still around or if the phenomena are still happening.

The experience can vary quite a bit depending on the phenomena, so we're talking about mainly two different types of things. One is the idea of an apparition or ghost sticking around after their death for quite a long time, which seems to be pretty rare. More common are the imprints, or place memories. That kind of thing is fairly common all over the world—not just in specific places we call haunted, but even in peoples' homes people experience things.

Q: Do you put much stock in spirit photography?

They can support the human experience, certainly, but when it comes down to it, none of the technology has been designed to pick up the things that we experience. There is no technology that is designed to pick up human consciousness in the body, let alone outside of the body.

The problem with the camera is that cameras are not better than people think they are. I have a lot of friends who are in photography and a couple of folks who work for some major companies, and the reality is that cameras do not take pictures of things that are invisible to the human eye—unless it's infrared, in which case we're doing something that is heat-sensitive and not what people typically think. If it's invisible to the human eye, it's going to be invisible to a flash and to a camera.

With ghost cases, we're talking about the ghost somehow affecting the camera—affecting the film, or the mechanism of the camera. We certainly have a lot of evidence that people's consciousness can affect computers. And if an object can move, certainly a camera can be affected.

There are many other explanations regarding spirit photography. This could be an effect of a ghost on the camera, but it's not a ghost. The image itself is not a ghost.

Q: What is your favorite haunt?

My favorite place, where I've probably had more experiences than anyplace else, is the Moss Beach Distillery restaurant, which is just south of San Francisco. It's haunted by a woman who was murdered in the early 1930s. Local historians have collected stories from people even as far back as a week after her death. She was murdered as part of a lover's triangle, so it's one of those classic ghost stories. People saw her ghost fairly regularly through probably the 70s. Since the late 70s, she hasn't been seen as much as she has been felt.

What's interesting about this case is that a lot of things have happened on the investigations we've been on—including with a lot of the TV crews. Although the biggest problem with TV shows is that the crews tend not to want to include themselves in talking about the experiences. So it something happens while the camera is turned off, they're not willing to talk about it if they see it. So we've actually had a lot of really good witnesses to evidence that have occurred there, except they're not willing to talk about it because they don't want to become part of the story. And then, of course, they complain that we have nothing on camera.

I've worked with about five mediums or psychics over the last 14 years at the Distillery. At the restaurant, they all had not only encountered the same person, but each psychic was able to add to and pick up different information that was later confirmed by some of the other folks as well as by some of the witnesses. So, in other words, we're getting psychic sensitives who are picking up information that the people living in the area or people who are working there can also confirm by their experience. That's very positive for us. She [the ghost] is pretty cooperative, generally.

Q: Where is parapsychology going?

For one thing, the funding in the United States has been drying up, and a lot of the organizations have been in danger for quite a while—partly because of the skeptics' movement more than anything else. It's a shame for people who are psychic practitioners and the ghost hunters—nobody seems to want to support the research. Because the research is not just in the lab, it's also outside the laboratory. But in general, I think it has gathered a little bit more momentum with some mainstream scientists who are more and more willing, at least amongst their peers, to discuss these experiences. And especially with physicists, the quantum physicists who are more interested in physics of consciousness. I think that's where it's been heading—looking at consciousness, which is extremely important when you're talking about ghosts, because that's what a ghost is by definition.

West Coast

West Coast

California

THE SAN FRANCISCO-OAKLAND BAY BRIDGE

SAN FRANCISCO BAY, CALIFORNIA

The Golden Gate Bridge is world-famous for attracting suicides, but its neighbor, the 4.5-mile San Francisco-Oakland Bay Bridge, boasts the bay area's most impressive and reliable ghost. Little-known outside the local populace, this phantom is so frequently spotted that instead of watching for the apparition, some commuters watch for other drivers' double-takes when *they* see the ghost.

The double-decker bridge built in 1936 now carries about 280,000 commuters between the San Francisco Peninsula and the Berkeley-Oakland area daily, making the phantom one of the most-seen in the world. But he looks so ordinary, so real, that few people realize they've just seen a ghost.

I first heard about him at a friend's party in Berkeley. Nearly everyone had seen him more than once, some dozens of times. They said that around 1948, a man's car ran out of gas and he had to walk back to a phone to summon the bridge tow truck. He was hit by a speeding car and killed instantly.

You can only see him out of the corner of your eye, they told me, and he looks absolutely real. If you try to see him straight-on, he disappears.

He always stands in the same location, but his posture can vary. Usually, he appears to be looking around, perhaps for the tow truck. He is on a narrow footpath right next to the road, dressed in a 40s-style hat and raincoat.

Late that night, I left for my San Francisco hotel. Though excited, I really didn't expect to spot the ghost. At my request, my friends had not revealed anything about his location, other than he was somewhere on the upper deck, westbound into San Francisco.

The span was midnight-quiet, the night clear and cool. As I drove, I continually scanned both sides of the bridge. I reached the Yerba Buena Island tunnel, where the eastern and western spans connect, without seeing anything strange. As I emerged onto the suspension bridge on the west side of the island, I saw no other traffic, though I did vaguely note a man standing in the shadows near the third tower on the northwest side of the bridge. He wore a coat and hat, but the bridge light that illuminated him from above revealed little detail except for rumples in his coat and the tilt of his hat.

I thought he was a cop using a bridge phone, but as I passed him, I realized he had no squad car. He was all alone, on foot. That seemed odd. And then it hit me—I had *possibly* seen the ghost of the Bay Bridge. I didn't really believe it, but I felt a little thrill as I jotted down the exact location before going to bed. I called my friends the next morning to report what I had seen—and where.

I had, indeed, seen the apparition.

So, if you're driving on the San Francisco-Oakland Bay Bridge, you might spot a pedestrian at the edge of the road. The only peculiar thing about him is that he disappears if you try to look at him straight on. But don't worry—if you see him but it takes a moment to register, you may not be out of luck. Just let your eyes dart briefly to the side again. As often as not, this ghost is likely to still be there.

—Tamara Thorne
Author,
Independent Paranormal Investigator

chickens, and other farm animals. Nearby, vast herb and vegetable gardens exist much as they did when the 960-acre compound (built in 1787 and rebuilt after an earthquake in 1812) was young. There is a lavenderia—a laundry pool where the natives washed the Spaniards' clothes and they themselves bathed. (A sign points out that the Chumash, unlike the Spaniards, enjoyed bathing themselves.) Nearby, beautiful fountains splash and bubble.

Despite the idyllic beauty, you may sense a darkness, a heaviness, as well. And if you do, you may also encounter one of the many hauntings. History books tend to gloss over the fact that the 21 California missions (La Purisima was the 11th) were founded by the Catholic Church and Spanish king to increase the strength of their empire, and the indigenous population was treated essentially as slaves, working long hours, not allowed to leave the compound, and forced to give up their beliefs for new ones. This is something it's

MISSION LA PURISIMA

MISSION LA PURISIMA STATE
HISTORIC PARK
2295 PURISIMA ROAD
LOMPOC, CALIFORNIA 93436
WEBSITE: *www.lapurisimamission.org*

The restored Mission La Purisima de Conception near Lompoc, California, looks much like it did when it was inhabited by Spanish priests and a working population of "neophytes"—the Chumash natives of the central coast. The low, neat buildings include chapels, living quarters for the padres and soldiers, kitchens, a springhouse, and weaving, and other workrooms are spread out, surrounded by gentle hills dotted with oak trees. A central pasture is home to goats, donkeys,

Photo by Tamara Thorne

difficult to ignore when you ghost hunt at the mission. It's in the air. You feel it.

The hauntings are everywhere. Cold spots are common. Sounds are, too. You may hear phantom singing and guitars and flutes inside the chapels. Male voices are overheard in the weaving room. Native chanting rises in many areas, and, after dark, hoofbeats sometimes break the silence.

Park rangers have admitted to seeing apparitions. Chief among them is that of Frey Payeras, who was in charge of the mission for many years and comparatively well-liked among the Chumash. His grave in the main chapel was uncovered in the 1930s during a restoration. Only the top half of his skeleton was found. The lower half was buried at the Mission Santa Barbara, a hundred miles south. (There is no mystery here, despite attempts to create one. Payeras rose high in the church and his body became a holy relic, to be shared. This was common at the time.) Payeras appears as an old padre in white robes near his grave and in his former quarters, where the bedding is frequently mussed by unseen hands.

Another monk walks the gardens in the morning and evening, and a soldier appears near the barracks. Even the ghosts of the padres' pampered greyhounds occasionally wander through the buildings, especially in the long hall that leads to the wine storage area. Another active haunt is in the padre's kitchen. He is Don Vicente, murdered there in the 1820s.

—Tamara Thorne
Author,
Independent Paranormal Investigator

LAUREL CANYON AND LOOKOUT MOUNTAIN ROAD

HOLLYWOOD, CALIFORNIA

Up in the Hollywood hills, above the hustle and bustle of the city and not far from the allegedly haunted ruins of Harry Houdini's old burned-out mansion, lies the intersection of Laurel Canyon Boulevard and Lookout Mountain Road. It is an area of frequent ghost sightings.

In the summer of 2000, I was hired to do tarot readings for a birthday party at a house on Lookout Mountain Road. It turned out to be quite a festive event, lasting for about six hours and attended by actress Fairuza Balk and many other people who worked in the entertainment industry. Around midnight, it began to break up.

I packed my tarot cards, got into my car, and began heading home. I reached the bottom of Lookout Mountain and then turned left onto Laurel Canyon Boulevard. It was at that moment that I spotted an old-fashioned carriage pulled by two white horses racing madly down Lookout Mountain Road toward the intersection. Oddly, there was no galloping sound.

The silent apparition lasted for only a second or two before vanishing into thin air, and at the time I thought I had simply imagined it due to the fact that I was extremely tired and my eyes were strained from hours of card readings. However, I later discovered that other people had also witnessed the same thing at the very same location.

Upon further research, I also learned that this apparition was said to be responsible for a number of traffic accidents at the intersection of Laurel Canyon and Lookout Mountain Road. Apparently, some drivers, upon seeing the phantom carriage suddenly appear, would slam on their brakes or swerve to avoid hitting it, resulting in a collision with other vehicles.

—Gerina Dunwich
Independent Paranormal Investigator

Santa Susana Pass Road

Chatsworth, California

The Santa Susana Pass Road, which winds through the rocky sagebrush-covered hills connecting the Los Angeles suburb of Chatsworth to the east side of Simi Valley, was once a dusty stagecoach trail back in the 19th century. It was also home to Spahn's Movie Ranch—a deserted former studio ranch infamous as the Manson Family hideout in the 1960s.

Before being reduced to ashes by a wildfire in 1970, Spahn was the site of at least one grisly murder. A ranch hand and stuntman by the name of Donald "Shorty" Shea was brutally stabbed to death there after attempting to evict Manson and his followers from the ranch. His decapitated body was buried in an unmarked grave on the property.

The area has a strange and disturbing feeling to it, and an inexplicable sense of "dread" seems to hang heavily in the air, especially in the still of night. Some people have even reported seeing the ghostly figure of a headless man standing on the rocks high above the road.

One dark and chilly night while I was driving through the thin wisps of fog along the Santa Susana Pass and hoping to catch a glimpse of the headless ghost, a pair of bright headlights from a black 60s model sedan suddenly glared in my rearview mirror. It startled me a bit, as I had not seen or passed another car for many miles. The vehicle tailgated me for quite some time, making me rather nervous. But as soon as I drove past the site where Spahn's Movie Ranch used to be, the "phantom car" seemed to mysteriously vanish into thin air.

—Gerina Dunwich
Independent Paranormal Investigator

Biltmore Hotel

506 South Grand Avenue
Los Angeles, California 90071
Tel: 1 (213) 624-1011
Website: *www.thebiltmore.com*

Americans have always been fascinated by the idea of stardom. Perhaps that is why some call Los Angeles the "land of

broken dreams." Many a high school drama student has packed his or her things and moved to the land of glitz and glamour in hopes of becoming a star. More often than not, it ends in heartache. Such is the story of the Black Dahlia.

Elizabeth Short was born on July 29, 1924, in Hyde Park, Massachusetts. With a persona much larger than the life she lived, Elizabeth knew she was destined for fame, so at age 19 she left home for Los Angeles. However, she never fully realized her dreams of becoming a Hollywood star. Instead, she settled for a life of mundane jobs and short relationships. Her friends nicknamed her "The Black Dahlia" because of the popular dark movie *The Blue Dahlia* starring Alan Ladd and Veronica Lake. Elizabeth had jet-black hair and a penchant for black clothing, and so she became the Black Dahlia.

On January 8, 1947, Elizabeth was picked up by a boyfriend named Red Manley for a night on the town. After their evening out, they returned to a hotel where Manley had rented them a room. The next morning, Elizabeth told her suitor she planned to move back home. Before she left, she said, she was going to visit with her sister at the Biltmore Hotel in Los Angeles. Manley agreed to take her there but could only drop her off. When Manley left her, she was making phone calls in the lobby of the Biltmore. He, along with the employees of the hotel, were the last to see her alive.

On January 15, 1947, six days after Manley had dropped Elizabeth off at the Biltmore, she was found dead in a nearby abandoned lot. When police arrived on the scene, they determined that the body had been posed in such a way that appeared almost seductive. Her face had been sliced

so that her once beautiful smile extended from ear to ear. And to top it off, she had been sliced in two just above the waist with what police later discovered to be a butcher knife.

To this day, the "Black Dahlia Murder" has yet to be solved. No one has given up hope, however—not even Elizabeth. The ghost of the Black Dahlia has been seen roaming the halls of the Biltmore Hotel. Witnesses report seeing a woman in a black dress with a sense of urgency and distress in her eyes. She has been seen pacing the lobby and waiting by the telephone. She has even shared rides with elevator passengers. Perhaps she is searching for her killer or just waiting for her sister to arrive. Just as in the identity of her murderer, we may never know.

—Tom Iacuzio
Founder,
Central Florida Ghost Research

CALICO GHOST TOWN

10 MILES NORTH OF BARSTOW, CALIFORNIA
GHOST TOWN ROAD EXIT OFF OF
INTERSTATE 15
TEL: 1 (760) 254-3340
WEBSITE: *www.calicoghostwalk.com*

Calico Ghost Town, founded in 1881, is a historic silver mining town where some people struck it rich and others lost everything. Like most western towns, Calico rip-roared with saloons and bordellos, but it was also considered more family-oriented than other boom-towns. The ghosts of Calico are many and varied, including friendly town drunks, billiard players, miners who still toil, and a whole host of schoolhouse ghosts—children, school teachers, and frequently spotted, generally playful shadow people who are often seen on the schoolhouse roof. Another famous ghost is that of a border collie named Dorsey who acted as the mail carrier.

Calico thrived until the late 1890s when the world value of silver plummeted. Still, Calico continued on thanks to rich deposits of borax in the Calico Mountains. But by 1910, better sources were found and the town began to fall into ruins, though it was never entirely deserted.

Photo by Tamara Thorne

In 1950, Calico was purchased and lovingly restored to the glory of its richest era by Walter Knott (who went on to found Knott's Berry Farm, Disneyland's closest southern California rival and home of the biggest month-long Halloween haunt in the state). Later, Knott donated the town to the County of San Bernardino. Since 1967, it has been a County Regional Park, dedicated to preserving the town's history.

People who experience the Calico Ghost Walk often come up to me after the tour to tell me about their own experiences with the ghosts. The interesting thing is that a great many of these people (of all ages) tell me of their sightings in detail— the same details that have been reported by other visitors months or even years earlier. They coincide perfectly.

One evening after one of our recent ghost walks, a mother and her 14-year-old son told me about their sighting. While at the school house, a curtain in the front windows was pulled back by a small hand, and a young girl's face peeked out. This was reported two weeks earlier to me at the same exact window pane while on a private tour. I never told anyone about the sighting. Yet it has since repeated several more times.

Calico Ghost Town is famous for the "Lights of Calico" that traverse across the hills and canyons around the town. It is rare to give a ghost walk where not one soul on the tour spots one of these fantastic moving lights or energy clouds. People have reported these lights even in the campground below town.

Walking through Calico is like stepping back into the heyday of a lively silver mining camp—except the inhabitants who remain make this a true ghost town. By learning the real history of Calico in the 1800s, it is easier for us to understand the ghost sightings that we have had in the past and are still experiencing today.

—Bill Cook
Calico Ghost Walk

RMS QUEEN MARY

1126 QUEENS HIGHWAY
LONG BEACH, CALIFORNIA 90802
TEL: 1 (562) 435-3511
WEBSITE: *www.queenmary.com*

The *RMS Queen Mary* made her maiden voyage on May 27, 1936, and led a colorful life as a transatlantic ocean vessel as well as a troop ship during World War II. During the ship's years of service, she completed 1,001 Atlantic crossings before being permanently docked in Long Beach, California, on December 11, 1967. She's seen her share of both good times and tragedies.

During World War II, the ship was painted military gray and given the ominous name "The Gray Ghost." Prisoners committed suicide on the ship during her military service. Allied soldiers died from heat exhaustion during a heat spell in the Indian Ocean, when 16,000 troops were aboard a ship designed to comfortably accommodate only 3,000. And while running a submarine-evading zig-zag pattern in 1942, the *Queen Mary* accidentally cut through the much smaller *Curaçao*, sinking the escort vessel in a matter of minutes. Ghostly legends abound aboard the floating hotel today.

According to psychic Peter James, there are more than 600 active ghosts on the ship today. Some of the more prominent spirit personalities include: Jackie, a young girl who was believed to have drowned in the second-class swimming pool; a man in black who has been spotted in some of the administrative offices and has been known to open and close doors, appear, then disappear, and move objects around the office; and an engineer in the boiler room who was crushed by one of the water-tight doorways on the lower decks.

Additionally, visitors have reported hearing phantom scrapes and screams from when the *Queen Mary* sliced through the *Curaçao*, and many have smelled cigar smoke, though no smoking is allowed on board. People have seen the specters of people dressed in vintage clothing, as well as other semi-materialized body parts floating around the ship.

—Jeff Belanger
Founder, Ghostvillage.com

HOTEL DEL CORONADO

1500 ORANGE AVENUE
CORONADO, CALIFORNIA 92118
TEL: 1 (619) 435-6611
WEBSITE: *www.hoteldel.com*

On November 25, 1892, Kate Morgan checked into the Hotel del Coronado. She never checked out, and by the many ghostly reports coming from the hotel over the decades, she's never left.

Built in 1888 by Elisha Babcock and H.L. Story, their vision for the resort was for it to be the "talk of the Western world." A luxurious hotel overlooking the sparkling waters of the Pacific Ocean was built—it's a place that has accommodated dignitaries and celebrities from all over the world. Today, the resort and spa still lives up to its opulent reputation, and the ghost of Kate Morgan is still experienced and seen to this day.

Kate was an attractive woman in her mid-20s when she checked into the hotel by herself on Thanksgiving evening, 1892. Many of the hotel staff who interacted with her during her stay reported she seemed ill or unhappy. She claimed she was waiting for her brother to join her at the hotel—

though he never showed. On November 30, 1892, Kate's lifeless body was found on the exterior staircase leading to the beach. She had a gunshot wound to her head, which the local authorities determined to be self-inflicted. Inside her room there were no personal belongings and nothing to identify her except the name she checked in with: "Lottie A. Bernard." After sending sketches of this woman around the country, she was eventually identified as Kate Morgan from Iowa. Apparently, she and her husband had an argument on the train while en route to San Diego. Her husband got off at an earlier stop, and Kate went on to the Hotel del Coronado expecting her husband to show up, but he never did.

Kate has been blamed for televisions and lights going on and off by themselves, for mysterious cold spots, perfume smells that seem to have no source, and for making an appearance as a semi-translucent woman in the hotel as well as on the staircase where she took her own life.

—Jeff Belanger
Founder, Ghostvillage.com

WINCHESTER MYSTERY HOUSE

525 SOUTH WINCHESTER BOULEVARD
SAN JOSE, CALIFORNIA 95128
TEL: 1 (408) 247-2101
WEBSITE:
www.winchestermysteryhouse.com

Any homeowner will tell you that you're never finished working on your home. Items will need fixing, rooms painted, you'll add little touches and additions here and there as time and money allow. The Winchester House takes this idea to an entirely different level. In 1884, Sarah L. Winchester, widow of William Wirt Winchester and heiress to the Winchester Repeating Arms Company fortune, purchased an eight-room house on 150 acres in San Jose and began making a few additions—additions that would keep three shifts of carpenters, architects, and construction workers busy for 38 years until Sarah's death in 1922. By the end of her life, Sarah turned the eight-room home into a 160-room Victorian mansion with three working elevators, 47 fireplaces, hand-inlaid parquet floors, silver and gold chandeliers, Tiffany windows, staircases that lead to nowhere, doors that open to brick walls, other doors that open to the outside on the second floor with a straight drop down, and many other architectural oddities. There weren't formal blueprints; Mrs. Winchester would just sketch out rooms on paper and even on tablecloths for the workers to follow.

Why did she do this?

Sarah's husband died in March of 1881 of tuberculosis while the couple was living in New Haven, Connecticut. Their only daughter died 15 years earlier during her infancy. Sarah was having a difficult time getting over the death of her husband, so

Photo courtesy of the Winchester Mystery House, San Jose, California

a friend of hers suggested she contact a Spiritualist medium. The medium claimed her husband William was present and "He says for me to tell you that there is a curse on your family, which took the life of he and your child. It will soon take you, too. It is a curse that has resulted from the terrible weapon created by the Winchester family. Thousands of persons have died because of it, and their spirits are now seeking vengeance." The medium told her to head west; her husband would guide her and she would know when she found the right home. The medium told her to start a new life and to build a home for herself and for the spirits who had fallen at the hands of a Winchester rifle. She was told she could never stop building the house or the curse would take her as it did her husband and daughter.

So Sarah Winchester built. If her plans conflicted with a room built earlier, they simply built around. Rooms are contained within rooms, and the floor plan is certainly chaotic at times. Sarah spent a great deal of time in a room she called "The Séance Room."

Sarah Winchester is said to be still wandering her house today, causing disembodied footsteps, murmuring voices, and cold spots. Psychics have gone in and identified many other spirits who they also believe call the Winchester Mystery House home. Whether these really are the souls of those killed by the famous rifle, or whether they're more a figment of the imagination, is up to each visitor to decide.

—Jeff Belanger
Founder, Ghostvillage.com

THE WHALEY HOUSE
2482 SAN DIEGO AVENUE
SAN DIEGO, CALIFORNIA 92110
WEBSITE: *www.whaleyhouse.org*

Built in 1856 by Thomas Whaley, a merchant from New York, the house was used for business purposes as well as the family residence. The building served as county courthouse and seat, theater, granary, and store. The property was the town gallows before the house was built. The most regular spirits present today are: Thomas Whaley, Anna Whaley (wife), James Robinson (hung on the property before the house was built), and a small girl (around 3 years old).

Back in 1993, I visited the Whaley House. Some might remember that there used to be some very spooky-looking mannequins in the upstairs bedrooms. I walked past the master bedroom and I heard the spirit voice of Anna Whaley. She explained to me that she did not like *her dress* on that mannequin and that people visiting were spooked by the mannequins. She found it disrespectful.

I went up to the caretaker and said, "Excuse me, I hope you do not think I am crazy, but Anna told me she doesn't like her black dress on that mannequin." The caretaker looked at me and said, "I believe

Photo by Bonnie Vent

THE WHALEY HOUSE

you. Not many things in this house actually belonged to a Whaley family member, but that is indeed Mrs. Whaley's dress." The lady also remarked that she and Anna were the only ones who knew that fact, so of course she believed me. This caretaker was June Reading, who was instrumental in saving the house.

I came back to the house a few months later and found that all of the mannequins had been removed, and the black dress was now laid out on the bed. As I was standing there, Anna's spirit thanked me for delivering her message. Little did I know that in the year 2000, a battle would ensue in court over what was and what was not Whaley property. I told every docent who would listen to save Anna's black dress. To this day, I do not know if it was my insistence or some documentation left by June Reading, but the dress was saved. There is a theater stage there now, but if you look at old pictures of the Whaley House, you will see Anna's black dress laid out on the bed.

Up to this point, I only had a spirit voice and the word of June Reading, who passed in 1998, as proof of that being Anna's black dress.

In August of 2003, I was researching through newspapers from the 1887 to 1888 timeframe. In the *San Diego Union* I found an article about a Gala Ball held at the Hotel del Coronado in 1888. Anna is included on the guest list. There is a detailed description of Anna's black dress! This must have been the occasion that caused her to buy the dress from Paris. Ten years after first communicating with Anna's spirit, I have found tangible proof of what she told me in a local newspaper printed in 1888.

—*Bonnie Vent*
Spirit Advocate, San Diego Paranormal Research Project

Oregon

MCMENAMIN'S GRAND LODGE
3505 PACIFIC AVENUE
FOREST GROVE, OREGON 97116
TEL: 1 (503) 992-9533
WEBSITE: *www.thegrandlodge.com*

In 1920, plans and construction commenced to build a series of grand complexes called the Masonic Home and Children's Cottage. Throughout the years, these buildings were a combination poorhouse, elder care, and orphanage for Master Masons and their families, before being bought and renovated by the McMenamins in the fall of 1999.

Photo by Todd Baker

Following its renovations, legends and stories began to circulate regarding the Grand Lodge being plagued by strange apparitions and occurrences. Staff and clientele have noted particular locations that have shown to have a consistent amount of paranormal or unexplained activity. Among these "hotspots" are a couple of the guest rooms in the main lodge—especially room 211, the second and third floor hallways, the Gift Shop, the Doctor's Office Bar, the Equinox Meeting Room, the Billy Scott Meeting Room, and the Children's Cottage.

Some of the more frequent paranormal complaints from staff and visitors alike have been the appearance of odd smells, locked doors unlocking themselves from the inside, cold spots, disembodied footsteps, the playful movement of objects from one location to another, knocking, whispering, laughing, and the distinct, uneasy feeling of being stalked by "presences." Also witnessed by numerous people is the apparition of an elderly woman on the second floor, as well as an elderly man on the third. Other apparitions include fleeting glimpses of children-shaped shadows darting in and out of rooms in the Children's Cottage.

An official investigation was held here in October of 2003. Pacific Paranormal Research Society did receive electromagnetic as well as a few photographic anomalies on our visit to the Equinox Room, the second floor hallway, and in the Children's Cottage. In our visit to the main lodge, we experienced a few cold spots in the hallways and the distinct feeling that we were being watched or followed.

However, the most profound evidence was collected during our investigation of the Children's Cottage. One photograph, taken outside the Cottage following this investigation, showed an oddly pink, bright orb (page 204).

In this building, we all heard the distinct sound of footsteps upstairs when we were downstairs. Then, investigating upstairs, we heard running that simulated that of children's small, bare feet, coming from the downstairs hallways. Later that evening, a previously closed door at the end of the downstairs hallway was found to have mysteriously opened and then later closed again of its own accord.

At the end of our investigation, one person in our group abruptly left the building after hearing tittering and giggles from inside one of the rooms that he swears were from a little girl.

—Todd and Martina Baker
Pacific Paranormal Research Society

13TH DOOR HAUNTED HOUSE

OLD REGAL CINEMA AT WASHINGTON SQUARE MALL
10125 SW WASHINGTON SQUARE ROAD
TIGARD, OREGON 97223
TEL: 1 (503) 730-4579
WEBSITE:
www.hauntingproductions.com

"The hauntings are nothing but a big plus for me!" asserts Ray Latocki, owner and operator of The 13th Door, a seasonal haunted house attraction. "Doing a haunted house in a facility that is already haunted brings me a lot more customers. It's been great for business!"

Ray Latocki has a lot to be excited about. Not only does his chilling haunted house pull in hundreds of people every year, his walk-through attraction also appears to be pleasing to his handful of ghostly roommates. "I think they stay for the entertainment," he says. "They seem

Photo by Todd Baker

to enjoy interacting with me, the props, my employees, and especially my customers."

Once a Regal Cinema built in the late 1970s, the grayish hulk of a building has four cavernous theatres and an elongated room upstairs where the projector rooms used to be located. Prior employees of the movie theater insist they have experienced a plethora of unexplained phenomena, including the faint sounds of a music box, doors opening and slamming on their own, being pushed down the stairs, children's muddy handprints on the film screens, and film reels flying off their projectors and being flung toward employees.

There are approximately five ghosts that have been documented and encountered here. There is an older, grumpy man in black that is nicknamed "Lurch," a little girl aged 8 to 10 in a pioneer dress, a woman in her 30s, a young man in his late 20s, and a "ghost cat." There is a legend of a young man committing suicide in the brightly painted blue storage room located upstairs. Although the police claim to have no recollection of this, prior theater employees say it is indeed true.

Latocki admits that some of the ghosts he rubs elbows with can be a trite rambunctious. "I don't mind the cold refrigerated breezes, the tapping, touching, footsteps, voices, dark shadows, or when they steal or bring me my building materials," he says with a laugh. "But I have had employees refuse to work in Theatre One and have threatened to quit after one night in there. Plus, I've heard quite a few of my customers describe to me in awe about the wisps of white that were running after them through the haunt. They think it's some amazing sort of special effect or illusion, but, believe me, I could not create something like that on my own!"

While The 13th Door may serve up scares to the living for a living, Ray admits that there are times that the ghosts have the upper hand. "When I'm alone at night, and I am followed or watched constantly by their dark shadows, that is just the most overbearing feeling I've ever had. Even though I know they won't hurt me, it's still just a creepy feeling."

—Todd and Martina Baker
Pacific Paranormal Research Society

FRANK-N-STEINS PUB & GASTHAUS
185 EAST CHARLES STREET
MT. ANGEL, OREGON 97362
TEL: 1 (503) 845-2633

Some places simply look as though they should be haunted. Frank-N-Steins Pub & Gasthaus, with its castle-like façade accented with gargoyles, bats, and medieval torches, is one establishment that doesn't disappoint. Perhaps spirits from corpses in what used to be Unger Mortuary next door were attracted to the lively atmosphere of a pub and chose to stay.

Photo by Ellen Morrison

Starting out its business life as a small grocery in 1906, its next incarnation as public house stuck. Stein Pub became Frank-N-Steins when a tavern owner named Frank bought it. Present owners Eulace and Ellen Morrison kept the intriguing name upon acquiring it in 2004. And what a suitable name it is as well, being in the downtown area of a German-settled community that boasts the largest Oktoberfest on the West Coast each September.

Ellen contacted Trail's End Paranormal Society of Oregon to investigate the basis for patrons' stories of a disappearing lady in the "Lottery Dungeon" and her own feelings of being watched when alone. Two investigations have produced EVP; electromagnetic field spikes; and images of ectoplasmic mists, orbs, and an incredibly bright *dancing* orb. This energetic sphere of spirit energy chose to reveal itself in several frames during a late-night investigation on February 8, 2005, in the area of the pub used for karaoke, adjoining the small dance floor. Textured contrails are long enough to reveal several loops taken in its speedy path. EVP captured the same night revealed a whispering female voice saying, "I'm sorry," and a louder "Yes," when asked if there was a message to be given to a living person. More investigations and historical research is planned.

"Where'd that lady go?" asked a friend of Eulace's one Sunday night just after closing. She'd seen a woman walk by the restrooms toward the bar and, when she looked again, she was gone. Convinced Eulace and some other friends were playing a trick on her, she checked all over the pub for the woman who must have been in

on the prank, without success. It was when the realization came upon her she'd probably seen a ghost that she wished she'd taken more careful notice of details so she could describe the woman.

—Sara Lessley
Investigator, Newsletter & Website Editor,
Trail's End Paranormal Society of Oregon

Washington

THE BUSH HOUSE
300 FIFTH STREET
INDEX, WASHINGTON 98256
TEL: 1 (360) 793-2312

The Bush House Country Inn, established in 1898, is nestled in the scenic town of Index on the Skykomish River and encircled by the Cascade Mountain range. This historic hotel served the small community of Index during the time of active mining and lumber operations in the Pacific Northwest.

Situated in one of the most beautiful areas in Washington State, the hotel is open for guests during the summer months, offering generous meals and lodging, but, according to accounts, it never closes for some of its past inhabitants and visitors. Staff and guests have reported numerous unexplained phenomena in the

Photo by Maureen Nelson

hotel. The odors of cigars and perfume have been experienced on the second floor guest accommodations area when no guests are present. One guest reported that after reorganizing some of the furnishings in his room to allow for a more comfortable extended stay, he left the hotel briefly, and when he returned, he was unable to open the door to his room. Once the door was opened with assistance from the staff, a strong gust of wind rushed out the door and past the bewildered guest and staff. The furniture he had so carefully arranged earlier was now in a complete state of disarray. He immediately cancelled his planned extended stay.

During an investigation by members of the Evergreen Paranormal Group, a number of anomalies were captured on film and video tape. The second floor guest area also produced many variations in the electromagnetic field meters brought along for the investigation, and more than a few chills were experienced by the group on the landing and in the third-floor attic space. The staff refused to talk about the third-floor space or allow entry to it. Some had been shaken by experiences they could not explain in that area.

The staff offered the explanation that the activity was due to Anabelle, a one-time extended guest of the hotel who had received news that her lover, a local miner, had been killed. She committed suicide by hanging herself in room number 9. A medium in attendance at the investigation claimed that her name was Alice and that she still resides in her room, occasionally walking the second-floor corridor. It was in room 9 that the guest who had rearranged the furniture met with an unwelcome site when he returned to his room.

As if the sounds, scents, and unaccounted-for movements of furniture and kitchen utensils were not enough to interest a skeptical guest, the cottage next to the Bush House is full of its own unusual events. Even though it is no longer regularly offered for guest quarters, the investigators were offered a chance to walk through it and visit the small chapel on the second floor that the family maintained. Though no one had been in the cottage recently, a large crucifix appeared to have been thrown across the floor and broken. The hotel staff recounted the story of a group of young skiers who had attempted to stay in the home, only to leave midway into the night with little explanation as to the reason for their departure. A film documentary was also made based around the appearance of two children in the window of the cottage when it was locked and empty.

—Henry Bailey
Independent Investigator,
Conjecture.com

THE OXFORD SALOON & EATERY

913 FIRST STREET
SNOHOMISH, WASHINGTON 98290
TEL: 1 (360) 568-3845
WEBSITE: *www.oxfordsaloon.com*

The Oxford Saloon & Eatery, established in 1910, is one of the oldest restored saloons in the Northwest. Housed in the Oxford Building (built in 1889 as Blackman Dry Goods Store), this fine old place, totally restored in 1992, has the look and feel of an 1880s saloon. There are two floors with original and restored fixtures of the period throughout. The main floor still has the original large, oak back bar.

Now serving fine food and drink, this historic saloon once served the local logger population and was a haven for gambling and the services of local ladies of the night on the second floor.

The Oxford is reputed to be home to no less than eight of its past visitors. Kathleen, the Madame of the upstairs brothel, and Henry, the ghost of a policeman who met his fate by being stabbed in the lower-floor gambling parlor, are two of the more prominent ghosts often making an appearance.

Incidents recorded by the staff have included full-body apparitions, scents of lavender perfume, and continued movement of objects. In at least one case, the apparitions have been so disturbing that one of the cooks refused to venture downstairs alone to retrieve supplies for meals.

The ladies' bathroom is reportedly occupied on occasion by at least one resident spirit who enjoys playing pranks with the customers, and the dance floor often attracts the attention of one of the ghostly patrons who has been known to pinch the rear ends of some of the ladies.

An investigation by the Washington State Ghost Society resulted in a number of EVP recordings, strange photographic phenomena, and unaccounted-for EMF meter readings that were exceptionally high. Both unexplained cold and hot spots were noticed by the researchers during an all-night investigation.

A medium in attendance with the group conducted a séance and stated that the second floor, in particular, still retains the oppressive energies of the ladies who worked in the brothel. While now an antique shop, the second floor has been home to a haunted doll, which has been said to be responsible for a variety of strange phenomena that continue to occur in the shop.

The Oxford has been investigated by numerous paranormal groups in the state and by a number of psychics. It has been featured in local television programs and is perhaps one of the most haunted locations in Washington State.

While it features a menu of fine food and music on one of the most haunted avenues in the state, First Street, in Snohomish, Washington, it attracts many customers in search of one of the many long-deceased visitors to this beautiful old saloon.

—Henry Bailey
Independent Investigator,
Conjecture.com

MURPHY FAMILY FARM
(PRIVATE RESIDENCE)
219 BUNKER HILL ROAD
LONGVIEW, WASHINGTON 98632

Kristie, one of our team's researchers, bought a farmhouse almost four years ago. Little did she know at the time that her life would be forever changed by this house. The farmhouse was rebuilt in 1920 after a fire destroyed the original structure. On the property stands a barn that dates back to the early 1800s. Within a mile of this house lay five different cemeteries dating back to 1800. Could the ghosts who haunt this property be former owners of the house? Or are they restless spirits traveling from the nearby cemeteries? No one knows for sure, but the Southwest Washington Paranormal Research (SWPR) team was called out to investigate this property back in March of 2004.

Since the first week the Murphy family moved in, they noticed strange things happening, such as lightbulbs burning out frequently, and radios and televisions turning on and off by themselves. The family also experienced times of feeling as if they were being watched even though they were alone. At first, the activity was relatively mild but soon turned into something much more sinister. They started to feel not so welcome in their new home. On one occasion, Kristie was coming down the stairs and felt a strong feeling of being pushed as she reached the middle of the stairway—almost causing her to break her foot and tailbone. After she stood up in pain, she walked to the kitchen and saw three figures: a man, a woman, and a teenage girl, all wearing clothes from the 1800s. She thought she might be going crazy and that it was just her imagination until others in the house started to experience the activity. She knew that her house was haunted.

One experience her son had to endure was being pushed out a window by unseen hands—the fall caused him to have a fractured back. The family has reported seeing a lady walking through the hall upstairs and hearing their names being called out when no one is there. Just about everyone who has visited the Murphy Farm has experienced some type of phenomena, whether it be shadows of figures, figures at your bedside, cold spots, or footsteps running up behind you. Visitors claim to feel even more uncomfortable in the barn and office area where there is always a heaviness to the air. Kristie and her sister-in-law, Stacey, decided to start documenting the events that were happening.

Kristie and Stacey contacted SWPR, and we set out to capture all of the paranormal activity that we could. They were soon welcomed as researchers on our team. We have been able to capture some incredible activity on this property including this photo. During a few of our official

Photo by Stacey Green

investigations, we have been able to document cold spots throughout the house and barn area. We have captured electronic voice phenomena and many ectoplasm pictures. Though no EMF readings have been detected, motion detectors have been tripped in the main house. We noted an increase in activity between the hours of 10 p.m. and 4 a.m..

—Kimberlie Travis
President & EVP Specialist, Southwest
Washington Paranormal Research

Rutherglen Mansion
Bed and Breakfast

420 Rutherglen Road
Longview, Washington 98626
Tel: 1 (360) 425-5816
Website: *www.rutherglenmansion.com*

The Rutherglen Mansion sits on top of Mt. Solo in Longview, Washington. It was built for John D. Tennant, vice president of Long-Bell Lumber Co., his wife, and his two children. They moved in on February 1, 1927. Tennant built and managed the lumber mill, which was Longview's first industry.

Tennant died in 1949 and the family sold the mansion. It served as a nursing home for 18 years. In 1972, Reuben Grendahl bought the mansion for his family. After the death of Reuben's wife, the Grendahls moved across the driveway to the carriage house. He then rented the house out and it became a girl's home and eventually a meeting spot for a church. In 1994, it became a restaurant and bed and breakfast that offers not only a hospitable atmosphere but a haunted one as well. Countless stories pass amongst employees as well as guests about sounds, sightings, and frequent cold spots throughout the house. It is said to be haunted by an old lady named "Alice" who is seen frequently sitting at a window looking out. Also there are rumors that a bride and groom who were once married there haunt the place. No evidence supports any bride and groom dying at the property that we could find. But the mansion was a nursing home for 18 years, and that might explain the old lady who they call "Alice."

On a prior visit, Southwest Washington Paranormal Research (SWPR) researcher Kim Travis actually witnessed a portrait fly off of a fireplace mantel. With all of this in mind, the SWPR team decided to return to Rutherglen Mansion for another investigation.

For our investigation, we decided to use digital photography, EMF detectors, thermal scanners, and various recording devices. We also had several video recorders monitoring locations where paranormal activity had been reported.

One of the first paranormal occurrences happened as two of our team members were investigating the private dining room. While one was sitting near the fireplace, the other noticed that the fireplace tools were rocking gently in their holder. The team tried to recreate the event by having other people sit in the same chair, but nothing happened, although many pictures containing orb anomalies were captured in this area. All of the researchers felt as though unseen eyes throughout this investigation were watching them.

—Kimberlie Travis and
Christine Bridges
Southwest Washington
Paranormal Research

PORT GAMBLE

KITSAP PENINSULA—1 MILE EAST OF THE HOOD CANAL BRIDGE ON HIGHWAY 104
PORT GAMBLE, WASHINGTON
WEBSITE: *www.experiencewashington.com/ City_C178.html*

In 1853, Port Gamble was formerly named after Lt. Robert Gamble, who was wounded in the War of 1812. The location also inspired Andrew Pope and William C. Talbot of the Pope and Talbot Company of San Francisco to establish an industry here. Both men were exploring the Northwest looking for a site for a sawmill to supply the lumber needs of California, and Port Gamble was the ideal location for their needs.

Captain Josiah P. Keller, who was part of the Pope and Talbot Company, later arrived in Port Gamble with his family and the necessary machinery to start the Puget Sound Mill Company in 1853. When the mill closed in 1995, it was the oldest continuously operating sawmill in the United

States. But Port Gamble's legacy lives on, and the community thrives knowing its history has been preserved.

Many of the community members who helped build Port Gamble are still there today in spirit and continue to make their presences known to the modern-day residents and visitors. From the woman who greets people from her third-floor window at the Walker-Ames House, to the stage manager who overlooks many of the activities that needed to be done at the community hall and theatre—many souls of the past are still here.

James A. Thompson still occupies the Thompson House. He was a sawyer from Maine who built the first part of the house in 1859. Evergreen Paranormal's sensitive, Maureen Nelson, received a clear impression of James upstairs during our group's preliminary walk-through of the house. Nelson was taken back one evening when she saw a photo of Mr. Thompson months after first encountering him—it was the same man she saw in her impression.

Other public buildings in town also have experienced supernatural phenomena, such as the general store, where under the store a male's voice was recorded,
though no one (living) was around who could have spoken the words. Events such as these remind people who work there and visit that although the years continue on, these ghosts remain.

Evergreen Paranormal was able to document some interesting EVP on audio tape as well as some on digital video. There are several video segments of orb movement, and one interesting account of Maureen Nelson sensing the presence of a woman in one of the buildings in town. Then, within seconds of recording, some paranormal mist moved from left to right on video. In the basement of this same building, Nelson asked if there was anyone in the building who wished to speak to us, and several seconds later, a male voice said, "Yes." There were no men in the building during that time. The group did find that moon phases seemed to play a part on the level of haunting activity— seemingly, such activity doesn't happen during new moons.

Port Gamble is located on the Northeast corner of the Olympic Mountain range and overlooks the Hood Canal Bridge.

—Maureen Nelson
Evergreen Paranormal Group

Alaska/ Hawaii

Alaska/Hawaii

Alaska

THE ALASKAN HOTEL

167 SOUTH FRANKLIN STREET
JUNEAU, ALASKA 99810
TEL: 1 (800) 327-9347
WEBSITE: *www.ptialaska.net/~akhotel/ index.html*

In Alaska's capital city of Juneau, one of the oldest buildings in town is also the most haunted. The three-story, 46-guest-room Alaskan Hotel was built in 1913 by James and John McCloskey, and entrepreneur Jules B. Caro. Juneau was a city that needed to grow quickly in order to accommodate the many miners who came to the area in hopes of striking it rich during the Alaskan gold rush. Originally a hotel and bordello, the establishment is Juncau's longest-running hotel, and in its early days, it was a place for miners to spend some of the gold

Photo by Jeff Belanger

they worked so hard to find. It's with one of these early miners that the ghostly legends of the Alaskan Hotel begin.

According to local lore, in the early days of the inn, a miner and his new bride came to Juneau and stayed at the hotel. The miner told his bride he would be gone for three weeks while he worked some of the mines in the mountains and streams of the area. Three weeks came and went, and when her husband didn't return, the woman found herself almost out of money. Faced with being forced out into the street, she turned to prostitution in order to survive. The story goes that her husband returned a few weeks later and was so furious at his bride for what she had done that he murdered her in one of the rooms of the hotel.

No matter the lore, the ghostly encounters have been happening for many years. Scott Fry, a local musician, was the manager of the Alaskan Hotel for 12 years. Fry said, "Room 218. I used to get people saying, 'She's in my room.' I've had people tell me that she was touching them, or they could see her sitting on the bed. A friend of mine told me if you walk up the top of the stairs, you could see her in the mirror by [room] 308. I've also had people tell me she was in the bar coming down the stairs. The bar has a lot of mirrors in it, and it's easy to see things out of the corner of your eye, especially if you're tired."

Dan Ward has worked at the Alaskan Hotel off and on since 1974. Though he's never personally experienced anything supernatural here, he has heard accounts from some of the staff at the hotel. He said, "Housekeepers used to always say there's one particular room where things would get moved around. They'd put towels someplace and come back five minutes later and they'd be somewhere else. I actually had a desk clerk one time who had just started—he was working the graveyard shift. He was sitting at the desk reading a book and you know how you kind of sense somebody walking up to you? He did that, and he looked up and he just got this image of a blond girl in a white dress. But when he actually got his head up there, there was nobody there."

—Jeff Belanger
Founder, Ghostvillage.com

Hawaii

USS ARIZONA

PEARL HARBOR, HAWAII
WEBSITE: *www.nps.gov/usar/*

The sunken hull of this once-mighty battleship is now a monument. A few bits of it are near the waterline, all rusting metal and twisted steel. Attached to the deck is the flagpole that never lowered her banner to the enemy. Below the waterline, the hull still holds the mortal remains of the crew. The *USS Arizona* has been a tomb since the morning of December 7, 1941, when she was hit by a Japanese bomb. The hull still leaks oil from her bunkers even after all these decades. It is as if the ship is still bleeding her life fluids. The many who visit the modernistic memorial built on pillars astride the broken hull are silent for the most part, respectful of this place. More than a few feel that the place is haunted. The story of the ghost is a U.S. Navy yarn told to me long ago by a Chief petty officer. It has its roots in World War II. Then, as now, the warships entering and leaving Pearl Harbor pause and salute the sunken battlewagon. Some say the ship was cursed from the start. When she was launched, a bottle of water was used to christen her rather than wine or spirits. It was a politically correct move at the time, but old salt-water sailors knew that nothing good could happen by not following the traditions of the sea.

The story goes that on the morning of the attack, the officer of the deck wasn't at his post. He was distracted and for personal reasons left his station for a few moments. It was in his absence that the

Japanese planes made their surprise sortie. The officer died in the blast that killed the ship and sent her to the shallow bottom of the harbor. The unfortunate guilt-ridden man now haunts the ship, walking the deck at low tide and looking out near the flagpole. He haunts the wreck at night and is seen in the dim light of dawn. They say that when you take pictures at the monument, many times odd things happen on the film. Orbs appear on film, there are foggy spots, and every once and a while a misty shadow is seen lurking in the background of the photograph.

—Richard Senate
Psychic Investigator/Author,
Carson Valley Ghost Stalkers

USS ARIZONA

Western Canada

Western Canada

British Columbia

ROEDDE HOUSE HERITAGE MUSEUM

1415 BARCLAY STREET
VANCOUVER, BRITISH COLUMBIA V6G 1J6
TEL: 1 (604) 684-7040
WEBSITE: www.roeddehouse.org

Distant ghosts glide by as you gaze at this beautiful heritage home in Vancouver's West End, and you're drawn back to a time when apartments were non-existent and homes such as this dotted the neighborhood— a time when life was simple and families were close.

Built in 1893, this Queen Anne, with towers, gables, balconies, chimneys, and large bay windows, sits unassumingly. Clapboard siding gave the house its distinct character, and it was rumored

vancouverparanormal.com]. gregory

Photo by Jan Gregory

that the famous architect of the time, Francis M. Rattenbury, built the home. The garden features a gazebo where ladies held afternoon teas on beautiful days.

Gustav and Mathilda Roedde moved into the home with their six children and three Saint Bernards shortly after the construction was complete.

Life was grand, and Mrs. Roedde was a fine cook and baker. From family accounts, the smells of baking permeated the house. Aromas of cinnamon, spices, fresh baked bread, and apple pie were everywhere.

Amid all this happiness, tragedy was also a part of the family's story.

Anna Henrietta, the first of the six children, died at the age of 5 after eating poisonous berries. After her death, Mathilda was arrested and charged with poisoning her daughter. In time, the courts found her not guilty, but that did not alleviate the heartbreak of losing Anna.

Another tragedy shook the family in 1925 when another child, Anna Catherine,

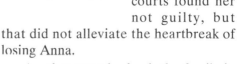

was killed while on duty at St. Paul's Hospital. On that fateful day, one of the other nurses asked Anna if she would switch shifts. Anna was agreeable, but this decision cost her. A mental patient mistook Anna for the other nurse and stabbed her to death.

Christmas Day was Anna Catherine's birthday. Every Christmas afterward was met with sadness over the loss of another beloved child. To this day, the name "Anna" is not used in the house due to the tragic deaths of the two Annas.

Vancouver Paranormal had the privilege of entering the Roedde House and seeing for ourselves how the family lived. The furnishings are late-19th century, and each room is divided with a receiving room complete with piano and fireplace. From the entranceway, a beautiful staircase leads up the bedrooms, a sewing room, and then continues up to the tower. The rooms are small by today's comparison, but warm.

Going through the rooms of the house, you feel that someone is watching you and you almost "hear" the family going about their activities. Cold spots float past, and some rooms are dark and feel occupied. The staff often feel watched when they attend to their duties. The bedrooms are silent, occupied only by mannequins in ancient clothing reflected in hazy mirrors. In the hallway, the very faint smell of spices can be detected. Can it be that Mathilda is still baking something for her family to enjoy? Or perhaps the tantalizing smell of cinnamon and cloves was simply imagined by this ghost hunter.

—Kathy Zuccolo
Vancouver Paranormal

FAIRACRES/BURNABY ART GALLERY

6344 DEER LAKE AVENUE
BURNABY, BRITISH COLUMBIA V5G 2J3
PHONE: 1 (604) 205-7332
WEBSITE: *www.city.burnaby.bc.ca/
cityhall/departments_parks/
prksrc_fclts_gllrya.html*

The stories at what is now Burnaby Art Gallery abound about a woman who casts a pale blue light. Some claim to feel sadness when beholding the quiet figure as she glides about the silent halls. But still there are unquiet rumors of a vicious and vengeful apparition. Could this apparition belong to Mrs. Grace Ceperley, the original owner of the house? She's been depicted in recent televised programs as a woman who chased all and sundry out of the house, but was she simply a woman in love with her home and not wanting to leave it?

Photo by Jan Gregory

Fairacres is situated on the northwest slopes of Deer Lake in Burnaby, British Columbia. Its English countryside style is oddly at home amidst the cedars and pines of Canada's west-coast rainforest.

Standing at Fairacres, one feels awe and certainly the presence of someone within, quietly watching—perhaps passing the upper windows, momentarily pausing, and wondering about us below.

Prior to the city of Burnaby purchasing this fine old home to serve as a gallery, no accounts of hauntings had ever been reported, though certainly the estate has had its share of colorful residents. Several families have called the mansion home, including a Catholic group of missionary monks who had a rectory within these old, vine-covered walls. The most remarkable group residing here was a religious cult calling themselves "Temple of the More Abundant Life," but they were finally ousted when reports of abuse and other complaints began to surface. None of these claims were ever legally validated.

It was after the home was converted to a gallery that reports started happening. People reported seeing a woman in pale blue moving about the hall. Marisa Ferrari, one of the office staff, heard monastic chanting and saw a bright white flash of light near the foyer where she worked. Caterers reported seeing the apparition of a young girl at the top of the inner stairwell, and the Vancouver Paranormal team experienced a large, crackling blue flash while in that very stairwell.

Coat hangers have been flung about the kitchen floor during a brief time when the staff were called to another room. Loud crashes have been reported without cause, and doors have jammed and locked. Without fail, whenever the gallery seems to be too loud from one activity or another, the fire sprinklers turn on. Workmen in the lower basement have reported that their laid-out tools were replaced on their hooks while their backs were merely turned.

Playful pranks or malevolent menace? Maybe you should visit the home and ascertain this for yourself. Having been through the entire house with gadgets and gears, we can tell you it is certainly haunted. The attic alone will transport you back decades, and the old smells are like perfume to the enthusiastic ghost hunter. Mrs. Ceperley seems to be no avenging wraith, no harridan of evil, but a quiet spirit who simply loves her home.

—Jan Gregory
Founder, Vancouver Paranormal

THE VOGUE THEATRE

918 GRANVILLE STREET
VANCOUVER, BRITISH COLUMBIA
TEL: 1 (604) 331-7900
WEBSITE: *www.voguetheatre.com*

Built in 1941, the Vogue Theatre was the hottest ticket in Vancouver. With nouveau art deco and acoustics, it soon became the place to go for one's entertainment dollar. Canadian and international stars of the day were all seen parading across its stage. Dramas and dance numbers, Broadway musicals, and one-man shows were all housed at the Vogue. All of the best-known entertainers of the period performed there, displaying their craft to enthusiastic audiences and, rumor has it, some remain to this day.

The main theater section features rows of plush, red seats, and ornate wooden carvings hearken back to a time of Vaudeville and stage drama. Row upon row of chairs sit like silent sentinels in the dark thick air of the theater, and the balcony box windows seem blind and gaping.

Though the Vogue Theatre is old by Vancouver's standards, perhaps others may consider the building not old enough for tales of ghosts, phantoms, and specters to take hold. Perhaps people would only believe in spirits finding a home in a location after centuries have passed? Maybe, but it seemed that from the start, odd things have been happening in the Vogue.

The earliest stories were about a young woman who may have been an actress forced to suicide by the rejection of her lover. Pregnant, alone, and unwanted, this young woman ended her life and returns to the theater to haunt the lower dressing room located under the stage. Wispy, shadowy entities are seen from time to time in the projector room. A strange, dark male image sits in there, sometimes alone, and sometimes with other spectral figures. The smells of alcohol and cigars have also been known to fill the air.

There are stories of empty chairs filling with misty forms, and distant laughter and applause have also been heard. On more than one occasion, ethereal actors move across the dusty stage. An encore from beyond?

Both patrons and employees have claimed to come across these unknown spirits who haunt the Vogue. From Vancouver Paranormal's investigations inside the theater, we have experienced the thick, unrelenting air which, like an invisible net, makes walking difficult. We have heard disembodied voices that seem to call out, but no one is there. We have also seen dark shapes gliding past, glimpsed quickly from the corner of our vision.

The washrooms downstairs also seem to have a "Peeping Tom" kind of spirit, who seems to enjoy scaring and spooking both men and women alike. An e-mail we received from one patron claimed to have been using the washroom, and beside him another gentleman was peering into the mirror and combing his hair. The patron was astonished to see the fully developed apparitional image slowly fade away, and the washroom became intensely cold.

—Jan Gregory
Founder, Vancouver Paranormal

DEAD MAN'S ISLAND

HMCS DISCOVERY (CANADIAN NAVAL BASE)
1200 STANLEY PARK DRIVE
VANCOUVER, BRITISH COLUMBIA V6G 3E2

North from Vancouver's downtown core, you approach a scenic location known as Stanley Park, and snuggled deep in cedar trees with the Pacific Ocean as a backdrop is the home of *HMCS Discovery*. This Canadian naval base has been in existence since 1943, but the island where it stands has been used by a series of First Nations people since pre-history. The island has a long, spooky, and chilling history of sacrifice and slaughter. Rumors about strange lights, weird moaning chants, and spectral figures roaming about were whispered at night when the settlers went to bed.

And now the small, pretty island where the *HMCS Discovery* is berthed is aptly named "Dead Man's Island."

Legend has it that in the 1700s, two tribes, the Northern and the Southern Salish people, were at war, and during one bitter battle, the Southern tribe took women, children, and elders hostage.

These hostages were marked for certain death. So it came about that the Northern tribes surrendered, hoping for a peaceful exchange, but they were cruelly slaughtered and more than 200 Northern warriors died.

Through time, because of the horrific acts, the island became known as a poisoned land or a land of enchantment, and then these stories were forgotten. It then became a burial place, first for the Salish First Nations and then for the new European settlers. Pioneers described how eerie the island looked, with its small cedar fences surrounding old burial mounds like ragged headboards jutting out of the ground and piercing the rain forest fog, forever marking its occupants' final sleep. It's a lonely, uneasy, disquieting place.

Once the Europeans came, the Salish people were pushed away from this mysterious pocket of land. The Europeans moved in and used the grounds for their own cemetery purposes, often disturbing the native dead. Among the dead buried on the island, aside from God-fearing pioneers, were the scoundrels and dregs of Vancouver's earlier community. Seamen suicides, Canadian Pacific Railway construction casualties, Chinese lepers, prostitutes, bandits, and other ruffians who fought each other in the grills and saloons of Gastown (Vancouver's original name)

were also buried there. Victims of the Great Vancouver Fire and smallpox epidemic all ended up in the wet, mossy, and muddy soil of Dead Man's Island.

In 1887, Mountain View Cemetery was finally built, and the burials on the island came to a stop. But then, when it got dark, the stories began.

Strange tales of screams have been reported coming from the island. The sounds are described as inhuman screams that make the blood turn cold. Others have reported seeing a fluorescent glow on the island, twisting and writhing as though in great agony and then changing into a human form. There have been spectral shapes seen moving in the fog, with red, glowing eyes and voices like broken glass, hissing out names of those who would disturb their sleep. And in this forest graveyard with vines covered in deep jade-colored moss, where souls lie in broken rest and reportedly still walk in the night, the *HMCS Discovery* sits.

—Jan Gregory and Kathy Zuccolo
Vancouver Paranormal

DEAD MAN'S ISLAND

Central Canada

Central Canada

Alberta

THE GUILTY MARTINI

10338-81 AVENUE
EDMONTON, ALBERTA T6E 1X2
TEL: 1 (780) 433-7183

The Guilty Martini is housed in a very nondescript brick building in the heart of Old Strathcona—a trendy area in Edmonton. Built at the turn of the century, the building used to be a carriage house at one time. It was originally owned by W.J. Scott and Sons, and horse-drawn carriages were constructed in the main floor of the building while the family lived upstairs. In the 1950s, it was an apartment building, and at the turn of the 21st century, the building has gone through many businesses, each with rumors of ghostly activity.

Photo by Rona Anderson

The main culprit of the ghostly activity is a specter called "Dapper Dan." It isn't known who this person was in life, but what is known is that he is mischievous and does not enjoy the "nightclub scene" with the loud music and drinking.

A lot of activity happens when the staff is first setting up for the nightclub's customers. Staff have reported that their shoulders have been touched and hair pulled. Ashtrays have been pushed off edges of tables, and liquor bottles and glasses rearrange themselves and clank together. Lights go on and off with no one touching the switch, and there are inexplicable extreme drops in temperature. In the upstairs lounge area, staff have seen a distinct outline of a person behind a curtain when no one was there, and black shadows going across the wall. One woman saw a shadowy image shaped like a big man in a lumber jacket come toward her. Two men were having a conversation when a black wraith-like shadow passed between, startling them both.

What has unnerved many have been the sounds of a person going up and down the stairs and walking around the upstairs floor when no one was found to be up there. One waitress saw a man's arm come through the cigarette machine and reach out to grab her! A club manager had thought she was alone after hours in the bathroom, when suddenly the stall door slammed shut on her.

There is a staircase starting from the west end of the upstairs lounge that goes to the rooftop. Reports of "unsettling feelings" and dark shadows have come from the stairwell. On one investigation, we took a picture in the stairwell, and a huge, cloudy vortex was caught on camera, floating horizontally across the stairs. Audio recordings were taken in the upstairs lounge as well as the stairwell to the roof, and on it are several short growls as well as one distinct animal *roar* in reply to, "Can you give me a sign that you exist in this building?" When asked, "Is it possible to see you at all?" the response was a very clear man's voice responding, "Yes."

On a good night, you just might be able to catch "Dapper Dan" leaning over the balcony, scowling at the nightclub patrons.

—Rona Anderson
Paranormal Investigator/Psychic,
Paranormal Explorers

FORT EDMONTON PARK
70000-143 STREET
EDMONTON, ALBERTA
TEL: 1 (780) 496-8787

Renovating a house can bring out both contractors and entities. Can you imagine what happens when buildings from different parts of the country are uprooted and transported together to one site? One of Edmonton's famous historical tourist attractions and Canada's largest living history park has haunted buildings throughout it.

Fort Edmonton Park represents four historical periods in Edmonton's history: the 1846 fur trade fort, and the streets of 1885, 1905, and 1920. In 1966, the fort was reconstructed (after being demolished in 1915). The fort itself contains various inner buildings and structures. Buildings were found from the four different eras and brought into the park. The uprooting and reconstruction of the structures have stirred up some ghostly happenings in the park.

Photo by Rona Anderson

Just before Halloween 2003, our group, accompanied by a local news photographer and a reporter, went to Fort Edmonton to spend most of the night in the Firkins house. Dr. Ashley Firkins originally owned the house, which was built in 1912. In 1992, the house was donated to the park. He was an Edmonton dentist and had a wife and son. As far as history shows, no one had actually died in the house.

Upstairs in the children's bedroom, the photographer captured an amazing purple-colored figure beside one of our group's members on the bed—he could not explain, technically, how it showed up on his camera. There was a definite presence of a small boy with a red ball in the house, but nothing overly negative or threatening was sensed.

In the study/sitting area, one particular piece of furniture seems to attract ghostly pictures. A female visage shows up in the middle of the bookcase, and an orb we captured with our camera appeared in the window and had a male face inside of it.

The rest of the park is just as haunted as the Firkins house. As it gets dark, up and down the different streets you can feel energies watching you out of the windows. Talking to the staff who work there, stories of unexplained thumps, footsteps, and the feeling something is behind you are very common. It's a fascinating place to go to see life the way it was during Edmonton's history.

—Rona Anderson
Paranormal Investigator/Psychic,
Paranormal Explorers

THE CHARLES CAMSELL HOSPITAL
12804 - 114TH AVENUE T5M 3A4
EDMONTON, ALBERTA

The existing Charles Camsell Hospital was built in 1967 and closed its doors in 1996. The original part of the building housed a tuberculosis sanatorium in the 1950s, mainly looking after aboriginal patients. Some people were forcibly placed into the hospital, and patients with certain "defects" were involuntarily sterilized. In 1982, a young man working on the roof fell to his death. The hospital has seen more than its share of the dark and tragic side of human suffering.

Sitting abandoned since 1996, the building gives off a haunted impression, and people walking by say they can feel many eyes looking out at them from the hospital windows. There are Satanic symbols and graffiti on the walls, and parts of the hospital are in slow decay. The setting absolutely invites ghost hunters to come in.

The fourth floor of the hospital housed the psychiatric wing. The patient isolation rooms and rumors of shock treatments make it a hot spot for confused and earthbound spirits. On video camera and a digital recorder, an anguished female scream was caught by our group on the fourth

Photo by Rona Anderson

floor, and it was verified that it did not belong to anyone in the investigation group. A major psychic impression picked up in the psychiatric wing was of a teenage girl, extremely distraught, pulling out her nails, which left her with bloody hands. She was waiting for her parents and kept repeating, "When are they coming to get me?"

On the second floor is the surgical wing, and blood stains are still on the floor in one room. We captured a male voice on our recorder in Operating Room 6 calling out "Karen" and some unearthly groans. The most startling audio was something "slamming" its hand down hard on the metal shelf we had left the recorder on. Seconds after that, the recorder shut off.

In the auditorium, we tried to communicate with whatever entities resided there, and everyone with a camera caught at least one picture with orbs floating in it. A psychic impression given in the auditorium was of a very sad, older aboriginal man with mobility problems looking for his wife. Our recorder caught this spirit lamenting, "We did not choose to be here."

Down in the morgue area, an elevator decided to start operating on its own. Footsteps above us on different floors were heard walking with a very loud clomp. The hospital is very active with unseen patients walking around.

At the time of this writing, the hospital is up for sale. The future of the building will probably entail being torn down or renovated for other purposes. The new tenants will surely be sharing the space with the previous "tenants."

—Rona Anderson
Paranormal Investigator/Psychic,
Paranormal Explorers

THE DEANE HOUSE

FORT CALGARY
806 9TH AVENUE SE
CALGARY, ALBERTA
TEL: 1 (403) 269-7747
WEBSITE: *www.fortcalgary.com/ deane.htm*

Fort Calgary was built in 1875 at the junction of the Bow and Elbow Rivers because the region had become a haven for whiskey traders and outlaws. The North-West Mounted Police were charged with establishing order here because rail lines were being laid, opening up vast regions of Canada to trade and settlement. The area grew up quickly into the city of Calgary. In 1906, the fort's superintendent, Captain Richard Deane, felt the living quarters weren't suitable for his wife, Martha. For the eyebrow-raising sum of $6,200, Captain Deane had a stately home built at the fort. He called the home: "Certainly the best house in Mounted Police occupancy at that date." Martha would never step foot in the house. She died of illness before she could move in. The fort closed in 1914, and the land was bought by the Grand Trunk Pacific Railway—they tore down all of the buildings except for the Deane House. The house became the station agent's quarters, and the building was relocated to the southeast corner of the property. In 1929, the house was sold to C.L. Jacques, a local entrepreneur who had the building moved again, this time across the Elbow River to the opposite bank, where it would become a boarding house. From 1933 to 1968, the house saw many dark days. There was a suicide in the attic, as well as a murder/suicide that occurred when a husband stabbed his wife to death and then took his own life as their children watched in horror. Two others dicd of natural causes in the building, and there are two unconfirmed reports of other murders that took place, one on the front steps.

In the 1980s, the building became a part of the Fort Calgary–preserved historic site. Today the Deane House is a restaurant with many haunted legends inside.

One common apparition spotted at the Deane House is an old native man with long, black braids who has been seen in the basement of the house. The apparition told one woman, "You shouldn't be here, this site is sacred," and then he faded away.

Bob Pearson, the interpretation coordinator for Fort Calgary said, "There was an old telephone that wasn't connected to anything. Not only is it not connected, I've discovered there's nothing inside it—it doesn't have any inner workings. Some people reported that they could hear the phone ring. They go in and try and answer it, and of course there was no one there."

Others have claimed to smell cigar smoke, hear voices, and an antique piano located on the second floor has been known to play when no one is supposed to be in the room. One of the workers will walk up the stairs to investigate, only to hear the music stop as they approach the top of the stairs. When they open the door to the room with the piano, there is no one there.

A scared staff member once reported seeing a dark apparition come down the stairs inside the house. The employee noticed this man had no legs below the knees. The ghost floated right by the staff member toward the door and dissipated into nothing.

—Jeff Belanger
Founder, Ghostvillage.com

EMPRESS THEATRE

235 MAIN STREET
FORT MACLEOD, ALBERTA T0L 0Z0
TEL: 1 (800) 540-9229
WEBSITE: *www.empresstheatre.ab.ca*

Many performers at the Empress Theatre have claimed to look out into the audience during rehearsals or performances and see a hairy-armed character sitting in the balcony. At a second glance, the ghostly man whom they call "Ed, the Phantom of the Empress" disappears.

J.S. Lambert began construction on his franchise of the Famous Players theater chain in 1910 on the now-historic Main Street of Fort Macleod. The first part of the 20th century was a time of rapid growth for the city. Lambert's theater would serve as the stage for vaudeville, concerts, lectures, live theater, and, eventually, moving pictures. In 1937, the theater was sold to Daniel Boyle, who made some significant renovations to the building—adding a balcony and moving the projection booth above the new balcony. He also made decorative enhancements such as updated light fixtures, window covers, and light-up neon tulips on the pressed-tin ceiling in honor of his wife.

The ghostly legends of the theater begin in the 1950s when a janitor who worked there as his second job died under mysterious circumstances at the local auction market. Locals say they smelled his phantom cigar smoke in the theater for many years after his death. Stories circulated of seeing the hairy-armed man in the bathroom mirror only to turn around and find him gone.

After Boyle's 1937 renovations, the theater wasn't touched again until 1982, when the Fort Macleod Provincial Historic Area Society took over the building.

EMPRESS THEATRE

Forty-five years of customers, performances, popcorn and candy fights, and sug-
ary treat spillage wore heavily on the
building. The Historic Area Society poured
$1 million into renovating the theater back
to its original splendor. The ghost encounters continued throughout the renovations
and after they were completed.

Diana Segboer was born and raised in
Fort Macleod, as were her parents.
Segboer has worked in various capacities
at the Empress Theatre including the role
of general manager. Her first personal encounter happened in the early 1990s, when
she was taking the concession booth inven-
tory while the theater was closed. "I walked
in through the lobby and went around into
the concession booth," she said. "I heard
some footsteps coming up the staircase,
and I thought '*Hmmm, I thought I was
alone, but hey, maybe Mike* [another theater employee] *was in the building*.' The
footsteps kept coming and kept coming,
and pretty soon I heard them right beside
me and then they stopped. And you could
feel the air just change—it went from regular air to almost frigid air. I just put down
my notepad that I was writing on and I
walked out the front door."

During her years of employment at the
theater, other unexplained phenomena,
such as footsteps or even hearing someone whistling a tune only to find no one
there, almost became commonplace. But
her most profound encounter happened in
the balcony. The theater has pretty standard theater seats that fold up to allow
more aisle access between rows, but these
seats are not spring-loaded. When the
seats are up they stay up, and when they're
down, they stay down…usually. Segboer
said, "I was upstairs in the balcony and was

putting the seats up, and in the next row,
the row that I had just finished, they were
coming down as fast as I was putting them
up. One by one."

*—Jeff Belanger
Founder, Ghostvillage.com*

Manitoba

THE FORT GARRY HOTEL
222 BROADWAY AVENUE
WINNIPEG, MANITOBA R3C 0R3
TEL: 1 (204) 942-8251
WEBSITE: *www.fortgarryhotel.com*

Built in 1913, the Fort Garry Hotel is a
majestic, 14-story, chateau-style structure that is both a national landmark and
beacon of pride in the Winnipeg skyline.
But beneath the opulent façade, and back
in the hotel's history, lie some tragedies
and some ghosts.

The Grand Trunk Pacific Railway built
a fort in 1911 where their east and west
lines joined. The company then built the
hotel to offer plush accommodations to
luxury railway passengers. For many years,
the first landmark rail riders saw as they
approached Winnipeg was the Fort Garry
Hotel.

The hotel has experienced and survived floods and even a major fire, and
today the building represents the spirit of
the city—and some of that spirit seems
intent on staying around forever.

The second floor is said to be the most
haunted, and room 202 is the epicenter of
activity. Sebastian Ritchie was over from
England staying at the hotel on business

in November 2003. Ritchie said, "I was staying in thc infamous room 202. At the time, I knew absolutely nothing of its spooky reputation whatsoever. In the early hours of the morning of November 20, I woke to see, by a crack of streetlight filtering in between the curtains, the outline of a figure standing at the end of my bed. I could barely make out more than the haggard silhouette of the head, and the shape of the body, clad in some kind of robe or cloak. I was literally petrified but, after a time, the figure dissolved into nothing, and I assumed it had been a trick of the light or an optical illusion.

"On my last day at the hotel, on leaving the breakfast room, I got into the elevator with a couple of other guests and pressed the number 2 button. 'Have you seen a ghost?' A woman asked me. 'No, why, should I have seen one?' I replied, and she said, 'The second floor's supposed to be haunted.' On checking out later that morning, I asked one of the staff at the front desk about the haunting, and he grinned back at me and said, 'Actually, it's not just the second floor. Room 202 is one of the rooms that is supposed to be haunted."

Dark figures are the most prominent sighting at the hotel, though a ghostly woman in a ball gown and strange ghost light that glides down the halls of the hotel have also been reported.

—Jeff Belanger
Founder, Ghostvillage.com

Ontario

THE OLDE ANGEL INN

224 REGENT STREET
NIAGARA-ON-THE-LAKE, ONTARIO L0S 1J0
TEL: 1 (905) 468-3411
WEBSITE: *www.angel-inn.com*

According to local Niagara-on-the-Lake tales, Captain Colin Swayzc of the British Army was staying at the inn that was to become the Olde Angel during the War of 1812. In late May of 1813, United States forces captured Fort George and the surrounding area. British soldiers retreated, except Captain Swayze. Swayze stopped by the inn to see the innkeeper's daughter, with whom he'd fallen in love. The American troops were closing in, burning the buildings as they routed out the British forces. Swayze hid in one of the large wooden beer barrels in the basement, but the Americans found him and shot him. Before leaving, they burned the inn to the ground. But Captain Swayze's story doesn't end here.

In 1815, John Ross rebuilt the inn and renamed it the Sign of the Angel Inn as a loving gesture to his wife. According to a newspaper clipping quoted by the current owners of the inn, the ghost stories started as early as 1820.

Today the Olde Angel Inn looks a lot like it did almost two centuries ago—hand-cut beams adorn the first-floor ceiling, and plank floors resonate with every step inside. And according to the current owners, some of those resonating footsteps belong to Captain Swayze.

The inn has been in the Ling family since March 1992. According to Samantha

Ling, the Olde Angel Inn's general manager, several guests have reported ghostly occurrences over the years that she admits are too similar to dismiss. Many guests have claimed to see Captain Swayze at eye level while they were in their beds in the inn. Ling said, "They wake up, and he is by their bed—like he's come up through the floor. So he's sort of at eye level with them, and his feet are still below the floor. He appears to them, but as soon as they start to sit up, he disappears."

The staff have also had their share of strange encounters. One night, the bar manager was cleaning up after closing when he heard footsteps in the dining area. He feared someone had just broken in, so he ran into the room to see who it was. No one was there, but curiously, all of the silverware on the tables was scattered.

Today, the British Union Jack flag flies over the inn, but not just because it's an English pub—the British colors also fly to appease Captain Colin Swayze. Captain Swayze may still hold a grudge over his untimely death to this day. It's been said that kegs of American beer often malfunction at the bar, while the kegs filled with British and Canadian ales work properly.

—Jeff Belanger
Founder, Ghostvillage.com

THE HERMITAGE RUINS

ANCASTER, ONTARIO
TEL: 1 (905) 529-4327
WEBSITE: *www.hauntedhamilton.com/ local_hermitage.html*

From the depths of the Dundas Valley emerges a beautiful tale of love lost at the Hermitage Ruins in Ancaster,

Ontario. The town itself is very rich in history and is the third oldest community in Ontario, the other two being Kinston and Niagara-on-the-Lake. The land surrounding the Hermitage Ruins have been connected with much folklore and legend, and people from all over Canada have heard the stories that surround this historic site. Disembodied voices are said to be heard by the sensitive visitor. If you listen very carefully, you can hear the death all around you. Some say that pain, suffering, sadness, and death echo forever like a lost soul trapped in time.

The first owner of this alluring land was Reverend George Sheed of Presbyterian faith, who came to Ancaster in 1830. He bought the land that same year and had a small, humble home built soon after. The home was then sold to Colonel Otto Ives, who immigrated to Canada from Greece as a result of eloping with the daughter of a high-ranking dignitary. Along with them, they brought her niece. Twenty-two years later, the land was sold to George Leith, who financed the building of a new two-story mansion on the property. The house was then bought by his youngest daughter, Alma Dick-Lauder, who continued to live on the property until 1942—even after several fires devastated the home to its

Photo by Stephanie Lechniak-Cumerlato

current state of ruins. The ruins were eventually transferred over to the City of Hamilton, and plans were made to secure the falling stones and preserve it as a tourist attraction.

The Hermitage, along with the strip of road called Lover's Lane, has its own elusive and enduring ghost story. In the late 1800s, a coachman named William Black lived on the property and caught the eye of Colonel Otto Ives's niece. A torrid love affair blossomed between the two, and when William Black approached her uncle to ask permission to marry his niece, Otto Ives became enraged and denied it. The coachman, distressed and heartbroken, headed to the back of the property and hung himself from the wooden rafters of the carriage house. When Otto Ives found William's dangling body, he immediately cut it down and buried it at a nearby crossroads, which is now known as Lover's Lane. To this day, local lore states that on the night of a full moon, you can catch a glimpse of William Black walking between the carriage house and the ruins, calling out and grieving for his lost love.

Glowing corpses that sink into the ground, a woman walking on a no-longer-existing second floor of the building, and seeing the ruins of the mansion completely back to its former glory—glowing candlelight and all—are only a few of the reported sightings that haunt this obscure land. Founding Partner of Haunted Hamilton Daniel Cumerlato believes he experienced firsthand the ghosts of William Black and his beloved, walking as dark silhouettes, arm in arm, toward the trees, then vanishing into thin air. Ghost walks are conducted regularly at this location, where you can hear many more haunted

tales on eerie, moonlit nights. Perhaps you might want to partake in them one evening—unless, of course, you're afraid of the shadows that lurk in the trees!

—Stephanie Lechniak-Cumerlato
Founding Partner,
HauntedHamilton.com

BATTLEFIELD HOUSE MUSEUM
77 KING STREET WEST
STONEY CREEK, ONTARIO L8G 1H9
WEBSITE: *www.battlefieldhouse.ca*

To date, strange and interesting reports have circulated about the ghost that is said to linger and reside in the Battlefield House. While no one has seen an actual apparition, it is said that Mary Jones Gage makes her presence known at this Stoney Creek landmark in more dignified ways.

Photo by Stephanie Lechniak-Cumerlato

Battlefield House was the homestead of the widow Mary Jones Gage and her two children, James and Elizabeth, who journeyed to the area from New York State in 1790. Mrs. Gage received a grant of 200 acres in exchange for

BATTLEFIELD HOUSE MUSEUM

swearing allegiance to the Crown. During the War of 1812, the Gage residence was forced to become headquarters of the invading American troops who occupied the house. Since then, it has been turned into a lovely museum that has carefully restored the original charm of the home.

Reports include antique pieces, ones that Mrs. Gage would have used, disappearing from a room, only to be found days later in a completely different area of the house. It is also said that Mr. Gage likes to fiddle around with the electrical currents, the vacuum cleaner, and the computers. One incident even had an old musket, which works fine normally, suddenly jam up and not work. Of course, it could only be the handiwork of a kid who has come to visit the museum for the day, as staff members unconvincingly speculate.

Why would Mary Jones Gage still be living within the walls at Battlefield House? One reason stands most prominent. Currently, the whereabouts of Mrs. Gage's body is a mystery. Her remains were said to have been interred in a lead-lined casket in the First United Church in Hamilton that burned down in 1969. This fire destroyed what was meant to be her final resting place when she died in 1841, and her remains, along with those of several other early settlers, were to have been relocated to the Woodland Cemetery in Burlington, Ontario, where a plaque in their memory was erected. Mary Jones Gage and her headstone disappeared and never made it to Burlington.

Most say that her lost soul found its way back to her home at the Battlefield House. A clairvoyant toured the house a few years back and was disturbed by a pervasive aura of violence in a front bedroom.

The psychic also sensed a benevolent spirit with a strong personality and said the house had some connection to children. This would make perfect sense because the house saw 10 of James Jr.'s kids and 16 of Elizabeth's.

There is also said to be a high energy on the battlefield itself, as we have received several reports from people who have actually been witness to ghostly, misty soldiers walking across the field, as if they were marching to battle. As with most other haunted battlefields, sounds of cannons firing can sometimes be heard and sounds of war echo prominently throughout the park.

—*Stephanie Lechniak-Cumerlato*
Founding Partner,
HauntedHamilton.com

Dingle Park

Corner of Dunn and Front Streets Oakville, Ontario

Dingle Park is a small downtown park in the Heart of Oakville. This lovely park is situated on the shore of Lake Ontario and affords a beautiful view of the Toronto skyline on a clear night. However, this is not what most people wish to visualize as they tour Dingle Park.

In its heyday, Dingle Park was the local swimming hole where local people and visitors alike would cool off in the waters of the lake and perhaps have tea at the Worn Door Step—the teahouse just up the street. Over the years, the waters of the lake have claimed a number of lives at this site. The most notable story is that of a young family who were visiting in town on a hot Sunday afternoon. Following a tea stop at the Worn Door Step, the parents and their 3-year-old daughter strolled to the park so the young girl could have a swim before heading home.

Something went tragically wrong and the little girl drowned. The death has left many stories of what happened that fateful day. Many reports have been heard about a young girl's ghost who is often seen at night dancing upon the rocks that now line the shore of Dingle Park. The constant theme of the sightings is always the same—the young spirit is barefooted and wet, as if just returning from a swim. Her physical body may be gone, but her spirit lives on, proving once again that those from the other side can make their presence felt.

—Jennifer Tyrrell,
Paranormal Investigator,
Field Investigation Research for Entities

MARKET SQUARE

CORNER OF WILLIAM AND NAVY STREETS
OAKVILLE, ONTARIO

As the sun goes down in beautiful downtown Oakville, the atmosphere of the day changes to a surreal one of eeriness and expectation. The quaint town shops along Lakeshore Road close and bring a quietness to the area. The connection to the spirit world becomes enhanced, and those who are prone to the feelings of "the other side" relish this time of day.

One of the many reported haunted locations in Oakville is Market Square—an area that dates back to 1835. Today's Market Square, a lovely park with small businesses surrounding the area, differs vastly from the Market Square of the 1800s. In its early days, Market Square

housed the Town Hall of Oakville, along with the "lock-up" or jailhouse.

As we toured in Market Square one evening, we knew the history of a spirit named Philip and his panache for being "available" in the area. That evening, we had a medium on the tour who immediately picked up on his presence within the square. She began communicating with Philip and was assured that he is a friendly spirit and likes the company of the tour guides and wanted them to feel welcome in his square.

Our first encounter with Philip was the first of many strange things that occur on a regular basis as we tour Market Square. There are strange sounds and noises heard routinely, and the faint smell of smoke is a constant reminder that there is a presence. Close to Halloween, the acrid smell of something burning is very distinctive and has our tour participants feeling creepy as they listen to the stories and wonder how close they are to the spirit world. Inevitably, this experience will drive the conversation for the remainder of the tour.

Last Halloween, our guides were so intrigued by the distinction in the smell of something burning on this particular tour that they elected to back-track to Market Square. Upon further investigation, they found that the historical plaques that were on the walls of the Square told of the 1800s Town Hall and jailhouse being completely destroyed by fire—not once but twice!

The experiences of Philip and of Market Square are but one of many ghostly happenings in Oakville, especially at Halloween, when the veil is thinnest between the worlds.

—Jennifer Tyrrell,
Paranormal Investigator,
Field Investigation Research for Entities

MARKET SQUARE

Saskatchewan

KING GEORGE HOTEL
240 MAIN STREET
MELVILLE, SASKATCHEWAN S0A 2P0
TEL: 1 (306) 728-2208

The King George Hotel is a three-story brick hotel in the heart of Melville. Built in 1911, today the hotel features a bar and restaurant and offers 10 guest rooms on the second floor. The guest rooms on the third floor are sometimes used during warmer months, allowing the King George to accommodate more guests. At one time, the third floor was a more active part of the hotel—the guest rooms bustled with activity, from both the living as well as a phantom maid.

Vaughn Smith was a touring bar musician back in the 1980s and 90s. He and his bandmates checked into the King George Hotel one Sunday afternoon in the fall of 1985. Smith was staying in a room on the third floor at the end of the hallway. This particular room had two entrances— one for the bedroom, and one for a small sitting room that was part of the suite. "While washing up, I heard some strange noises emanating from the bedroom," Smith said, "but I attributed them to the old steam heaters. I locked up both doors and went for dinner with the rest of the band at a local restaurant."

Melville was one of the few towns Smith's band performed in that actually had a movie theater. Smith tried to no avail to convince some of the other members of his band to go with him to take in a movie. After dinner, he went back to his room at the King George before the movie.

"I distinctly saw a woman, who I assumed was the housekeeper, walk into the hallway toward the entrance to my bedroom," Smith said. "When I turned down that hallway, I noticed my bedroom door was open, although I had locked it before I left. So she must have gone into my room, but there was no one in there. I wanted to find her as I needed more towels. Thinking the woman must be in my sitting room, I unlocked the door to discover she wasn't there either. This was an old hotel, and when someone walked along the floor near you, you could hear it. Still thinking I had somehow missed her, I washed my hands and prepared to go to the movie. Then I heard the strange noises coming from the bedroom again. I walked into the bedroom, and as I listened to the steam heaters, the noises, which were a low mumbling sound, changed direction and emanated from the sitting room. That's when it hit me that it was really strange that I didn't see the woman anywhere. So being a natural hero, I got the hell out of there as fast as I could and went to the movie."

After the movie, Smith returned to find his room unlocked, though he had locked it again before leaving for the movie. Smith's brother, who was also in the band, noted that his door was also left unlocked. That night, the band was going to have a mini rehearsal in Smith's sitting room, but it was canceled when the lead singer and his wife refused to stay in the room. "I can't stay in your room," Smith recounted the lead singer saying. "It's got a bad vibe in there. I don't like it. There's something really wrong in your room."

The next day, after Smith returned from lunch, he found his bed made and fresh towels left on top. "I didn't think anything of that," Smith said. "Although usually the maids didn't touch the band rooms until the end of the week because we're notorious slobs. I thanked the lady at the front desk, who was also the co-owner of the hotel, for sending someone to clean my room but mentioned that it wasn't necessary. She just looked at me and asked me what I was talking about. She literally had no idea. I told her about my clean room and the towels. She said that her daughter cleans the rooms on Sunday mornings and doesn't return until the following Sunday. I told her about seeing the woman go into my hallway, and she had no explanation for that or my clean room. She just shrugged and didn't offer anything else. My room was made up two more times that week and no one else's was."

Smith figured this ghost wasn't out to harm him; in fact, she seemed to be intent on making him comfortable.

The current owners claim that several of their bar regulars have also reported a dark, male figure that opens a door, walks to one area of the bar, and then disappears late at night near closing time.

—Jeff Belanger
Founder, Ghostvillage.com

KING GEORGE HOTEL

Eastern Canada

Eastern Canada

New Brunswick

FORT LATOUR

FORT LATOUR DRIVE
SAINT JOHN, NEW BRUNSWICK

In 1631, the self-appointed governor of Acadia, Charles de LaTour, established a fort at Portland Point near the mouth of the St. John River. Fort LaTour (also called Fort Sainte Marie) was a strategic location to facilitate fur trading in New France. When one self-appoints himself governor, there's a good chance that another might step up and feel more entitled. Such was the case with D'Aulnay de Charnisay, who also claimed the governorship of the region. Charles de LaTour's wife, French actress Madame Francoise Marie de LaTour, is considered Canada's first heroine because of the way she gallantly defended the fort from Charnisay's four-day attack while her husband was in Boston.

On Easter Sunday, the fifth day of battle, the fort was finally captured while the men were praying at their Easter service. Charnisay bribed his way into the fort, and Madame de LaTour agreed to surrender on the condition that the men's lives would be spared.

Charnisay agreed, then immediately broke his word. He forced Madame de LaTour to watch as he had each one of her men hung in front of her. Within three weeks, Madame LaTour died—one bit of lore says her death was caused by a broken heart, another says she was poisoned by Charnisay. She was buried near the fort, but her gravesite has been lost to history.

Charnisay built Fort Saint Jean on the western side of the harbor. Soon after, he met with his own untimely death by drowning while canoeing off the coast. Charles de LaTour then married charnisay's widow and became the undisputed Governor of Acadia. But Madame LaTour's story didn't end with her death, if we're to believe some of the local legends.

Some locals have repeatedly seen a woman in an old-fashioned gray gown strolling along the bay close to the former Navy Island in Jervis Bay. Several people have uncovered some pine coffins in the area while excavating, though historians knew of no graveyard nearby. Some of the workers who made the discovery were quick to spread the word that the remains were that of Madame LaTour's, but none of the claims have ever proved to actually be true—they were some other woman's bones.

Canada's first heroine may still be walking the bay, waiting for her grave to be found so she can receive a burial and monument befitting a hero. In the 1950s, the original site of Fort LaTour was finally discovered by archaeologists. Today, a fenced-in grassy hill with a plaque and a Canadian flag flying proudly overhead marks where the fort once stood. Nearby, the Harbour Bridge casts its shadow over the site.

—Jeff Belanger
Founder, Ghostvillage.com

Nova Scotia

THE GARRISON HOUSE INN
350 ST. GEORGE STREET
ANNAPOLIS ROYAL, NOVA SCOTIA B0S 1A0
TEL: 1 (902) 532-5750
WEBSITE: *www.garrisonhouse.ca*

Built in 1854 and originally called the Temperance Hotel, the Garrison House Inn is a three-story mansion with seven unique rooms to rent and views that overlook the 20-acre National Park of Historic Fort Anne. The building operated as a hotel until 1920 when a wealthy doctor purchased the building to house his family and his practice. In 1971, it went back to being an inn when a new owner bought the building. Today, the inn is full of antiques and furnishings from the late-19th century. But one of its guest rooms holds another kind of old relic from the past. The ghost of a little girl named Emily has been said to make her presence known on some foggy summer nights. She's only shown herself to women, and she's become an endeared soul to the staff of the inn.

—Jeff Belanger
Founder, Ghostvillage.com

ANGUS MACDONALD BRIDGE
BRIDGE OVER HALIFAX HARBOR CONNECTING THE SISTER CITIES HALIFAX AND DARTMOUTH, NOVA SCOTIA

The Angus MacDonald Bridge (named after a famous Nova Scotian politician) has long been said to be cursed. Over the span of 200 years, three bridges have been constructed on this site, and intrigue is connected to all three.

The first construction, a foot bridge, fell unexpectedly during a winter storm. Legend has it that a Mi' kmaq (the local native tribe) may have originally placed a curse on the bridge, causing it to fall. Years later, the second, a railway bridge, also fell on an otherwise pleasant day. And the third, the present Macdonald Bridge, has had its share of mystery—the first being a worker falling to his death while it was being constructed in the 1950s. Following this accident, a local Mi' kmaq Indian chieftain was asked to remove the curse. He obliged by performing a ceremony in which he literally "buried a hatchet," though some believe the curse still lingers.

—Andy Smith
Owner/Tour Guide, Tattle Tours:
A Ghost Walk of Historic Halifax

KEITH'S BREWERY
1496 LOWER STREET
HALIFAX, NOVA SCOTIA

Scotsman Alexander Keith purchased a local brewery in 1820 shortly after immigrating to Halifax, Nova Scotia, and over the years, he established a reputation for fine beer and a keen sense of business.

Photo by Andy Smith

Keith was a remarkable man—among his distinctions, he was twice mayor of Halifax, a president of the provincial Legislative Council, a director of the Bank of Nova Scotia, and a Grand Master of the Freemasons. But locals knew him best for his hospitality. He loved his beer and the art of brewing; so much so that he built his home (which still exists on Hollis Street, Halifax) next to his brewery. On top of that, he had a tunnel built from his home to the brewery so that he could visit it and inspect the operations at any time, night or day.

After 50 years of business and community activities, he died at 78. And while he lies buried in the local Camp Hill Cemetery, many believe his spirit never left the brewery. On rare evenings, visitors to Keith's Brewery (still in operation) have sensed a spirit lurking in the recessed rooms, tunnels, and hallways of the brewery.

—Andy Smith
Owner/Tour Guide, Tattle Tours:
A Ghost Walk of Historic Halifax

KEITH'S BREWERY

Asia

Asia

UBIN GERMAN GIRL TEMPLE

NORTHERN COAST
PULAU UBIN
SINGAPORE
TEL: 65 9686-4869
WEBSITE: *www.find-german-girl.org*

This is a tragic story, not even known to many Singaporeans today, of how a young German girl died in Pulau Ubin (which means "Rock Island"on Malay) at the outbreak of WWI, and thereafter she became immortalized in a Chinese temple. The power of the spirit of the German girl was so real and efficacious that it not only attracted local worshippers but someone wicked who stole her remains.

In the tranquil coastal village of Pulau Ubin, northeast of Singapore, there was a coffee plantation owned by a German merchant who lived on the island with his family.

Photo courtesy of Singapore Paranormal Investigators

According to the islanders, in August 1914 when the British came to confiscate the plantation, a young girl, the daughter of the plantation owner, became frightened and ran away. On the fateful evening, the girl lost her way, fell down a steep cliff, and was killed.

Meanwhile the rest of the family was captured by the British authorities and interned. A few days later, her body was found by local Boyanese workers from the plantation. The body was covered by termites so they threw soil over the corpse. Often after that, when the local workers and residents passed the spot, they would say a prayer. Eventually, her remains were exhumed and placed in a Chinese temple on a hill on the island. Gamblers began to pray at the temple for good luck, and several of these gamblers were successful and attributed their success in winning to the spirit of the German girl.

When the war was over, the German plantation owner and the rest of the family were freed. They returned to Pulau Ubin to find out what had happened to their daughter but because of language difficulties were unable to determine where her remains were. They left Pulau Ubin and Singapore, never to return.

The remains of the German girl were kept at the temple on the hill until 1974, when the property became the site of a granite quarry. Several local people exhumed the remains consisting of hair, an iron cross, and some coins and put them in a porcelain urn.

A new temple on the quarry property was then built for the remains. The coins were somehow lost (or probably ransacked) at the time the remains were moved in 1974. Even the porcelain urn placed at the center of the altar in the new temple was said to be empty; it is only a symbolic replica of the original, because the original urn with the remains inside was stolen.

Singapore Paranormal Investigators (SPI) has been pondering some theories regarding the stolen remains. One theory is that the porcelain urn itself was a valuable antique and it was stolen by relic hunters. The other speculation is that the remains of the white girl have a strong spiritual force, and therefore the urn was robbed by people who practice black magic or sorcery.

Despite that the physical existence of the German girl corpse was no more in the 1970s, her spirit was made immortalized at this Chinese temple. Worshippers came to give offerings that include perfumes, cosmetics, mirrors, flowers, and fruits to the deceased German girl.

It has been reported to SPI that people have encountered moving shadows outside the temple at night. Recently, some members of a filming crew who reenacted the legend for movie production got possessed on the spot—one vomited repeatedly after touching the urn, and the other, who was dressed in a German girl costume, suddenly started to speak in German. They believe that somehow her spirit is lingering in the temple as perhaps an angel goddess. On a lighter note, the German girl spirit was said to kindly give blessing to the worshippers, sometimes helping them win lotteries.

What is the true identity of the German girl? How did a mortal white girl transform into a Chinese deity? What could have happened to the remains? Did they ever really exist? Is it just a legend?

In the past few years, SPI has been investigating the place via a fusion approach of interviewing the villagers, digging into the historical records, and even consulting some spiritual mediums.

Hopefully one day, SPI will be able to shed some light on the mystery, especially in the hope that the descendants of her kin would be able to reunite with the German girl.

—Sunkist Lee
SPI Elite Member, Department of
Historical Research, Singapore
Paranormal Investigators

SYONAN JINJA AT MACRITCHIE RESERVOIR

MACRITCHIE RESERVOIR, SINGAPORE
WEBSITE: *http://syonan-jinja.spi.com.sg*

Abandoned in the thick jungle of the MacRitchie Catchment area are the ruins of Syonan Jinja, which means "Shinto Shrine of Syonan" or "The Light of the South," dating back to World War II. Built by the British and Australian POWs to commemorate Japanese soldiers who died fighting in the invasion of Singapore, Syonan Jinja could be said to be a replica of the now-controversial Yasukuni Shrine in Japan.

The original structure of

Photo courtesy of Singapore Paranormal Investigators

Syonan Jinja was a temple with no walls. It was raised from the ground by a stone platform graduated with a few steps, and the sloping temple roof rested on wooden pillars that stood at regular intervals around the perimeter of the platform. Tons of smooth stone pebbles that should have been used for the reservoir filtration were taken instead for paving the garden of the shrine.

When the war ended, the temple was promptly obliterated by fire, leaving the whole place ground zero except for some traces of stone ruins.

As the years went by, all traces of the shrine—mainly its foundation and the 90 stone steps of access—were overwhelmed by dense jungle growth. The fountain, made from a massive granite boulder, is still intact today. However, underneath the fountain, a secret tunnel was found freshly dug by some unknown people, with a purpose unknown too.

There are some debates circulating that Syonan Jinja was not destroyed by the returning British but by the Japanese themselves. A conspiracy is speculated of covering up a secret treasure left over by the Japanese on the event of a hurry retreat. A gruesome rumor says that a company of Japanese Imperial Guards who were absolutely loyal to the Emperor vowed to protect the secrecy of the treasure with their blood. A mass ritual suicide, which is called "Sappuku," therefore, took place at the Jinja.

Recently, Singapore Paranormal Investigators probed into this mystery and discovered what may be a link to the famous legend of Yamashita Gold. According to some records, in 1981 an Indonesian gardener named Sappari, who worked at the reservoir during the occupation years, suggested that something very valuable had been buried close to the Jinja. His account indicated that just before the defeat looked imminent in 1945, Japanese soldiers in trucks drove up to the reservoir and undertook what Sappari described as "a lot of activity."

Nowadays, the access path to Syonan Jinja is blocked with fallen trees and other obstacles beyond your imagination. The swamp is infested by various snakes, scorpions, biting spiders, and millions of mosquitoes. There is waist-deep water to cross and many opportunities to get disoriented and lost. Superstitious trekkers who lost their directions to Syonan Jinja would blame it on the haunting of the Japanese spirits who protect the Jinja from intruders.

—SPI Elite Team
Singapore Paranormal Investigators

Fort Canning Park

City Hall, Singapore
Website: *www.spi.com.sg/haunted*

Fort Canning used to be a symbol of authority in Singapore. In 1861, the fort was named in the honor of Viscount Charles John Canning, the first viceroy of India. The hill underwent several name changes. The Malays called it Bukit Larangan or "Forbidden Hill" for several possible reasons:

(1) It reputedly contains the royal tomb of Sultan Iskandar Shah, the Malay ruler of the Kingdom of Singapura, who is said to have forbidden ordinary people to come to the hill because his concubines and wives used to bathe at a spring there.

(2) The Malays were fearful of climbing the hill as they thought the palace of their ancestor kings had once stood there.

(3) The site had sightings of fabled lion for which Sri Tri Buana, ruler of Temasek, later named the island Singapura, or "Lion City."

(4) Besides the fabled lion, the Malays believed that the hill is haunted by many other ghosts and spirits.

A legend that is associated with Fort Canning is about a national treasure of gold, which belonged to the sultans of the ancient kingdoms. The hill was mystified with all sorts of spooks and ghouls dwelling there. In particular, there is one guardian spirit in a form of a huge python that was said to safeguard the national treasure at Fort Canning. Only those who know the magic word and speak it to the python spirit will have the treasure revealed, otherwise their hearts will be eaten away when confronted.

There is, however, some clue to the legend of the national treasure from the archaeological evidence of a 14th-century prosperous town at Fort Canning. During the construction of the 30-million gallon capacity reservoir in 1928 on the hill, many Hindu Javanese gold jewelries dated to about 1360 were excavated. Ruins of ancient brick buildings were unearthed, too, which gave support to the possibility that a wealthy ancient palace once stood.

In 1822, the founder of modern Singapore, Sir Stamford Raffles, claimed the hill for his residence, naming it Government Hill. Until the mid-19th century,

Photo courtesy of Singapore
Paranormal Investigators

Singapore's governors were residents here; thus the epithet "Government Hill" as well as "Central Park."

The park walls are made up of tombstones, and Fort Canning Park was once a graveyard for some 600 Christian graves. This used to be the old Christian Cemetery until 1865. The only graves left are at the corner of the park. Those tombstones that were removed were set into the wall surrounding Fort Canning Green.

Nowadays, you can still see a strange sight of walls made of tomb slabs that line the former cemetery. Those are the famous men and women who gave their lives to the young colony. They are the elite people having titles of lieutenants, generals, sergeants, and so on. Most of them died at about mid-age during battles. Their short histories are embedded in the walls.

—SPI Elite Team
Singapore Paranormal Investigators

OLD FORD MOTOR FACTORY
UPPER BUKIT TIMAH ROAD, SINGAPORE
WEBSITE: *http://ford-factory.spi.com.sg*

On the west side of Singapore, between Bukit Batok and Bukit Timah, situated in a deserted compound is the Old Ford Motor Factory. The Ford factory has a remarkable history and a haunted reputation.

The company Ford Motor Works was making history when they decided to build a new factory at Bukit Timah to replace their old premises on Anson Road. The new spacious Art Deco factory was the first car assembly plant in Southeast Asia. But history of a less salubrious kind was also made at the Ford factory.

During World War II, fierce battles were fought around the areas of the Ford factory. High casualty was inflicted on both armies. A whole Malay regiment was fought to the last man, defense posts got wiped out overnight, bombs dropped nonstop, and many places were engulfed in fire. Of the battles fought in Bukit Panjang, Choa Chu Kang, Bukit Batok, and Bukit Timah, the Ford factory miraculously remained the one place spared from any damage.

Swiftly, the Japanese fought in a hard and bloody way to win the battle at Bukit Timah, which once was used as supply storage by the British. Hopes of defending Singapore diminished. On February 15, 1942, the head of the Allied forces, Lt. General A.E. Percival, surrendered to General Yamashita of the Japanese Forces. Ford factory was chosen as the venue for the British generals to sign the surrender documents.

After that, the Ford factory was occupied as a Japanese military headquarter during the occupation in Singapore. No official record was known about the actual activities that occurred in the military headquarters, but rumors said that many anti-Japanese coalition forces were

Photo courtesy of Singapore Paranormal Investigators

OLD FORD MOTOR FACTORY

taken inside and executed there. Interrogation, tortures, and slaughtering of the anti-Japanese people that took place in the cells of the compound were not of a rare routine.

The factory has been abandoned for ages since the end of the war. In the last decades, some tire companies used to have their offices there but they moved out after a while. Day and night, the factory was left vacant with the building structure left almost untouched. If the stone-tape theory of ghost were true, the vengeful spirits would be absorbed by the walls of the factory, preserving the uncanny energies from the violent deaths. Wandering spirits that pass by may dwell, too, for it has been deserted for so long.

—SPI Elite Team
Singapore Paranormal Investigators

MOUNT PLEASANT CEMETERY

UPPER THOMSON ROAD, SINGAPORE

Located beside the Police Academy on Thomson Road, Mount Pleasant Cemetery is not a place for the fainthearted, especially for people scared of spirits.

The cemetery was once part of the 86ha Bukit Brown Chinese Cemetery on Lornie Road. The land was acquired by the colonial government in 1919 and opened as a cemetery in 1922. George Henry Brown bought the place and named it Mount Pleasant, but it was also known as Brown's Hill. There was a misconception that Bukit Brown was named so because there used to be a coffee plantation over the hill. Nonetheless, due to the construction of the Pan-Island Expressway, the cemetery was split into two.

While both cemeteries share the same history, Mount Pleasant Cemetery contradicts its name.

Surrounded by jungle and wilderness, it has an eerier atmosphere than Bukit Brown. Visitors are far fewer at Mount Pleasant Cemetery. In fact, many drivers pass by the area without realizing what is there.

There is a narrow, snaking pathway leading deep into the cemetery with a metal chain strung across to keep cars out, but there is no other clue that this is a cemetery. Soon after passing the chain, you can see the tombs on both sides, some of them cracked with age.

But at night, the tombs are barely visible because of the tall Angsana trees surrounding them; the cemetery plunges into pitch darkness. What makes the cemetery notorious is not the dead in the tombs, but sightings of the evil spirit Pontianak and the sounds of her spine-chilling laugh as she flies over the trees at night.

According to Malay legend, the Pontianak is a vengeful female spirit that originated from women who died during childbirth and are cursed.

Before the place was bought by George Brown, it was a local Javanese village in medieval times that was dominated by Malay Bomohs or shamans who practiced black magic. One popular black art during that time was to create and control such Pontianak vampires as servants, some even as assassins. The Javanese village vanished in time, and the land turned into a cemetery in the last century. But those Pontianaks remain and roam free there.

Gruesome rumor has it that, at Mount Pleasant Cemetery, men died on open ground with their bodies shredded—guts and male organs were stripped off and scattered around the cemetery. That gave rise to the fear that the mythical creatures were the suspected killers.

Some people want to believe that the Pontianak sightings are really some of the many monkeys or animal predators that inhabit the area. In fact, it was reported that in 1896 a tiger was shot at Mount Pleasant. But for believers, the area is extremely haunted and is a location to be avoided.

—SPI Elite Team
Singapore Paranormal Investigators

Japan

MT. OSORE

OSOREZAN, AOMORI PREFECTURE, JAPAN
WEBSITE: *www.soultrackers.com/ soultrackers/invest/famous/ mtosore.html*

I lived in Misawa, Japan from 2002 to 2004 during part of my enlistment in the U.S. Air Force. While in Japan, I learned about some beliefs of spirituality and the paranormal that prevail in their culture. I was told of a particular mountain, only a few hours drive from the base, called Mt. Osore, or "Fear Mountain." This mountain is a dormant volcano with a shrine at the center. Mt. Osore is also referred to as "The Gateway to the Dead." This is one of three Reizan sites in Japan. This means "Mountains dedicated to gods or Buddha." The Japanese believe that their deceased loved ones go to

these locations to cross over to the other side, similar to our stairway to heaven or tunnel of light.

I have been to Mt. Osore twice. On the first trip, a friend and I made the two-hour drive from Misawa to Mt. Osore. Even before we got out of the truck, the smell of rotten eggs was very distinct. When we opened the doors, the thick smell of sulfur clung to the mountain air and was a strong reminder of the volcano that we were on. Yellow stains were visible throughout the grounds, marking all of the natural sulfur vents. Five temple statues stood watch over the entrance to the left. When we passed through the large gates of the entrance, I had an overwhelming psychic sensation as if there were thousands of people watching me. I have been in the field of paranormal investigation since the 1990s, and this location had the most overwhelming, powerful force that I had ever felt in my life.

While walking the vast grounds, we could see several buildings and the first of many temples. There was a mix of older

Photo by Jonathan Williams

and newer style Japanese architecture all around. Toward the back of the compound were trails that led throughout the volcanic terrain. A Buddha statue known as Jizo, protector of those condemned to hell, sat on one of the hills. There was also a 9th-century temple dedicated to all the souls of the unborn. The sulfuric lake in the center had a large beach area, and everywhere you looked there were piles of rocks, big and small, tall and wide. Each stone represented someone's beloved ancestor whose soul resided in the mountain. I was awestruck as I stared across the hills. There were thousands of rock piles as far as the eye could see.

To walk through Mt. Osore was like being in an episode of the *Twilight Zone*. I had strong feelings of death and sensations of being watched. This is one of the most energy-rich places that I have ever been to, and I will never forget the experience.

—Jonathan Williams
Operations Director, SoulTrackers
Paranormal Investigations

Jamaica

Jamaica

Montego Bay

ROSE HALL GREAT HOUSE

ROSE HALL PLANTATION
MONTEGO BAY, JAMAICA
TEL: 1 (876) 953-2323

Rose Hall was once the home of Annie Palmer—a woman the locals feared in her day. Even today, her legend is used to scare children across the island of Jamaica, and she is best-known as "The White Witch of Rose Hall."

Built in 1770 on Montego Bay, Rose Hall Plantation was an island paradise—though only for those who lived in luxury within the house. For the slaves who worked the sugar cane plantation, Rose Hall could sometimes be deadly.

Annie Palmer was born Annie Mae Patterson in the early 1800s and grew up in Haiti. She had a Haitian nanny who taught her voodoo from a young age. When Annie was 10, her parents died under mysterious circumstances, and her nanny raised her until she was 18. Ever ambitious, Annie wanted wealth and wanted it quickly—she came to Jamaica and enchanted local plantation owner John Palmer. They were soon married, and Annie became mistress of the plantation. But Annie was hungry for more excitement and had gotten bored with her husband. She demanded that some of the slave men come to her bedroom so she could have her way with them. When she grew tired of these lovers, she would have them killed so they couldn't tell anyone else. According to the legend, Annie's husband died mysteriously one evening, and Annie inherited everything. She married twice more, and again, two more husbands died. Each time, she acquired more wealth. And all the while, she brought slaves into the Great House for her pleasure before having them dispatched when she grew tired of them.

The other slaves were suspicious, but they didn't say anything publicly out of fear of the White Witch. According to Beverly Gordon, a native Jamaican and the current manager of the Rose Hall Great House, Annie Palmer not only beat the slaves in daylight but she also brought them back to the mansion for further torture. Gordon said, "Where the ladies' and gentlemen's rooms are now, that's what she used as her dungeon, and those two pits went 16 feet down. That's where she kept the slaves if they were caught trying to run away from the property. She would get them there, throw them in the pit, and then leave them there to die without food or water, no medical attention whatsoever. She was gruesome, awful."

In 1971, a group of psychics came to Rose Hall to try and trap the spirit of Annie Palmer. Gordon said, "They tried to raise Annie, and she was giving them a hard time. She came out of the tomb, they were trying to get her back in, and they could not. On her tomb, they placed three crosses on three sides. They wanted to trap her spirit back inside the tomb and they could not, so they did not put the fourth cross on. They just left that side open."

Today there are ghostly phenomena in every corner of Rose Hall. People report hearing doors slam on their own, and men's screams echo through the chambers and hallways. Apparitions have been sighted and even photographed throughout the building, but especially in the bedrooms.

—Jeff Belanger
Founder, Ghostvillage.com

South Africa

South Africa

Cape Town

FLYING DUTCHMAN
CAPE OF GOOD HOPE
CAPE TOWN, SOUTH AFRICA

Legends of phantom ships on the seas and harbors of the world go back many centuries. Today, some of these ghost ships are incorrectly labeled with the generic term of *Flying Dutchman*. This isn't fair, because, though there may indeed be many phantom ships, there's only one *Flying Dutchman*, and the centuries-old ghostly legend behind that ship got its start off the Cape of Good Hope at the southern tip of South Africa.

In 1641, Captain Hendrik van der Decken swore to get his ship around the Cape of Good Hope and home to Amsterdam, even if it took him until Doomsday. The ship was lost, though it seems, from the dozens of sightings of the ghost ship throughout history, that Captain van der Decken kept his word—the ship is still trying to make its way around the Cape.

In earlier legends dating to the mid-1800s, some ships reported being hailed by this vessel—though they didn't realize it was a ghost ship. Captain van der Decken calls across and asks if the vessel will carry some personal letters of the crew onward

for them. To allow the *Dutchman*'s row-boat across and to accept the letters certainly spells doom. Sightings of the vessel continued in mariner reports from reputable sailors aboard Royal Navy ships throughout the 1800s and into the 20th century. The ship is described as having full, billowed sails, even when no wind is present. Witnesses also claim the ship glows an eerie red at night. The *Flying Dutchman* is considered a bad omen for any ships that spot it.

—Jeff Belanger
Founder, Ghostvillage.com

CASTLE OF GOEDE HOOP (GOOD HOPE)
BUITENKANT STREET
CAPE TOWN, SOUTH AFRICA
TEL: 27 21-787-1249
WEBSITE: *www.castleofgoodhope.co.za*

The largest of South Africa's buildings is also the oldest...and the most haunted. The Castle of Goede Hoop (Good Hope) in Cape Town was built between 1666 and 1679 by the Dutch East India Company to serve as a replenishment station for ships sailing by the Cape of

Good Hope. The pentagon-shaped castle was constructed on the shore so high tides would fill its moat. There was a dreaded *Donker Gat* (dark hole) dungeon used to hold prisoners, who would be chained to the walls and tortured. If an extra-large wave came crashing up the shore during high tide, the hole could fill with water within seconds and drown the prisoner chained below. One can imagine the mental anguish of hearing the waves getting louder and louder as the tide rose—hoping the next crest doesn't fill your watery tomb.

The castle also served as an execution site for convicts, escaped slaves, and rebellious natives. There's small wonder why this place is haunted.

One of the most profound sightings at the castle involves a tall, glowing figure that is seen pacing between the Oranje and Leerdam bastions. The spectral figure would occasionally stop his march to lean over the castle wall to view the street below. The sound of phantom footsteps have also been reported in this area when no living person is present to make the sounds.

It's rare when we can put a name from history to a ghost, but in the case of the Castle of Goede Hoop, we can: Governor Pieter Gysbert van Noodt. In April of 1729, van Noodt ordered seven soldiers to their deaths for desertion. One of the seven stood on the gallows and announced that the group was wrongly accused and condemned van Noodt to "divine justice." The seven were hanged, and van Noodt died later that same day of unknown causes. Today, van Noodt has been seen walking the grounds and been heard cursing under his breath before disappearing.

Other resident ghosts include the curly-haired specter of Lady Anne Barnard, who lived at the castle in the late 1700s and has been known to make her appearance at parties, and a phantom black hound that leaps at visitors but vanishes inches before colliding with the frightened visitor.

Today the castle is an Africana museum offering daily tours.

—Jeff Belanger
Founder, Ghostvillage.com

Iran

Iran

Yazal Province

CHAK CHAK SHRINE

ORDAKAN
YAZAL PROVINCE
IRAN

Clinging to the side of a mountain in central Iran, the ghost of a beautiful woman is seen at what is now called the Chak Chak shrine. The shrine has weathered the ravages of time because of the protection offered by the towering cliffs that shelter it from the sweltering heat of the dry, Iranian desert.

The woman in life was Nikbanou, a Persian princess, who lived in the seventh century. During her life, the Arabians invaded her land on horseback to establish Islam in her homeland. Fearing for her safety, she fled to the mountain and was forced to stay there as the religion spread quickly. Here she lived until her death, where her corpse was left for the vultures. The dead are not buried, for Zoroastrians believe the dead body will contaminate God's pure earth, so the deceased are taken to two outcrops that are called the Towers of Silence. The dead are left here for the vultures to devour and for the bones to be bleached in the sun.

Goshtasb Belivani is a priest in Iran's pre-Islamic religion. He told the story of the young man, having left the body of his dead father and feeling ill, and, being completely overcome with grief and exhaustion from the trip, lay down and fell asleep. He woke up with a jolt and, regaining his awareness, saw a beautiful woman with long, dark hair and wearing a green gown standing just to his side. Her gaze brought him such calm that he found himself in tears and feeling totally at a peace, a place where, in his emotional body, he had never been before. She offered him a cool drink, and as he took the drink from her hand, she disappeared. After finishing the drink, he then fell into a deep sleep and didn't awake until mid-morning. When he awoke, he was filled with joy and had an energy that he had not experienced since he was a child. Over the rest of his lifetime, the man returned to the cliff where he saw the apparition to honor the lady who had given him new life and in hope of seeing her once again.

Word spread fast, and many people sick with disease or crippled went to find what quickly became a shrine to the "lady in green" and her curative powers. Tales of the many miraculous cures bestowed by the apparition brought the sick and the diseased from all over the world.

—Janice Cottrill
Investigator, Researcher, and Writer,
Cottrill Investigations

Oceania

Oceania

Australia

COMMISSARIAT STORES

115 WILLIAM STREET
BRISBANE CBD
QUEENSLAND, AUSTRALIA
WEBSITE:
www.queenslandhistory.org.au

Reputed to be Queensland's first stone building, construction of the Commissariat Stores began in 1827 and was completed in 1829 through the utilization of convict labor. Built as a secure store, the walls of the building were constructed to a thickness of up to 1.2 meters, with the majority of the building set into the surrounding riverbank. A pier at the front of the building facing the river allowed for delivery of government supplies directly from vessels anchored in the Brisbane River; however, this was demolished to make way for the modern Riverside Expressway.

The Commissariat Stores building has served a number of purposes since its construction, initially as a store for government supplies through its early years, a repository for the Queensland State Archives, a migrant depot, and finally as the headquarters for the Royal Historical Society of Queensland. More recently, much of the interior has been converted into a convict museum documenting the early years of Brisbane settlement.

With such a colorful history, it is not unusual to believe that a ghost or two may reside within its walls. Those who have worked within the building over the years relate experiences of hearing strange noises when no other workers are about, of phantom footsteps in vacant sections of the building, of having office materials moved with no explanation, and of the feeling of an invisible presence. However, the most well-known phenomena relates to a door located at the side of the building, accessed via a ramp on the second floor.

It is said that at times when the building's employees have left for the day and the doors have been locked, a strange phenomenon may be experienced by knocking on this door. Lucky visitors may hear the ghost who inhabits the Commissariat Stores directly after knocking on the door. Although no employees remain in the building, footsteps may be heard on the floorboards approaching the doorway from inside the building. The footsteps will continue up to the inner side of the door and abruptly stop, giving the impression that a worker inside is about to open the door; however, it is merely a common prank played by the resident spook.

While it is uncertain where this ghost originated, there is a possibility that the haunting may date back to the initial construction of the Commissariat Stores. In September 1828, while a working gang was excavating the footings for the building, a convict named John Brungar had an altercation with another convict named William Perfoot. Before the overseer could intervene, Brungar struck Perfoot in the head with a mattock. An early written source documenting the incident stated that as a result, Perfoot's head "was cleft asunder." Brungar was subsequently transported back to Sydney where he was hanged for the murder. The question remains: Does convict Perfoot's ghost walk the halls of the Commissariat Stores, or is the resident ghost from more recent times?

—Liam Baker
Founder, Brisbane Ghost Hunters

VICTORIA PARK

(BELOW CENTENARY POOL)
GREGORY TERRACE
BRISBANE
QUEENSLAND, AUSTRALIA

The story of the Victoria Park ghost is probably the most famous "haunting" in Brisbane's history. The site of this tale has been partially destroyed by the new Inner-City Bypass; however, the tale will live on in the hearts and minds of those who were lucky enough to have played a part in the week-long saga.

The episode began in November 1965, after a group of local children overheard rumors suggesting a ghost had been observed within a tunnel beneath the rail line bordering Victoria Park. The following night, the intrepid ghost hunters crept down in the hope of spotting this spook.

One boy, lagging behind the rest of the group as they passed through the tunnel, experienced more than he could have imagined. As he endeavored to catch up to his friends, he was accosted by a misty green, armless, legless, headless apparition that seemed to materialize from the wall of the tunnel.

Seemingly "mesmerized" by the specter, the boy was dragged by his friends to the nearby Royal Brisbane Hospital—his companions feared he had been possessed by the ghost. The ensuing tale, as related by the children to hospital staff, made sensational newspaper headlines the next day and within a short time, thousands of local residents were lining both sides of the tunnel in the hopes of catching a glimpse of the ghost. For the next week, the Victoria Park ghost became the major talking point of Brisbane, not to mention a fantastic opportunity for family outings.

The nearby lake, frequented by local children as a swimming hole previous to the ghost's appearance, was promptly filled with barrels of oil, old mattresses, and broken furniture before being set alight by locals in an attempt to shed some light over the scene and coax the ghost from its hiding place. Children threw firecrackers, and the local Brisbane teenage gangs tussled over territory. Food vendors moved about the crowds selling their wares, and the police were called in regularly to calm the overanxious crowds. One impatient man arrived on the scene with a flamethrower, asking the throng at the mouth of the tunnel to stand clear while he "persuaded" the ghost from its slumber!

But at the end of the week-long drama, the ghost of Victoria Park remained a mystery. One newspaper in Brisbane published a long-exposure photograph taken within the tunnel, showing what they believed to be the answer to the ghostly riddle. The photograph exhibited a strange mist emanating from an open drain in the floor of the tunnel, possibly the result of gases produced by rotting vegetation, and it was declared that the "ghost" had now been explained in logical terms. However, this did not take into account three previous sightings in the vicinity in 1903, 1922, and 1932. As a result, many believe that the elusive Victoria Park ghost is patiently waiting to make another appearance in the future.

—Liam Baker
Founder, Brisbane Ghost Hunters

ARCHERFIELD AIRPORT
BEATTY ROAD
ARCHERFIELD
QUEENSLAND, AUSTRALIA

Archerfield Airport is Queensland's major center for general aviation activities. However, during World War II, Archerfield became an important military air base for the Royal Australian Air Force, United States Air Force, and the Dutch Air Forces. During this time, a variety of bombers, fighters, and transport aircraft became common sights above the suburb of Archerfield. Unfortunately, as eventually occurs at any airfield, pilot error and mechanical failure occasionally take their toll.

Several accidents occurred during the war years at Archerfield, the vast majority of which transpired fortunately without the loss of life. However, on March 27, 1943, a C-47 Dakota transport plane crashed into dense bush on the outskirts of the air base

moments after takeoff, resulting in the death of all 23 military and air force personnel on board. At the time, the accident was deemed as the worst air disaster in Australian aviation history.

In more recent years, a warplane buff visiting the site experienced an event he will never forget. "I was walking across one of the airfields on my way back to a group of friends when I spotted a man dressed in what appeared to be World War II flight gear," he said. "I can remember him vividly, right down to his flight jacket, goggles, and cap. As there were a number of wartime aviation buffs visiting the airfield that day, I thought nothing of it—must have been someone getting into the spirit of things by turning up in costume. We passed each other and the friendly chap acknowledged me with a gesture and a nod, as did I to him, and I continued to walk back to rejoin my friends. When I arrived back, I asked my colleagues who the chap in the World War II flight gear was. It was at that point that one of the more knowledgeable of our group told me that I had just met the ghost of Archerfield!"

The ghost, who regularly visits the vicinity of the airfield, has been seen by many residents of the area, and while there have been numerous, non-fatal accidents over the years at Archerfield, the jovial spirit in question is rumored to have resulted from the C-47 Dakota incident of 1943. While there have been a few sightings within the airport grounds themselves, the majority of sightings take place along the road outside of the airport.

Stories abound of a lone airman, dressed in full period flight uniform, sometimes walking through the site but most commonly seen traversing alongside

Beatty Road, which runs along the boundary of Archerfield Airport. Some observers say that as they pass by and glance at the airman in curiosity, their gaze will be acknowledged with a wave and a smile.

—Liam Baker
Founder, Brisbane Ghost Hunters

RICHMOND BRIDGE

BRIDGE STREET
RICHMOND
TASMANIA, AUSTRALIA

Located in the Southern region of Tasmania, the town of Richmond is considered to be the most important historic town in the state. One of the town's most important claims to fame, however, is the Richmond Bridge—the oldest surviving road bridge in Australia still in regular use. Built between 1823 and 1825 by convicts laboring under appallingly harsh conditions, the bridge and associated roadway provided an integral link between the fledgling colony of Hobart Town and the penal settlement of Port Arthur.

Photo by Liam Baker

The residents of Richmond are no strangers to unexplained phenomena and ghostly occurrences—many of the town's buildings harbor specters and tales of times long since passed. However, the beautiful stone bridge traversing the Coal River in the center of town holds a special place in the hearts of the locals—at least three ghosts are associated with the structure.

The most well-known haunting associated with the bridge dates back to 1832 and is still a common occurrence to this day. The ghost in question is that of a convict overseer named George Grover, also referred to as Simeon Groover, who perished upon the bridge. Transported to Tasmania for the crime of stealing, Grover completed his term of incarceration and attained the position of convict overseer and "flagellator"—a term given to those within the colony placed in charge of administering floggings to insubordinate convicts.

Well-known for his constant maltreatment and cruelty toward the convicts in his care, Grover's reign of terror came to an end in 1832 when, while drunk on the job, the convicts took their revenge. Grover was set upon and beaten, after which, badly injured, he was thrown from the parapet of the bridge to the rocky riverbank almost 30 feet below. Many locals and visitors to the bridge have reported witnessing Grover's ghost still pacing the length of the bridge as he did in life.

Another well-known ghost of the place is that of a large, black dog. Affectionately known as "Grover's Dog," the animal appears on the bridge after dark and usually only materializes before lone women and children. Local lore holds that the dog is a friendly spirit of the bridge, manifesting in order to ensure women and children safe passage across the bridge at night. One local woman reports that the animal has appeared by her side on numerous occasions while crossing the bridge at night. However, upon reaching the opposite end of the bridge, the dog promptly disappears.

A third ghost has been seen by many walking across the bridge. Some locals who have witnessed this particular spirit say he is a very smart-looking chap, complete with a straw bowler hat and walking cane. However, others who have reported observing this ghost believe it may belong to that of a convict who, weary from the appalling conditions and immense workloads, jumped to his death below.

—Liam Baker
Founder, Brisbane Ghost Hunters

PORT ARTHUR HISTORIC SITE

ARTHUR HIGHWAY
TASMAN PENINSULA
TASMANIA, AUSTRALIA
WEBSITE: *www.portarthur.org.au*

Established in 1830 as a timber-getting camp, Port Arthur was upgraded to a fully operational penal settlement in 1833. Intended as a punishment station for the incarceration of repeat offenders, Port Arthur earned a reputation as "hell on earth" for those imprisoned within its limits. Forced into hard labor under a regime of harsh punishment and discipline, hundreds of convicts lost their lives in the pursuit of repaying their debts to society. The spirits of many unfortunate convicts, as well as the military officers and their families, have remained as a result of Port Arthur's colorful history.

The Port Arthur historic site has as many ghosts as it does buildings, with far too many to list. Unexplained events at the site are commonplace, with ghosts and associated phenomena occurring around virtually every corner. However, there are some locations within the precinct where ghostly phenomena are most frequent.

The Parsonage holds the reputation as one of the most haunted buildings at Port Arthur, with quite regular ghostly occurrences dating back to the late 1800s. Common experiences include the smell of rotting flesh, unearthly moaning, unexplained knocks and rapping noises that emanate from the walls and floors, sudden drops in room temperature, billowing curtains within the rooms even though all windows are closed, and strange lights that appear in the windows after the building has been locked for the night. The apparition of a melancholy young woman also inhabits the Parsonage and has been witnessed by visitors on numerous occasions.

The old Powder Magazine, located within the heart of the precinct, is topped by an impressive guard tower, which provided a perfect vantage point from which to observe the movements of convicts and soldiers in the settlement below. On occasion, phantom moans and shouting have been heard from the tower, and visitors

Photo by Liam Baker

have reported observing soldiers within the area directly behind the tower dressed in their regulation red uniforms. The ghost of an overzealous guard is also said to haunt the walkway below the tower, an invisible hand grabbing unsuspecting visitors by the arm as they pass by.

The Port Arthur Church also has its fair share of ghosts. Since the building was gutted by fire in 1884, bizarre lights have been witnessed at night within the shell of the church, with the occasional sound of ringing bells emanating from the bell tower—all remaining church bells are now housed in a glass case at the base of the bell tower. It is said that during the construction of the church, two convicts had an altercation that resulted in the death of one of the pair, falling to his death after heavily striking his head upon the bell tower wall. Later, when ivy began to grow upon the wall in the vicinity of the accident, the section of sandstone where the convict's head had impacted mysteriously remained bare.

—Liam Baker
Founder, Brisbane Ghost Hunters

Hobart Penitentiary Chapel

Corner of Brisbane and Campbell Street
Hobart
Tasmania, Australia
Website: *www.key.org.au/pchs*

Built in 1831 primarily as a house of worship for the ever-growing number of convicts and free settlers, the Hobart Penitentiary Chapel has seen many alterations over the years. Closed to free settler worship in 1845, and greatly enhanced into a fully operational penitentiary in 1857

with the addition of cells and an execution yard, the resulting complex was described as hellish confinement by those imprisoned there. Part of the complex was demolished in the 1960s during further construction; however, much of the site has remained in original condition for mroe than a century. In more recent times, the previously demolished section of the chapel has been painstakingly rebuilt to the original design in order to restore the site to its former glory.

The entire site exhibits a haunted atmosphere, regularly seeming unusually cold with an overwhelming sense of despair and hopelessness. For some, the oppressive ambience of the place can become so overpowering that they are forced to leave, complaining of headaches and breathing difficulties. The ghosts of the Penitentiary Chapel roam freely within the confines of the outer walls, each section of the site having at least one resident spirit and a myriad of reported unexplained phenomena. However, some sections of the chapel display a larger volume of inexplicable occurrences on a more regular and spectacular level than elsewhere within the precinct.

The Penitentiary Chapel is also haunted by the ghosts and memories of convicts whose lives were abruptly terminated through execution. The first execution

Photo by Liam Baker

was undertaken within the confines of the penitentiary in 1857, with a total of 32 convicted felons being executed in the years leading up to the final hanging in 1946. It is within the vicinity of the still-existent gallows that many visitors are exposed to the haunted atmosphere of the site, with experiences ranging from an overwhelming sense of fear, feeling hot and smothered even in winter when the temperature is low, the sensation of being grabbed by unseen hands, and the overpowering smell of blood and decomposition in the area directly below the trapdoor.

The solitary cells located beneath the floor of the chapel are also renowned for ghostly activity. Affectionately nicknamed the "Dust Hole" by convicts unfortunate enough to have spent time within this section of the penitentiary, the 36 solitary cells were constructed with insufficient ventilation and a complete lack of lighting. Closed in 1847 due to concerns over the prevailing inhumane conditions of these cells, the oppressive atmosphere and the spirits of many still reside beneath the Chapel flooring. Those willing to venture into the depths of this section report experiencing noticeable fluctuations in temperature, hearing footsteps and voices from within the empty cells, and catching momentary glimpses of spectral prisoners moving about in the darkness.

—Liam Baker
Founder, Brisbane Ghost Hunters

FREMANTLE ARTS CENTRE AND HISTORY MUSEUM

(PREVIOUSLY FREMANTLE ASYLUM)
1 FINNERTY STREET
FREMANTLE
WESTERN AUSTRALIA
WEBSITE: *www.fac.org.au*

The building within which the Fremantle Arts Centre and History Museum now resides has had a very colorful and varied history. Constructed in the early 1860s through convict labor, the building began its life as Western Australia's first lunatic asylum, fulfilling its chief purpose of housing the insane for 40 years. However, during the early 1900s in response to the suspicious deaths of two inmates and a subsequent government inquiry, the Fremantle Asylum was condemned and decommissioned.

By 1909, the building was again in use as a homeless women's shelter and continued its life as such until the outbreak of World War II. Throughout the war years, the asylum building acted as the headquarters for the American Forces, during which time the majority of the complex fell into disrepair. Following the war, the building was utilized for a number of purposes until a restoration project was undertaken in 1970 and the Arts Centre and History Museum were installed. While the building has been exposed to a variety of uses and modifications over time, the 40 years spent as a lunatic asylum seems to have played a pivotal role in relation to the haunted atmosphere and spirits found within its walls.

FREMANTLE ARTS CENTRE

As with many haunted locations, staff of the Arts Centre and History Museum regularly report unexplainable knocks and raps, as well as the sound of phantom footsteps within the corridors. Certain sections of the building seem prone to noticeable fluctuations in temperature, and the sensation of an invisible presence is always nearby. Many tourists who have ventured into the site claim to have witnessed apparitions and unexplainable phenomena within the building; some occurrences have terrified observers to such an extent that they have fainted as a result of the experience or immediately fled! There is no doubt that a multitude of spirits haunt the vicinity of the asylum due to its unpleasant past, with a handful of apparitions frequently observed haunting their respective sections of the site.

However, the most prevalent and well-known resident ghost is that of an aging woman. Always witnessed or sensed on the first floor of the asylum building, but most regularly within a specific room on that floor, the story relating to the wretched apparition is one of the most heart-wrenching tales of the asylum. Confined within its walls following her daughter's abduction, the woman in question slumped into a deep depression. Unable to cope with her terrible loss, she chose to leap from a first-floor window in order to bring an end to her grief. Ever since, her spirit has been seen by many of the visitors to the asylum complex, walking the halls of the first floor in search of her long-kidnapped child.

—Liam Baker
Founder, Brisbane Ghost Hunters

THE PRINCESS THEATRE
163 SPRING STREET
MELBOURNE
VICTORIA, AUSTRALIA
WEBSITE:
www.marrinertheatres.com.au

The present-day Princess Theatre was constructed in 1886, replacing an earlier theater building on the site dating back to 1854. Highly valued as Melbourne's oldest theater, the building's façade is beautifully designed with an incredibly lavish interior fitted during extensive renovations undertaken in 1922. However, the theater's most distinctive feature is a purpose-built sliding roof, which opens to the sky and provides ventilation to the theater below. The Princess Theatre has hosted a number of renowned performers and stage shows, including *The Phantom of the Opera*. But this theater is also home to a phantom of a different kind, one who has chosen to stay on long after his final act.

On the night of the March 3, 1888, during the final act of the well-known opera *Faust*, the famous baritone Frederick Baker fell victim to an unfortunate turn of events. Playing the part of Mephistopheles, Baker was required to descend through a trapdoor in the stage while portraying his character's plunge into hell. However, during his descent, Baker suffered a massive heart attack and vanished beneath the stage. Unbeknown to the audience, Baker was rushed into the theater boardroom in the hope that he would be stabilized. Unfortunately, there was little anyone could do, and Baker died shortly after. From this moment on, Frederick Baker's ghost took up residency within the theater.

Many present and former staff of the Princess Theatre talk of their own personal hair-raising experiences with the ghost of Frederick Baker, or "Federici," as he was aptly nicknamed during his career. The most common ghostly occurrences within the theater range from unexplainable balls of fluorescent light that hover about the stage and dress circle, mysterious noises within the wings and corridors, and an ever-growing list of bizarre accidents and equipment malfunctions during performances. Many performers who have undertaken shows at the theater even claim that Federici's ghost has passed them within the halls of the building. However, a great many performers and regular visitors to the theater have witnessed the apparition of Federici in all his glory.

The most regular area of the theater within which Federici's ghost is seen is the dress circle. Dressed in evening attire complete with cloak and top-hat, Federici's spirit has been observed on numerous occasions sitting or standing within the dress circle staring at the stage as if scrutinizing a performance. At times, the apparition lingers within its seat for an extended period, allowing astonished spectators the opportunity to study the ghostly figure in detail. Federici's ghost has become such a welcome visitor to the theater that his appearance on the opening night of a new performance is regarded as good fortune. Consequently, the theater staff always ensure a vacant seat within the dress circle on such an occasion!

—Liam Baker
Founder, Brisbane Ghost Hunters

NORTH HEAD QUARANTINE STATION

NORTH HEAD SCENIC DRIVE
MANLY
NEW SOUTH WALES, AUSTRALIA

The North Head Quarantine Station is the oldest and longest surviving station of its kind in the world, operating from 1828 until as recently as 1984, although in a diminished capacity in its latter years. The station was activated in order to address the serious issue of communicable diseases such as cholera, smallpox, and the bubonic plague entering Sydney Harbor aboard vessels carrying goods and early immigrants. Settlers aboard vessels suspected of carrying such infections were forced to disembark at the station at the mouth of Sydney Harbor and were placed under rigid quarantine until they were deemed healthy. Hundreds died under quarantine during this process, resulting in the haunted nature of the site today.

Quite unlike most haunted sites, the number of apparitions observed across the Quarantine Station site is incredible. Virtually every building and open area of the station has at least one apparition associated with it; a number of visitors leaving the site after dark have witnessed ghostly figures crossing in front of their vehicles as they navigated North Head Scenic Drive on their way from the station. Lights regularly turn themselves on in many of the locked buildings, staff and visitors commonly report strange sounds such as phantom footsteps on many of the verandas, and people are frequently touched or grabbed while walking through the site.

Of all the apparitions regularly witnessed throughout the site, two lingering spirits are by far the most frequent and remarkable. The more recurrent of the two ghosts is that of a traditionally dressed Chinese man, usually witnessed within the vicinity of the Asiatic quarters. The second apparition, that of a young girl in a white dress with pigtails, is less commonly observed. However, many of those fortunate enough to have caught a glimpse of this ghost have initially mistaken her for a flesh-and-blood child.

Unfortunately, a few buildings within the site known for their extreme paranormal activity were destroyed by fire in 2001, one being the station's original hospital building. Renowned for numerous apparitions of former patients observed laying in the old hospital beds as well as walking the wards, the loss of this building was a tragic event. However, plans are afoot to reconstruct this complex on the surviving building footings in the near future, after which the ghosts of the hospital may return!

Photo by Liam Baker

Since the tragic fires, one section of the station continues to exhibit a high level of unexplained phenomena. A seemingly innocent corrugated-iron structure on the site houses the station's shower block (pictured above). This block is notorious for doors slamming shut, lights inexplicably turning on and off, exploding lightbulbs, bangs and crashes against the corrugated iron walls, and the sounds of phantom footsteps pacing the rows of showers and toilets. If spirits and bizarre occurrences are what you seek, this section of the station is the best location for ghost hunting.

—Liam Baker
Founder, Brisbane Ghost Hunters

MONTE CRISTO HOMESTEAD

HOMESTEAD LANE
JUNEE, NEW SOUTH WALES, AUSTRALIA
TEL: 61 (02) 6924-1637
WEBSITE: *www.montecristo.com.au*

Monte Cristo is a late Victorian-era mansion that was built in 1884. The home sits high on the hill overlooking the New South Wales town of Junee and stands a testament to its builder's, Christopher William Crawley, financial empire. The mansion's religious name and grand stature are contrasted with a dark past that has led some ghost hunters to call Monte Cristo Australia's most haunted house.

Reginald Ryan has owned the Monte Cristo since 1963 and is an expert on the home's history. He knows all about some of the cruelty that went on at mansion. He said, "There was a girl pushed off the balcony. She was a maid and was pregnant at the time, and she died [from the fall]. One of the young boys that was working and boarding here didn't get up for work one morning, and the boss said, 'Come to work,' and the boy said he was too sick. The boss thought he was acting and set fire to the straw mattress, and the boy didn't get out in time and was burned to death."

The Crawleys had a history of treating their servants poorly—whether by cruel words, beatings, and possibly worse. After Christopher Crawley's death in 1910, his wife, Elizabeth Lydia Crawley, became a shut-in. She confined herself to an upstairs bedroom that she had converted into a chapel. She lived for 23 more years and only left the property on a handful of occasions the rest of her days.

Matt Bowden of the Australian Ghost Hunters Society (AGHS) visited Monte Cristo in 2001. Bowden said, "I experienced a few cold spots—especially in a room called the Drawing Room, where the lady of the house, Mrs. Crawley, would sit and sew. I experienced a cold spot in the corner of that room. At the time, there was a psychic on our tour, and she informed me that Mrs. Crawley was sitting in a chair next to where I was standing. I didn't see it, I couldn't exactly feel her presence as such, but I certainly felt a definite cold spot. I actually had a digital thermometer with me at the time—a piece of my ghost hunting equipment—and there certainly was a drop in temperature when I looked at the reading."

According to Ryan, there are at least 10 ghosts haunting Monte Cristo. Some psychics who visited the estate in the late 1990s for an Australian television show felt a woman who was murdered in the house was among the 10. Though no records of a murdered woman have been found there, it is possible that if something did happen, the Crawleys were held in such high regard that the local police probably wouldn't have asked too many questions. Other ghosts include members of the Crawley family and some of their many servants.

—Jeff Belanger
Founder, Ghostvillage.com

New Zealand

THE BLACK DOG OF MOERAKI
SOUTH ISLAND
OTAGO, NEW ZEALAND

Moeraki is a windswept peninsula in Otago, on the southeast coast of New Zealand's South Island. Today it's a popular tourist spot; famous for the rugged coastline, little blue penguins, Moeraki lighthouse, and a phenomenon of nature known as the Moeraki boulders. The boulders are giant, spherical balls of granite that dot the coastline in small groups. Some say they are a result of the natural action of the waves rolling the great rocks in the surf, others say they are meteorites, and then there are those who believe them to be of a more spiritual nature. Whatever their source, they are a site well-worth seeing.

Before the coming of the Europeans, Moeraki was inhabited by Maoris—small tribal groups who would travel around the coast, fishing and hunting. It was common in those days for the Maoris to keep dogs inside their fortifications that they called their "Pa." The dogs were kept for several reasons: guard dogs, pets, and in lean times, they were a source of food. One such dog, a particular favorite of the Kuia (ancient woman), was a great black brute, ill-tempered and stand-offish, but usually a great watchdog barking at all that moved. He was always a great comfort to the Kuia, for the dog slept just outside her whare (house) and next to the chief's. Throughout the day, he was forever hanging around the camp looking for food scraps.

It's rumored that one night the chief, who was coming out of his hut to relieve himself and not looking where he was going, tripped over the wretched sleeping animal. The old chief fell down and hurt his leg, and the dog howled in fright and promptly bit him, adding to the chief's woes. The dog ran off snarling and snapping. In a fury, the chief ordered the useless animal be caught, killed, and served up for dinner.

Later that day, while eating kai (dinner), the Kuia looked around for the old dog to give him some scraps. Of course, he wasn't to be found. She asked of the chief, "Where is the black dog?" The chief replied, "You're eating him!" Up jumped the enraged Kuia, overturning all the kai. She stood back and cast a Makutu (curse) on the chief. It was indeed the last dinner the chief ate—the legends say he choked on a bone of the dog and died as a result of the Makutu.

In her curse, the Kuia said that no one on Moeraki was ever to hurt a black dog again, and from that time to present day, the appearance of a large, black dog on the foreshores at Moeraki is to be considered a bad omen.

Some years later, when the Europeans had arrived and the settlement at Moeraki became a fishing village and lighthouse station, strange stories of a black dog approaching at night started to be told. In some accounts, the dog would fall in and walk just in front of people walking home, seeming to guide them to their homes. Other times the dog would weave in and out, barking and growling, causing people to become confused and fall. In a number of cases, people who complained of seeing the dog weave ahead of them suffered serious injury, broken limbs, and on at least two occasions, death.

For more than 150 years, the story has been told, many people have seen the dog,

no one claimed ownership, and he has never been seen in daylight hours. Just hope that if by some strange twist of fate you find yourself in Moeraki, the dog that walks you home is not large and black and he does so in a straight line.

—Dorothy O'Donnell
Web Owner, Ghosts and Other Haunts

WAITOMO CAVES HOTEL
RD7 OTOROHANGA
NORTH ISLAND, NEW ZEALAND
TEL: 64 7 878-8204
WEBSITE:
www.waitomocaveshotel.co.nz

The Waitomo Caves are home to curious little creatures called *Arachnocampa luminosa*—better know as glowworms. The insects glow a fluorescent green in their larval stage and are indigenous to New Zealand. Inside the dark caves, visitors look up into what, at quick glance, may look like a starlit sky, but is actually thousands of glowworms attached to the ceiling of the cave. Once outside of the cave, visitors may glance high above them to the majestic Victorian building perched at the top of the hill looking down on them.

The Waitomo Caves Hotel was originally called the "Government Hostel at Waitomo" and was built in 1908, though the area grew so quickly in popularity that another wing was added in 1928 to accommodate more guests. The style is New Zealand Victorian, and the building boasts a very unique and asymmetrical design. Visitors may come for the glowworms and incredible views, but some of them also come for the ghosts.

Hotel guests have reported an entity playing little tricks on them, such as moving shoes around their room or hanging items on the doorknob. One female guest, who was staying in room 12B with her brother, spilled some makeup powder on the floor. When she turned around, she found a small human footprint in the powder that did not match hers or her brother's feet. The siblings then noticed that the room order numbering in their hallway went 9, 10, 11, 12A, 12B, 14, 15... they were actually staying in what should be room 13.

Apparitions have been seen in the dining room, and some staff members report getting an uneasy feeling in the back corridor. And the Waitomo Caves' glowworms aren't the only balls of light showing up in tourists' photographs—some guests report many strange orbs in the photos they take within the building.

—Jeff Belanger
Founder, Ghostvillage.com

STATE HIGHWAY 4

10 KILOMETERS SOUTH OF MAPIU
NORTH ISLAND, NEW ZEALAND

Approximately 10 kilometers (6.2 miles) south of the town of Mapiu, along the side of Highway 4, is a ditch where people have reported seeing a Maori (person of Polynesian-Melanesian decent) woman standing by the road in the middle of the night. "Nathan" and "Brodie" sent in their encounter to my Website:

"My friend and I were in his truck coming from Palmerston North, and on the way we went through a little town called Mapiu between Taumarunui and Te Kuiti. When we were about 10 kilometers south of Mapiu, we came across something weird— we saw an old Maori lady, about 40 or 50 years old, dressed in old rugged clothes and standing in the ditch on the side of the road just staring at us. She looked lost, but it was about 2 a.m. and it was raining hard. We slowed down, but did not stop. This got us thinking that it was very weird, but then we thought nothing more of it and carried on. But last week, my friend was talking to a work mate who he had never met before, and this guy started talking about some random Maori lady at the same place we had seen her about 10 months prior. We had never mentioned anything to anyone about her, but this guy described her to a T. And now all sorts of stories are coming up from everywhere— from people we don't even know. Apparently this Maori woman was hit by a truck that was speeding and it killed her. Exactly one year later, the driver died on that same part of the road."

—Dorothy O'Donnell
Web Owner, Ghosts and Other Haunts

STATE HIGHWAY 4

United Kingdom

United Kingdom

England

DENHAM CHURCH
DENHAM ST. MARY
SUFFOLK, ENGLAND

Denham Church stands in the small village of Denham St. Mary in Suffolk. Nearby stands Denham Hall, which is divided into a number of flats. The church, hall, and surrounding areas have been the scene of many paranormal events over the years.

There are at least 11 different ghosts in and around the hall, including a monk who walks an old footpath, a lady who has been spotted walking over a nearby bridge, and another ghostly lady who walks out of the church gate just as you walk past.

A misty figure that floats down a steep hill leading from the church has also been witnessed, as have two very evil-looking red eyes in the steep bank of the same hill.

Two other ghostly ladies have been seen here—one walks up the path of an old cottage at the foot of the hill, and the other is seen wearing Victorian clothes and walking the gardens of the hall in daylight.

Suffolk Paranormal Investigations have received a recent report regarding a farm worker's ghost that has been seen by locals around the farm building. He died around 1920 in a rather nasty accident in which he lost his head under the wheels of a horse-drawn cart. It is said his ghost is headless.

A number of strange things have been reported inside the hall, including small colored lights which move around the walls, a bloodstain on the floor which comes and goes, and footsteps and whispering that can be heard within. But by far the most interesting haunting is "The Chain" that can be heard dragging along the road from the church. It stops at a spot that was a crossroads many years ago. When it stops, a luminous ball hovers around one meter above the ground for five or six minutes before it fades away.

We have researched this case and found a very interesting story to this haunting.

A young girl, about 16 years old, lived in the village, and she was very beautiful. All the local men fell in love with her. Their wives and girlfriends were not happy, so they said she must be a Witch as she was bewitching the men folk.

She was found guilty of witchcraft and locked in the church for a number of days awaiting her fate. She was bound in chains, dragged down the road, and thrown into a well to drown; her body was then dragged along the road and buried at the crossroads.

Many years later, she was dug up by workmen, and they found that her remains were still in chains. She was given a full Christian burial in a churchyard near Bury Street in Edmunds, but the ghostly chains can be heard to this day.

—Richard Keeble and
Shantell Ainsworth
Suffolk Paranormal Investigations

THE LAIRS/PIPERS VALE

IPSWICH
SUFFOLK, ENGLAND

Set beside the River Orwell, the "Lairs," as it is affectionately known by locals, is a valley of natural beauty, but behind the façade, a different story begins to unfold. Suffolk Paranormal Investigations decided to investigate this after a wave of sightings.

After researching the area and talking to locals, we were surprised by the amount of people telling the same story. Strange balls of light around the Orwell Bridge and dancing over the River Orwell are seen regularly. The bridge has been the site of several suicides since being built in 1982.

A white figure, the feeling of being watched, and cold spots that witnesses walk through have all been experienced in one particular area of the valley. The sound of horses' hooves has been heard, and a white figure on a horse has been seen here by a number of witnesses, spanning a number of years.

Jeff, an Ipswich resident, related the following experience to us: "I used to take my dog out for a walk down Pipers Vale, Ipswich. Twice I heard the sound of a horse coming from behind me. I turned round

and was going to wait and let it pass, but there was no one on the open area. I was really surprised, as I had heard it clearly. A different time, I was walking in the same place with my wife and son and I heard it again. No one else had. I thought I was imagining things. I do not believe in ghosts, but my wife said that maybe that's what it was. About five years later, a neighbor told me they had heard the same thing close to where I had."

Margaret Catchpole was a notorious horse thief and jail breaker who was born in Suffolk in 1762. By her 30s, she was working in service for the Cobbold family in Ipswich. She was famed for her horsemanship after riding bareback from Nacton to Ipswich for a doctor to help her sick mistress.

The route Margaret had taken that night coincided with the sightings of the figure on a horse and the sound of hooves.

The lane where people have reported the white figure, cold spot, and feeling of being watched leads to a huge oak tree where Margaret used to tie her horses.

—Richard Keeble and
Shantell Ainsworth
Suffolk Paranormal Investigations

THE QUEENS HEAD HOTEL

79 MARKET STREET
ASHBY-DE-LA-ZOUCH
LEICESTERSHIRE, LE65 1AH
ENGLAND

Not for the faint-hearted, the Queens Head Hotel is a 17th-century, three-story coaching inn with a black-and-white beam façade. On the ground floor level is a nightclub area where the Spirit Team began our investigation of the many accounts of spirit activity that have been reported in the building. We set up video cameras to cover the nightclub, with a camera specifically covering the bar. On the first floor, cameras were set up at various points in the attic bar.

The staff of the Queens Head recount many sightings of a tall, dark, imposing man in the hotel. At first, they believe he is simply a patron, only later they realize there is no one around—the dark man disappears. His presence makes the staff feel very uneasy, as though they are in the presence of evil. Voices have also been heard when no one else is around to account for them. During our investigation of the nightclub area, several of our members described this phantom man, though they had no prior knowledge of him.

The spirits of children have been seen and heard inside the hotel as well. They seem afraid of the larger entity, as though he controls them, or did. We placed a 20-pence coin on its side on the bar and asked if anyone could cause it to fall. The coin immediately fell, though the phenomenon was not repeated when we tried again. Many orbs were visible in there.

The upstairs bar was very misty during our time there, like people had been smoking, but no one had. Dank smells came and went without explanation. One of our senior members felt his arm being touched, EMF meters confirmed high levels of electromagnetic energy, and a child was seen sitting on the stairs wearing a gray school uniform. The child spirit was later seen standing by the fireplace. When we asked the spirit to come forward, a footstep was heard.

While reviewing one of our video camera monitors that was placed in an upstairs room, we observed the screen blank out for a moment, as though someone walked in front of the camera, but no one (who was living) could have been in the room to do so.

—*Annmarie Godsmark*
Spirit Team

THE TOWER OF LONDON
LONDON EC3N 4AB
ENGLAND
TEL: 44 (0) 870-756-6060
WEBSITE: *www.hrp.org.uk*

The Tower of London has seen a millennium of British history. The fortress has been home to the Crown Jewels, it's served as an armory, a prison, a mint, a royal palace, and a place of execution from some royals and other notable enemies of the king. Today, the Tower of London is considered one of the most haunted places on earth.

The Tower's earliest structure was built by William the Conqueror of Normandy between 1066 and 1067 C.E. King William I chose the site along the shores of the river Thames because of its defendable position. He had the initial structure built into the southeast corner of the early Roman city walls. The central White Tower was the tallest building in London for many centuries. Today, more than 20 towers make up the Tower of London fortress.

Ghost encounters have occurred all over the grounds and in almost every building. One of the most predominant specters at the tower is that of Anne Boleyn. Boleyn was the second of King Henry VIII's six wives. Henry VIII found his wife guilty of infidelity and treason. She was beheaded at the tower on May 19, 1536.

Some have reported seeing her headless ghost walking the grounds, and reports (and even the lyrics of an old folk song from 1935) claim some see her with her head tucked underneath her arm.

Photo by Jeff Belanger

Today, there are many people who live and work at the Tower of London. The Yeoman Warders (better known as the Beefeaters), and their families live in accommodations within the tower. No one knows the tower's ghostly legends better than members of this elite guard.

Yeoman Sergeant Phil Wilson has been a Yeoman Warder and full-time resident of the tower since 1996. Wilson relayed an account told to him by a retired Yeoman Warder. Wilson said, "He told me that he lived in one of the quarters around the casements, which are in the outer circle of the tower. His story goes that he was fast asleep one night, no problems at all, and then he was shaken awake by his wife, who said, 'Who were those two children standing at the end of the bed in white nightgowns?' Of course he woke up and had seen absolutely nothing. She then went on to describe these two children as looking quite distressed, and they were in long, white nightgowns cuddling each other in front of a Victorian fireplace. Of course, there was no Victorian fireplace there at all. So you put it down to a dream or whatever. Anyway, [the couple] moved from the quarters to somewhere else, and they started redecorating the quarter and found there was actually a false wall behind which was a Victorian fireplace. So that gave that story a bit more credence."

Perhaps the saddest ghostly tale within the tower is that of the two princes—12-year-old King Edward V and his 9-year-old brother, Richard, Duke of York. The two boys were murdered under suspicious circumstances in 1483, and their bodies were hidden—buried near the foundation of the White Tower. Could this retired Yeoman Warder's wife have caught a glimpse of the two princes?

There are almost as many ghost stories within the Tower as there are cobblestones in its walkways.

—Jeff Belanger
Founder, Ghostvillage.com

ROBIN HOOD'S GRAVE

BARNSDALE FOREST
WEST YORKSHIRE, ENGLAND

Deep in the heart of West Yorkshire, amidst the hustle and bustle of industrial towns, there lies a forgotten grave, hidden within the dark, mysterious remains of the once-great Barnsdale Forest. Here, under the twisted shadows of ancient trees, lies Robin Hood's grave, cast up like a great ship of stone wrecked in the Kirklees everglades. Fallen pillars and twisted railings are all that remain of the famous outlaw's tomb. It was here, in 1347, that the famous outlaw was bled to death by the evil prioress of Kirklees and her lover, Red Roger of Doncaster, though no one knows the reason why. It could have been murder, mischance, poor nursing, an inevitable death from medieval medicine (bleeding), or a more sinister reason such as vampirism (that is, the people who drink blood, not the undead), Pagan sacrifice, or thwarted passion. No matter the reason, Robin died without the Last Rites of the Church and was buried in unconsecrated grounds on the crossing of ley lines. Small wonder, then, that we hear today of hauntings in this area and tales of black magic ceremonies in the vicinity.

Over the past few years, reports of paranormal phenomena around the gravesite have been reported to the Yorkshire Robin Hood Society. One of the earliest stories was from an elderly lady who used to visit her aunt in Hartshead, near Kirklees, many years ago. She and a friend reported hearing Robin calling for Marian and seeing flashing lights in the sky, and, on one occasion, they found a silver arrow in a field near the grave.

In the early 1980s, I was told by a local man named Roger Williams how he saw an apparition of a white lady on two occasions when he was clandestinely visiting the grave. On both occasions, 1963 and 1972, he saw the same woman gliding across the grass and has since stated, "Wild horses would not drag me up there again."

I personally had a terrifying experience at the graveside when I saw a hideous specter, which I identified as Red Roger of Doncaster—a shadowy form was nearby him, which I assumed to be the prioress. I felt a terrific force of evil in the area. Similarly, Mark Gibbons, a paranormal researcher, saw a white figure in the woods and vowed never to go to the grave again. Two reporters, Judith Broadbent and Sue Ellis, experienced strange happenings when they visited the grave in the mid-1990s, and Sue was taken seriously ill immediately afterwards. A gamekeeper employed on the estate had his gun go off unexpectedly near the grave—he lost two of his teeth and narrowly missed serious injury. He also swore that he saw Robin's apparition in the nearby priory gatehouse where Robin died.

During the Yorkshire Robin Hood Society's (YRHS) investigations, which originally started out as purely historical, Otley psychic Evelyn Friend became aware of the evil forces in the area and sought to bless the land by conducting an exorcism on the four points of the ley lines, which stretch from Hartshead Church, to Castle Hill, the Three Nuns Inn, and Alegar Holy Well in Brighouse. The Vicar of Brighouse at that time, the Reverend John Flack, was asked to perform a blessing service at the graveside, but was refused permission from the landowner and forbidden to become involved in the situation.

Shortly afterward, his church was vandalized for occult purposes. Two bishops were asked to intervene and use their position to press for the ceremony, but both declined in no uncertain terms. In fact, they were decidedly "not amused" and completely disassociated themselves from the matter and advised Miss Friend and the YRHS to leave well enough alone.

In the meantime, the deterioration of Robin Hood's grave and Kirklees Priory gatehouse continues, the disturbances are still happening, and the general public are forbidden to visit.

—Barbara Green
Yorkshire Robin Hood Society

ORDSALL HALL

ORDSALL LANE
SALFORD, ENGLAND
TEL: 44 (0) 161-872-0251
WEBSITE: *www.salford.gov.uk/ ordsallhall*

Ordsall Hall is home to one of England's many "White Ladies"—a misty, white female form that has been seen floating around the grounds. But the inside of the hall may even be more haunted. Strange occurrences with electrical equipment, knocks, footsteps, doors opening and closing, and even the witnessing of actual ghosts have all been reported inside.

The oldest part of the building was constructed sometime before 1177 C.E. because the name "Ordeshala" appears to have paid a feudal tax in the old public records of that year. Ordsall Hall is best-known for being the home of the Radclyffe family. Margaret Radclyffe, whose exact date of birth isn't known, but was either in 1573 or 1574, is the center of most of the ghostly speculation. Margaret had a twin brother named Alexander who went off to fight in Ireland in 1599. He died in battle and never returned home. Margaret died soon after of a broken heart. The official report called it "strings around the heart," which today we know of as angina brought on by stress. The legend says Margaret Radclyffe is forever waiting for her brother to return from Ireland, and she won't go until he does. Her spirit is blamed for most of the unexplained phenomena at Ordsall Hall.

Les Willis has lived in Salford his entire life and has been a guide at the hall since 1992. He recounted a story regarding the previous supervisor who was living at the hall with his wife when they received a call in the middle of the night from the elderly people's home across the street. Willis said, "It was three o'clock in the morning when this telephone call came asking, 'What's your wife doing outside walking around on the grounds?' And he said, 'She's actually sleeping next to me.' Somebody from the elderly people's home had actually spotted some white shape and thought it was the supervisor's wife."

Willis has also had his own unexplained experiences while working at Ordsall Hall. This happened during a break with one of his colleagues. He said, "We were off downstairs and I had just noticed through the corner of my eye something going up the stairs—and we could hear footsteps. We both heard the same thing."

Ordsall Hall's Website was home to one of the Internet's earliest and most popular "GhostCams." A camera is set up in the Great Hall, which broadcasts a picture of the inside of the building every 15 seconds—allowing online ghost hunters to try their luck at spotting the ghost of Margaret Radclyffe.

—Jeff Belanger
Founder, Ghostvillage.com

MUNCASTER CASTLE

RAVENGLASS
CUMBRIA
CA18 1RQ
ENGLAND
TEL: +44 (0) 1229 717 614
WEBSITE: *www.muncaster.co.uk*

Muncaster Castle was once the court of a great fool—Tom Fool to be exact. Thomas Skelton, better known as Tom Fool, was the court jester for the Pennington family during the latter half of the 16th century. Always the prankster, Skelton was known for his humorous antics in the court, for giving bad directions to travelers who came by the castle, and also for performing a murderous deed for his master when required. Tom Fool's presence is still felt at Muncaster, and his ghost has become the scapegoat for almost every little thing that goes wrong inside, be it supernatural or not. But Skelton is by no means the only spirit here.

Built around 1258 C.E. by Gamel de Mulcastre, the castle sits on a picturesque setting in West Cumberland by the River Esk. The castle has served as a fortress to ward off marauding Scots from the north, it was an outpost to protect trade routes from Carlisle, and it's been home to the Pennington family, a family of great influence in the region, for almost 800 years.

"There's always been the ghost stories about Muncaster," Peter Frost-Pennington said, who has been living at the castle since 1987. "At least initially, we didn't really talk about them outside the family at all."

The most profound phenomena at Muncaster occurs in the Tapestry Room. Until the mid-1990s, the Tapestry Room bedroom was part of the main castle and was not used as part of the accommodations the castle rents to guests. Only friends and family stayed in the Tapestry Room, but the practice didn't last very long because so many people who stayed in that room claimed they couldn't sleep because they heard an infant crying for hours—though no infants were anywhere in the Castle. The crying phenomenon at Muncaster has been happening for many years, and the event has been known to happen not for a fleeting moment, like so many paranormal encounters—it has at times gone on for multiple hours.

On the Castle's grounds, there have been numerous reports of a "White Lady"—believed to be the ghost of Mary Bragg, who, in 1805, was a housekeeper in Ravenglass and was in love with the footman at Muncaster. Mary Bragg was brutally murdered along the road to Muncaster by henchman sent by another woman who was in love with the Muncaster footman. Frost-Pennington said, "She's this white lady who appears on the main roads around Muncaster and sometimes in the garden. Some people have even reported that they thought they'd hit someone. They were driving on the road, and this figure in white jumps out in front of them—they hit this young girl in front of them. They stopped the car and there's nothing to be seen.

"People have often seen darting figures, or sometimes she's a solid figure that looks like you or me. Other times, she's just a sort of miasma or mist, but a fairly thick mist. And we do get sort of odd clumps of mist hanging around hills around here on occasion, but people I've talked to are sure it wasn't just a bit of the mist. They say, 'Oh, no. It wasn't like that at all. It was different—it was a definite blob.'"

—Jeff Belanger
Founder, Ghostvillage.com

THE MARSDEN GROTTO

COAST ROAD, SOUTH SHIELDS
TYNE AND WEAR, ENGLAND NE34 7BS
TEL: 44 (0) 191-455-6060

This building is located on the northeast of England's coast and was built into the limestone cliffs by a man nicknamed Jack "the Blaster" Bates. The building's history dates back as far as 1782, and it's a very interesting building even to look at. Over the years, many deaths have taken place at the now refurbished inn and restaurant. These include killed smugglers, washed-up sailors, and suicides by leaping from the cliff tops above.

There were several unexplained occurrences that happened prior to any of our overnight investigations at the grotto. There have been unexplainable knockings on the current manager's flat door, which is located inside the premises. When the manager answered the door, no one appeared to be there. The main door to the beer cellar has been heard rattling and shaking as if a person is locked inside, but when opening the door, the staff find the cellar is empty. A chain is used in the bar to keep the customers from getting behind the bar area. This chain has been heard rattling and clanking while no one is in the

vicinity. Faint voices and mutterings have also been reported when no one is around. There is also a set of mysterious bare footprints that can't be washed away; they keep on returning every time the wooden floor is cleaned. The ghost of a man has been seen on the premises, along with numerous reports of black shadows. This is why The Answers People Seek team was asked to join North East Ghost Inspectres on investigating any paranormal activity at the grotto.

Many believe the numerous deaths are responsible for the amount of ghost sightings and unexplained occurrences that are continuing to be seen and reported. Our investigations seem to raise even more questions. We experienced power and electrical drainages along with many unexplainable lights and sounds recorded on digital cameras and digital sound recorders. Much of the information our psychics have provided has been researched and confirmed as correct. On one occasion, we invited a local newspaper reporter along to the investigation. She was open-minded, but quite skeptical also; that is, until she claimed to have seen the ghost of a man in the lower cave bar. You could tell she was visibly shaken up by the whole experience.

Our team has really enjoyed researching the building and seeking out some of the answers to the paranormal questions it raises. Through our research and overnight investigations dated 19th of November 2004 and 17th of December 2004, we believe the place to be very active, and we look forward to continuing our ongoing research to discover what is there and why.

—Paul Roberts
Founder, The Answers People Seek

Ireland

GILLHALL ESTATE
LURGAN ROAD
DROMORE COUNTY DOWN
NORTHERN IRELAND

Gillhall Estate consisted of a vast estate of land, farm buildings, and an impressive house that had been built between 1670 and 1680 by John Magill. Sadly, the house is no longer standing after a fire in 1969, which rendered it unstable and a hazard. The house was then demolished by the Territorial Army.

Gillhall was as impressive inside as it was out. Many of the rooms were so large that they required a fireplace at both ends for enough heat. There were remarkable carvings inside the house, an example being the barley-sugar banisters and the carved swags of foliage on the staircase.

Gillhall was also renowned for its reputation of being one of the most notorious haunted houses in Ireland. This was due to the Earl of Tyrone who made a pact with his cousin, Lady Beresford. The story goes that as children, Lady Nichola Beresford, John Power, and Lord Tyrone, vowed that whoever died first would come back in the form of a ghost to prove to the other that there was a life after death. One night in 1693 while she was staying at Gillhall, Lady Beresford was visited by the ghost of Lord Tyrone who told her that there was indeed a life after death. To convince Lady Beresford that he was a genuine apparition and not just a figment of her imagination, he made various predictions, notably that she would have a son who would marry his niece, the heiress of Curraghmore, and the more shocking prediction that Lady Beresford would die on her 47th birthday.

His predictions all came true. To further convince Lady Beresford of his visit, he touched her wrist, which made the flesh and sinews shrink. Lady Beresford wore a piece of black ribbon around her wrist to hide the damage for the rest of her life. When the fifth Earl of Clanwilliam brought his bride to Gillhall in 1909, it is said that she found the ghosts of Gillhall too much to bear and so the house was abandoned by the family. In 1910, the Earl and his wife bought Montalto in Ballynahinch. From then onward, Gillhall stood empty and deserted, except for the small portion of the house in which the recent owner's land steward and his family could live. In 1945, the land steward, who was a local man by the name of Mr. Robert Matchet, and his family were surprised when they received a visit by two American soldiers who told them of a room in the house where they could find a pane of glass in the window with a verse written on it. The soldier told of how his grandmother had been a servant in the house at the time and had told him the story of how one of the young ladies in the house had been mischievous, and so to punish her, the girl's father had locked her in this room for a short spell of time. While she was in the room, the young girl took her diamond ring and proceeded to write the following on the window.

The beauty of holiness
Is best understood
To him that beauty beheld
By the fair and the good.

No one had previously known about this until the Americans' visit.

By 1966, the house was in an advanced state of decay. It was then that the Irish Georgian Society carried out much-needed repairs, without which it would definitely have been past saving. The Society hoped that having made the house watertight they could restore the house further at a later date. Unfortunately, it was shortly after their first attempt at restoring the full glory of Gillhall that the house fell victim to fire. Gillhall may not be standing, but the its legend certainly lives on. People are still known to pass the gates of Gillhall as quickly as possible for fear of seeing the infamous ghost.

—Warren Coates
Chairman, Northern Ireland
Paranormal Research Association

SPRINGHILL

20 SPRINGHILL ROAD
MONEYMORE
COUNTY LONDONDERRY BT45 7NQ
NORTHERN IRELAND

Springhill is a 17th-century house that was once the home of 10 generations of a single family from Ayrshire. In the late 19th century, a certain Miss Wilson was residing at Springhill and saw a tall female apparition standing at the top of the moonlit stairs. The ghost approached a door to a room and mysteriously threw its hands up in the air in a grief-stricken manner before vanishing. The same room was occupied in later years by another guest, Miss Hamilton, who reported having witnessed excited servants pouring into the room before the door to the room opened, a light shone in, and the activity ceased. Miss Hamilton was dumbfounded to hear that the owner of the house had papered over that particular door. A governess reported having heard two children in the next room to

hers holding a casual conversation about a ghostly woman standing by the fireplace.

Teddy Butler, an administrator of the property for a number of years, saw a woman in black at the foot of the stairs. He also heard the sounds of marching and heavy footsteps on the stairs and landing, and he even collided with a woman going through the back door in the middle of the afternoon. This woman is said to have been the wife of Colonel Conyngham who served in the Crimea. Her portrait disappeared from Springhill a few years ago, mysteriously reappeared wrapped in brown paper, vanished again, and it hasn't been seen since.

—Warren Coates
Chairman, Northern Ireland
Paranormal Research Association

LEAP CASTLE

COUNTY OFFALY
NORTHERN IRELAND

According to the legends, Leap Castle was built on a Druidic site. When the O'Carroll family came here, they had a nasty habit of murdering people and dropping the mortal remains down a hole in the wall called an "oubliette." Once in the hole, the remains were promptly forgotten about. One O'Carroll chieftain murdered his own brother, a priest, for starting Mass too promptly. Hence, the top floor of the castle is called the Bloody Chapel. It was, however, lower down in the castle that "It" is experienced—an elemental force of evil with the head of a sheep and the stench of death.

The small, windowless room below the oubliette was the final resting place for scores of victims who were initially locked in a hidden dungeon off the Bloody Chapel. This room had a drop floor, and prisoners were pushed into the room where they fell to their deaths—either impaled on a spike below, or if they were unfortunate enough to miss the spike and die a quick death, they slowly starved in the midst of rotting, putrid corpses.

Around 1900, workmen who were hired to clean out the windowless room discovered hundreds of human skeletons piled on top of each other. It took three full cartloads to remove all of the bones, and one theory is that some of the remains were those of Scottish mercenaries hired by O'Carroll who had them murdered when it came time for payment. Mysteriously, among the bones, workmen also found a pocket watch made in the 1840s. Could the dungeon still have been in use back then? No one will ever know.

Shortly after the gruesome discovery in the dungeon, playful dabbling in the occult may have caused the reemergence of the evil spirits. In 1659, ownership of Leap Castle passed in marriage from the O'Carroll family to an English family, the Darbys. The Darby family turned Leap into their family home, with improvements and additions and landscaped gardens. In the late-19th century, descendants Jonathan and Mildred Darby were looking forward to raising their family here. The occult was the fashion of the day, and Mildred Darby did some innocent dabbling, despite the castle's history and reputation for being haunted.

In 1909, she wrote an article for the *Journal Occult Review*, describing her terrifying ordeal:

"I was standing in the Gallery looking down at the main floor, when I felt somebody put a hand on my shoulder. The thing was about the size of a sheep. Thin, gaunt, shadowy...its face was human, to be more accurate...inhuman. Its lust in its eyes, which seemed half-decomposed in black cavities, stared into mine. The horrible smell one hundred times intensified came up into my face, giving me a deadly nausea. It was the smell of a decomposing corpse."

The spirit is thought to be a primitive ghost that attaches itself to a particular place. It is often malevolent, terrifying, and unpredictable. The Darbys remained at Leap until 1922. Being the home of an English family, it became the target of the Irish struggle for independence. Destroyed by bombs and completely looted, nothing but a burned-out shell remained. The Darbys were driven out.

The castle lay in ruin for decades. But then, in the 1970s, it was purchased by an Australian, who had a white Witch brought in from Mexico to exorcise the castle. She spent many hours in the Bloody Chapel and when she emerged, she explained that the spirits at Leap Castle were no longer malevolent, but they wished to remain.

In the 1990s, the castle was sold to the current owners. They are aware of the castle's troubled history. Shortly after moving in, they began restoration of the castle. However, a "freak accident" left the owner with a broken kneecap, which delayed restoration work on the castle for nearly a year. One year after his "accident," the owner was back at work when the ladder he was standing on suddenly tilted backwards away from the wall, causing him to jump to the ground. The result was a broken ankle and more delays with the restoration. The owners say they would be happy to share the castle with the spirits as long as there are no more "occurrences."

LEAP CASTLE

Recently, the christening of the owner's baby daughter took place in the Bloody Chapel. For the first time in centuries, the castle was filled with music, dancing, laughter, and most of all, love. To quote those in attendance, it was a "happy, pleasant, wonderful day."

Have the troubled spirits of Leap Castle finally found peace? Assuming they haven't left, one can only hope they have.

—Warren Coates
Chairman, Northern Ireland
Paranormal Research Association

GLENARM CASTLE

COUNTY ANTRIM
NORTHERN IRELAND
WEBSITE: *www.glenarmcastle.com*

There was once so much paranormal activity here that the mistress of the house had every room exorcised except the attic—from which, according to the story, all of the ghosts immediately fled. The son of the owner says that there used to be a terrible stamping noise from the attic and that one night, the noise was so loud, he was sent to investigate. He switched on the light at the bottom of the stairs and went up. Suddenly, the light turned itself out, and he realized that whatever was making the noise had gotten behind him. Somehow, he managed to get back down the stairs and never went up again. The noises continued for years afterward. After a skeleton was found on the grounds, the theory formed that the house is haunted by someone who was murdered there.

—Warren Coates
Chairman, Northern Ireland Paranormal
Research Association

COOLEY WELLS

PORTAFERRY
COUNTY DOWN
NORTHERN IRELAND

There is an ancient set of holy wells situated seven miles north west of Portaferry. Over the past several years, the Northern Ireland Paranormal Research Association have had several people contact us about strange goings-on, ranging from hearing voices to seeing figures of people walking about the site.

On four different occasions, we conducted investigations at the site with amazing results. Working with a trained medium, we were able to make contact with a fisherman called "Paul" who worked on the site in 1874. Paul was very amused that we were taking an interest in him and this place. Paul told us that he knew he had passed on but did not want to leave this place, which is understandable considering this is one of the most peaceful and beautiful places one would ever want to see.

After working with Paul for some amount of time, we began to recognize some energy that came from this spirit: love, trust, happiness, but mixed in with all of this, we all felt a deep sense of not belonging and wanting. We all knew that a spirit rescue was needed.

Photo by Warren Coates

The following night, we returned to the wells with digital cameras, camcorders, and night-vision equipment. After some time, we began the spirit rescue. I asked Paul if he would mind if I took a few photos, which I did. There was no smoke or mist on the night I took them.

The medium, aided by the rest of the team, finally said goodbye to Paul, and all present felt the whole place change and get lighter as Paul the fisherman finally moored his boat for the last time.

—Warren Coates
Chairman, Northern Ireland
Paranormal Research Association

MALAHIDE CASTLE

MALAHIDE
COUNTY DUBLIN
IRELAND
TEL: 353 (0) 1 846-2184
WEBSITE: *www.malahidecastle.com/
malahidecastle/ghost.asp*

Malahide Castle was the fortress of the Talbot family from 1185 to 1973. Located northeast of Dublin on the Irish coast, the name "Malahide" literally means "on the brow of the sea." Lord Richard Talbot first arrived in the area in 1170 from Shrewsbury in England, where his family were also lords. King Henry II's son, Prince John, confirmed Talbot's lordship of the Malahide land. The earliest parts of the castle were built around 1185, and as time went by and new generations of Lord Talbots came into power, they built onto the structure, turning the castle into one of the most breathtaking landmarks in Ireland. The castle was home for the Talbots and their servants for almost eight centuries except for a brief period between 1649 and 1660, when Cromwell granted the castle and its lands to Miles Corbet.

The most renowned of the Talbots' servants was Puck. Puck served the Talbots in the first half of the 16th century. He was a 4-foot-tall bearded man who lived in one of the castle's turrets, keeping a vigilant watch for attack. (Today the stairs ascending to his former chamber are referred to as "Puck's staircase.") Puck was reclusive, but tidy and loyal. The lore of the castle says he kept to himself mostly, his quarters were always clean, and after the other servants left food out for him outside of his chamber door, the next morning they would always find his plates and utensils cleaned and waiting for pickup. There are two differing tales surrounding Puck's death—one version says he hung himself in the Minstrel's Gallery within the castle for no apparent reason. The other version of the story says Puck was in love with a relative of Lady Lenora Fitzgerald. The infatuation angered some in Lady Fitzgerald's court, who stabbed Puck through the heart outside of Malahide Castle. No matter how Puck died, his ghost has been spotted on many occasions since. A ghost of small stature has been seen peering out of the turret window, walking along outside, on his staircase, and in the Great Hall where, in 1976, a man from Sotheby's auction was appraising some items for an upcoming auction when he saw the short, bearded man looking at him from the staircase. This man had no prior knowledge of Puck or any castle ghosts, but when he described who he saw to people who worked in the castle, they knew he had seen Puck.

Another curious bit of lore involves the carved chimneypiece in the Oak Room within the castle. The sculpture portrays the ascent of the Virgin Mary. According to the legend, during the years that Miles Corbet ruled Malahide Castle, the depiction of Mary vanished. After Corbet left and the Talbots returned, so too did Mary in the sculpture.

Malahide Castle also has its own version of the White Lady—believed to be the mysterious and unknown woman whose portrait hangs in the Great Hall. The legend says she occasionally leaves her painting to wander the grounds.

—Jeff Belanger
Founder, Ghostvillage.com

Saint Katherine's Abbey

(The ruins are in a valley about 2 miles east of the village of Shanagolden, County Limerick)
Ireland

Saint Katherine's was one of Ireland's earliest nunneries. Built circa 1298 for the Order of Saint Augustin, the abbey was in operation until 1541. The haunting stems from the story of the earl and Countess of Desmond, who were on the run during a battle in the area. The countess was struck by an arrow, and the earl believed his wife was killed and he hurried to bury her beneath the chapel's altar. The legend goes that she wasn't dead, and, when she regained conciousness, she screamed for help but no one was close enough to help her. Today people claim to still hear the countess's cries for help.

—Jeff Belanger
Founder, Ghostvillage.com

Scotland

Ravenspark Asylum
Sandy Lane
Irvine, Scotland

The Ravenspark Asylum was in use from approximately 1846 to 1995, but it now lies deserted with its many corridors and wards still furnished with broken electrical equipment, hospital beds, and wheelchairs. The clothing and suitcases of its former inmates and staff appear to have been abandoned almost suddenly, giving the building an extremely eerie atmosphere. The hospital housed the insane, elderly, and unwanted. It is alleged that there are bodies of paupers buried in unmarked graves in the overgrown hospital gardens.

This location is a favorite of Ghost Hunters Scotland due the huge amount of paranormal activity recorded since our first visit. On many occasions, we have recorded banging doors, whispering, the sound of running footsteps, and even physical attacks. Our equipment has often been drained of all power even though it had been recharged that day. Although there is absolutely no electricity in the building, readings from our EMF readers have been very erratic. We have also captured strange light anomalies and orbs on digital camera, and have recorded EVP and movement on camcorder. Our trigger objects have also been moved.

The hospital is home to some resident spooks. Quite often, the team is followed by a childish spirit who trails after us in the dark corridors. This spirit identified himself as Peek-a-boo Pete to one of our mediums. Through our research, we discovered this was likely to be a man named

Peter Brown, who was known by the locals in the 1960s as "Peek-a-boo Pete" and who had the mental age of a child. There is one particular room that always affects our sensitives and visiting mediums—the physio room. The forlorn and silent spirit of a young boy called Iain sits trapped in his tiny wheelchair in this room. A very sick woman who also haunts this room and Ward 3 is known to impose her illness on those who can sense it. The asylum is also home to the spirit of a very aggressive orderly who makes it very clear he does not want us there. Maybe he was the one responsible for physically pulling the other side of the door of the Annick Ward closed to prevent our team from trying to continue our investigation.

The Ravenspark Asylum is now waiting to be redeveloped into luxury apartments very soon. Something tells us that the new tenants will encounter some very unwelcome house-guests.

—Debra Campbell and Alex Dorrens
Ghost Hunters Scotland

SOUTH BRIDGE UNDERGROUND VAULTS

MERCAT TOURS LTD.
MERCAT HOUSE, NIDDRY STREET SOUTH
EDINBURGH EH1 1NS
SCOTLAND
TEL: 44 (0) 131-557-6464
WEBSITE: *www.mercattours.com*

Edinburgh's South Bridge was built in 1785. Its 19 arches span the Cowgate Ravine and connect the central part of the city with a flat area of land to the south that was needed for further growth of the city. In Medieval times, it was important for people to live as close as possible to the castle for protection. But as time went on, concern for a marauding invading army waned, and the populace spread out. Soon, housing filled in the valley, abutting right against the bridge itself. What were once open arches were now sealed in. The impoverished and those who made their living selling their services and wares upon the bridge itself soon used these enclosed arches as workshops, storage facilities, and even homes.

The living conditions were less than ideal, but the poor had no other choice as far as shelter went. To add to the problems of living under the bridge, the construction wasn't watertight. Rainwater made its way down the walls and cracks and pooled in the lowest areas.

During the Irish Potato Famine of 1845 to 1847, the destitute Irish came over to Scotland seeking a better life. Many had no money, no employment, and very few prospects, so they settled in the vaults. Prostitution, whiskey stills, gambling, fights, and murders were all taking place in the vaults in the latter half of the 19th century. By the early 20th century, the vaults were permanently sealed off in hopes of cutting out the stronghold of Edinburgh's dark side. The vaults stayed shut until the 1980s, when they were rediscovered by a local property owner. Soon after, sections of the vaults were open to the public for walking tours. But the tour guides and guests soon discovered they weren't alone in the underground vaults.

There are many spirits that seem to still be calling the underbelly of the bridge home. There are many children, including Jack, a young boy in late 18th-century dress, who some local psychics believe died during the bridge's construction. Other guests have heard children's laughter, and some adults have reported feeling a child's hand slip into theirs as they walked along the tour. But the most sinister of the South Bridge vault spirits is the one they call Mr. Boots.

If someone seems intentionally frightened, or if a psychically sensitive person feels threatened, it's attributed to Mr. Boots. Des Brogan, one of the founders of Mercat Tours and coauthor of the book *Hidden and Haunted: Underground Edinburgh* (Mercat Tours, 1999) said, "We call him that because he wears knee-length boots, very rough trousers that fit into the boots, and a very dirty ruffled white shirt. He's unkempt and unshaven, and he has very bad breath. We know this because people can smell it. If our guide is telling stories, he will appear behind the group. And only some people in the group will see him. But as soon as he's spotted, he disappears."

—Jeff Belanger
Founder, Ghostvillage.com

GLAMIS CASTLE
GLAMIS BY FORFAR
ANGUS DD8 1RJ SCOTLAND
TEL: +44 (0) 1307 840393
WEBSITE: *www.glamis-castle.co.uk*

Glamis Castle offers a potpourri of paranormal activity and tales. The castle has several ghosts to its legend (including a White Lady and a Gray Lady), a monster, a vampire, and a woman accused of witchcraft who was burned at the stake. The castle has been in the Lyons family since 1372, when the land was presented to the family by Robert of Bruce. Castle construction began around 1400 and continued for centuries as the family added on to the majestic building.

Royalty did not always favor the Lyon family. In the 1537, Janet Douglas, Lady Glamis, was accused of using sorcery to try to kill King James V. She was burned at the stake in Edinburgh and is said to be the "White Lady" who haunts the castle grounds and especially its clock tower.

Another legend of the castle involves the Earl of Crawford and the devil. Apparently, the earl loved to play cards, and one Sunday he could find no one to gamble with him because even the servants were afraid to gamble on the Church's day of rest. In a drunken stupor, the earl allegedly exclaimed that he would play cards with the devil himself. Then a knock came at the door, and a tall man dressed in black walked in to play cards. The door was shut and servants heard shouting and swearing from within the room. One servant was said to put his eye up to the keyhole to try and see what was happening, but was blinded by the fire and light that shot out. The earl came out to reprimand the servant, and when he turned around, the man in black was gone. A few years later, the earl died. The folklore says the room had such an aura of evil that they sealed it off. For many years, the family and staff reported hearing footsteps and shouts coming from inside the room where they believed the devil and the earl were still playing cards.

There is also a "Gray Lady" at Glamis who has been seen wandering the grounds. Though her identity in life is a mystery, she's been spotted walking around outside the castle for many years.

The vampire in the castle's legend is said to be that of a servant woman—when she was discovered, she was sealed in a secret room.

The "monster" of Glamis is a curious bit of folklore that began in 1821 with the first son of the Earl of Strathmore. According to the legends, the boy was born in Glamis but was severely deformed. The boy was said to have no neck, undersized arms and legs, and had the overall appearance of a large egg. He was also said to be covered with hair. The family expected the child to die, so they hid him in a secret chamber within the castle and announced to everyone that the child was stillborn. But the child didn't die. The boy, who was the true heir to the castle, grew up and remained a hidden secret in the castle. As each of the earl's other sons reached the age of 21, they were shown their hideous brother who was still living in the castle. After seeing the deformed man, each son lived an unhappy existence the rest of his days. Supposedly this "monster" lived for a century and died in the 1920s.

The lore is as much a part of Glamis Castle's history as are the real royal figures who have called these grounds home. Today the castle is most renowned as the childhood home of Elizabeth Bowes-Lyon, who became Queen Elizabeth and mother of the current queen.

—Jeff Belanger
Founder, Ghostvillage.com

Wales

RUTHIN CASTLE HOTEL

RUTHIN
NORTH WALES, UNITED KINGDOM
TEL: 44 (0) 1824-702664
WEBSITE: *www.ruthincastle.co.uk*

The lush, rolling hills of North Wales are steeped in romantic lore as well as the blood of numerous battles. What better location for a 700-year-old haunted castle?

For anyone who enjoys creature comforts to go along with their desire to experience a ghostly encounter, this castle is the perfect combination. Built in 1207 for King Edward I, much of the original structure is in evidence today. Colorful peacocks wander among moss-covered walls. Fifty-eight beautifully appointed rooms are available to guests, along with a banquet room where the Medieval Banquets are held in the evenings. You can still see the remnants of the oldest parts of the castle, which is some of the oldest construction that can be found in Wales. The castle grounds also have drowning and whipping rooms as well as dungeons. Is it any wonder that restless souls wander the grounds?

While several different ghosts are said to roam the premises, the most well-known locally is the "Gray Lady," who has been seen walking the battlements at night. She has also been glimpsed in the banquet hall and outside the castle. She is believed to have been the wife of the second-in-command at the castle sometime around 1282, when it was occupied by the armies of Edward I. Her husband was having an affair, so she ended the life of his mistress with an axe. For her crime, she was executed and as a murderess, she couldn't be buried in consecrated ground. Her grave can be seen today outside the castle walls, covered with stones. Many guests have reported seeing her dressed from head to toe in gray and walking her solitary course.

—Kathy Conder
Lead Investigator, Encounters
Paranormal Research and Investigation

RUTHIN CASTLE HOTEL

THE SKIRRID MOUNTAIN INN
LLANVIHANGEL CRUCORNEY
ABERGAVENNY, MONMOUTHSHIRE NP7 8DH
WALES
TEL: 44 (0) 1873-890258
WEBSITE: *myweb.tiscali.co.uk/skirrid/*

Welsh locals say that at the exact moment of Jesus' death on the cross, a bolt of lightning came down and split the 1,600-foot-tall peak of a Monmouthshire mountain in two. Today the mountain is called Skirrid Mountain, and at its base lies the Skirrid Mountain Inn—which also has its share of legends. The inn also boasts one of the oldest pubs in all of the United Kingdom. There is written record of the building as far back as 1104 C.E., though it may be even older than that. Due to its remote location, the public house was used for many civic events beyond a drink and a meal—the building has also served as the place for town meetings, a courthouse—where judges would preside over local cases—and even the site of execution. A worn beam by the stairwell bares witness to where the hangman's rope brought 182 people to their deaths over the centuries. The unlucky person would stand on a lower step as the rope was tightened around his neck. Because there isn't much clearance below, the victim wasn't as lucky as those who were hung by a gallows where the fall itself might snap the neck, offering an instant death. The many people executed at this inn slowly suffocated to death as their windpipes were crushed. It's no surprise that the Skirrid Mountain Inn is not only old, it's also quite haunted. But ironically, the most dominant presence is not one of the many who met their end in the stairwell, it's the spirits of Landlady Fanny Price, who died of consumption in the smallest bedroom in the inn in the early 1800s, and her immediate family, who owned the property during that time. The Price family's mortal remains lay in the churchyard a short distance away from the inn.

"She walks the pub at night," Daryl Hardy, the inn's current coowner said. "Apparently, one of the other major characters in the pub—we can't tell whether it was her father or her husband—but he's called Henry Price, he pretends to be a soldier marching up and down outside on the cobbles. You can hear sort of horses' hooves outside on the cobbles. Or he'll be up in the loft banging on the chimney breasts, trying to scare the guests."

Glasses continually fly off the shelves behind the bar. Hardy claims they lose about 10 to 15 glasses per week this way. Another supernatural event witnessed by eight people in the pub one night happened when a small stack of money—paper bills with coins on top—traveled down the entire length of the bar, hovered in mid-air for a moment, then dropped to the floor as the witnesses watched in stunned silence.

The three upstairs guest rooms also have their share of activity. One of the more humorous anomalies occurred when a guest complained he couldn't sleep because some unseen force was spinning the toilet paper roll in the bathroom all night. Not unfurling the paper, just playfully spinning it and keeping the poor man awake.

Many strange and misty photos have been taken by the bar and in the stairwell where so many met their doom.

—Jeff Belanger
Founder, Ghostvillage.com

LLANCAIACH FAWR MANOR HOUSE

NELSON
TREHARRIS
CF46 6ER WALES
TEL: 44 (0) 1443-412248
WEBSITE: *www.caerphilly.gov.uk/visiting/museums/llancaiachfawrmanor.htm*

The first written documentation that the Llancaiach Fawr Manor House existed is on a work itinerary written by John Leland in 1537. The house was built for the Prichard family and, considering the building's 4-foot-thick walls, they intended the home to be a stronghold against attack. As the years went by and the family's wealth grew, they built on to the manor, turning the home into an increasingly substantial building.

In 1601, a feud between the Prichard and Lewis families erupted when a man named Lewis William was murdered. Edmund Lewis successfully accused a servant of Edward Prichard for the crime, and the servant was hanged for the killing. Edward Prichard felt his servant wasn't the right man, and he was angered by the actions. The feud lasted the rest of Edward's life and on into the next generation.

Today, members of the Prichard family are said to still be haunting their grand home. King Charles I, who was once a visitor to Llancaiach Fawr, is also said to make appearances within the manor. Other ghosts include several children who have been heard playing by the front door. Guests and staff have reported feeling their clothing being tugged on by these children's spirits. The Llancaiach Fawr Manor House is also home to an Internet-based "Ghostcam," where online ghost hunters can watch for spectral activity in the building.

—Jeff Belanger
Founder, Ghostvillage.com

LLANCAIACH FAWR MANOR HOUSE

Paranormal Investigator Profile

Dr. Hans Holzer

DR. HANS HOLZER is the author of more than 130 books, many of which cover the supernatural. He received a Ph.D. in parapsychology from the London College of Applied Science. He's been studying the paranormal for more than 60 years and has investigated haunted locations all over the world. He currently lives in New York City. He was the first to coin the term "the other side of life."

Q: What was your first encounter with a spirit?

My first visual experience was when I lived in New York City with my father in a penthouse apartment on Riverside Drive. I was asleep in bed, and I woke up and there was my mother dressed in a white nightgown, pushing my head back onto the pillow. My head had slipped off the pillow. At that time I was subject to migraines. Had I not had my head back on the pillow, I probably would've

Photo courtesy of Hans Holzer

had one, and there would've been dizziness and I would've been out of business for a day. I said, "Oh, hello, Mama." And she disappeared.

Q: Is that the event that triggered your interest in the subject?

It's not a question of whether I had experiences. My interest has nothing to do with personal experiences. Nothing in my scientific view does not have an explanation. The question is, sooner we get it or later we get it, but there has to be an explanation. You can't say nobody knows. I don't accept that.

Q: How does the spirit world interact with our own?

What I have learned in my investigations is that there are seven levels of consciousness on the other side of life that are concentric with our world. It's not up or down, it's just concentric. We can't see it because it moves at a different rate of speed than we move.

There's three levels when you are born. You are born with a physical outer body, a duplicate inner body, and at the very moment of birth—that's very important—the moment the child is supposed to see the light during childbirth; that is, when the soul or the spirit is inserted from the pool of available spirits from the other side.

Q: What is the most important part of a ghost investigation?

We are living in a technological age. And some of the investigators that I've met believe in all sincerity that running around with Geiger counters and cameras and instruments that can measure cold spots will be the way to investigate a haunting or a ghost. That's wrong. Because if you really are an investigator of the paranormal, and you're dealing with ghosts or hauntings, you're dealing with a human being—nothing more, nothing less. Therefore, you should have with you a good trancemedium who can lend her body or his body temporarily for that entity to speak through so you can find out what the trouble is. That's the way it works—not a Geiger counter.

Q: Do you put any stock in the camera during an investigation?

I have worked with psychic photographers. That's a special form of mediumship. Psychic photography is a gift. Some have it. I've used these people in haunted places. When there was something there, they would photograph it.

Q: What is something funny that happened to you during an investigation?

I was one of the first to investigate the Whaley House in San Diego in 1960. I was there with [psychic medium] Sybil Leek and Regis Philbin, whom I've been friends with for a long time. He was hosting a local television show, and the three of us went there. While we were there, the older woman, she appeared—it was a very white figure, and Regis got excited and turned on the flashlight, and of course that was the end of the phenomenon. And I keep reminding him of that.

Q: Have you ever been afraid doing this work?

Fear is the absence of information. Fear is created by not understanding something. You bring on the fear. There is no object to fear. I've never been afraid during an investigation. I shouldn't be in this business if I was.

There's nothing out there that isn't one way or the other human. Hollywood notwithstanding, there are no monsters out there. There is no other supernatural race, no devils, no fellows in red underwear. It doesn't exist.

The paranormal is part of our experience—we just don't always understand it as such.

Q: What have you learned about yourself during all these years of investigations?

My purpose is that I have a job. First of all, the other side, being a bureaucracy and being a well-ordered world, invests in people's abilities. When the other side decides some individuals have very good minds and good hearts, then they are given talents with the proviso that they will use those talents for the betterment of the world and mankind. If you don't, they won't like it. So they make it very plain: You have a gift. Use it. I found out early enough that they had something in mind for me. I accepted that it's an assignment. I noticed that what happened to me was kind of programmed: I met some people who were important for my career or for my enlightenment—it was all arranged. So I finally said, "Friends, I noticed you're running my life. It's okay with me. I will do it." And I hear this in my right ear: "We will guide you, help you. Use your gifts. You have two separate paths—one has to do with science, parapsychology research, and the other has to be the entertainment business. But you combine them to let the world know what you find."

And that's what I do.

Europe

Europe

Czech Republic

CHARLES BRIDGE
PRAGUE
CZECH REPUBLIC

Built in 1357 and commissioned by Charles IV, Charles Bridge connects the Old Town and Malá Strana and crosses the river Vltava. Originally called *Kamenný most* or the Stone Bridge, the Gothic structure was built by architect Petr Parlér who also oversaw the building of Prague Castle. Local legends say they mixed egg yolks in with the mortar to make the bridge stronger. The bridge has survived much traffic and natural threats such as floods. Today it's used as a historical landmark and a footbridge. But tourists and street merchants aren't the only ones who wander across this bridge—this site also has its share of ghosts. In the Middle Ages, when a leader executed a person, the leader wanted the world to know about it. Posting decapitated heads (and other severed body parts) on popular landmarks was common practice all over Europe. But there were 10 particular local lords who had the misfortune of having their heads stuck on poles on the Charles Bridge for years until the flesh rotted away and their skulls were picked clean by the birds. Today, these 10 lords are said to be walking the bridge—especially at night—singing sad songs and scaring those who pass by wondering who the source of the singing is. But the 10 ghosts aren't the only lore belonging to the Charles Bridge. A water goblin is said to live under the bridge, who devours the souls of those who drown from falling or jumping off the bridge.

—Jeff Belanger
Founder, Ghostvillage.com

France

THE CATACOMB MUSEUM
1, PLACE DENFERT-ROCHEREAU
75014 PARIS
FRANCE
TEL: 33 (0) 1-43-22-47-63

*A*rrete! *C'est ici L'Empire de la Mort* reads the sign over the archway 20 meters below the city of Paris in the silent tunnels of a very old limestone quarry. "Stop! Here is the Empire of the Dead" is the translation. Once you walk through the arch, you're greeted by millions of human bones. Rows of skulls stare out at you from a retaining wall of leg and arm bones. The skulls form macabre patterns throughout the maze-like tunnels. There are patterns of skulls displayed in valentine heart-shapes, Christian crosses, arcs, and columns of bones and skulls all adorn the edges of the tunnels. The human re-

Photo by Jeff Belanger

mains housed in here—more than 6 million bodies representing 30 generations of Parisians—were moved to the underground tunnels between 1785 and 1859 because the cemeteries of Paris were overflowing with rotting corpses. With so many dead disturbed, it's little wonder why so many consider these tunnels to be haunted.

The limestone quarries began in 60 B.C.E. by the Romans. They used the build materials to construct ramparts and buildings for the city that would become Paris. Over the centuries, the city grew—its buildings became taller, and the city spread across the landscape. More building materials were needed, and the only direction left to go was down.

More than 300 kilometers of tunnels were carved under the city of Paris—a city that was constantly growing in population and size. As the buildings closed in around the cemeteries that were once on the outskirts of town, there was no longer room for the bodies. As the rotting bodies spilled into the streets and buildings, people who lived close by found themselves getting sick from the terrible smell. So the bodies were moved into the quarrying tunnels below the city. People have claimed to hear voices in the tunnels. Darting shadows have been seen by those who pass through, and some psychically sensitive people have claimed to get impressions from some of the various skulls and bones that are intertwined with so many others.

—Jeff Belanger
Founder, Ghostvillage.com

Germany

HEIDELBERG CASTLE
D-69117 HEIDELBERG
GERMANY
TEL: 49 (0) 62-21-53-84-14
WEBSITE: *www.cvb-heidelberg.de*

The majestic Heidelberg Castle in southwestern Germany sits on a hillside overlooking the Neckar River in the valley below. Prince Elector Ruprecht III built the first part of the castle between 1398 and 1410 to serve as a regal residence in the inner courtyard. Years later, other major buildings were added on to the castle. Fountain Hall was erected between 1476 and 1508 by Prince Elector

Phillipp, and, in coming centuries, other rulers added on to the fortress. The castle saw plenty of turmoil: it was destroyed during the 30 Years' War (1619–1649), it was rebuilt by Prince Elector Karl Ludwig between 1649 and 1680, and it was brought to ruin again by French troops in the latter half of the 1600s. After a third rebuilding attempt in the mid-1700s, a lightning bolt wrought heavy damage to a large section of the castle. The building was abandoned and was slowly pillaged for building materials so the town of Heidelberg could grow. In 1800, the pilfering stopped, and the castle slowly returned to its splendor. The castle is located very close to an area of religious importance. Could spirits from a bygone area have been plaguing the castle all of those centuries, helping the misfortunes along?

In the valley, just across the river, there is an area of religious significance dating back to the Celtic era. The area holds Celtic ruins, Roman ruins, and even the ruins of a theater built by the Nazis during the 1930s. Locals have reported hearing wailing voices from the castle through the valley. Others have seen hooded apparitions walking between the castle and the sacred site.

—Jeff Belanger
Founder, Ghostvillage.com

The Netherlands

THE ANNE FRANK HOUSE
PRINSENGRACHT 267
AMSTERDAM
THE NETHERLANDS
TEL. 31 (0) 20-5567105
WEBSITE: *www.annefrank.org*

Anne Frank was one of the many Jewish victims of the German Nazis. In 1940, when the Nazis invaded the Netherlands, anti-Jewish sentiment quickly grew. In July of 1942, Anne, her sister, Margot, and her parents went into hiding in a building on Prinsengracht. They constructed an annex that incorporated the back side of the house and the upper-most floor of the building for hiding.

For two years, Anne, her family, and four others sought refuge in the well-crafted hiding space. It was during these two years that Anne wrote her now-famous diaries of daily life of living in fear of being discovered and the horrible isolation of hiding. Sadly, the group was betrayed and was reported to the Nazi authorities, who deported them to concentration camps.

With so much mental anguish, it's not too surprising that some have reported supernatural activity in the annex. Cold spots are reported throughout the annex, and the ghost of a young girl has been seen silently looking out of the window.

Today, the Anne Frank House is a museum offering tours and exhibits.

—Jeff Belanger
Founder, Ghostvillage.com

THE ANNE FRANK HOUSE

Poland

NIEDZICA CASTLE
ASSOCIATION OF THE ART HISTORIANS—
CASTLE TEAM, NIEDZICA
NIEDZICA
POLAND
TEL: 48 18-262-94-89
WEBSITE: *www.zzw-niedzica.com.pl*

On an ancient hill of limestone and shale 30 meters above the Dunajec River is one of southern Poland's most haunted locations: Niedzica Castle. The castle holds secrets of hidden treasures, ancient artwork, and a ghostly woman who is said to appear every night. A small sign along the road leading up to the castle features a ghostly caricature, warning those who approach of the spectral resident.

The castle is situated on a small peninsula into the river. From a distance, it's easy to understand why one would build a castle in this location—not only are the views breathtaking, but the position is highly defendable. There are cliffs, then water on three sides, and only one feasible approach if one were to try to mount an attack. The current castle was built in 1325 by the Hungarian Berzevichy family, though this wasn't the first fortress on this spot—earthen walls stood to mark the former stronghold. The castle was originally called Dunajec Castle, and it had several owners over the centuries.

The history behind the ghostly legends here stem from one of the castle's early owners, Sebastian Berzevichy, who went to Peru in South America. There he married a local woman and they had a daughter named Umina, who went on to marry an Inka royal who held his family's treasure. In the 1860s, when the war between Spain and Peru was coming to an inevitable head, the Berzevichy family moved to Europe to escape the war and made their way back to Niedzica. They brought the Inka family treasure with them so it wouldn't be captured by the Spanish. The local legend holds that Umina was murdered in front of the castle by a potential treasure thief who was never caught, and Umina's ghost began to appear every night to scare off any who sought the gold. Umina's father hid the treasure and created a cryptic document so the riches could be located again one day. But no one has been able to break the code in the document. Today Umina is referred to as the castle's "White Lady," and reports of her sighting still come in from locals and visitors.

Today, Niedzica Castle is a museum with archaeological and historical exhibitions from the Spisz region and offers several suites that can accommodate up to 35 guests. The Association of the Art Historians operates the castle today.

—Jeff Belanger
Founder, Ghostvillage.com

MOUNT SLEZA
SUDETY MOUNTAINS
SOBOTKA
POLAND

The Sudety Mountains are in southwestern Poland and run along the border with the Czech Republic. Local legends say this mountain range was formed after the fallen angel Lucifer was cast out of heaven and into hell. The entrance to the underworld was alleged to be located in the region where the mountains now stand. Once Lucifer was cast below, the angels of heaven closed the entrance by piling rocks and dirt on top, forming the Sudety Mountains.

One would think that locals would simply avoid such a place, considering its evil lore, but this isn't the case. These mountains are also said to be rich with gold and crystals, but these same mountains are also said to be guarded by a spirit who protects the mountains' treasures. Mount Sleza is said to be where this spirit dwells and is sighted most often. Some say that those who find the right cavern or who are willing to dig into Mount Sleza may find the entrance to hell in these mountains.

—Jeff Belanger
Founder, Ghostvillage.com

WAWEL ROYAL CASTLE
TOURIST SERVICE OFFICE
WAWEL 5, 31-001
KRAKÓW
POLAND
TEL: 48 (0) 12-422-51-55 EXT. 291
WEBSITE: *www.krakow-info.com/wawel.htm*

Wawel Hill in Kraków has been home to human activity for almost 50,000 years. Archaeologists have uncovered evidence of settlement from the Paleolithic, Neolithic, and Bronze ages. There was evidence of this area being a farming community as well as a trading hub. Between 1506 and 1548 C.E., King Sigismund I the Old had the Polish royal palace built on this very hill. Wawel Hill is the very heart of Poland—where their kings were crowned, ruled, and laid to their eternal rest within the vaults under the cathedral. The ghosts of these royal spirits are said to still visit the castle today. Though ghosts aren't the only anomalies of note for locals and tourists, dragons allegedly also once walked here.

In a 200-foot-long cave on the western slope of Wawel Hill is *Smocza Jama*—the Dragon's Den. Some believe the dragon was a serpent goddess who lived in the hill. The dragon posed quite a problem for those who lived in the region as it made quick meals of the livestock and local virgins. Prince Krak is the man credited with defeating the dragon. Today the cave holds a statue of a dragon and millennia of human record, as prehistoric man through modern humans in the 16th century of the common era all used the cave as a home.

According to one local legend, all of Poland's deceased kings gather for a conference on December 24th every year in an underground chamber in Wawel Hill. One of these kings, King Kazimir, once told the tale of exploring some of the many caves of Wawel Hill when he was a child. Inside one of the tunnels he found a glowing stone that produces a magical energy that feeds and protects Kraków.

One of the castle ghosts is King Sigismund I the Old's jester, Stanczyk. It's said that whenever Poland is in danger, Stanczyk is seen in his jester's costume along the battlements of Wawel Castle.

—Jeff Belanger
Founder, Ghostvillage.com

WAWEL ROYAL CASTLE

Romania

Bran Castle
Bran
Romania
Website: *www.draculascastle.com*

In the Romanian village of Bran, about 15 miles southwest of Brasov in the Carpathian Mountains, lies Bran Castle. Built in 1377 to protect the city of Brasov from invasion, today the castle is more commonly referred to as "Dracula's Castle" because it was once a residence of Prince Vlad Tepes, aka "Vlad the Impaler," son of Vlad Dracul (*Dracul* meaning "Devil"), who was a knight of the Dragon Order. Vlad used to sign his name "Draculea" or "Draculya" or "The Devil's Son." He's now best-known as the historical basis for Bram Stoker's *Dracula*.

Between 1456 and 1462, Vlad Tepes was a strict ruler of Wallachia, but to his credit, he increased trade and the strength of his army. According to his legend, he was ruthless against any who stood against him, and his infamy grew in his battles against the Ottoman Empire. Though not the only military leader to incorporate this practice, Vlad was known to impale his captives on long spears—many times while they were still alive. Dying in this way could sometimes take hours if one was unlucky.

Bran Castle may still be home to some of the many tortured souls who died at Vlad's hand. In the courtyard, there is a fountain that conceals a hidden tunnel some 50 meters below the surface. Guests who know where to look and listen have claimed to have heard moans coming from within the tunnel. But victims aren't the only spirits said to haunt the castle. Many believe Vlad himself still passes through the castle and its grounds. He seems to be most active in the chamber he once used. People have photographed strange, glowing mists and light streaks within his room. Today, the castle offers tours six days a week for those who want to walk were Vlad once stood.

—Jeff Belanger
Founder, Ghostvillage.com

Choosing an Investigator

What to Look for in a Paranormal Investigator

People who are dealing with a haunting in their homes go through a range of emotions: There is certainly fear from not understanding the events happening around them. There may be confusion or even anger toward the entity that they believe has invaded their private space. Some are thrilled by the notion of sharing their homes with spirits and don't want them to go away, but they would like to understand the phenomena transpiring.

As you can see from the myriad of ghost hunter television shows, the many thousands of Websites covering the supernatural, and even by the number of contributors to this very book, there are paranormal investigators everywhere.

For people who believe they may have a haunted home or business, they may find that sharing their very personal supernatural experiences with a total stranger can be more daunting than the event itself. But there are individuals and groups out there who offer a lot of help in understanding and dealing with these paranormal events. Their objective is to study and learn about these phenomena and to help spread knowledge about the subject.

Some things to expect from a paranormal investigator include help with background research on your property. They're looking for deaths, accidents, or other events that may have been the trigger for the ghostly phenomena. They may ask you personal questions about any medications you may be taking, or your drug and/or alcohol usage. They may ask about other personal family matters, such as violence from or emotional problems with members of your family. They will explore the areas of your home where you experience the phenomena most often. Some investigators will use equipment, such as thermometers or meters that measure electromagnetic fields, or they may take video and audio recordings, while others may bring in psychics or other more esoteric tools such as dowsing rods or a pendulum to try and connect with any entities who may be present.

Good paranormal investigators ask a lot of questions, and they are professional in how they conduct their research and how they deal with you. The vast majority of groups do not charge for their services, though you should ask, up front, if they do. You will want to ask how long this person or group has been doing this work and how many places have they investigated. Some investigators may even offer you references. Many groups today have legal forms that they will sign, promising not to disclose any information about your case without your consent—these are the kinds of behavior and practices that should put you at ease.

There are also various paranormal investigation certifications that larger organizations offer to their members who pass a required test. Some of these certifications are rather easy to obtain, while others are certainly more valid. When you are engaging the services of a paranormal investigator, you should speak with them over the phone or maybe in person at a neutral location, such as a coffee shop, and see what rapport you have with that person. A good investigator will help you understand what you're going through, identify if there is, in fact, a haunting, and can get you further help if required.

The following section is a directory of paranormal investigators from all around the globe. While their inclusion in this directory is not an endorsement, these are individuals and groups who are actively doing this work. They're waiting to help.

Paranormal Investigator Directory

New England

Christopher Balzano
FOUNDER
MASSACHUSETTS PARANORMAL CROSSROADS
WEBSITE: www.masscrossroads.com
E-MAIL: alosa1066@hotmail.com
SERVING: EASTERN MASSACHUSETTS AND
SOUTHERN NEW HAMPSHIRE

Jeff Belanger
FOUNDER
GHOSTVILLAGE.COM
WEBSITE: www.ghostvillage.com
E-MAIL: info@ghostvillage.com
TEL: 1 (508) 966-5057
SERVING: WORLDWIDE

Thomas D'Agostino
WRITER, PARANORMAL INVESTIGATOR,
RESEARCHER
RHODE ISLAND PARANORMAL
WEBSITE: www.riparanormal.org
E-MAIL: ramtail@aol.com
TEL: 1 (401) 568-9840
SERVING: NEW ENGLAND

Brendan Keenan
RESEARCHER
THE PARANORMAL RESEARCH SOCIETY
OF NEW ENGLAND
WEBSITE: www.prsne.com
TEL: 1 (203) 375-6083
SERVING: UNITED STATES

Ronald Kolek
EXECUTIVE DIRECTOR
THE NEW ENGLAND GHOST PROJECT
WEBSITE: www.neghostproject.com
E-MAIL:
neghostproject@comcast.net
TEL: 1 (979) 455-6678
SERVING: NEW ENGLAND

Andrew D. Laird
DIRECTOR AND FOUNDER
THE RHODE ISLAND PARANORMAL
RESEARCH GROUP
WEBSITE: www.triprg.com
E-MAIL: triprg@yahoo.com
SERVING: NEW ENGLAND, EASTERN NEW
YORK, AND NEW YORK CITY

Brian McIntyre
RESEARCHER
THE PARANORMAL RESEARCH SOCIETY
OF NEW ENGLAND
WEBSITE: *www.prsne.com*
TEL: 1 (203) 375-6083
SERVING: UNITED STATES

Lydia L. Rapoza
CURATOR
CRANSTON HISTORICAL SOCIETY
WEBSITE:
www.cranstonhistoricalsociety.org
E-MAIL: rilydia@ix.netcom.com
TEL: 1 (401) 944-9226
SERVING: RHODE ISLAND

Sarah Louise Robinson
E-MAIL: slrobinson213@yahoo.com
SERVING: MASSACHUSETTS, CONNECTICUT,
NEW HAMPSHIRE, AND RHODE ISLAND

Bill Washell
FOUNDER
MAINE'S PARANORMAL RESEARCH
ASSOCIATION
WEBSITE:
www.mainesparanormal.com
E-MAIL: meparanormal@yahoo.com
TEL: 1 (207) 782-2032
SERVING: MAINE AND NEW ENGLAND

John Zaffis
FOUNDER
THE PARANORMAL RESEARCH SOCIETY
OF NEW ENGLAND
WEBSITE: *www.prsne.com*
E-MAIL: jzaffisjr@snet.net
TEL: 1 (203) 375-6083
SERVING: UNITED STATES

Mid-Atlantic

Linda J. Andrews
DIRECTOR AND FOUNDER
EASTERN SEACOAST PARANORMAL
RESEARCH AND STUDIES
WEBSITE: *www.esprs.net*
E-MAIL: director@esprs.net
TEL: 1 (856) 692-5434
SERVING: EASTERN SEACOAST FROM NEW
ENGLAND TO NORTH CAROLINA

Joshua Braathen
CO-FOUNDER
J & J GHOST SEEKERS AND ASSOCIATES
WEBSITE: *www.jjghosts.com*
E-MAIL: josh@jjghosts.com
TEL: 1 (570) 350-2944
SERVING: EAST COAST OF THE
UNITES STATES

Tom Brobst
CO-FOUNDER
EASTERN PENNSYLVANIA
GHOST RESEARCHERS
WEBSITE: *www.epgr.net*
E-MAIL: webmaster@epgr.net
TEL: 1 (832) 213-1141
SERVING: CENTRAL AND
EASTERN PENNSYLVANIA

Dwayne Claud

LEAD INVESTIGATOR
WESTERN NEW YORK PARANORMAL
WEBSITE: *www.wnyparanormal.com*
E-MAIL: wnyparanormal@aol.com
TEL: 1 (585) 382-3644
SERVING: WESTERN AND CENTRAL NEW YORK, NORTHERN PENNSYLVANIA, AND EASTERN OHIO

Joanne Davis

E-MAIL: Roxydav@aol.com
SERVING: DELAWARE, PENNSYLVANIA, MARYLAND, AND NEW JERSEY

Jason Gowin

INVESTIGATOR
GHOST HUNTERS INCORPORATED
WEBSITE: *www.wasted-days.net/ghi*
E-MAIL: gow2099@hotmail.com
TEL: 1 (607) 742-0614
SERVING: NORTHEASTERN PENNSYLVANIA AND SOUTHERN TIER, NEW YORK

L'Aura Hladik

CO-FOUNDER
NJ GHOST HUNTERS SOCIETY
WEBSITE: *www.njghs.net*
E-MAIL: laura@njghs.net
SERVING: NEW JERSEY, NEW YORK, AND PENNSYLVANIA

Robert Husak

FOUNDER/LEAD INVESTIGATOR
TRP PARANORMAL INVESTIGATIONS
WEBSITE: *www.trpparanormalinvestigations.com*
E-MAIL: Robhusak@trpparanormalinvestigations.com
TEL: 1 (740) 947-2458
SERVING: OHIO, WEST VIRGINIA, KENTUCKY, AND WESTERN PENNSYLVANIA

Dave Juliano

DIRECTOR
SOUTH JERSEY GHOST RESEARCH
WEBSITE: *www.sjgr.org*
E-MAIL: help@sjgr.org
TEL: 1 (877) 478-3168
SERVING: NEW JERSEY, DELAWARE, AND EASTERN PENNSYLVANIA

Jess Kroh

CO-FOUNDER
EASTERN PENNSYLVANIA GHOST RESEARCHERS
WEBSITE: *www.epgr.net*
E-MAIL: webmaster@epgr.net
TEL: 1 (832) 213-1141
SERVING: CENTRAL AND EASTERN PENNSYLVANIA

Alison Lynch

LEAD PARANORMAL INVESTIGATOR
REAL HAUNTINGS
WEBSITE: *www.realhauntings.com*
E-MAIL: RealHauntings@yahoo.com
TEL: 1 (201) 858-2694
SERVING: NEW YORK, PENNSYLVANIA, NEW JERSEY, AND CONNECTICUT

Laura Schmidtmann

FOUNDER AND LEAD INVESTIGATOR
SYRACUSE GHOST HUNTERS
WEBSITE: *pages.prodigy.net/kas9865*
E-MAIL: kas9865@prodigy.net
SERVING: CENTRAL NEW YORK

Nikki Turpin

CO-FOUNDER
LONG ISLAND GHOST HUNTERS
WEBSITE: *www.geocities.com/lighosts*
E-MAIL: lighosts@yahoo.com
SERVING: NEW YORK AND CONNECTICUT

Dominick Villella

PARANORMAL INVESTIGATOR
PARANORMAL INVESTIGATION OF NYC
WEBSITE: *www.paranormal-nyc.com*
E-MAIL: dom@paranormal-nyc.com
TEL: 1 (917) 656-4334
SERVING: NEW YORK CITY AND
SURROUNDING AREAS

Jonathan Williams

OPERATIONS DIRECTOR
SOULTRACKERS PARANORMAL
INVESTIGATIONS
WEBSITE: *www.soultrackers.com*
E-MAIL: soultrackers@yahoo.com
SERVING: MAINLY THE UNITED STATES,
BUT WE HAVE OVERSEAS OFFICES
THROUGHOUT THE WORLD.

Vincent Gale Wilson, Jr.

PRESIDENT
THE MARYLAND PARANORMAL
INVESTIGATORS COALITION
WEBSITE:
www.marylandparanormal.com
E-MAIL: vwjr.md@verizon.net
TEL: 1 (443) 474-4005
SERVING: DELAWARE, MARYLAND,
AND VIRGINIA

South

Keith Age

PRESIDENT
LOUISVILLE GHOST HUNTERS SOCIETY
WEBSITE: *www.louisvilleghs.com*
E-MAIL: bruno11111963@yahoo.com
TEL: 1 (502) 644-7013
SERVING: KENTUCKY AND INDIANA

Melanie Billings

WRITER/PARANORMAL INVESTIGATOR
WEBSITE: *www.Hauntster.net*
E-MAIL: greywolf73@earthlink.net
SERVING: NORTH AND SOUTH CAROLINA

Valkerie Carver

CO-FOUNDER
TIDEWATER PARANORMAL INTESTIGATIONS
WEBSITE: *www.geocities.com/
grovecrm/TPIA4.html*
E-MAIL: valkerie@cavtel.net
TEL: 1 (757) 747-9331
SERVING: THE GREATER VIRGINIA AREA

Susan Crites

FOUNDER
WEST VIRGINIA SOCIETY OF GHOST HUNTERS
WEBSITE:
www.wvsocietyofghosthunters.com
E-MAIL:
info@wvsocietyofghosthunters.com
TEL: 1 (304) 754-6983
SERVING: EASTERN PANHANDLE OF WEST
VIRGINIA AND THE SHENANDOAH VALLEY

Barbara Eyre

CO-FOUNDER, INVESTIGATOR, WEBMASTER
NORTH CAROLINA PIEDMONT PARANORMAL
RESEARCH SOCIETY
WEBSITE: www.ncpprs.org
E-MAIL: investigations@ncpprs.org
TEL: 1 (704) 585-2886
SERVING: THE FOOTHILLS, PIEDMONT, AND
TRIAD REGIONS OF NORTH CAROLINA

Thomas Iacuzio

FOUNDER
CENTRAL FLORIDA GHOST RESEARCH
WEBSITE: www.cflgr.org
E-MAIL: centralfloridaghost
research@yahoo.com
TEL: 1 (386) 445-7510
SERVING: CENTRAL FLORIDA, BUT WILL
TRAVEL, IF NECESSARY

Angie Madden

CO-FOUNDER
PARANORMAL INVESTIGATORS OF GEORGIA
WEBSITE: www.pi-ga.com
E-MAIL: paranormalinvestigators
ofgeorgia@yahoo.com
SERVING: GEORGIA, SOUTH CAROLINA,
TENNESSEE, ALABAMA, NORTH CAROLINA

Donna L. Marsh

FOUNDER
ADSAGSONA PARANORMAL SOCIETY
WEBSITE: www.apsociety.com
E-MAIL: info@apsociety.com
TEL: 1 (615) 871-9858
SERVING: TENNESSEE, SOUTHERN AND
WESTERN KENTUCKY, NORTHERN GEORGIA,
AND NORTHERN ALABAMA

Bloody Mary

MYSTIC, MEDIUM, PARANORMAL
INVESTIGATOR
BLOODY MARY'S TOURS, INC.
WEBSITE: www.bloodymarystours.com
E-MAIL: bloodymary@cox.net
TEL: 1 (504) 915-7774
SERVING: NEW ORLEANS-BASED, BUT WILL
TRAVEL INTERNATIONALLY

Scott McClure

HISTORIAN, LEAD INVESTIGATOR,
AND WEBMASTER
WEST CENTRAL GEORGIA INVESTIGATORS OF
PARANORMAL ACTIVITY
WEBSITE: www.wcgipa.com
E-MAIL:
wcentralgaghost@bellsouth.net
TEL: 1 (770) 574-9467
SERVING: GEORGIA, ALABAMA,
AND TENNESSEE

Jason McCurry

FOUNDER
HAUNTEDLIVES PARANORMAL SOCIETY
WEBSITE: www.hauntedlives.com
E-MAIL: helps@hauntedlives.com
SERVING: ALABAMA, GEORGIA, MISSISSIPPI,
AND TENNESSEE

Christine Rodriguez

PARAPSYCHOLOGIST
EAST COAST HAUNTINGS ORGANIZATION
WEBSITE: *www.ghostecho.com*
E-MAIL: investigations@ghostecho.com
SERVING: EASTERN UNITED STATES

Rick Rowe

FOUNDER & LEAD INVESTIGATOR
THE PARANORMAL & GHOST SOCIETY
WEBSITE:
www.paranormalghostsociety.org
E-MAIL: AngelOfThyNight@aol.com
SERVING: FLORIDA, NATIONALLY, AND
INTERNATIONALLY, IF NEEDED

Scott Schneider

INVESTIGATOR
NORTH CAROLINA PIEDMONT PARANORMAL
RESEARCH SOCIETY
WEBSITE: *www.ncpprs.org*
E-MAIL: pyritepirate@aol.com
SERVING: PORTIONS OF NORTH AND
SOUTH CAROLINA

Belinda Swindell

LEAD INVESTIGATOR
HAMPTON ROADS PARANORMAL RESEARCH
GROUP
WEBSITE: *www.geocities.com/hrprg.geo*
E-MAIL: webmaster@hrprg.zzn.com
TEL: 1 (757) 485-3128
SERVING: SOUTHEAST VIRGINIA AND
NORTHEAST NORTH CAROLINA

Stanley Wardrip Jr.

FOUNDER/LEAD INVESTIGATOR
CAPE FEAR PARANORMAL INVESTIGATIONS
WEBSITE: *groups.yahoo.com/group/
CF-Paranormal/*
E-MAIL: CFParanormal@aol.com
TEL: 1 (910) 452-2893
SERVING: EASTERN NORTH CAROLINA

Mike Watkins

FOUNDER/LEAD INVESTIGATOR
NORTHWEST GEORGIA PARANORMAL
INVESTIGATION TEAM
WEBSITE: *www.nwgapit.com*
E-MAIL: mike@nwgapit.com
TEL: 1 (706) 639-9481
SERVING: GEORGIA, ALABAMA,
AND TENNESSEE

Great Lakes

Wendy Blackmer and Jodi Williams

PARANORMAL INVESTIGATORS
GHOSTSEEKERS OF MICHIGAN
WEBSITE: *www.ghostseekers-of-michigan.com*
E-MAIL: comments@ghostseekers-of-michigan.com
SERVING: MICHIGAN MAINLY, BUT WILLING
TO TRAVEL

Shawn P. Blaschka

LEAD INVESTIGATOR
WAUSAU PARANORMAL RESEARCH SOCIETY
WEBSITE: *www.pat-wausau.org*
E-MAIL: blaschkas@aol.com
SERVING: CENTRAL WISCONSIN

Dino Brancato

FOUNDER
GHOST CHASERS OF MICHIGAN
PARANORMAL INVESTIGATORS
WEBSITE:
www.ghostchasersofmichigan.com
E-MAIL:
ghostchasersofmichigan@hotmail.com
TEL: 1 (866) 446-7874
SERVING: MICHIGAN, OHIO, INDIANA,
AND WEST VIRGINIA

Nicole Bray

FOUNDER AND PRESIDENT
WEST MICHIGAN GHOST HUNTERS SOCIETY
WEBSITE: *www.wmghs.com*
E-MAIL: founder@wmghs.com
SERVING: ALL AREAS OF WEST MICHIGAN

Bea Brugge

CO-FOUNDER
WORLD PARANORMAL INVESTIGATIONS
WEBSITE: *www.wpiusauk.com*
E-MAIL: wpiusa2004@sbcglobal.net
SERVING: OHIO AND SURROUNDING STATES

Kathy Conder

LEAD INVESTIGATOR
ENCOUNTERS PARANORMAL RESEARCH
AND INVESTIGATION
WEBSITE: *www.encounterspri.com*
E-MAIL: kathy@encounterspri.com
TEL: 1 (860) 608-2214
SERVING: MICHIGAN AND THE
NEW ENGLAND AREA

Janice Cottrill

INVESTIGATOR, RESEARCHER, AND WRITER
COTTRILL INVESTIGATIONS
E-MAIL: jjaniceneon@aol.com
SERVING: MICHIGAN, OHIO, ARIZONA,
AND FLORIDA

Bob Freeman

SENIOR INVESTIGATOR
NIGHTSTALKERS OF INDIANA
WEBSITE:
www.cairnwood.blogspot.com
E-MAIL: caliburn@comteck.com
TEL: 1 (765) 395-3615
SERVING: INDIANA

Justin Hammans and John-Michael Talboo

CO-FOUNDERS
PROOF PARANORMAL—INDIANAPOLIS,
INDIANA
WEBSITE: *www.proofparanormal.com*
E-MAIL: proofparanormal@yahoo.com
SERVING: MIDWESTERN UNITED STATES

Rick Hayes

PARANORMAL COMMUNICATIONS
CONSULTANT, FOUNDER OF LIFESGIFT
LIFESGIFT
WEBSITE: *www.lifesgift.com*
E-MAIL: rick@lifesgift.com
SERVING: WORLDWIDE

Rob Husak

FOUNDER, LEAD INVESTIGATOR
TRP PARANORMAL INVESTIGATIONS
WEBSITE:
www.trpparanormalinvestigations.com
E-MAIL: trpparanormal@hotmail.com
TEL: 1 (740) 947-2458
SERVING: OHIO, PENNSYLVANIA, WEST
VIRGINIA, INDIANA, AND KENTUCKY

Stephanie Lane

WEBMISTRESS
DEADOHIO.COM
WEBSITE: *www.deadohio.com*
E-MAIL: webmistress@deadohio.com
SERVING: NORTHEAST OHIO

Brian Leffler

FOUNDER
NORTHERN MINNESOTA PARANORMAL
INVESTIGATORS (N.M.P.I.)
WEBSITE: *www.nmpi-scary.com*
E-MAIL: krcguns@yahoo.com
TEL: 1 (218) 778-0279
SERVING: MINNESOTA, WISCONSIN, AND
THE UNITED STATES

Edward Shanahan and Amy Cooper

PSYCHIC FEELERS AND INVESTIGATORS
THE UNEXPLAINED WORLD
WEBSITE:
www.theunexplainedworld.com
E-MAIL: edward_shanahan@prodigy.net
SERVING: CHICAGOLAND AREA, ILLINOIS,
AND MAY TRAVEL

Jennifer Smith

FOUNDER/LEAD INVESTIGATOR
DEADFRAME PARANORMAL RESEARCH GROUP
WEBSITE: *www.deadframe.com*
E-MAIL: info@deadframe.com
TEL: 1 (330) 475-4957
SERVING: EASTERN UNITED STATES
AND SOUTHERN CANADA

Troy Taylor

FOUNDER
AMERICAN GHOST SOCIETY
WEBSITE: *www.prairieghosts.com*
E-MAIL: ttaylor@prairieghosts.com
TEL: 1 (217) 422-1002
SERVING: THE UNITED STATES

Great Plains

Michael D. Adams

LEAD INVESTIGATOR
MISSOURI PARANORMAL RESEARCH SOCIETY
WEBSITE: *www.missouriparanormal.com*
E-MAIL:
sherry@missouriparanormal.com
SERVING: MISSOURI AND ILLINOIS

Lynette Baker
TEAM LEADER / WEBMASTER
CENTRAL IOWA GHOST HUNTING TEAM
WEBSITE: *www.midiowa.com/cight*
E-MAIL: cight@pcpartner.net
SERVING: CENTRAL IOWA

Vicky Glidewell
FOUNDER AND PSYCHIC-MEDIUM
TULSA GHOST INVESTIGATORS
WEBSITE: *www.tulsaghost.net*
E-MAIL: TulsaGhost@sbcglobal.net
SERVING: TULSA AND NORTHEASTERN
OKLAHOMA

Joe Leto
FOUNDER
DES MOINES IOWA EXTREME PARANORMAL
ADVANCED RESEARCH TEAM (DIEPART)
WEBSITE: *www.diepart.com*
E-MAIL: joe@diepart.com
TEL: 1 (515) 250-2108
SERVING: IOWA

Sueanne Pool
PSYCHIC/MEDIUM
KANSAS CITY GHOST HUNTERS
WEBSITE: *www.kcghost.com*
E-MAIL: dtpool@swbell.net
SERVING: AMERICAN HEARTLAND

Tim Pool
PRESIDENT
KANSAS CITY GHOST HUNTERS
WEBSITE: *www.kcghost.com*
E-MAIL: dtpool@swbell.net
SERVING: AMERICAN HEARTLAND

Lee Prosser
E-MAIL: rozwizca@sbcglobal.net
TEL: 1 (918) 342-4962
SERVING: OKLAHOMA

Debra Prosser
E-MAIL: rozwizca@sbcglobal.net
TEL: 1 (918) 342-4962
SERVING: OKLAHOMA

David P. Rodriguez
FOUNDER AND LEAD INVESTIGATOR
P.R.I.S.M. - PARANORMAL RESEARCH AND
INVESTIGATIVE STUDIES MIDWEST
WEBSITE:
www.DoYouSeeDeadPeople.org
E-MAIL: info@doyouseedeadpeople.org
SERVING: NEBRASKA, IOWA, SOUTH
DAKOTA, KANSAS, MISSOURI,
AND MINNESOTA

Erik Smith
PRESIDENT
OKLAHOMA CITY GHOST CLUB
WEBSITE: *www.okcgc.com*
E-MAIL: okcgc@yahoo.com
SERVING: OKLAHOMA AND
SURROUNDING STATES

Southwest

Henry Bailey
EDITOR/INDEPENDENT INVESTIGATIONS
CONJECTURE.COM
WEBSITE: *www.conjecture.com*
E-MAIL: hsbailey@msn.com
SERVING: TEXAS, NEW MEXICO, ARIZONA,
AND LOUISIANA

Michael Carrico and Osvaldo Luna

CO-FOUNFERS/LEAD INVESTIGATORS
L.V. PARANORMAL INVESTIGATIONS
E-MAIL:
lvparanormalinvestigations@yahoo.com
SERVING: LAS VEGAS VALLEY

Kira Connally

PARANORMAL INVESTIGATOR
MYSTIC GHOST
WEBSITE: *www.mysticghost.com*
E-MAIL: kjc@blueivvy.com
TEL: 1 (817) 715-8163
SERVING: NORTH AND CENTRAL TEXAS

Peter James Haviland

PRESIDENT, LEAD INVESTIGATOR
LONE STAR SPIRITS PARANORMAL
INVESTIGATIONS
WEBSITE: *www.lonestarspirits.org*
E-MAIL:
Investigations@lonestarspirits.org
TEL: 1 (281) 446-2276
SERVING: TEXAS

Janice Oberding

DIRECTOR
NEVADA GHOSTS AND HAUNTINGS
RESEARCH SOCIETY
WEBSITE: *www.HauntedNevada.com*
E-MAIL: Janice@hauntednevada.com
SERVING: NEVADA AND CALIFORNIA

Ginger Pennell

CO-FOUNDER
SPIRIT QUEST PARANORMAL
WEBSITE:
www.spiritquestparanormal.com
E-MAIL: info@spiritquestparanormal.com
TEL: 1 (281) 733-7301
SERVING: NATIONWIDE

Chris Peterson

PRESIDENT
UTAH GHOST HUNTERS SOCIETY
WEBSITE: *www.ghostwave.com*
E-MAIL: MrMan320@aol.com
TEL: 1 (801) 565-0949
SERVING: UNITED STATES

Richard L. Senate

PSYCHIC INVESTIGATOR/AUTHOR
CARSON VALLEY GHOST STALKERS
WEBSITE: *www.Ghost-Stalker.com*
E-MAIL: HaintHunter@aol.com
TEL: 1 (775) 267-9974
SERVING: NORTHERN NEVADA

Rocky Mountains

Bryan Bonner

FOUNDER
ROCKY MOUNTAIN PARANORMAL RESEARCH
SOCIETY
WEBSITE:
www.rockymountainparanormal.com
E-MAIL:
bryan@rockymountainparaormal.com
TEL: 1 (720) 201-1234
SERVING: COLORADO AND REFERRALS TO THE
WORLD

Marie Cuff

PRESIDENT
IDAHO SPIRIT SEEKERS
WEBSITE: *www.idahospiritseekers.com*
E-MAIL: idahospiritseekers@yahoo.com
TEL: 1 (208) 899-6131
SERVING: IDAHO, OREGON, AND WASHINGTON

Bill Cook

DIRECTOR
GHOST UNIVERSITY
WEBSITE: *www.GhostUniversity.com*
E-MAIL: info@ghostuniversity.com
TEL: 1 (760) 220-6626
SERVING: INTERNATIONAL

Chris Elder

FOUNDER
GHOSTS OF IDAHO
WEBSITE: *www.GHOSTSOFIDAHO.ORG*
E-MAIL: GOI@ghostsofidaho.org
SERVING: IDAHO

Gerina Dunwich

INDEPENDENT PARANORMAL RESEARCHER
WEBSITE: *www.freewebs.com/gerinadunwich*
E-MAIL: gerinadunwich@yahoo.com
SERVING: LOS ANGELES, SAN FERNANDO VALLEY, AND VENTURA COUNTY (CALIFORNIA)

Kelly A. Winn

VICE-PRESIDENT
IDAHO SPIRIT SEEKERS
WEBSITE: *www.idahospiritseekers.com*
E-MAIL: idahospiritseekers@yahoo.com
TEL: 1 (208) 899-6131
SERVING: IDAHO, OREGON, AND WASHINGTON

Jim Eaton

PARANORMAL INVESTIGATOR
GHOSTSTUDY.COM
WEBSITE: *www.ghoststudy.com*
E-MAIL: jim@ghoststudy.com
TEL: 1 (916) 201-9005
SERVING: CALIFORNIA, OREGON, AND WASHINGTON

West Coast

Todd & Martina Baker

FOUNDERS
PACIFIC PARANORMAL RESEARCH SOCIETY
WEBSITE: *www.NWPPRS.COM*
E-MAIL: martina@nwpprs.com
SERVING: PACIFIC NORTHWEST AND THE WESTERN UNITED STATES

Bridget Emery

INDEPENDENT PARANORMAL INVESTIGATOR
E-MAIL: queenmarylady@yahoo.com
SERVING: SOUTHERN CALIFORNIA

Sara Lessley

INVESTIGATOR, NEWSLETTER & WEBSITE
EDITOR
TRAIL'S END PARANORMAL SOCIETY OF
OREGON
WEBSITE: *www.trailsendparanormal
societyoforegon.com*
E-MAIL: sara@trailsendparanormal
societyoforegon.com
SERVING: OREGON AND SOUTHWESTERN
WASHINGTON

Tamara Thorne

AUTHOR, INDEPENDENT PARANORMAL
INVESTIGATOR
WEBSITE: *www.tamarathorne.com,
www.hauntster.com*
E-MAIL: tamara@tamarathorne.com
SERVING: SOUTHERN CALIFORNIA

Kimberlie Travis

PRESIDENT & EVP SPECIALIST
SOUTHWEST WASHINGTON PARANORMAL
RESEARCH
WEBSITE: *www.swpr.org*
E-MAIL: Spiritchaser74@aol.com
TEL: 1 (360) 430-9888
SERVING: OREGON AND WASHINGTON

Bonnie Vent

SPIRIT ADVOCATE
SAN DIEGO PARANORMAL RESEARCH
PROJECT
WEBSITE: *www.sdparanormal.com*
E-MAIL: info@sdparanormal.com
SERVING: INTERNATIONAL

Eastern Canada

Don Lightbody

DIRECTOR
ATLANTIC CENTER FOR PARANORMAL
RESEARCH AND INVESTIGATION
E-MAIL: stardust1@eastlink.ca
TEL: 1 (902) 852-4258
SERVING: NOVA SCOTIA AND PRINCE
EDWARD ISLAND

Andy Smith

OWNER/TOUR GUIDE
TATTLE TOURS: A GHOST WALK OF
HISTORIC HALIFAX
E-MAIL: andysmith@ns.sympatico.ca
TEL: 1 (902) 494-0525
SERVING: NOVA SCOTIA

Central Canada

Rona Anderson

PARANORMAL INVESTIGATOR/PSYCHIC
PARANORMAL EXPLORERS
WEBSITE:
www.paranormalexplorers.com
E-MAIL: paranormal1@telus.net
TEL: 1 (780) 430-1238
SERVING: ALBERTA AND CANADA

Stephanie Lechniak-Cumerlato and Daniel Cumerlato

FOUNDING PARTNERS
HAUNTED HAMILTON
WEBSITE: *www.hauntedhamilton.com*
E-MAIL: info@hauntedhamilton.com
TEL: 1 (905) 529-4327
SERVING: HAMILTON AND NIAGARA REGION
(AS WELL AS WORLDWIDE)

Sheal Mullin

FIELD AGENT/EVP SPECIALIST
PARANORMAL INVESTIGATOR'S SOCIETY
CANADA
WEBSITE: *parasociety.freewebpage.org*
E-MAIL: shealtm@primus.ca
TEL: 1 (905) 361-7454
SERVING: ONTARIO

Jenny Tyrrell

OWNER/OPERATOR
FIELD INVESTIGATION RESEARCH FOR
ENTITIES (F.I.R.E.)
WEBSITE: *www.ontarioghosts.org/
oakvillewalks/*
E-MAIL: starry1ca@hotmail.com
TEL: 1 (905) 339-9450
SERVING: HALTON AND SURROUNDING AREAS

Western Canada

Jan Gregory

FOUNDER
VANCOUVER PARANORMAL
WEBSITE:
www.vancouverparanormal.com
E-MAIL:
vancouverparanormal@yahoo.com
TEL: 1 (604) 255-1505
SERVING: VANCOUVER AND
LOWER MAINLAND

Europe

Warren Coates

CHAIRMAN
NORTHERN IRELAND PARANORMAL RESEARCH
ASSOCIATION (NIPRA)
WEBSITE: *www.nipra.co.uk*
E-MAIL: warren@nipra.co.uk
TEL: 44 (0) 28-9145-8822
SERVING: IRELAND

Alex Dorrens

RESIDENT SENSITIVE
GHOST HUNTERS SCOTLAND
WEBSITE: *www.ghosthunters.org.uk*
E-MAIL:
lonewooolf@ghosthunters.org.uk
SERVING: UNITED KINGDOM

Annmarie Godsmark

ASSISTANT GROUP MANAGER
SPIRIT TEAM
WEBSITE: *www.spirit-team.co.uk*
E-MAIL: enquiries@spirit-team.co.uk
TEL: 44 (0) 24-7672-7932
SERVING: EUROPE

Barbara Green

YORKSHIRE ROBIN HOOD SOCIETY
WEBSITE:
www.robinhoodyorkshire.co.uk
E-MAIL:
bgreen@juliet33.freeserve.co.uk
TEL: 44 (0) 14-8438-6566
SERVING: YORKSHIRE

Elaine Jonson

PARANORMAL INVESTIGATOR
PARANORMS—SEEKERS OF TRUTH
E-MAIL: paraspirit@aol.com
TEL: 44 (0) 77-9188-7904
SERVING: UNITED KINGDOM

Richard Keeble and Shantell Ainsworth

SUFFOLK PARANORMAL INVESTIGATIONS
WEBSITE: *www.geocities.com/ suffolk_paranormal*
E-MAIL: Ghosthunter9@msn.com
SERVING: EAST ANGLIA, UNITED KINGDOM

Paul Roberts

FOUNDER
THE ANSWERS PEOPLE SEEK
WEBSITE:
www.theanswerspeopleseek.com
E-MAIL:
theanswerspeopleseek@msn.com
TEL: 44 (0) 19-1416-8801
SERVING: NORTHEAST ENGLAND

Central America

Sharon Scott

INDEPENDENT PARANORMAL INVESTIGATOR
E-MAIL: mexgringa2003@yahoo.com
SERVING: TIJUANNA, SOME MEXICO AREAS, AND SOUTHERN CALIFORNIA LOCATIONS

Asia

Kenny Fong

FOUNDER
SINGAPORE PARANORMAL INVESTIGATORS
WEBSITE: *www.spi.com.sg*
E-MAIL: kenny@spi.com.sg
TEL: 65 96280722
SERVING: SOUTHEAST ASIA

Oceania

Liam Baker

FOUNDER
BRISBANE GHOST HUNTERS
WEBSITE: *free.hostdepartment.com/b/brisghost/*
E-MAIL: brisghost@optusnet.com.au
SERVING: PRIMARILY BRISBANE, BUT ALSO ALL OF AUSTRALIA

Dorothy O'Donnell

WEB OWNER
GHOSTS AND OTHER HAUNTS
WEBSITE: *www.nzghosts.co.nz*
E-MAIL: greyghostnz@gmail.com
TEL: 64 21 2570001
SERVING: NEW ZEALAND

Glossary

This is a quick glossary to help you understand some of the insider terms that are occasionally used in some of the listings by the various paranormal investigators, all of whom take a slightly different approach to their research.

Apparition—a recognizable manifestation of spirit energy, such as a semi-translucent figure of a human or animal or a recognizable part of a human or animal.

Dowsing—using tools such as bent wires, a forked stick, or a pendulum to facilitate spirit communication. The practice was originally used for finding underground water sources but has been adapted by practitioners for finding more subtle energies.

Ectoplasm—a smoky film of residue believed to be left behind by spirits. Also known as "spirit matter" or "mist." Also referred to as the shortened version of "ecto."

Electromagnetic Field Detector (EMF)—a handheld device used to measure electromagnetic fields in the immediate vicinity of the device. Many paranormal investigators have adapted this device for supernatural investigations because they believe spirit energy affects EMF readers. EMF detectors measure in milligauss—some investigators believe a reading between 2.0 and 7.0 milligauss indicates spirit presence.

Electronic Voice Phenomena (EVP)—unexpected, oftentimes unexplainable, disembodied voices captured via audio-recording media. Many paranormal investigators will use standard recording devices to try and capture these mysterious voices as part of evidence collection during an investigation.

Ghost—a recognizable, non-interactive figure that is witnessed in a specific area performing the same actions over and over. Also known as a "residual haunting."

Medium—a person who can act as a go-between for the living and the spirit world.

Orb—a spherical ball of light often thought to be spirit energy. Orbs often appear in photographs (especially digital photographs), but are sometimes witnessed with the unaided eye.

Planchette—the device used to indicate letters/messages on a channeling board (also known as a *Ouija* board). Original planchettes had small holes in them that held writing implements. The user would place their hands on the small table-like device, and messages would be written out by the pen.

Poltergeist—German for "noisy ghost," this is a phenomena during which the physical environment is interacted with by an unseen force. It can include loud knocks, objects breaking, or other malevolent events that are more often heard than seen.

Psychic—a person who can see, hear, and/or sense spirits.

Residual haunting—a psychic impression left on a location by a specific event. A ghost may appear regularly and perform the same actions over and over like a movie playing.

Séance—a meeting involving a medium or channeling device with the purpose of spirit communication.

Sensitive—a person who is psychically intuitive and can pick up vibrations from spirits.

Spirit—an interactive, intelligent entity not from our physical plane.

Index

C

F

G

M

O

P

About the Author

Jeff Belanger leads a very haunted life. He's been fascinated with the supernatural since age 10, when he investigated his first haunted house during a sleepover. Since then, he's been a writer and journalist for various newspapers and magazines, and in 1999 he launched Ghostvillage.com as a repository for his writings on the subject of the supernatural. The site has since grown to become the largest paranormal community on the Web, attracting hundreds of thousands of visitors per year.

Over the years, Jeff has interviewed hundreds of people about their experiences with the profound. His objective approach to the subject makes the supernatural accessible to a wide audience. He's also the author of *The World's Most Haunted Places: From the Secret Files of Ghostvillage.com* and *Communicating With the Dead: Reach Beyond the Grave*. Jeff is a regular guest on many regional and national radio programs, has lectured across the United States on ghosts and the supernatural, and has been featured on television programs about the paranormal. He currently haunts Bellingham, Massachusetts, with his wife, Megan.